# RED GOLD OF AFRICA

# " RED GOLD
# OF AFRICA *Copper in*
*Precolonial History and Culture*

# Eugenia W. Herbert

THE UNIVERSITY OF WISCONSIN PRESS

Published 1984

The University of Wisconsin Press
114 North Murray Street
Madison, Wisconsin 53715

The University of Wisconsin Press, Ltd.
1 Gower Street
London WC1E 6HA, England

Printed in the United States of America

For LC CIP information see the colophon

*To Basil Davidson, through whom I first discovered Africa, and to my colleagues in the history department at Mount Holyoke College.*

Incipit vita nova.

*All art is a dialogue. So is all interest in the past. . . . The more precisely we listen, and the more we become aware of its pastness, even of its near-inaccessibility, the more meaningful the dialogue becomes. In the end, it can only be a dialogue in the present, about the present.*

— M. I. Finley

# CONTENTS

## Part III: COPPER IN TRADITIONAL AFRICAN SOCIETY

# ILLUSTRATIONS

---

## BLACK AND WHITE ILLUSTRATIONS

Figures 1–7 are of "les mangeurs du cuivre":
copper mining and smelting in Katanga. De Hemptinne,
1924 (from *Mwana Shaba,* no. 172, 15 December 1969).
Photos Thomas Jacob

## COLORED ILLUSTRATIONS                    (following page 216)

# MAPS, CHARTS, TABLES, AND DIAGRAMS

## DIAGRAMS

# ACKNOWLEDGMENTS

Any work that gestates for over a decade incurs an immense number of debts. A bulging correspondence file testifies to the willingness of scholars on three continents to share their knowledge, often with a total stranger. In some cases I have been able to acknowledge their help in footnotes, but if I cannot thank them all individually, I should at least like to do so collectively.

I am also indebted to the governments of Gabon and Cameroon for permission and help in pursuing researches in these countries in 1979 and 1982 respectively. In Cameroon, brass casters gave generously of their time and expertise, and I am especially grateful to Maître Fondeur Nsangou Gnamsié Mama of Fumban for allowing me to document work in his atelier in detail. In Yaoundé Tom Reefe offered warm hospitality, assistance, and friendship.

Many museum and library staffs have provided invaluable assistance over the years. The Interlibrary Loan Department of the Williston Library at Mount Holyoke College has been particularly assiduous in ferreting out obscure sources. I am grateful, too, to the College for a summer grant toward research in Gabon, to the Andrew W. Mellon Foundation for a faculty fellowship that enabled me to do field study in Cameroon and to complete the present manuscript, and to Wellesley College for a Mary Elvira Stevens Travelling Fellowship that made possible my first trip to Africa in 1969.

Five colleagues have been especially influential in giving direction and form to this work. When my interest went no farther than curiosity about the unexplained volume of the medieval trans-Saharan trade in copper, Raymond Mauny suggested I look into ritual uses of the metal. In a very real sense this marked an epiphany for me, and I have looked at economic history in a different way ever since. Several years later, Leonard Thompson urged me to expand the original, limited study into a book. Then in 1978 while I was at St. Antony's College, Oxford, I came to know Marion Johnson, who shared with me her superb knowledge of African economic history and a great deal else. Subsequently, she supplied me with the computerized print-outs of English Customs House records which for the first time provide a base for the quantitative study of the copper and brass trade with Africa over more than a century. As the manuscript took final shape, Jan Vansina went over it in minute detail, giving me the benefits of his incomparable experience and unrivalled command of the literature. But perhaps my most long-standing debt is to Robert Farris Thompson, whose friendship I have treasured for twenty years and whose encouragement had a very special meaning at a time when Africa was competing precariously with hearth and home.

My family and friends have provided the framework without which intellectual labors have little joy. My brother, Peter Warren, twice welcomed me in Africa, and my sister-in-law, Lillian Warren, joined one of these forays with her customary zest, as did my daughters, Cathy and Rosemary. They and my son Tim have accepted their mother's obsessions with good humor and have all been pressed into service of one sort or another, Rosemary even doing her stint as research assistant. My husband Bob has always been my staunchest booster and most astute critic (and a provider of titles without equal).

In addition, Nancy Neaher's personal and professional encouragement and her willingness to share her knowledge of Nigerian casting traditions have been invaluable. It was she, too, who made me aware of the importance of first-hand metallurgical experience. In this connection, I am very grateful to Leonard DeLonga and Brooke Lynes for initiating me into the mysteries of welding and lost-wax casting. Similarly, Jean Verdussen contributed the fruits of his long experience in Katanga copperworking and rare source materials from his own archives.

Old friends such as Sue Achenbach, Sunny and Harry Miskimin, Liliane Greene, and other comrades in the Center for Independent Study as well as newer friends such as Jane Crosthwaite, Toni Ellis, Bonnie Miller, and Nancy Frieden have shared the ups and downs of mortal existence with a generosity I cannot describe, much less repay. Carlyn Saltman, former student, now friend, I thank in particular for her part in the Great Cameroon Expedition and for jumping into the word-processing breach when time was running out. She is responsible for some of the photos in this volume, while Thomas Jacob took endless pains with many of the others. In various ways Dale Gadsden, Ellie Pieszak, Pat Prairie, and Stacey Klinsman also helped to prepare the manuscript. In the last stages of the work, I have been blessed with a model editor, Mary Maraniss, a true *nganga* of publishing.

For the last five years, Mount Holyoke College has been my spiritual home, a very real Abbaye de Thélème, and it is to my friends in its history department, including those no longer here—Susanna Barrows, Chuck Trout, and the late John Teal—that I affectionately dedicate this book.

# INTRODUCTION

Over the centuries thousands of tons of copper and its alloys were produced in Africa by indigenous metallurgists or were imported from across the desert and across the sea. The metal was cold-hammered, drawn into wire, cast into statues, fashioned into bracelets, vessels, staffs, masks, offered as bridewealth, exchanged for goods and services, deposited in shrines, buried with the dead, used to ornament the human body, swords, guns, canoe paddles, royal palaces. Fine wristlets were smithed light as a feather, massive anklets moulded heavy as a grindstone. Copper was used to mark the passage of girls to womanhood, to protect the young and the old from malefic forces, to consecrate kings and to propitiate gods and ancestors.

How were the quantities of metal obtained for these myriad uses, who made the objects, what was their function, who might possess them, why did they take the form they did? The answers to these questions may differ from culture to culture and to some extent from period to period, but the data gathered from a wide range of sources suggest a number of generalizations that can be applied to sub-Saharan Africa as a whole in the millennium and a half or more between the earliest uses of copper and the colonial era.

It is a curious fact that in tropical Africa — "golden Guinea" — much copper but little gold has yet been found by archaeologists between Rao near the Senegal mouth and Ingombe Ilede on the Middle Zambezi, that is, in the vast area stretching from the fifteenth parallel north to the fifteenth parallel south of the Equator. Undoubtedly more gold will be found within this area, but I would venture to predict that when it is, it will be limited to recent strata or to regions in close trading contact with the Muslim and Christian worlds, material evidence of a borrowed system of values. In a continent synonymous with gold to the outside world for more than a millennium, that metal had, I believe, only minor value or none at all except where there was a long history of exposure to Arab and European influence: the western Sudan-Akan region and Zimbabwe, in particular.

Traditionally, copper and iron have been considered the base metals of everyday use, while gold and silver have been the luxury metals *par excellence,* the ultimate expressions of value. So patently has this held true for western and oriental cultures that it has taken on the aura of a universal verity, buttressed by such unassailable factors as scarcity, purity, immutability, and intrinsic beauty. It is the thesis of this book that such a view does not fit the African experience. In sub-Saharan Africa the fundamental polarity centers on iron and copper alone. While iron has historically been the utilitarian metal and copper the metal of ornamentation and prestige, the polarity is clearly more complex, since iron is used just as frequently for ritual and decoration and to denote status. True, there are very few silver deposits to be found in Africa. Alluvial and surface deposits of gold are widespread, however, but were largely ignored precisely because in those areas less affected until recently by the European and Arab obsession with the yellow metal, indigenous peoples paid little attention to them. In contrast, copper was the supremely precious metal in the traditional African system of values. This notion of value has come increasingly to the fore as I have worked on the book and will be dealt with more fully in later chapters.

In the past, histories of metals and metallurgy have generally passed over tropical Africa in silence. This is altogether understandable, since so little material has been available. Nevertheless, in 1937 Walter Cline published a remarkable monograph in mimeographed form, *Mining and Metallurgy in Negro Africa,* drawing heavily on the ethnographic literature but also exploiting Arab and European travel accounts. Cline's work still stands as the basic text in the field of African metallurgy. In addition, Raymond Mauny's "Essai sur l'histoire des métaux en Afrique occidentale" (1952) and *Tableau géographique de l'ouest africain au moyen âge* (1961) have added greatly to our knowledge of metalworking in the western Sudan. Lars Sundström includes a valuable chapter and extensive bibliography on copper and brass in *The Trade of Guinea* (1965), although his approach is essentially synchronic and noninterpretative, a catalogue of data rather than a critical and historical appraisal of it.

These are virtually the only scholars who have dealt broadly with copper and copperworking in Africa or parts of Africa. None has adequately explored the role of copper in African societies, and all need to be updated with the archaeological findings of Thurstan Shaw, Merrick Posnansky, Frank Willett, D. W. Phillipson, Joseph Vogel, Brian Fagan, Jacques Nenquin, Michael Bisson, N. J. Van der Merwe, Pierre de Maret, and others. In addition, such art historians as William Fagg, Denis Williams, Robert Farris Thompson, Arnold Rubin, Philip Dark, Nancy Neaher, and Anita Glaze have produced valuable studies of the art and technology that were an integral part of the copper and bronze traditions of West Africa. Indeed, historians of African art have thus far pioneered in combining visual evidence, historical and ethnographic documentation, oral tradition, and field research. Only a few anthropologists have been able to match the breadth of their approach.

No one who has worked in African precolonial history needs to be reminded of the enormous gaps in source materials. Written documentation in Arabic exists only for the lands immediately south of the Sahara and for the coastal cities of East Africa, and it is often scanty and based on hearsay. From the second half of the fifteenth century it is, of course, supplemented by a wealth of European sources: bills of lading, account books, travelers' descriptions. Nevertheless these are all the work of outsiders, colored by the cultural biases of the writers and their preoccupation with mercantile interests. Few Arabs or Europeans penetrated beyond the desert or coastal fringes before the burst of enthusiasm for African exploration in the late eighteenth century, and most of those who did "went native" and left no accounts. As a result, written records for much of tropical Africa are nonexistent before the last century.

In some areas this void has been partially filled by the careful collection of oral tradition. The time-depth that can be reconstructed and the reliability of the content depend to a large extent upon the value the societies themselves place or have placed on the preservation of their past and upon the purpose to which they intend their history. Jan Vansina and others have demonstrated the usefulness of oral tradition: on a grand scale, it has been used to recover dynastic history and recapitulate population movements; on a more finite level, it has served to record craft techniques such as mining and smelting before all memory of them has been lost.

The archaeology of Iron Age Africa has made tremendous strides over the past two decades. The most extensive work has been carried out in Ghana, Nigeria, eastern Zaire and the lacustrine region, the Middle Zambezi Valley, portions of the Swahili coast, the Zimbabwe plateau, and eastern Transvaal. On the other hand, the forest areas of West Africa, and parts of the Congo Basin and the former Portuguese territories, remain virtual *terrae incognitae,* archaeologically speaking. In spite of these discontinuities, the chronology of metalworking in Africa is now on increasingly firm ground in a number of regions, with the discovery of ancient mining and smelting sites themselves as well as of objects manufactured locally.

These objects, together with the many others collected over the years from nonarchaeological contexts, provide the most tangible evidence for the importance of copper in African societies. They also tell us something of the technological and economic levels of the groups that made them. When Shaw published the account of his excavations at Igbo-Ukwu in 1970, for example, it created a sensation among African historians: the three pits yielded a wealth of copper and bronze objects without precedent in tropical Africa and revealed that there existed an autonomous metalworking tradition of great technical and artistic accomplishment at a surprisingly early date.

The plan of this book is very different from the order of my own researches. Starting as an economic historian with a special interest in the trans-Saharan trade, I was puzzled by the constant demand for copper and brass in West Africa, a demand that clearly could only be met by massive imports across the desert and later across the sea. Piqued by the suggestion of Raymond Mauny that I should look into the ritualization of copper, I began to examine its role in West African religious, social, and political systems, which meant, of course, looking at African art. Certain patterns began to emerge which, to my surprise, I found largely repeated in Central and Southern Africa, as Michael Bisson has confirmed, although copper was not the scarce commodity in these regions that it was in West Africa. At this point, too, I realized the need to map the sources of copper within tropical Africa that were worked in precolonial times, studying the technology employed and reconstructing wherever possible the routes by which both indigenously produced and imported metals were distributed.

The organization that has been adopted is, therefore, tripartite. The first part is devoted to indigenous copper mining and metallurgy and its social, political, and ritual aspects; part II reconstructs all aspects of the copper trade to, from, and within Africa that can be documented for the precolonial period; part III examines the multifaceted role of copper in African society and argues for its primacy over gold. In the conclusion I deal more generally with the notion of value and the significance of materials in preindustrial societies.

The history of copper in black Africa begins with the exploitation of the mines near Agadès about 2000 B.C. I have chosen to carry it up only to the eve of the colonial period, about 1870–80, because so much was altered under colonialism. This cutoff date is very approximate and not altogether satisfactory, since much of the ethnographic data on which I have had to rely are more recent; they have been used nonetheless when there is a reasonable probability that they apply equally to the earlier period. Geographically I have tried to survey the entire continent south of the Sahara, because of my conviction that many of the uses of copper and attitudes to it were comparable over large parts of Africa. The major omissions are Ethiopia and the Horn of Africa, the *oikoume* that remained in contact with the Mediterranean and Near Eastern world from antiquity and shared in its developments.

So much of the evidence bearing on the history of copper in Africa is fragmentary and buried in obscure sources that it has seemed useful to broaden the scope of the book in order to bring as much of it as possible together in one place. At the same time, I have synthesized and summarized a great deal of material to avoid a purely encyclopedic compendium of data. This *vue d'ensemble* will, I hope, be followed by several more-specialized studies of particular aspects of the topic.

The theme of copper has provided an opportunity to interweave elements of economic, cultural, and technological history on a continental scale that I have found irresistibly fascinating and challenging. It has forced me into areas where my own training gave me no special competence — mineralogy, metallurgy, archaeology, anthropology, art history — but which have so much to teach the historian of Africa. Surely the interdependence of scholars and of disciplines is one of the greatest attractions of this new field, and the readiness of other laborers in the vineyard to share insights and information one of its greatest rewards.

# RED GOLD OF AFRICA

# The Age of Metals

> When an art is so poor that it lacks metals, it
> is not of much importance, for nothing is made
> without tools.
>
> — AGRICOLA, *De Re Metallica*

The age of metals dawned about 8000 B.C., radiating from the hill country of western Asia and possibly from other seminal areas as well. For centuries, even millennia, gold, copper, and meteoric iron were collected and
used in their native state but not recognized as metals: they were simply
another form of stone, brighter and more beautiful, fit more for ornamentation than utility. As Cyril Stanley Smith has observed, "aesthetic curiosity, not necessity was the mother of invention,"[1] and it was the decorative qualities of native metals that first prompted man to investigate their
possibilities. Unlike other stones, metals are malleable (within limits) and
do not chip or flake when struck, properties that automatically suggested
other uses than those for flint or obsidian.

The development of true metallurgy, as opposed to the lithic use of native metals, followed from a sequence of critical discoveries, none of which
can be pinpointed geographically or chronologically nor even explained
except by conjecture. The first of these was the realization that heating
a lump of native metal changed its mechanical properties and made it more
workable. If native copper is cold-hammered, for example, it quickly becomes brittle, but if it is heated over an open fire and then hammered,
it can be shaped and hardened without cracking. This process of alter-
nately heating and cold-hammering, called annealing, made possible the
smithing of the first metal tools and weapons and gave copper an immediate practical supremacy over gold and silver, which would always remain
too soft for utilitarian purposes. It also made possible a great variety of
ornamental uses, since with annealing, copper could be hammered into
sheets as thin as 0.4 millimeter, sheets that could then be cut into ribbon
or rolled into beads.

A temperature of only a few hundred degrees suffices for annealing copper. To melt it, the heat must be raised to 1083° C., and this can only be
accomplished with a forced draft. Consequently the progression from annealing to melting could not have been as simple as might appear. Once
a molten state is achieved, however, the gangue components mixed with

copper tend to separate and float free, leaving the pure metal to be cast or smithed. The earliest flat axes were cast in open moulds, probably from refined native copper. They were then finished and given an edge by cold-hammering and annealing. In time, bivalve moulds and lost-wax casting permitted a more complex craftsmanship.

The next major milestone in the history of metallurgy was the smelting of ores, with its corollary, the perception that metals originally known only in their natural form could also be won from minerals of very different appearance. This is especially true of copper. Native copper is usually a dark purplish green, revealing its real color and shine when it is scratched. Pale blue azurite, ruby-red cuprite, yellow chalcopyrite, gray tetrahedrite, and iridescent bornite ("peacock ore") are all, however, incarnations of the same metal. The comprehension of this unity presupposes a remarkable leap of imagination, and in a sense, the reduction of these compounds to pure copper is the quintessential alchemy. "It meant," Stuart Piggott notes, "a realization that a sort of transmutation of one natural substance into another was within man's power."[2] No longer was man limited by dwindling supplies of native copper. First the simpler oxides were smelted. Then, when these, too, grew scarce, metallurgists learned to recognize and smelt the more complex sulphides by roasting them first at subsmelting temperatures. The earliest reduction of oxide ores seems to have occurred soon after 4000 B.C., with the roasting and smelting of sulphides following later.[3] In a sense, it is a continuous process of discovery that has led in our own century to the use of ores with lower and lower metallic content, making greater and greater demands on technological skills.

Many ingenious explanations have been offered for the discovery of smelting. For a time, the most appealing was the "camp-fire" theory—that a piece of copper ore accidentally fell into a campfire and was smelted on the spot. Coghlan effectively disproved this theory by embedding a lump of malachite (copper carbonate) in an open charcoal fire and showing that it did not turn into metallic copper: while the temperature was high enough for smelting, too much oxygen was present, so that only a nonmetallic cuprous oxide was produced. Another explanation of the origin of smelting is that man had already learned how to melt native copper and that bits of oxide clinging to it were accidentally smelted during such a heating. This theory presupposes the association of native copper with an appropriate oxide, as well as the achievement of a reducing atmosphere, a possible but not very likely set of circumstances.

A more convincing hypothesis links the discovery of smelting to pottery-making. Early pottery kilns were capable of reaching temperatures of more than 1100° C. If a copper oxide such as malachite were used as a pigment to glaze a pot and a properly reducing atmosphere attained within the kiln, metallic copper would be produced. It is not fortuitous that in much of the western Sudan the potter is the wife of the blacksmith, but whether this association goes back to the early period of metalworking there is no way of knowing. All that can be said is that the pairing of potters and smiths is a natural one, since both need to know soils and minerals as well as the techniques of manipulating heat.

Unless it is carried out with a high degree of competence, smelting produces copper containing many more impurities than are found in the native metal. At first the pattern of impurities would have been purely random, but in time, observation would have shown that certain impurities were actually desirable, making the metal more workable in one way or another. The earliest alloy to be produced intentionally, accidental though its discovery may have been, was arsenical copper. Arsenical coppers predominated throughout much of the eastern Mediterranean and Middle East during the so-called Early Bronze Age, before bronze itself became widespread. Arsenic does not help in casting or annealing copper, but it greatly improves its tensile strength and hardness when hammered. It has long been assumed that arsenical copper was superseded by tin bronze because the latter could be cast more easily, was harder and could hold a finer edge — or, alternatively, because the manufacture of arsenical copper released highly toxic fumes fatal to its smelters. Lechtman has shown the weakness of the toxicity argument and has emphasized that in terms of their metallurgical properties, arsenical copper and bronze appear to be virtually interchangeable.[4] Whatever the cause of the shift, the true Bronze Age was relatively short-lived, thanks to the scarcity of tin ores in much of the ancient world. In some regions, indeed, bronze was produced rarely or not at all.

Whereas bronze is an alloy of copper and tin — ideally in the ratio of 9:1 or 10:1 but in ancient practice extremely variable — brass combines copper and zinc. Some early brasses, such as those found in Egypt, may have been obtained accidentally in smelting copper ores containing natural amounts of zinc, but true brass was a Roman invention. Metallic zinc does not occur by itself in nature and is difficult to isolate from compounds because of its extreme volatility. Until the eighteenth century, therefore, the only means of producing brass in the western world was by heating metallic copper with calamine, a zinc oxide, until the zinc was freed from the calamine and dissolved in the copper. Modern standard brass contains two parts of copper to one of zinc, but in earlier periods the proportions varied as much as they did for bronze.

For the first few millennia, the history of metallurgy was preeminently the history of copper, although lead may have been more important than is generally realized.[5] The only native form of iron was meteoric iron, and it is by no means as common as native copper. It, too, had been fashioned into beads and amulets from earliest times, but like the soft iron often obtained as a by-product of the preparation of copper and gold, it was unsuited for tools or weapons. Iron ores reduce at a lower temperature than copper so that in theory they should be easier to smelt. In fact, however, the process is a good deal more difficult, since temperature is not the only factor. If the same technique is used as with copper, only a spongy bloom is produced, totally unfit for working. To insure a workable iron, a flux must be used during the smelting, and heat maintained over a longer period but at a temperature lower than the melting point of the metal. This helps to explain why the technique of smelting and forging iron was not discovered until about 1500 B.C. and remained for centuries a jealously guarded secret of the Chalybes and their neighbours the Hittites. As a consequence it was for long a luxury metal, like gold and silver the prerogative and gift of kings. Not until the last millennium before Christ did its use gradually spread. Even then, many areas were slow to adopt the new technology. This was particularly true of Egypt: iron did not eclipse copper and bronze as the metal of industry, agriculture, and warfare in the Nile Valley until sometime after about 500 B.C.[6]

2

Such a schematic summary of the history of metallurgy in the Near and Middle East conveys a tidy purposiveness which is belied by the detailed archaeological record. Actually, the picture is one of tremendous lags and discontinuities, with some areas taking centuries to adopt techniques common to almost adjacent peoples and with the use of stone continuing side by side with metals for long periods. And because metals remained valuable and scarce commodities — early mining and smelting were tremendously laborious, time-consuming, and often unsuccessful procedures — they were often reclaimed and reworked. Consequently, the absence of finds in a given region at certain levels of excavation is not incontrovertible proof that metals were not part of its material culture. Ronald Tylecote has commented, for example, that no gold artifacts have been discovered dating back before the end of the fifth millennium,[7] a circumstance that could be interpreted to indicate the exceptional value of the metal or the opposite.

The accumulating weight of evidence favors eastern Turkey and the Iranian plateau as a major cradle of early metallurgy, and suggests that it slowly spread from this nuclear area. The great river-valley civilizations were borrowers, not innovators, in this process, for the simple reason that they lacked ores and fuel. Not until the closing centuries of the pre-Christian era did the Upper Nile Valley become a center of iron, with the rise of Meroë under its Kushite rulers. But if they were not technical pioneers, the craftsmen of Egypt and Mesopotamia transformed the metals they received into artistic masterpieces.

The Near Eastern bias in archaeology and prehistory has recently provoked a salutary reaction that has had echoes in African history. Armed with a host of radiocarbon dates, Colin Renfrew has challenged the diffusionist assumptions of earlier generations and specifically the view that prehistoric Europe derived most of its civilization and technology from the Near East and the Aegean. Renfrew argues that at least some strands of the "complex web" of copper metallurgy were spun quite independently in Europe. The northern Balkans and Carpathian Basin, he maintains, were technically far more advanced than the contemporary Aegean; they need not have owed all their metallurgical skills to Greece or western Asia.[8] Recent finds of very early cast bronzes in Thailand may add fuel to this revisionist movement.

### 3

Until recently it appeared that Africa south of the Sahara did not follow the path traced in the Near East and Europe, that there was no Chalcolithic Period when copper was used as a stone, there were no ages of copper or bronze, no production of brass before the nineteenth century. All the available evidence pointed to a transition directly from stone to iron, or possibly to iron and copper simultaneously. This view is currently being revolutionized by discoveries in the Agadès region of Niger which suggest that there were two "copper ages," based on the exploitation of local metal, the first as early as 2000 B.C. This would be by far the earliest evidence of metalworking in sub-Saharan Africa, more than a thousand years before iron was smelted in the same area or before copper was worked at Akjoujt in Mauritania.[9]

At the same time, more radiocarbon dates are becoming available for ironworking, so that Taruga no longer seems isolated as it did just a few years ago. As Sutton notes, "western and equatorial Africa appears to be falling in line with the great radiation of ironworking through the Afro-Eurasian land-mass in the earlier and middle centuries of the first millennium B.C."[10] The earliest evidence for iron smelting at the Nok culture site of Taruga in central Nigeria dates to about the sixth century B.C., roughly contemporary with the earliest dates for sites to the east of Agadès in Niger. In the millennium stretching from about 500 B.C. to 500 A.D., ironworking spread over broad areas of the continent, albeit unevenly.[11]

West of Lake Victoria, Schmidt claims to have found evidence of ironworking about 500 B.C. as well, but this date is not universally accepted.[12]
Similarly, Phillipson's hypothesis of a two-stream diffusion of metalworking through eastern, central, and southern Africa has been sharply attacked
by Huffman for its theoretical confusion and lack of clearly defined diag-
nostic traits for the cultures he is tracking.[13] At present all that we can
say for certain is that ironworking had reached the Transvaal by about the
third or fourth century A.D.[14]

The spread of iron in subequatorial Africa has in the past been frequently
associated with Bantu dispersion. Guthrie's monumental work on comparative Bantu suggested that the vocabulary of ironworking was a relatively
late addition to proto-Bantu but was acquired before the main outmigra-
tion from the core area in the Congo Basin, reinforcing the view that the
spread of iron was, by and large, synonymous with the spread of Bantu-
speaking peoples. This conclusion has come under fire from both archaeologists and linguists. It does not, of course, fit with Phillipson's demonstration that the Iron Age cultures of East Africa, particularly in the
coastal hinterland of modern Kenya, preceded those closer to the conjec-
tural Bantu homeland. Furthermore, de Maret and Nsuka have carefully
examined a much larger number of metallurgical terms than Guthrie for
the most important zones and deny that there is "a single stem reconstructed
in the whole of the [Bantu] area which can be affirmed to have a meaning
directly related to metallurgy in Proto-Bantu"; that is, there are too many
stems present in the various languages to postulate derivation from a single ancestral, metalworking group. In addition, the most common of the
stems relating to metallurgy also occur in non-Bantu languages, although
the separation of Bantu- and non-Bantu-speaking groups long antedates
the age of metals.[15] It seems increasingly doubtful, therefore, that the Bantu
were responsible for the primary spread of ironworking in the heart of
Africa.[16]

But what of the broader question, the ultimate source of Africa's knowledge of metalworking? For a time, the most popular theory held that it
reached tropical Africa from Meroë, the "Birmingham of Egypt," located
on the Upper Nile near the confluence with the Atbara. A romantic elaboration of the theory suggested that blacksmiths formed part of the retinue
of the royal family fleeing westward after the capture of their capital by
Axumite invaders in the fourth century A.D. There are a number of weak-
nesses in this theory (not the least of which is the analogy with Birmingham, which made its fortune in finished metalwares, especially brass, not
in smelting). First of all, the heyday of Meroë's iron manufacture is now
believed to have been several centuries later than originally assumed, so
that in all likelihood it is somewhat later than Nok or at best barely con-

temporary. Then, too, Tylecote has shown a basic divergence in the types of furnaces used at the two sites.[17] Further, no traces of Meroitic culture have been found along the alleged diffusion route westward.

It seems more likely, as Mauny suggested almost two decades ago, that ironworking reached West Africa from the north across the Sahara, either from Carthage or from southern Morocco. The discovery of the "route des chars" — rock paintings of two-wheeled chariots along both the far-western and the central routes joining the Sudan with North Africa — virtually proves that contacts did take place between the two coasts of the desert during antiquity. The westernmost is the shortest in terms of the desert crossing, particularly since the Sahel almost certainly extended much farther north than it does today.[18] Mme. Lambert's excavations at Akjoujt would tend to confirm this path of diffusion: she has shown that copper mining and smelting took place on a large scale in western Mauritania, beginning about the sixth century B.C.[19]

There is no reason to assume, however, that metalworking spread to all of black Africa from a single source. Some time ago Huard proposed this possibility even for the central Sudan–Lake Chad region,[20] and while his specific reconstruction now seems unlikely in view of the Niger, Nok, and Akjoujt dates, the idea of multiple sources and multiple centers of secondary dispersion is altogether plausible, especially in the light of the linguistic complexity that Ehret and others are finding in connection with metalworking vocabulary.[21] An early cradle of African metallurgy appears to have developed in Ethiopia, probably derived not from the Nile Valley but from Bronze Age predecessors of the Axumites who crossed over from southern Arabia to the coastal region north of the Bab al-Mandab Straits during the fifth century B.C. and subsequently pushed inland to the Tigre and Amhara highlands.[22] Whether offshoots of these peoples carried the Iron Age to East Africa or whether there was a parallel diffusion from the coast are questions that remain to be answered.

Is there a possibility that ironworking was invented independently in tropical Africa? The case for independent invention has been argued most determinedly by Lhote and Diop.[23] As we have noted, the assumption that metalworking is too complicated a process to have been discovered more than once has already been undermined by discoveries in eastern Europe. It is further weakened by the abundant evidence that pre-Columbian Andean civilizations developed a sophisticated tradition of working in copper, tin, silver, and gold — but not iron — without any known contact with the Old World.[24] The laterite soils so frequently encountered in Africa are rich in easily smelted, if low-grade, iron ores. Anthropologists have documented native techniques in some of the few regions where smelting persisted until recent times; nothing shows more clearly than Jean Rouch's documentary of Songhay smelting the basic simplicity of the methods used, coupled with the infinite skill of the blacksmith.[25]

Claims of independent invention have thus far met with little acceptance. Many of Lhote's and Diop's hypotheses are based on inaccuracies or are purely speculative. But until recently the most telling argument against an independent discovery was the absence of a sequential development in tropical Africa from copper to copper alloys to iron. There is no precedent for mastering the techniques of smelting iron without a preliminary apprenticeship in other, more easily worked metals — even the remarkable skills developed by Andean metallurgists did not lead them to the discovery of ironworking before the Spanish conquest. Now the picture is changing in the Sahel, but it is still probable that this indicates an extension southward of the metallurgy of the western Mediterranean. Elsewhere, in Africa all the evidence points to the priority of iron. Many African languages, for example, either do not distinguish between iron and copper or refer to the latter as "red metal" or "red iron."[26] While Fagan has noted that indigenous techniques of smelting copper in Zambia are elementary enough to have been discovered on the spot,[27] there is no proof that this happened nor any archaeological evidence that copper smelting antedated the exploitation of iron.

Even if the basic technology of ironworking came to Africa from outside, African smiths added a bewildering variety of local innovations and adaptations. In several cases they achieved a fusion of the direct process with incipient cast-iron production resulting in a bloom of high-carbon steel produced directly from the smelting furnace and subsequently decarburized in the forge. They also invented the induced-draft furnace and partial preheating of bellows-driven air. So varied are the furnace and bellows types, however, that they cannot really be used to plot the diffusion of ironworking in any detail, beyond the likelihood that bowl furnaces were probably the earliest. Their occurrence in Southern Africa and irregular distribution in the rest of the continent seem to be survivals of Early Iron Age technology.[28]

When the first Europeans arrived in the fifteenth century, the use of metals was universal in tropical Africa. Only three cultural groups had no knowledge of metalworking: the Pygmies of the equatorial forest, the San of South Africa, and the inhabitants of Fernando Po. Certain ethnic groups were so skilled in smelting and smithing that their products were long preferred to European imports. The weapons of the Songye, wrote Frobenius, were so perfectly fashioned that no industrial art from abroad could improve upon them. Their iron blades were cunningly ornamented with damascened copper and their hilts inlaid with the same metal.[29] The Marave blacksmiths of the Zambezi were renowned even to the Portuguese for their iron, which when heated was "malleable like lead . . . but when cold . . . hard as steel. . . ."[30]

## 4

Everywhere and at all times, the discovery of metals has been recognized as an event of Promethean proportions. African peoples have rarely failed to account for their acquisition of iron in myth, legend, or tradition. Sometimes it is ascribed to the gods, sometimes, more prosaically, to cultural borrowings or wandering smiths. Historians have generally viewed ironworking as the watershed in African history. In his pioneering *Old Africa Rediscovered,* Basil Davidson went so far as to declare that "it was the smelting of iron that hammered on the doors of ancient Africa and broke them down," producing the "civilizations . . . which give pre-European history there its central interest and its main achievement."[31]

Judgments of the role of iron and of those who work it have often been more guarded, tinged with wonder but also with awe and fear. The Delphic Oracle saw it as the instrument of destruction as well as of civilization: "Smiting is there and counter-smiting, and woe on woe."[32] The Koran would echo this ominous view of iron. Though never the primary metal of war and peace in Africa, copper, too, partook of this ambivalence, invoking the awesome power of kingship and execution at the same time that it connoted fertility, healing, and protection. It was distinct from iron, sometimes antithetical to it, sometimes complementary and enhancing.

# Part I

# COPPER RESOURCES AND COPPER METALLURGY IN PRECOLONIAL AFRICA

Map 1. Sources of copper in Africa, precolonial period

# "Ancient Workings" in sub-Saharan Africa

> . . . A land whose stones are iron-ore and from
> whose hills you will dig copper.
> — Deuteronomy 8:9–10

Richly endowed with gold and iron, Africa is relatively poor in copper. It is not quite so poor, however, as the map of ancient workings would seem to indicate. Outcroppings of malachite and azurite are common over large areas of Central and Southern Africa, and possibly over smaller areas elsewhere — outcroppings that are too modest to qualify as mines or to interest modern developers but which were altogether sufficient for the needs of local smelters and craftsmen. In addition, several of the occurrences identified in this century were not exploited by indigenous metallurgists because of their mineralogical complexity. The prime example is the Zambian Copperbelt, one of the richest copper deposits in the world, which was not discovered until the 1920s because it lacked the usual surface indications, in particular the easily recognized traces of oxidized ores.

The term "ancient working" has customarily been used for any mining operation carried out before the colonial era, that is, before the late nineteenth century. Prospectors and geologists sent out by European concerns quickly learned to look for them as the surest indicators of deposits worth pegging, and with good reason: "Apart from five of the large orebodies now being exploited in the Copperbelt of Northern Rhodesia [Zambia] which were disclosed by applied geology, all of the operating copper mines in Africa were marked by the presence of old workings." So wrote J. A. Bancroft, who spent most of his professional life in Central Africa as a mining engineer. His list included the Mindouli and other small mines in equatorial Africa, the Bembe mine in Angola, Katanga, Messina in the northern Transvaal, Tsumeb in Namibia, and O'Okiep in Namaqualand.[1] He could have added the mines of Phalaborwa in the eastern Transvaal, the deposits in Zimbabwe and neighboring Botswana, Akjoujt in Mauritania, and Takedda in Niger.

The difficulty with these ancient workings is that it is impossible to determine from the visual evidence alone just how ancient they are. Fortunately, several sites have recently been examined by archaeologists and prehistorians and dated by radiocarbon, while for others there is written evidence of age. Still others, however, remain an historical enigma. What follows is a survey of ancient workings that have been identified, with the evidence for dating. The technology used to exploit them, as well as estimates of output, will be discussed in a later chapter.

## THE SOUTHERN SAHARA AND SUDAN

In 1354–55 the peerless traveller Ibn Battuta journeyed to the Sudan and made a long detour on the return trip to Morocco in order to visit the flourishing trading city and center of copperworking at Takedda. The ore, he wrote, was dug outside the city, then brought into town to be cast into bars for trade with the south.[2] The name Takedda has since vanished from the map; it is clear from his description, however, that it must have lain to the east of the Niger Bend on the caravan route to Ghat and Egypt. There are widespread surface indications of copper in Aïr, and in 1950 Brouin proposed the identification of Takedda with modern Azelick, west of In Gall and the site of a large ruined city.[3] This identification was accepted by Mauny and others but fiercely contested by Lhote, who went so far as to suggest that Ibn Battuta was not talking about copper at all but about salt.[4]

More recently, the careful field studies of Bernus and Gouletquer have established beyond reasonable doubt that Azelick was Ibn Battuta's Takedda and that copper, not salt, was its primary industry. They argue convincingly that it came to a virtual end with the destruction of the city by the Sultan of Agadès, probably in the latter part of the fifteenth century. Its powerful position already undermined by the gradual exhaustion of the copper ores and possibly also of fuel for smelting, Takedda was unable to withstand the rising power of the sultanate; for the same reasons copper would not have been worked under the new rulers. Only then did the salt pans at nearby Teguidda n-Tesemt become the major industry of the area.[5]

What is more startling is the emerging antiquity of copperworking in this region, now dated by radiocarbon to the first millennium B.C. or possibly a little earlier. It may be still older near Agadès, to the southeast of Azelick. Here Grebenart has identified three sites with copper-smelting furnaces. On the basis of furnace typology and carbon 14 results, he distinguishes two "copper age" periods, the one falling in the early-to-mid first millennium B.C., which is not out of line with Azelick or Akjoujt nor with the spread of ironworking to the Sudan. Dates for the earlier copper age, however, are mostly a full millennium earlier, some as old as 2000 B.C. (which would be even older when calibrated). The occupation sites close to the furnaces show copper associated consistently with stone tools. Further, the pottery has affinities with the "Saharan neolithic" to the north, so that in this area, at least, copperworking seems to have antedated iron by many centuries.[6]

Until the discoveries at Azelick/Takedda and Agadès, the copper mines at Akjoujt in western Mauritania had been believed to be the oldest south of the Tropic of Cancer. Oxidized ores are found throughout the region, reaching to a depth of 70 feet at some points, occurring elsewhere simply as small stainings of green and blue dotting the arid landscape. In a few places near Akjoujt itself there are even traces of native copper.[7] The Grotte aux Chauves-souris (Grotto of the Bats) was one of the principal ancient mines. A man-made hollow in the north face of the Guelb Moghrein, it comprises three chambers, of which two were excavated by Nicole Lambert in 1968. Radiocarbon dates obtained from samples of charcoal used in the preliminary treatment of ore within the mine indicate that mining flourished in the fifth century B.C. and may have begun even earlier. New dates from the uppermost chamber of the Grotto show that the mine was also worked in the fifteenth to seventeenth centuries A.D. While there is still a long gap between these sets of dates, it seems plausible that there was more of a continuity of smelting than was previously suspected. The dating of a furnace at Lemdena to the early first millennium A.D. and the finds of copper in Senegalese sites of the same millennium tend to support this continuity.[8]

The workings in the Nioro-Siracoro region of northern Mali and adjacent southern Mauritania have not yet been carefully studied. The only evidence for early working is contained in brief geological surveys carried out during the colonial period to determine whether the deposits might warrant modern exploitation. Since the verdict was negative, they were never examined more closely. Nevertheless, nine sites appear to have been worked in the past, with one in particular, Boullé Kadié, showing signs of extensive surface mining.[9]

Mauny has argued for the identification of Nioro with the Dkra mentioned by al-'Umari, an Arabic writer of the fourteenth century. Al-'Umari had no first-hand acquaintance with the western Sudan but gathered his information from members of the retinue of Mansa Musa, Sultan of Mali, passing through Cairo on his celebrated pilgrimage to Mecca. The Sultan, al-'Umari was told, "possesses a city called Zkra [or Dkra] where there is a mine of red copper whence bars are brought to the city of Niani [the royal residence]."[10] At the time of the pilgrimage (1324–25), the Nioro deposits would have been the only ones within the Malian Empire: both Akjoujt and Takedda lay well beyond its borders.

Unfortunately, oral traditions from the Nioro region are completely silent about these mines, perhaps an indication that their exploitation did not long survive the legendary "rex Melli" and has been entirely forgotten. As far as the toponym Dkra is concerned, it may be a transliteration of Diara, an ancient capital of Mali located only about five miles from Siracoro. Diara in turn is considered a derivative of *dyakule, dyakwalle, dyakwale,* all variants of "copper" in Sarakolle and Azer, languages spoken in the region.[11]

The fourth and last copper occurrence of significance in the Sudan is to be found at Hufrat en-Nahas in the extreme southwestern corner of Bahr al-Ghazal. These "holes of copper" lie just east of a range of hills forming the Nile-Congo watershed, not far from the banks of the Umbelasha River, a seasonal tributary of the Bahr al-Arab. The old workings are spread over an area more than a half-mile square and consist of a thousand-odd shafts scattered around two large hills known as Um ("Mother").[12]

In 1912 Frobenius collected a tradition in Kordofan ostensibly referring to Hufrat. According to his informants, the Nap of Naphta or King of Kordofan was the "richest man in the world," thanks to his control over the output of mines of copper and gold. His capital was supposed to have been in the vicinity of Hufrat, although the site is a long distance from the modern Kordofan.[13] An equally extravagant tradition that seems to have caught the fancy of at least one British officer in Egyptian service early in the present century equated the deposits at Hufrat with King Solomon's mines.[14]

These traditions, needless to say, cannot be taken very seriously, but the sheer extent of the ancient workings at Hufrat en-Nahas has suggested to modern geologists that the deposits must have been worked for several centuries at least.[15] The first known reference to them is contained in W. G. Browne's *Travels* of 1793–96. Browne's information is not first-hand—he never reached the mines—but based on accounts of merchants trading with Darfur. From them he learned that copper was "brought from the territory of certain idolatrous tribes bordering on Fur," from mines which he located at "Dar al-Nahas" (rather than Hufrat en-Nahas) in Fertit, twenty-three and one-half days march almost due south of Cobbé.[16] Since no archaeological work has been done at the site, it is impossible to set a more precise *terminus a quo*. The mines continued in production throughout the nineteenth century until the Mahdist uprising of the 1880s.[17]

Elsewhere in West Africa there are minor deposits that show signs of possible early workings, for example at Ougarta in southern Algeria and at Tessalit in northern Mali. It now appears, however, that the apple-green mineral extracted at Tessalit was used to produce beads rather than metal.[18] Farther to the south, in the Gaoua region of Upper Volta–Ivory Coast, deposits of commercial importance were accidentally discovered in the 1930s during the prospection of pits sunk by the indigenous Lobi for both water and gold, but these do not seem to have been exploited earlier for copper.[19]

Dieterlen and Griaule claim that local copper deposits were worked "autrefois" by the Dogon, but presumably this claim is based on hearsay, since it is uncorroborated by geological or archaeological evidence.[20] There have been similar reports of copper mines in Hausaland, Bornu, Adamawa, Azandeland, southeastern Nigeria, and Chad, none of them substantiated by first-hand observation;[21] what seems likely, therefore, is that information about centers of copper trading or copper smithing was mistakenly interpreted to refer to the actual mining and smelting of the metal.

Several observations stem from this survey of ancient workings in Saharan and sub-Saharan West Africa. First of all, the very early furnaces in the Agadès area would seem to long predate Phoenician settlement on the North African coast and to imply Libyan-Egyptian influence, or, more improbably, independent invention of copper metallurgy. From Agadès, the technology probably spread to Azelick and environs, where it may have been carried on for the better part of two millennia. Akjoujt, however, is more than two thousand kilometers to the west of Agadès and was probably an outpost of Maghrebian-Spanish metalworking traditions rather than an offshoot of Agadès and Azelick.

Until recently it appeared that in both areas the period of exploitation was relatively brief. With growing evidence to the contrary, we can well wonder how miners and smiths found adequate water to wash the ores and fuels to smelt them. Only Hufrat combined substantial mineralization of easily worked ores with ample timber and water.

## CENTRAL AND SOUTHERN AFRICA

The copper resources of Central and Southern Africa are infinitely richer than those to the north. Most were worked for centuries and some continue to be competitive in the world market.

A discontinuous band of mineralization in the form of nonstratified or vein deposits extends from the Middle Niari River of the Congo Republic to northern Angola.[22] The "terre noire" of the Niari-Djoué mineral fields was long exploited for copper, lead, and iron by indigenous metallurgists, while gold in the region went unnoticed until the arrival of the Brazza Mission in 1882.[23] The most important areas of mining in the north were at Mindouli and M'Boko Songho (Sundi: *nsongo* = copper), but localized deposits throughout the region and to some distance in the north were also exploited at various times. At Mindouli itself, mining was concentrated in an area two square kilometers in extent along a chain of rocky hills. Four major mines were in operation, the largest of which comprised 150 to 200 pits, still actively producing at the end of the nineteenth century. At M'Boko Songho the Grande Mine consists of an impressive "chapeau de fer" some 500 meters long by 100 meters wide: a red tumulus hooded with hydroxides of iron, rising out of the middle of a swampy valley richly endowed with oxides of copper and lead as well as iron. Mineralization at both Mindouli and M'Boko Songho lay near the surface and did not extend to any great depth, making them relatively easy to work.[24]

How far back can we date mining in this area? Dupont, one of the first Europeans to reach M'Boko Songho, declared in 1887: "I believe that the total deforestation of this region may be due in part to the centuries-old metallurgical operations, for they must be very ancient."[25] It seems quite probable in fact that these are the mines of the "Land of the Anziques," referred to by Pigafetta in the sixteenth century as lying beyond the Kingdom of Loango and north of the Congo River.[26]

Across the Congo to the south lie the mines of northern Angola, chief among them Bembe, some 70 miles south of São Salvador and about 120 miles inland from the port of Ambriz. Within a few decades of their arrival in 1481, the Portuguese had taken full measure of the abundance of copper produced in the Kingdom of Kongo. "In this land of Manicongo," wrote Pacheco about 1508, "there is no gold . . . but there is much fine copper."[27] Since both Bembe and Mindouli lay within the frontiers of the kingdom in the early sixteenth century, either one or both may have been meant. Indeed, there is little reason to doubt that copper exploitation throughout the lower Congo region antedates the advent of the Portuguese.

Pacheco's report of abundant copper was echoed in subsequent dispatches of Portuguese officials and in the accounts of Pigafetta and the captive Andrew Battell.[28] So flourishing were the Bembe mines that by the 1530s the Portuguese were determined to take them over. Ruy Mendes, factor of the mines, brought in German miners to construct smelting furnaces along the latest central-European lines. They apparently remained for several years at least and fed the myth of rich deposits of silver, as well as copper, in the hinterland of the province of Sonyo, south of the Congo mouth.[29] The Niari mines, in contrast, were probably spared Portuguese ambitions because of their inaccessibility: it is highly unlikely that any European reached them before the late nineteenth century.

In addition to the Bembe region there are copper outcroppings in a number of other parts of Angola. The mines of Dombe Grande, only five leagues from the sea just south of Benguela, were worked at least from the sixteenth century.[30] The "good and abundant copper" which they produced did not fail, too, to interest the Portuguese, who hoped to divert it from trade with the "Lands of Prester John" to their own markets.[31] Two centuries later, Capello and Ivens learned of these mines and noted that they showed "symptoms of having been worked in remote times."[32] North of Dondo, inland from Luanda, Monteiro also found heaps of blue and green carbonate ores and was able to clear several old workings.[33] Widespread indications of copper have been identified in the hinterland of Novo Redondo and to a lesser extent in the Mossamedes region, but it is not clear whether these, too, were worked before the nineteenth century and if so, for how long and on how great a scale.[34] The same may be said for the deposits of Bié, east of Benguela.[35]

Duarte Lopes, who visited São Salvador in the late sixteenth century, describes mines of metal lying to the east of the Kingdom of Kongo.[36] A few years later, the Portuguese governor, Rebello de Aragão, learned from native informants of a "great lake where there is much iron and copper, a lake of remarkable size from which rise many rivers and whence they say are born the waters of the Nile,"[37] a rumor curiously like that which inspired Livingstone in his last years to look vainly for the fountain of the great river systems of Central Africa.

Were these intimations, however vague, of the copper mines of Katanga, whose fame had spread even to the capital of Manicongo and the Atlantic coast? Or did they refer to the much more modest and nearer deposits localized in the basin of the Lubi River in Kasai? Or were they simply another will-o'-the wisp retailed to the Portuguese in response to their often credulous greed for metals? It is impossible to say. Rebello fixes the latitude for his great lake at 16° which in fact is the latitude of Bembe and thus not at all helpful. He himself tried to traverse Africa from the Cuanza to "Monomatapa" (Zimbabwe) but pushed only as far as Bié, still far to the west of Katanga.[38] Lekime, on the other hand, claims that Katangan copper was reaching the Atlantic by the sixteenth century, without, however, offering any proof that it was truly Katangan and not from sources within Angola.[39] Since the Portuguese tried so desperately on repeated occasions to gain control over the Bembe mines, recognizing their importance to the African economy as well as to their own, the silence of the documents about deposits as rich as those of Katanga argues strongly that they did not know of their existence and that there was no direct trade with the Atlantic coast before 1800. Even in the nineteenth century, copper from Katanga seems to have been traded directly only as far as Kasai, and any metal that reached the coast was reexported from that region.[40]

The earliest indisputable written references to the copper of Katanga are contained in a report of Governor Lacerda of Mozambique in 1798. Like Rebello before him, Lacerda had conceived the grand design of crossing the continent from one coast to the other. In preparation, he gathered all

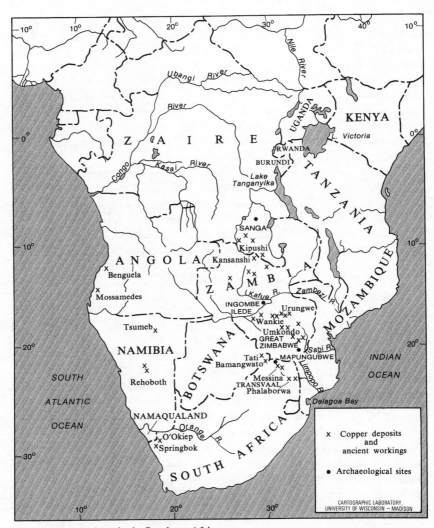

Map 2. Copper deposits in Southern Africa

the information he could find about the interior, particularly about the lands of Kazembe, reputed to be rich in copper and gold. One object of the mission was to divert the trade in copper, "brass," and slaves from the Zambezi Valley to the west coast, where it would be more amenable to Portuguese control. Lacerda died at Kazembe's court before reaching Katanga itself. Eight years later, however, two half-caste traders at last set

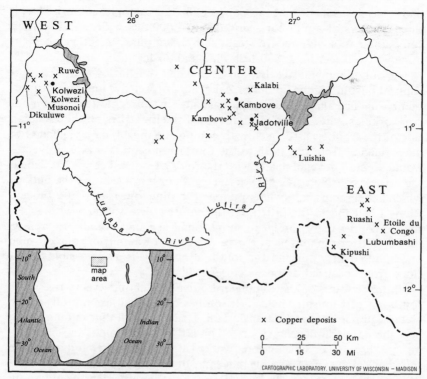

Map 3. Copper mines in Katanga

foot in Katanga, and it is in the journal of one of them, Baptista, that
the word *catanga* first appears in the literature, referring to the country
of "green stones" (malachite).[41] There has been some difference of opinion about the etymology of the name Katanga, which by the nineteenth
century referred to both the chief and the territory.[42]

Documentary evidence for the exploitation of the Katangan mines thus
dates back only to the late eighteenth century. Evidence of other kinds,
nevertheless, indicates a much greater antiquity. First of all, there is the
sheer extent of the ancient workings. Eye-witness accounts and oral traditions concur that by the later nineteenth century mining and smelting had
dropped off sharply or ceased altogether in most areas, so that the bulk
of the extraction must have taken place before about 1850. Surveys carried
out by mining geologists between 1901 and 1906 identified more than a
hundred ancient copper workings, a "discovery" unprecedented in the history of mining for so short a period. Some of the workings were of re-

markable size: The Star of the Congo mine, for example, comprised a pit three-quarters of a mile long, and 600 to 1,000 feet wide, an excavation comparable to some modern steam shovel dug pits.[43] Another open-cut mine was 720 feet long, 480 feet wide and 30 feet deep at one end.[44]

The only Katangan site that has been dated thus far by radiocarbon is Kipushi, just inside the border of Zaire, about forty-five miles west of Lubumbashi. The ancient mining pit has long since been destroyed by modern workings, but a series of undisturbed smelting sites on the Zambian side of the frontier, associated with mining at Kipushi, have yielded C-14 dates ranging from the ninth to the fourteenth century A.D. These dates would seem to dovetail neatly with the finds of worked copper at Sanga, the earliest of which may date to the eighth or ninth century, the bulk of which belong to a slightly later period according to revised dates. Indeed, Phase I at Kipushi (ninth to twelfth centuries) is associated with an H-shaped copper ingot similar to those found at Sanga. In all probability, the copper for the burials at Sanga came from Kantangan sources some one hundred fifty miles to the south, although it is also possible that it came from localized desposits closer still.[45]

Six miles south of the Katangan border and about seventy-five miles southwest of Kipushi, Michael Bisson has carried out excavations of the greatest importance at Kansanshi Hill. He has shown that mining began here about the fourth century A.D.[46] This is the earliest dated "ancient working" yet discovered. Since the ores worked at Kansanshi are similar to those found in Katanga, it is possible that some of the Katangan mines may have been worked at an equally early date. The same argument would apply to other deposits in Zambia, but as yet there is no proof.

The confusion that has arisen over whether any of the Copperbelt mines were worked in the precolonial era stems partly from the definition of Copperbelt and partly from conflicting accounts of early observers. Brooks claims that the term should be restricted to the five mines of N'Changa, N'Kana, Roan Antelope, Mufulira, and Chambezi, that he saw all of the surface evidences before modern mining was started, and that none "had any evidence whatever of previous extraction by natives or anyone else and showed no ore at the surface which would have attracted such work." On the other hand, Phillipson documents small ancient workings at both Chambezi and at Roan Antelope, although at the latter, powdered malachite may have been used as medicine rather than to produce copper.[47]

Outside the Copperbelt proper, virtually all the Zambian mines later pegged by Europeans were on ancient workings: not only Kansanshi but also Bwana M'Kubwa, Sable, Silver King, Kalulu, Chifumpa, Lukasashi. The most extensive of these were at Kansanshi and Bwana M'Kubwa (which is sometimes included in the Copperbelt although the mineralization is

of a very different sort).[48] At Kansanshi, European surveyors found ancient workings covering an area about 7,000 yards in diameter from which
thousands of tons of malachite had been extracted by indigenous miners.
The earliest survey of Bwana M'Kubwa in 1904 described

> two principal old copper workings, parallel and about 30 feet apart, on the
> northeastern slope of the Kopje. One of these is almost continuous and un-
> broken for a length of 750 yards, the width of the excavation varying from
> five feet to 23 feet. The second run of workings extends in the aggregate to
> a distance of 293 yards, the width . . . averaging four feet and its depth two
> feet to 30 feet — in fact the old working had been carried to a depth of 160 feet.[49]

"Chirupula" Stephenson remembered the old working simply as "a thousand yard long gash with sheer walls 30–40 feet high, stained green (malachite), wide enough for two wagons to travel side by side — except where
huge trees had grown."[50]

The mines of the Hook of the Kafue above the confluence of the Mungwa
River, including those of the so-called Big Concession and Mankoya, were
considerably less extensive, and the workings themselves have not been
dated. Nevertheless, archaeologists reconstructing the Early Iron Age in
Zambia from the growing number of excavated sites have theorized that
these mines may have supplied the copper found in the Middle Zambezi
Valley from the third or fourth centuries of our era onward, since they are
the closest sources known.[51] This question will be discussed in more detail
later.

Summers' monumental mapping of ancient workings in Zimbabwe and
neighboring areas of Botswana and the Transvaal lists some 148 copper
mines, of which about 80 lie within the present borders of Zimbabwe. A
few of these are associated with gold, but most were probably worked for
copper alone.[52] According to Summers the only major copper deposit not
worked in the precolonial period was the Molly Mine (Mangula), but this
is disputed by Bancroft's testimony that he personally viewed old workings there.[53] It is hard to imagine that the rich malachite and chrysocolla
ores at Mangula would have passed entirely unnoticed.

The most extensive areas of ancient workings are in the Sinoia region
on the northern part of the plateau and in the Sabi Valley near the Mozambique border. The largest of the latter group, indeed probably the largest
in Zimbabwe, is Umkondo, described in 1906 as covering a space 1,500
feet long and 300 feet wide, with shafts sunk to a depth of 60 feet.[54] It
appears that virtually no gold was obtained in the area of Great Zimbabwe
itself, but copper was mined at what later came to be called Zimbabwe
Copper Mine.[55]

We can surmise that copper and gold were probably worked concurrently in Zimbabwe, since the same prospecting and mining techniques were used, although the refining methods differed. Portuguese sources of the sixteenth century refer to Mombara or Ambara as a major source of copper: this is probably Chedzurgwe, where archaeological excavations have dated the copperworking culture to about 1500 A.D.[56] The only copper mine itself for which a radiocarbon date is available is Umkondo. Here a wooden digging stick found in a shaft has yielded a date of about 1630 A.D. The mine was apparently still being worked in the late nineteenth century. At Aboyne, gold mining has been dated to about 1200 A.D.[57] Unfortunately, no mining or smelting area in Zimbabwe has been subjected to the same sort of study as Kansanshi, so that the development of the industry in any area or over the country as a whole cannot be dated sequentially.

Peripheral to the Zimbabwean deposits is an area of discontinuous mineralization extending from eastern Botswana to Messina in the Limpopo Valley to Phalaborwa in the Lowveld of the eastern Transvaal, the so-called Limpopo Mobile Belt. Copper was still being mined in the Botswana portions of the Belt during the nineteenth century, but no evidence is available for dating the beginnings of the industry. The artist and traveller Burchell was told that surface ores were so plentiful at some of these sites that mining was unnecessary — the ores could simply be gathered.[58] Livingstone, however, found many actual mines with the smoke (from fire-setting) still visible, although they were not very deep. "Copper," he wrote his father-in-law Robert Moffat, "has been worked very extensively at Chonuane. Enormous must the labour of extraction have been."[59] In the Tati region of Botswana, copper is associated with gold, as in Zimbabwe, but to the south in Bamangwato country, copper ores occur alone. Here ancient workings are numerous, some of them with large stopes, but the area has just begun to be explored.[60]

Extensive copper mining was carried out in the northern and eastern Transvaal in pre-European times and, on a more modest scale, in the Magaliesberg. Ancient workings once dotted the landscape down to the edge of the Highveld, readily recognizable in later times by the line of dense bush and trees that almost invariably grew up in the depressions that remained after indigenous miners had filled in the abandoned trenches and shafts. Trevor counted some 120 separate mines in the Messina area alone, just south of the Limpopo River.[61]

Archaeological work carried out by Van der Merwe and Scully at Phalaborwa in the Lowveld indicates that both iron and copper mining began here about the eighth century A.D., perhaps earlier. Copper mining was concentrated at Lolwe Hill, where it has been estimated that over the centuries more than 10,000 tons of rock containing the ores were dug from its shafts and galleries, to be smelted in the myriad furnaces of the surrounding plain.[62]

Attempts to date the Messina workings, on the other hand, have had to rely heavily on oral tradition, since modern mining has destroyed the ancient workings and made archaeological investigation impossible. These traditions have proven somewhat contradictory. One states that when the Venda moved southward across the Limpopo about two hundred years ago, they found the Lemba already mining copper and claiming that their ancestors had been the first to do so in this region. Another tradition, however, derives the Messina miners from the Musina clan, who originally crossed the Lebombo Mountains to settle in Phalaborwa and later migrated north and west to the Zoutpansberg to search for copper.[63] It was probably Messina copper which supplied Mapungubwe and other Greefswald sites fifty-five miles to the east, sites now dated to about the tenth to twelfth centuries.[64]

In the southern Transvaal, an Iron Age copper mine designated simply 47/73 has recently been examined by archaeologists on Olifantspoort Farm where it runs along the slope of a ridge parallel to the main crest of the Magaliesberg. It has not yet been dated, but the ores treated seem very similar to those worked at Uitkomst Cave, twenty-five miles to the southeast and dated by carbon 14 to the mid-seventeenth century. On the other hand, a copper chain and copper beads have been found at Broederstroom 24/73, also in the Magalies Valley, which date from the period 350–600 A.D., so that we can guess that copper was probably worked in the region far earlier.[65]

On the other side of the continent, ancient workings have been found in both Namibia and Namaqualand. The former, in particular, is besprinkled with copper ores, of which by far the most spectacular are the deposits of the Otavi Mountains. Tsumeb, "the green hill," is a mound of almost pure malachite, 180 meters long, 40 meters wide, and 12 meters high, extending to a depth of some 400 meters. Lesser deposits have also been mined at Otzisongati. The earliest travellers beyond the Orange River in the 1790s reported that copper was worked by the Bergdamas, who obtained it from Ovamboland, so that it is highly likely that copper mining in southwest Africa goes back at least to this period.[66]

In Namaqualand, European contacts were made more than a century earlier, so that we can date indigenous mining to the mid-seventeenth century at the latest. An expedition sent out from the Cape by Van Riebeck in 1661 wondered at the quantities of copper and iron jewelry, clearly of native manufacture, worn by the Namaqua. Stories of a "Copper Mountain" soon filtered back to the Cape, and the promise of mineral wealth provoked periodic "copper rushes" over the next two hundred and fifty years. The Copper Mountain itself consists of "six hills which stand out from the high range and show traces of verdigris on the surfaces."[67] In fact, copper is not limited to these hills, for deposits are spread from the Orange River southward to O'Okiep. At O'Okiep the area of mineralization covers about 600 square miles, although the zone of oxidation rarely extends deeper than 70 feet.[68]

The last area that needs to be touched upon is Uganda and the interlacustrine region. Bancroft includes the deposits at Kilembe in the foothills of the Ruwenzori in his sweep of ancient workings,[69] but he is the only one to do so. The surface covering of carbonates, oxides, and silicates would not have been beyond the capabilities of indigenous metallurgists, but if they did exploit these deposits, it must have been on a small scale, since early works do not mention the mine before its discovery by European prospectors in 1927, and later writers do not indicate that old workings were found in the course of modern mining.[70] On the other hand, there are scattered references to sources of malachite in Rwanda from which copper was produced for local consumption,[71] while in eastern Zaire near the Lomami River, Livingstone came upon the "Bakuss" smelting copper from ore and selling it to traders.[72] Undoubtedly many other localized deposits in Zaire have escaped the notice of outsiders altogether.

The extent of ancient workings in tropical Africa bears testimony to the longevity and to the volume of mining activity in a number of areas. Dating is often problematical, although we are at last beginning to accumulate both single dates and sequences for several sites of copper mining and smelting: second and first millennium B.C. for Agadès, fifth century B.C. for Akjoujt, fourth to ninth centuries A.D. for Kansanshi, eighth to fourteenth centuries for Kipushi, eighth to nineteenth centuries for Phalaborwa, thirteenth century for Harmony (also in the Lowveld), seventeenth century for Umkondo. Combining this evidence with the finds at Early Iron Age sites, it seems reasonable to speculate that copperworking began about the second or third century A.D. in parts of Central Africa. Mining may be too formal a term for what certainly started as the simple gathering of mineral-rich rocks from the surface of the ground, to be broken up and smelted in impermanent clay furnaces whose traces would long since have disappeared.

For the mines of Dkra and Hufrat, of the Niari Basin and Angola, there is only documentary evidence. Although this makes clear that copper was being worked in the western Sudan during the fourteenth century and in Congo-Angola by the time the Portuguese arrived late in the following century, it leaves unanswered the chronology of mining at Hufrat. One can hope that archaeology may be able to fill in more of the gaps, as it has at Akjoujt, in Niger, and in Central and Southern Africa, before it is too late.

# The Smith as *Nganga*: Ritual, Social, and Political Aspects of Copperworking

> La figure mythique du Forgeron-Héro-Civilisa-
> teur africain n'a pas encore perdu la signification
> religieuse du travail métallurgique: le Forgeron
> céleste . . . complète la création, organise le
> monde, fonde la culture et guide les humains vers
> la connaissance des mystères.
>
> — MIRCEA ELIADE,
> *Forgerons et Alchimistes*

The skill of ancient prospectors in uncovering copper wherever it was hidden no longer needs to be argued. Perhaps, as Summers has suggested, it was the skill of the botanist rather than the geologist — of people finely aware that certain patterns of vegetation were surer indicators of mineralization than particular rock formations.[1] Ironically, however, but also typically, the very thoroughness with which African copper deposits were identified and exploited had the effect not of inspiring respect for African metallurgists but of casting doubt on the African-ness of the ancient workings. While the assumptions underlying these theories have long since been laid to rest in most parts of the world, there continue to be occasional echoes from the "alien metalworker" camp, so that a brief discussion of this topic forms an appropriate prelude to a more general description of the ritual, social, and political implications of metalworking in precolonial African cultures.

In an article published in 1912, T. G. Trevor, Inspector of Mines for the South African government, distinguished between "ancient" and "native" workings in the Transvaal. The Bantu, he claimed, were incapable of both the effort and the skill demonstrated by the scale of copper mining. Furthermore, native consumption of copper in the form mainly of bangles and the like was too insignificant to account for the output that must have been achieved: "It is improbable," he declared, "that a ton of native copper could now be obtained in the whole of South Africa." He concluded, therefore, that the ancient mines of Rhodesia as well as those of the Transvaal must have been exploited by foreigners, most likely from southern

29

Arabia, who mined copper and gold well before the Christian era and exported them to overseas markets.[2]

This theme of civilizing foreigners was energetically elaborated in the 1920s by the South African physical anthropologist Raymond Dart, who argued that a succession of outsiders — Babylonians, Phoenicians, Arabs, and Indians — masterminded the development of South African mineral wealth. He appealed to rock paintings to strengthen his case, interpreting certain scenes as depicting contact between indigenous Bushmen and Babylonic-Phoenicians, easily identifiable thanks to their beards, Phrygian caps, and occasional white faces. In one picture a bearded foreigner in tunic and cap is allegedly attempting to clothe a naked Bushman girl at swordpoint, so great is his civilizing ardor. Declared Dart, "No arguments, however specious, can gainsay the positive witness of these mute commentaries upon the past history of our country, when as yet the Bantu invader was unknown."[3] Such theories, of course, found their counterpart in the attribution of Great Zimbabwe to immigrant Phoenicians or southern Arabians on the grounds that Africans were incapable of monumental building in stone.

On a more modest level, the anthropologist Stayt viewed the Lemba, the skilled smiths who exploited the copper deposits in the Messina area of the Transvaal, as descendants of early Muslim traders who settled on the coast between the twelfth and sixteenth centuries A.D. They were, he asserted, "Armenoid types" physically and had managed to maintain their intellectual and cultural superiority through endogamy, even though little linguistic evidence could be found to separate them from their Venda hosts.[4] Oral traditions collected subsequently by Van Warmelo seemed to confirm that the Lemba were regarded as foreigners who had come as traders to the Venda "from across the sea" (across the Limpopo?), and he and others have ascribed non-Negroid coloring and features to them.[5]

The argument for foreign influences was not confined to the Transvaal and Zimbabwe. Between 1925 and 1927 a lively dispute raged over the antiquity, origins, and scale of copper mining in Central Africa. T. A. Rickard, a well-known historian of metallurgy, argued that mining in Katanga was of recent origin, only a matter of a century or a century and a half, and that it was begun under the direction of Arab slavers, using forced labor and imported technology to produce metal for export to the Arab world, and later to the Atlantic via Angola. Like Trevor, Rickard minimized the role of the African market as a catalyst for indigenous production.[6] Rickard's main antagonist was a fellow engineer, G. L. Walker, who claimed a high antiquity for copper mining and smelting throughout Africa on the basis of a technology for which there had been sufficient evidence before it was disturbed by European intrusion. If copperworking had been introduced by Arabs, he asked, why would mining and smelting have been limited to the less complex copper carbonates, why would furnaces have been relatively small, why was there no evidence of bronze-making—in other words, why did the technology and level of social organization not reflect those of the proto-industrialized world?[7] Bancroft and other mining engineers familiar with the African scene tended to side with Walker and to agree that copperworking in Katanga long antedated the arrival of Arab traders, even if the latter may have stimulated demand on the eve of the colonial period.[8]

More recently, Summers has again raised the possibility of foreign influence on early mining on the Zimbabwe plateau, particularly influence from South India.[9] The weakest part of his argument, indeed the weakest part of all the arguments for foreign influence, is that mining techniques show so little difference throughout Central and Southern Africa and so little similarity to those in use outside sub-Saharan Africa from late antiquity onward, as we will see in the next chapter. Even Summers can cite only the most general similarities with what is known about methods in South India during the period in question, while the complete absence of any evidence of a windlass in Zimbabwean mining, for example, is hard to explain if it had ever been introduced—as it surely would have been by Indian or Near Eastern metallurgists. The one case of foreign influence that has been explicitly documented before the colonial period is the importation of German miners by the Portuguese to work the Bembe mines during the sixteenth century.[10] Since Portuguese policies in northern Angola seem ultimately to have had a disastrous impact on local mining, we do not know what effect, if any, these miners may have had.[11]

The tendency to assume that Africans were incapable of large-scale productive enterprise of course reflected the ideas of racial superiority that justified the European partition of Africa, while the picture of outside entrepreneurs and technicians directing a servile indigenous labor force in the mines seemed to offer a preview of the conditions that once again prevailed under colonial rule. Such assumptions also gained credibility from the fact that African metalworking was in decline in many areas during the nineteenth century. Several factors contributed to this decline, above all, competition from cheap European imports of copper, brass, and iron, and political upheavals within the continent itself, in particular the Yeke migrations into Katanga and the aftershocks of the *mfecane* (the "time of troubles") in the Transvaal and on the Zimbabwean plateau, replicating the earlier upheavals in northern Angola. What European explorers and prospectors of the latter half of the century found was an industry replete with signs of past greatness that seemed cruelly incongruous with the present.

Nevertheless, even Trevor was by 1930 more cautious than he had been eighteen years earlier in ascribing South African metalworking to non-Bantu metallurgists. [12] And indeed, the body of evidence built up since the work of Gertrude Caton-Thompson at Great Zimbabwe has only served to reinforce her picture of an indigenous technology which owed little or nothing to the outside world once the core of metallurgical knowledge spread throughout the continent in the centuries immediately preceding and succeeding the birth of Christ. The main centers of metalworking have failed to show evidence of either foreign technology or the foreign goods, settlement patterns, and language borrowings that could have been expected to accompany colonies of foreigners producing for an outside market. In the Transvaal itself, quite to the contrary, the pioneering work of Friede and his associates at the University of the Witwatersrand in reconstructing basic operations of Early Iron Age metallurgy has resoundingly confirmed its African character, contributing to the growing consensus that Bantu settlement of the region must now be pushed back into the first millennium A.D. and that these early Bantu introduced metalworking to the region. Similarly, the work of Warnier and Fowler on large-scale iron production in the Cameroon grassfields demonstrates the degree of specialization that could be achieved under the stimulus of a purely regional demand. Here a dense agricultural population and abundant supplies of ore and fuel combined to produce what has been aptly called "a nineteenth-century Ruhr." [13] There is no reason to believe that this area is unique: rather, the study of African technology and its social setting is still in its infancy.

## SMITHING AND THE SUPERNATURAL

Who, then, were these African metalworkers? Who mined and smelted the copper? Who fashioned it into the variegated forms found the length and breadth of the continent? What social and ritual roles were bound up with the working of metals?

In most general terms, copperworking has been the province of the specialist, that is, of the smith. The degree of specialization obviously depended on the volume of metalworking and its complexity, which themselves were determined by the availability of the raw materials and the market for finished products. Smiths of certain ethnic groups became famous for their art, but few regions seem to have been entirely without craftsmen of some sort. In some societies, especially those whose wealth allowed considerable stratification and a demand for sumptuary goods, copper- and brassworkers formed a craft group distinct from ironworkers, though it may be significant that in all of these cases with which I am familiar the artisans worked imported copper and brass: they were not concerned with the mining and smelting processes.

Much has been written about the ambivalence attaching to the person of the smith, not only in Africa but in other pre-industrial societies throughout the world. Feared, revered, despised — whatever the words used — smiths have traditionally been viewed as a people set apart from the rest of mankind by the nature of their work and the common practice of endogamy, or at least of marriage within prescribed groups. The use of the word *caste* in connection with African smiths rather than the more neutral if more awkward *hereditary occupational group,* however, can be misleading, denoting as it does not only apartness but a rigid social hierarchy of the sort familiar in India but not typical of Africa. True, the smith occupies a clearly inferior position among such peoples as the Tuareg, Masai, and Somali, but this is undoubtedly because, as Cline long ago pointed out, these pastoralists despise *all* those who do manual work.[14] Often, too, the smiths are ethnically different or at least regarded as "others." Among the Chaamba of the Sahara, for example, they are sedentary blacks, concentrated in oases and politically subservient to their nomadic Berber overlords.[15]

In the agricultural or mixed-farming societies that predominate south of the desert, this inferiority is decidedly rare. On the contrary, the smith plays a central and powerful role in both the natural and the supernatural spheres. In fact the distinction itself is false, since the roles are intimately connected and since such dualism is alien to African thought. The smith functions as priest, artist, shaman, magician, initiator precisely because his work demands not merely manual skills but the esoteric knowledge to manipulate the dangerous forces at play in the extraction of ores and in their transformation into finished objects. As Ndinga-Mbo expresses it, "In venturing into the bowels of the earth to extract metals, the goods of the gods who are believed to live there, the smith braves the order of nature. The other phases of metallurgy are equally acts that bring the smith into competition with the gods." To do this successfully and safely, the smith must be a master, *nganga,* a word that in Kikongo and related Bantu languages connotes a specialist, and to be a specialist generally demands not only mastery and skill but also the possession of magical powers.[16] "Opening a mine, extracting a mineral is equivalent to murdering a superior being, the Earth, this mother of mothers," writes Cissé of Mande belief, so that the smith must know the proper offering to make to the hyena, guardian of the earth.[17]

Indeed, throughout the western Sudan, the smith figures prominently in mythology. Songhay tradition gathered by Jean Rouch relates that the son of the *génie de l'eau* taught the ancestors of Songhai smiths how to change earth into water, that is, how to smelt metals by means of fire.[18] In Dogon mythology, the semidivine nature of the smith is even more explicit. According to Dieterlen, the smith has a different biological status from the eight ancestral families, since he has been formed from the placenta of Nommo, the offspring of the creator god and the earth: "Nommo and the smith are of red blood; Nommo and the smith are twins, both are red like copper." We will explore the implications of these expressions in a later chapter, but for now what is important is the Dogon belief not only in the magical powers of the smith (that he can, for example, change himself into all sorts of beings, animal and vegetable) but also in the necessity of endogamy—because he possesses a "mixed blood," derived in part from the sacrificial blood of the divinity.[19] Further, the processes by which he produces metal are often conceived of explicitly or implicitly in sexual terms, analogous to sexual intercourse and birth in their invocation of vital forces —hence the function of the smith as circumcisor.[20]

Kongo traditions identify the first king as a smith, while myths in western and southern Tanzania, in western Uganda, and in Burundi associate the introduction or perfection of ironworking with particular kings or with chiefly lineages.[21] As Vansina and Sutton have pointed out, these should not be taken literally but are intended to show the symbolic equality of king and smith, the importance, above all, of iron as a symbol of power.[22] The prominence of smiths in the epic of Sundiata underscores the same point.

Iron is the metal of the hoe and the spear, the key to the labors of peace and war; but the working of other metals was also ritualized as far as one can judge from the often imprecise documentation, particularly operations that identified the smith most clearly as magician: mining, smelting, and casting. Simple forging, on the other hand, seems to have been much less ritualized.

Accounts of copper mining and smelting in Katanga emphasize the secret knowledge of the master smelter, passed on from generation to generation, but also introduce the personage of the "maître sorcier," the nganga, as somehow distinct, unlike the composite figure of smith-magician described by Ndinga-Mbo in the Congo Republic. This master sorcerer* is present at all crucial stages of metalworking, collaborating with the chief and his fellow smiths (see fig. 1).[23] Thus before mining can begin in the Kakanda mine, the old Yeke chief N'Kuba, master of the Dikuluwe smelters, must invoke his predecessors and mentors to propitiate the spirits of the mine: "You who have preceded us, it is you who have opened for your children the entrails of the mountain. Grant that we may find treasure." The master sorcerer then drives three stakes into the ground where shafts are to be sunk as protection against cave-in and spits a mouthful of a bark decoction over the area to speed discovery of veins of copper.[24]

---

*The word *sorcerer* or *magician* seems preferable to *shaman,* used by Cline, because of the latter's rather particularistic derivation from northeast Asian and related cultures.

Monsignor de Hemptinne was the first Catholic missionary to reach Katanga (1910) and was eventually named apostolic prefect of the province. He settled initially in the village of Chief N'Kuba, obtaining a concession of the salt marshes in the region and exploiting them on behalf of the Church. He first observed copper-working at the Kakanda mine east of modern Kolwezi in 1911. In October 1924 he again prevailed on N'Kuba to reenact the procedures from start to finish, and it is the account of these two campaigns that de Hemptinne published as "Les mangeurs de cuivre" in the review *Congo* and subsequently as a booklet. He also filmed and photographed the 1924 campaign but apparently did not publish any of the photographs, and it has not been possible to track down the originals or the film. A number were published, however, in *Mwana Shaba,* journal of Géca-mines (successor to the Union Minière du Haut-Katanga), December 15, 1969, and it is from this source that the selection on these pages is taken. Although the quality is inevitably poor, the pictures represent a unique record of indigenous copper-working.

1. Rituals performed by the *maître-sorcier* before starting the bellows

2. Women washing the ore

3. Extraction of malachite

36

4. Making tuyeres by hollowing out small termite hills

5. Constructing the furnace from termite hills

37

6. Wiredrawing

7. Casting copper ingots in open moulds

38

To the east, in the Luishia area, the maître-sorcier precedes the miner to make fires around the periphery of the mine on which he throws green leaves of *mwenge* to purify it of evil spirits. In the evening he spreads some of the cinders from these fires in the mine pits, while others he mixes with certain roots, a pinch of powdered ore, and water. Each morning the miners rub this mixture over their entire bodies before beginning work. If a miner is accidentally touched by a stone of any size while mining, he stops as if dead, struck by the spirit of the mountain. His comrades carry him immediately to the sorcerer, who administers a special medicine that produces vomiting and diarrhea, then rubs him again with the original cinder mixture. The same ritual is used if a miner is called back to the village and then returns to the mine.[25] Ndinga-Mbo describes comparable propitiatory rituals among the Koyo and Akwa of the northern Congo Republic, one of the few areas, it would seem, where they have continued virtually to the present.[26]

From these accounts it becomes clear that only those with special ritual knowledge can perform the ceremonies that neutralize the malefic forces of the earth and make it render up its treasures, but that once these ceremonies have been performed, anyone can participate in extracting ore. In fact, according to Ndinga-Mbo, the *ngang'okuba,* the master of the forge, never stays on the mining site after digging the first hole but leaves it to the villagers, who then supply him with ore to be smelted in the next phase, an operation that is comparably ritualized.[27]

Among the Yeke the ritualization of the smelting process even extends to the preparation of the charcoal, clear recognition, no doubt, of the importance of the proper fuel to the procedure. When smelting is about to begin, the smelter washes his hands and face with an infusion of bark prepared by the maître-sorcier already referred to. From that point on, however, the smith is fully in charge: "He alone will know the furnace. . . . One senses in him an important actor confronted with a delicate and mysterious task." He throws the ritual water on the tuyeres along with a cluster of herbs, the charcoal is lit, the bellows operators set to work, and the crowd of onlookers takes up the chant:

> Ku Mulu wa Kalabi kudi kinonge.
> On the summit of Kalabi rises a high furnace,
> a high furnace with a large womb,
> the heritage of our father Lupodila,
> a high furnace where copper trickles and billows.
> O my Mother! O my Mother!

As de Hemptinne comments with Belgian understatement, "the mystery of the smelting furnace is not a simple operation of chemistry and physics."[28] Indeed, it is very close to parturition. Such symbolism is even more explicit, incidentally, in an iron-smelting furnace, photographed by Brian Fagan in Zambia, which was supported on four legs and supposed to embody the form of a woman giving birth, or in Tanzanian furnaces with sculpted female breasts. In Zambia, too, smelting of both copper and iron was accompanied by chants intoned by smiths without which the smelt would not, it was held, have succeeded.[29]

While no particular rituals are reported for the simple refining of smelted copper nor for casting ordinary ingots, Cline errs in asserting that they are absent for all casting.[30] Dark describes elaborate sacrifices of goats, cocks, and cows and special prayers that precede brass casting in Benin, for it is recognized that casting large pieces is dangerous business: if the pouring is not done just right, the mould can blow up and kill the craftsmen involved. The assistance of a host of deities is invoked — Ogun, Ehi, Edion, and Iguedhae, the legendary caster who is supposed to have introduced the art from Ife.[31] In northeastern Nigeria Gude smiths also performed rituals to insure success in casting:

> The craftsman . . . goes to the bush and brings back two different kinds of green leaves, a dried piece of vine and an earthworm mound. A piece of the vine is bitten off and chewed while the other ingredients are mixed together with water. A small amount of the concoction is rubbed on top of the mould. The remainder is taken to the furnace.
>
> The furnace is spit upon several times with the piece of vine that has been chewed, and the remainder of the concoction is rubbed on the inside of the furnace. The purpose of the ritual, according to the craftsman, is that should the molten brass find a hole in the mould, the medicine would suck it back and prevent it from running to the bottom of the furnace.
>
> During the ritual a prayer is offered which would be something like this: "God, this is the work which I have done myself. Help me for these things to come out of the fire well. If someone wants to spoil them for me, then destroy him. I want this metal to come out good and I do not want deceit to play a part in this work."[32]

Even more complex are the rituals surrounding the casting of *edan* by Ogboni smiths among the Yoruba. These brass cult objects may be made only by men past the age of fathering children (just what this age is Williams does not make clear), because the spells invoked during the manufacture of cult images — that is, the constant invocation of the *orisa,* or spirit — might impair the potency of younger men. Furthermore, younger men would have to fear the loss of children already born, as a result of the superior powers inherent in the art. The casting operation itself is surrounded with libations, vigils, sacrifices, and other rites. These, as Williams notes, give a kind of sacredness to the object even before it is cast and emphasize its close association with the earth, since the edan is conceived of as a vehicle for the spirit of the earth.[33] Clearly, then, the casting of sacred objects or even of forms of jewelry associated with status or ceremonial wear, as in the Gude case, is ritualized both because of the uncertainty of the process, the ever-present risk of failure or even danger in the casting operation, and because of the qualities believed to inhere in the finished product, qualities that derive, in turn, from the material, its form, and the transformation that gives form to the material.

One of the rare studies to state explicitly that the forging of copper is subject to the same interdictions as the forging of iron is that of Célis and Nzikobanyanka concerning Burundi. Here copperworking is a specialized occupation, but all coppersmiths are also capable of working iron. No women or strangers are allowed to be present during either forging or wire-drawing, and sexual relations are forbidden the night before work is undertaken. In theory, only the future owner of the bracelet being forged—and it is primarily a question of bracelets—is allowed to attend, perhaps for the practical reason of keeping an eye on his valuable copper, and he is supposed to offer banana beer to the craftsman to lighten his labors. Significantly, the word used to designate the recompense of the smith is not the ordinary word for wage but that used also for payment to a diviner. Once the bracelet is completed, its owner should never pass it over a fire, for fear of destroying it. There is, it is true, something of a paradox in the special status of the smith in Burundi, since he is always a Hutu (or, rarely, a Pygmy), never one of the ruling Tutsi, and yet may own cattle and build a house of brick.[34] According to tradition, copper- and ironsmiths were taught their art by the first ruler, Ntare Rushatsi, who wanted objects of copper—lances, bracelets, even a hammer—as symbols of royal authority and wealth. These same objects were then used in divination after his death.[35]

The privileged position of the coppersmith in Burundi is paralleled by that of the brass caster in West Africa. Benin is, of course, the best-known example. According to one tradition, the art was introduced by the Oba Oguola, and it has remained exclusively a royal prerogative, identified with the temporal and spiritual power of the dynasty.[36] Brass casters form a separate guild and consider their chief to be head of both the brass- and ironworkers, a point disputed by the latter. When large objects are being cast, the brass casters mobilize the blacksmiths to provide enough charcoal and to work the bellows necessary to have relays of molten metal at hand. As a sign of their superiority, they then dismiss the blacksmiths when the pouring is accomplished and before the moulds cool and are broken open. The king (*oba*) himself formerly attended the operation and richly rewarded casters for successful work.[37] According to Egharevba, the Oba Eweka II (1914–33) was a skilled brass smith.[38] In a related vein, a descendant of the royal family of Dahomey, where brass casters also formed an influential group, served as their titular head in the late 1960s.[39]

In Nupe, the culture hero Tsoede is said to have brought back with him from Idah workers in iron and brass to impart their skills to local craftsmen. As Nadel remarks, there may be some truth in these traditions, since the sacred bronze figures of Tada and Jebba are unlike anything known in Nupe and the north, and seem stylistically and technologically oriented toward the south, toward Ife and Benin, or possibly toward some as yet unidentified Nigerian tradition of metalworking.[40] Nadel's chronology, however, no longer fits with the age assigned to these pieces.

Among the Bagam of western Cameroon the brass caster had the status of attendant on the head chief, from whom he took orders directly and near whose quarters he carried on his work.[41] Other examples could be cited from other African societies that link the art of copperworking with the sacral character of kingship: the fact that the Bushoong smith, "though a commoner wears a hatpin of brass which is the privilege of members of the royal family,"[42] or that Yeke smelters wear the "kilungu," the shell so widely associated with chiefly rank in East Africa.[43] It might seem a contradiction then that the Yoruba Ogboni society has the right to cast in brass, but Williams and others have pointed out that this society functions in fact as a locus of power balancing or even competing with that of the king.[44] This association of copper and brass with power will be explored more fully in part III.


## POLITICAL CONTROL OF MINES
## AND THE ORGANIZATION OF WORK

Information about control of copper mines is often confused and confusing. It is highly unlikely, for example, that the King of Kongo "gave" the copper mines of Bembe to the Portuguese in the latter half of the sixteenth century, as Balthazar Rebello de Aragão relates, a cession which later provided the justification for Portuguese occupation of the mines in 1856.[45] Indeed, although Travassos Valdez claims the mines had long been unworked at this time, Monteiro states that they "belonged" to several surrounding towns which worked them but that the natives of other towns were also allowed to extract malachite on payment of a percentage of the ore.[46] At M'Boko Songho, north of the Congo, Dupont was also told that the mines belonged to neighboring towns.[47] More romantically, the mines of Kalabi in Katanga, visited by Capello and Ivens in the mid-1880s, were reputedly "owned" by a princess named Inafumo or Inafume.[48]

What Europeans referred to as rights of ownership should more properly be defined as usufructory rights, that is, rights of exploitation. In the words of Sundström, "As a basic principle, mines were not regarded as private property, but belonged to the tribe like any piece of land. A mining site belonged for the duration to whoever worked it."[49] Outside groups might be allowed to mine as long as they paid a percentage of the yield to the recognized overlord, as at Bembe. Similarly, San in Namibia paid a tribute which included copper ore to the Ovambo.[50] Suzerainty could, in fact, become very complicated: the Mwilu mines in western Katanga were under the immediate control of the master forgers of the region, who in turn were obligated to send bars of copper to their overlord, Quibiri, who ultimately sent them to his overlord, the Mwata Yamvo. When these lands were seized by Kazembe, he entered the chain of tribute immediately below the Mwata Yamvo.[51]

If local traditions can be accepted, many mines remained undeveloped because the indigenous peoples lacked the skills to work them. Thus according to one account, mining did not begin in the Luishia area until the early eighteenth century with the arrival of Kipai, who had learned the art of smelting copper from a "Mulenge" in the Zambezi Valley whom his mother had married. When mother and son later returned to her native Katanga, Kipai accidentally came upon outcroppings of malachite while hunting, and actively encouraged by the reigning chief, began to develop the resources of the area.[52] There is, however, an inherent implausibility in this story—that copperworking would have been brought from an area where ores are not found to one close to ancient centers of the art—and it may reflect internal political relationships rather than an accurate history of metallurgy in the region.

The most extensive account of the organization of copperworking in nineteenth-century Katanga is that reconstructed from oral traditions by Marchal and published in 1939. It concerns only the Luishia region (Jadotville district) but even for this limited sphere points up the differences from chiefdom to chiefdom, so that one must beware of broad generalizations. According to Marchal, the chief Katanga (like Kazembe, for example, the proper noun designated both the title and the place) had exclusive rights to most of the mines in the region. One particularly energetic chief, Katanga Kapururu, organized large-scale mining in the first half of the nineteenth century, directly employing both indigenous and foreign workers and encouraging agricultural production to feed them. During this boom period, nine hundred or more miners may have been employed in his domains, about a third of them foreigners, including slaves who obtained their freedom after three or four mining campaigns. Indigenous miners working under accredited smelters received copper or goods to the value of about 60 kilograms of copper per campaign, while foreigners were fed by the chief and paid 30 to 50 kilograms for about five months' work. In the nearby chiefdom of Kembe, in contrast, access to mines was open to any member of the local population and to friendly outsiders upon payment of a tithe to the chief. Each village had one or two teams of miners under the direction of the head smelter.

Potential competitors could be excluded from mining and smelting precisely because they lacked the skills, ritual as well as technological, which were jealously guarded within the families of master smelters. Early Yeke immigrants to Katanga, for example, came strictly as traders. Once they had conquered the country under their leader Msiri, their smelters, who had known only the working of iron in their homeland, had to be initiated into the secrets of copperworking by their allies, the Sanga smiths, or in the eastern and central areas by the Samba, with the result that their methods differed, as we will see in the next chapter. Once initiated, they formed powerful guilds into which they initiated their mentors and which dominated production throughout Katanga.[53] To some extent they killed the goose that laid the golden egg, for under Msiri production declined and by the turn of the century amounted to only a trickle.[54] To be sure, this was probably inevitable, in the light of historical events affecting Katanga and all of Africa.

The division of labor in many mining areas seems to have been a logical one: women and children did the surface gathering as well as the washing and sorting of ores (see fig. 2), while men worked underground.[55] Nevertheless, there may well have been exceptions on both scores. Ladame, a territorial administrator in the Belgian Congo writing in 1921, claims that women were rigorously excluded from Katangan mines and their environs; Marchal, speaking specifically of the Luishia region, confirms this.[56] But Carnahan, who visited Dikuluwe in 1920, offers a firsthand account: "Most of the miners were women, to the number of about two hundred, working under men, in the ratio of one capita, or boss, to fifteen women."[57] This was simple surface digging, however, or inclines of soft ore, whereas Ladame may have been referring to deep mining or to a different area.

Nonetheless, women may also have mined underground. Many observers have been struck by the narrowness of trenches and mineshafts in ancient workings in Africa as elsewhere.[58] Some have gone so far as to suggest a race of pygmy miners reminiscent of the gnomes that even Agricola firmly believed inhabited the darker recesses of mines. Schofield, on the other hand, theorizes that underground mining may have been performed by women and children to minimize the size of the hole needed, especially in difficult rock. In support of this view he notes that skeletons of women and young girls have been found in several Zimbabwean mines, as well as iron bracelets used only by women votaries of a particular cult, and draws obvious parallels with the employment of children in English mines until the nineteenth century.[59] Van der Merwe remains unconvinced. Commenting on shafts found at Lolwe (Phalaborwa) which were about 70 feet deep but only about 18 inches in diameter, he writes: "I cannot imagine a relay of pre-pubescent girls being lowered by their ankles to dig it, nor a tribe of enslaved Bushmen (as the locals suggested). There must have been some workings inside the blasted-out bench, providing a connection to the vertical ventilation shaft."[60] That is, the extremely narrow shafts may have been for air circulation rather than for extraction of ore.

Van der Merwe's comment raises the question we have only touched upon in passing: the use of slave labor. Though oral and literary sources suggest that slaves may have been employed in gold mining in West Africa,[61] evidence for their widespread use in copper mines is uneven. The earliest report is that of Ibn Battuta, who noted that slaves of both sexes were involved in the mining and smelting of copper at Takedda in the southern Sahara in the mid-fourteenth century.[62] More than five hundred years later, Herero slaves captured by the Nama are said to have ended up in the copper mines at O'Okiep in Little Namaqualand,[63] while at Hufrat en-Nahas, Gessi Pasha found much of the mining in the hands of slaves in the late 1870s when the entire area was controlled by the break-away slave raider, Suleiman Zubeir Bey.[64] As we have seen, traditions collected by Marchal refer to the use of slaves by Katanga Kapururu even before the conquest by Msiri about 1850; these same sources claim that Msiri then forced the labor of reluctant miners and monopolized the sale of copper.[65] Nevertheless, Crawford's account, much closer to the events, notes that it was "only with his copper and iron smelters [that Msiri was] wont to deal in any measure humbly," since he knew that they were the foundation of his greatness, so that while he may have forced ordinary miners into the pits, he seems to have handled his smelters much more gingerly.[66] De Hemptinne, for his part, makes no mention of traditions of slave or forced labor but describes a division of produce among Yeke in which each miner, including women, was entitled to his or her own diggings minus the requisite tribute to the chief.[67]

As we have noted, many ethnic groups living in the midst of copper-rich regions had no involvement in the industry at all, leaving that to specialist clans or peoples. And even among the latter, only a fraction were actually engaged in metalworking: "Every Bayeke is not a miner any more than is every inhabitant of the Borinage," as de Hemptinne, good Belgian that he was, expressed it. Even chiefs were not necessarily "mangeurs de cuivre."

Like hunters, "copper eaters" had to be admitted by initiation into the secret fraternity.[68]

The degree of specialization varied widely, as one might expect, from very part-time to full-time. In some areas, mining and smelting were perforce dry season occupations, although forging could take place at any time. In other regions and with other types of technologies such as the "four volant," the small, nonpermanent furnace of the Yeke, copperworking could be carried on throughout the year. In practice it was neatly adapted to the agricultural calendar: as soon as the sorghum was gathered in mid-May, the entire village moved to the mining site, where land was cleared and eleusine planted. This ripened in the course of the mining campaign, so that two agricultural and one mineral crop were harvested in well under a year. None of the accounts make quite clear whether the Yeke smith himself took part in any aspects of agriculture, however, or whether he could afford to be a full-time specialist.

At the other end of the spectrum, mining at Messina (Transvaal) was formerly in the exclusive hands of the Musina people, according to a tradition recorded by Van Warmelo in the 1930s. They practiced no agriculture at all, devoting themselves man, woman, and child to working the rich veins and casting ingots, which they exchanged for food with neighboring groups who apparently knew nothing of copperworking. The Musina preserved their monopoly and their ethnic separateness by restricting marriage to the two clans into which they were subdivided.[69]

Another form of specialization more narrowly concerned with the actual working of refined metal is that between ironsmiths and coppersmiths. Although in many areas, as we have seen, they were one and the same, elsewhere they formed distinct social groups. Where copperworkers did not themselves mine and smelt ores, relying on traded metal, they tended to become "jewelers" as opposed to smiths, properly speaking. The *niaka* among the Mossi and the Kpeene of the Senufo[70] had their counterparts in Benin, Akan, Hausa, and Nupe brass smiths, all of whom were differentiated from blacksmiths.[71] And though this specialization is most abundantly documented in West Africa, it also occurred elsewhere. A Hurutse in South Africa told the missionary Robert Moffat, "I am not an ironsmith, I work in copper."[72] Similarly, special craftsmen forge copper and brass in Burundi and draw copper wire in Kiziba on Lake Victoria.[73] Such specialization not only implies ample supplies of copper and its alloys but a demand capable of supporting it. It may also imply, at least in some cases, a secularization of the craft: one is born a smith, say the Mossi, but one becomes a jeweler.[74] Just how common this is, the existing documentation does not yet allow us to speculate.

Though forms of endogamy tended to keep copperworking the preserve of particular families, there are, as always, exceptions. According to Froehlich, any Konkomba (northern Togo) could work iron and make copper and brass into bracelets if he had been initiated into the secrets of the art; there is no smith "caste." True, during the colonial period, their art at times degenerated into little more than recycling telegraph wire into bracelets as fast as it was strung.[75] Furthermore, although "guilds" monopolized brass casting and smithing in highly developed cultures in West Africa, they were not always rigidly hereditary. Two large family groups reputedly were the earliest to practice casting in Nupe, for example, and most modern brass smiths at least claim descent from them, but unrelated boys may be taken in as apprentices and trained to the profession. Marketing of the wares is delegated to the women of these families when work is not done on commission.[76] In a curious twist to the high degree of specialization usually associated with casting, Afigbo notes that recent fieldwork in southeastern Nigeria suggests that casters within the Igbo Nri culture complex did not pursue their craft as a profession but undertook it to meet the ritual requirements of the society,[77] a situation perhaps analogous to that of Yoruba Ogboni casters.

One of the standbys of the history of metallurgy is the itinerant smith. This gypsy figure is now under attack by prehistorians, above all on the basis of ethnographic data.[78] In Africa there are only isolated examples of such smiths outside of southeastern Nigeria. Before we discuss them, however, a few clarifications are in order. First of all, since metals are often found in areas far from settlements or even in areas hostile to permanent settlement, it has been common to establish temporary mining camps at a distance from the home base. Thus Bisson found that the earliest groups exploiting the Kansanshi (Zambia) deposits beginning about the fourth century A.D. formed no permanent villages near the mines.[79] Similarly, Crawford, travelling in Katanga in the latter half of the nineteenth century, remarked on the absence of habitation in the vicinity of the Mirambo copper mines and was told that the natives came long distances to dig for metal, which they carried back to the villages to smelt[80] — possibly because of a lack of fuel and water in the area, though he himself does not offer any explanation for so arduous an undertaking. Secondly, entire peoples specialized in metalworking might migrate from one copperworking area to another: both the Musina and Lemba are said to have done this, according to different Transvaal traditions. Or individual craftsmen might introduce their arts from one center to another, as in the legends of Benin, Nupe, and a host of other societies. None of these phenomena, of course, qualifies as itinerancy. And since most areas of Africa had their own metalworking skills by the late first millennium A.D., the itinerant smith, had he once existed, would gradually have become obsolete. Certain ethnic groups, it is true, became famous for their fine craftsmanship, but in this case the objects they fashioned may have been more mobile than the creators.

The Lemba are a notable exception. Junod, who studied them around the turn of the century, describes travelling coppersmiths who obtained copper from miners in the Venda Mountains in the form of sticks called *ritsondjolo,* which they carried to the villages of their Sotho hosts and clients to make into bracelets of fine-drawn wire, a skill the Sotho did not possess. So prized were these bracelets that they had a ready sale everywhere and purchased corn, goats, cattle, and even wives. True itinerants, the Lemba would stay for a while in one area, then move on to another.[81] Less well documented are the smiths of Ondonga in Ovamboland (Namibia): Lebzelter simply refers to them as an "itinerant group" and notes that formerly the lords of Ondanga were masters of the copper mines at Otavi.[82]

The best-known domain of itinerant smithing is the southeastern coastal region of Nigeria, an area of mangrove swamps without local supplies of metal, even iron. Coastal peoples have long been served by smiths of the hinterland, of whom the most famous were the Awka and the Abiriba, both Ibo subgroups. By the nineteenth century, Awka smiths were organized into guilds, and operated as journeymen who set up shop in or near village markets. Gradually, fixed tours evolved, and certain circuits became the preserve of specific Awka kin groups who not only manufactured iron tools and weapons but also brass ankle plates, leg coils, and bells. Their market extended as far west as the Itsekiri and Urhobo beyond the Niger River. To the east, Abiriba metallurgists of the Cross River region occasionally settled in villages, but the largest number appear to have moved about the monthly fairs and markets which flourished under Aro patronage as part of the trading system that linked the coast with the hinterland. Aro traders, who themselves have no traditions of smithing or casting, furnished Abiriba brassworkers with raw materials in the form of copper and brass rods, and these were made into cult objects and personal ornaments. Neaher's field researches have shown that this pattern of itinerancy was well established, and indeed, still continues, if on a drastically reduced scale.[83] A comparable pattern obtained among Kpeene (Senufo) casters, who might live for years as "guests" in a settlement or who might follow market circuits to sell their wares.[84]

Specialist or jack-of-all-trades, artisan or artist, magician or courtier, the African copperworker was a technologist. Without a profound knowledge of his craft, there would have been traffic with neither gods nor kings. It is this knowledge that we will be discussing in the next two chapters.

# "Mangeurs de Cuivre": Mining and Smelting

*Kintengwe twayo kulyo mukuba.*

We are the furnaces,
we are going to eat copper.

The typical copper deposit worked by African miners lay on a slope or hill. Sometimes it was merely a *kopje*, sometimes a more majestic outcropping that received the name of mountain, such as the Koperberg of Namaqualand. At the surface of the ground there was often a layer of gossan or iron oxides covering the zone of oxidized copper ores which were the result of millennia of weathering by wind and rain. Below the oxidation zone, at varying depths, were the zones of secondary and primary enrichment: sulphide ores such as chalcocite, bornite, and the more complex chalcopyrites, compounds of copper, sulphur, and iron. Mineralization occurred in broad strata or in veins, embedded in a host of matrices ranging from loose shale and clay to hard quartz. Even within a small area, geological factors often intruded to give deposits very different configurations (diagram 1).

The oxidized ores found most commonly in Africa are the carbonates: malachite, $Cu_2(OH)_2CO_3.Cu(OH)_2$, with a copper content of 54.7 percent, and azurite, $2CuCO_3.Cu(OH)_2$, 55 percent copper. Cuprite, the red oxide of copper, has a metal content of 88.8 percent but is much rarer than either malachite or azurite. Chrysocolla, a hydrated silicate of copper, also occurs in the oxidized zone. Malachite was clearly the main source for the metallic copper produced by native metallurgists south of the Sahara. Since azurite occurs frequently with malachite, it, too, was probably worked in some areas.[1] Whether chrysocolla was identified as a copper ore is less certain;[2] in fact, the question has recently been raised whether it would have been technically possible to smelt ores containing a mixture of malachite and chrysocolla as at Azelick.[3] On the other hand, Azelick apparently was unusually well supplied with native copper, which would have been the easiest of all to work.[4]

Many, if not most, ancient workings in Africa were abandoned before the colonial period. Frequently stopes and shafts were filled in, leaving little trace. Some may have been deserted because of the exhaustion of

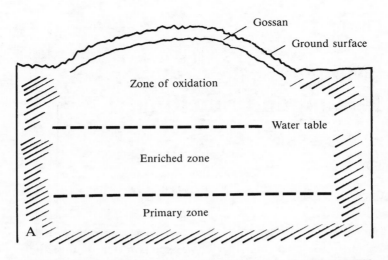

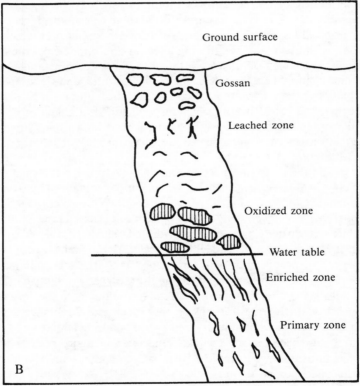

Diagram 1. Schematic diagram of copper mineralization.
        A. Section of typical copper deposit (after Tylecote, 1976)
        B. Enlargement of copper deposit (after Bateman, 1950)

oxide ores or because they had reached unmanageable depths. Others may have been the scene of accidents and considered unlucky.[5] Still others would have fallen victim to economic competition from the coast or to political upheavals such as the Yeke invasions of Katanga in the mid-nineteenth century.[6] The furnaces used to smelt copper ores were less solid than their counterparts used for iron and are almost uniformly in a state of ruin or have vanished altogether, leaving, at best, heaps of slag to mark their former presence. Even these slag heaps are frequently mistaken for iron-smelting slags because of the frequent association of copper and iron oxides.

Furthermore, eye-witness descriptions of copper mining and smelting, dating from the time when these activities were a living part of the cultural tradition, are rare. Consequently, to understand indigenous techniques we must fall back on travellers' accounts, on the occasional enlightened mining engineer who noted the remains of ancient mines uncovered during modern operations, on archaeological excavations and reconnaissances, and on the several reenactments of metalworking commissioned by investigators in the field, bringing out of retirement elderly specialists who had not yet forgotten how things had once been done. All of these sources of information have their limitations. Few travellers knew much about metallurgy; more important, they often met with extreme reticence or open hostility when they tried to inquire about mines, and were even barred from regions where mining was still taking place.[7] Mining engineers had little leisure to study the details of ancient workings and lacked the training and resources of modern archaeologists. Reconstructions, "command performances," no matter how willingly carried out, are artificial, and with the long period of time that has passed without practice, indigenous metallurgists have forgotten important aspects of the art and lost the expertise that comes from experience, the almost intuitive sense of the successful smelter who knows exactly what is going on inside the furnace at any moment. And even the archaeologist is limited to what objects can tell him, supplemented only by what may be remembered in oral tradition.

## THE "MANGEURS DE CUIVRE": CENTRAL AFRICA

The most colorful and complete description of a "command performance" is that published by Monsignor de Hemptinne, Apostolic Bishop of Katanga.[8] De Hemptinne mobilized an entire village of Yeke to conduct a campaign of mining and smelting at Kakanda mine (Katanga) in 1911 and again in 1924, and recorded the undertaking in print and on film. The "mangeurs de cuivre"—so called because of the nourishing and enriching quality ascribed to copper—responded to de Hemptinne's invitation with enthusiasm, he tells us, suggesting that the enterprise was viewed almost as a lark, leavened with festivity and mystery. His account conveys nothing of the sense of dreaded slave labor so commonly associated with mining. Of course, we must allow for the colonial situation and his exalted rank, but it may also be that mining in Katanga was simply a more benign pastime than elsewhere, thanks to the superficial character of most of the deposits and the relative ease with which they could be worked.

Men, women, and children departed for the mines under the leadership of their elderly chief N'Kuba. The actual mining was done by men only, either in open pits or underground, using picks similar to their axes, except that handle and blade were heavier than those of the axes and the cutting edge of the blade ran at an angle to the handle rather than parallel to it. As shafts were dug deeper, ladders made of fiber were lowered. At the bottom, three miners worked to dislodge the ore, filling cylindrical baskets made of fiber from the mbombo, manga, and other trees, measuring roughly 35 centimeters in diameter and 14 centimeters in height. Light but strong and rigid, these baskets could hold some 25 kilograms of ore and were passed to the surface by men and women stationed on the ladders (fig. 3). Where blocks of mineral were too heavy to fit into the baskets, they were raised by fiber ropes. Once on the surface, the chunks of ore were sorted and pulverized until they could be winnowed to separate the malachite from the matrix of rock.

When the miners struck rock walls too hard for their picks, fire-setting was used to break them up. The shaft was filled with wood to the desired height and left to burn until morning. By that time the heat had burst the obstructing stone and mining could resume. De Hemptinne does not mention using water for sudden cooling as part of the fire-setting process.

Mining might reach a depth of 35 meters, but generally went no deeper than 10 or 15. The excavation of a shaft proceeded at the rate of about 1 meter per day, but this pace could not be sustained for long, so that a shaft of 30 meters might represent three months' labor. As shafts grew deeper, lighting became a problem for which a burning bunch of straw provided only a temporary solution; no other type of lamp seems to have been remembered. Timbering was rarely necessary, because of the circular shape of the shafts and the solid nature of the terrain. Then, too, underground galleries were not long, the most extensive being only about 20 meters.

Malachite was the only mineral sought in this area; everything else was left behind as sterile rock. Consequently the size of the excavations may be a somewhat misleading indicator of the amount of copper ultimately recovered. In any case, when an ample supply of ore was in hand (formerly, after some three months' labor), mining ceased and smelting began, usually at some distance from the mines. The first step was the manufacture of charcoal. The best wood for the purpose was obtained from the mobanga tree (*Afrormosia angolensis*), an exceedingly hard wood that resisted all but the solidest and sharpest axes. A pyre of very dry dead wood (the tree is impervious to termites) was piled on top of enormous holes to a height of about a meter above the ground and set afire. When it had burned down to ground level, it was covered with a thick layer of earth. Forty-eight hours later it had been transformed into hard bright charcoal of the best quality.

The next step was the construction of the furnace (figs. 4, 5). The Yeke had no permanent furnaces but built them anew for each campaign, destroying them in the process of obtaining the smelted metal which collected in the bottom. As many as twenty or thirty might be built to smelt an abundant harvest of ore, each minutely supervised by a master smelter. Each furnace was constructed over a cleaned and leveled area about 1 meter square. In the center, the smelter hollowed a basin 40 centimeters in diameter and 5 or 6 deep. To get rid of any lingering dampness, he lit a small fire in the basin. A dozen small white-ant hills provided the raw materials for the furnace itself. Three of these served more or less intact for the tuyeres once they had been bored out with iron rods. They were arranged around the rim, at equal intervals and slightly inclined. For the body of the furnace, four or five whole anthills were smoothed on one side and set around the basin, gaps between them filled in, and the entire edifice built up to a height of 70 to 75 centimeters and propped up with several forked branches for good measure. The whole construction took only about a half-hour, and to the untrained eye, the furnace appeared perpetually in danger of collapse.

Smelting itself proceeded in several stages, closely watched over by the master smelter. First, a single layer of charcoal was placed in the basin and mobanga branches piled tightly over it to the top of the furnace. Once the fire was burning briskly, a layer of charcoal was added on top of the branches and then the ore itself on top of this, generally two baskets or 40 to 50 kilograms. Since the furnace was too small to contain the entire charge, the green malachite formed a cone at the summit of the pile and would have overflowed had not the smelter added more anthill clay to build the sides still higher. Gradually the smoke died down and flames spurted up to blacken the ore; at this point, the fire was left alone for an hour and a half, and attention turned to the manufacture of the bellows. These were made of two bags of antelope skin and operated by two sticks, opening and closing first one and then the other to force a continuous stream of air through each tuyere. A tube of fresh bark, kept moist until the last minute, connected the bag to the tuyere and was capable of withstanding the immense heat generated in the oven.

When the last of the mobanga logs had burned and the pile of ore had fallen into the body of the furnace, the smelter made a thick mud paste and spread it around the sides of the furnace to block all the apertures of the constituent anthills. Henceforth, virtually the only sources of air were the three tuyeres, and the only exit for the flames was through the opening at the top. The furnace was then filled to the brim with charcoal, the bellows operators set to work with furious intensity, and the actual process of fusion began. It was a magical scene:

> It is eleven o'clock at night. The furnaces spit fire. The workshop is a luminous oasis, delirious in the bosom of the silent forest, asleep under a limpid, profound and brilliantly starry sky.
> Soon the flames are transformed, a blue-green plume with gilded crest crowns the oven and projects strange lights on the ebony bodies.
> The molten metal begins to run into the brazier. (p. 22)

Once the operation was complete, the furnace was broken down, the embers swept to one side and the glowing mass of copper disclosed, "like an eye of rising sun gazing on the world." It would later be refined and worked in the leisure of the rainy season back home in the villages.

There were thus two phases of the smelting process as de Hemptinne describes it. The first involved dehydration in an oxidizing atmosphere — there were many holes in the furnace walls in addition to the open tuyeres. The second, the smelting proper, used a forced draft to raise the temperature to the melting point of copper (1083° C) and required a reducing atmosphere with a minimum of air, which was achieved once the holes were tightly sealed and the bellows attached. The first phase took about two-and-one-half hours, the second only about thirty minutes. A charge of about 50 kilograms of ore with a copper content calculated at more than 40 percent would have produced some 20 kilograms of metal, but in this demonstration the smelter was distracted by the photographers, the draft produced by the bellows was not adequate, and a portion of the ores remained unreduced; at the same time, some of the charcoal did not burn and adhered to the copper collected in the basin at the bottom of the furnace.

It has seemed well worth giving so much space to de Hemptinne's account — and we will return to it later in discussing other aspects of metallurgy — because of its remarkable detail and because the procedures, though carried out at official request rather than spontaneously, were performed by people for whom mining and smelting were living memories. De Hemptinne also includes a briefer description of smelting techniques used by the Luba of Mwilu, techniques which differ in some respects from those of the Yeke. At the time he collected his information, the copper industry was still very much alive in western Katanga, supplying the markets of the Lomami and Kasai. The Luba washed and sorted the malachite ore, then grilled it on an open pyre. Next it was washed again and carefully sorted before being reduced in a permanent furnace. The furnace was about the same size as that of the Yeke but served for both smelting and refining: the molten metal ran out of the bottom directly into solid, fixed moulds which could be used repeatedly. So skillful were the Luba smiths that they could pierce a hole to let the molten metal into the mould, then block it with a mass of white ash paste without losing a drop.[9]

There are several comparable descriptions by other observers. One, by the administrator Ladame, offers what seems to be a firsthand report, albeit brief, of smelting in the Luishia region of Katanga. Here the smelter began his operation with a round layer of charcoal. When this was already glowing, a quantity of ore was added, then alternate layers of charcoal and ore, building up a "sugar loaf" of decreasing diameter. As the layers were added, a wall of clay 3 to 4 centimeters thick was built around the pile to a height of about 80 centimeters, at which point it was entirely covered over. Then holes were pierced for the bellows' connections. The bellows themselves were activated by vertical poles. At the end of three or four hours, the liquefied metal was collected at the base. This process would combine the oxidizing-reducing phases of Yeke smelting, but it is hard to imagine building the entire furnace around a heap of glowing charcoal and ore, not simply reinforcing and extending it. Ladame also claims that at the time of writing (1921), there were many of these old kilns, "touching in their simplicity," still to be seen and deserving of a place in the colony's museums — how they escaped destruction when the smelted metal was retrieved is another of the points not clarified in his account.[10]

A more carefully reported demonstration of copperworking was carried out in 1961 near Solwezi, west of the Copperbelt in Zambia. Malachite ore was hoed from surface outcrops at Kansanshi, then taken to the smelting site, where it was broken down into chunks of green carbonate about a cubic centimeter in size. Since smelting had died out among the local Kaonde sometime around the First World War, all but one of the participants were over seventy years old but had memories of taking part in traditional smelting with their fathers. There were some differences of opinion about procedures, not only because of the long lapse of time but also because the men represented different totems, each of which may have had its preferred variations.[11]

The Kaonde, too, used the ubiquitous anthill to construct their furnace around a hole in the ground; similarly, a small, bored anthill supplied their single tuyere. The furnace was only about 40 centimeters high, little more than half the height of the Yeke and Luba furnaces. Bag bellows were prepared from the leg skin of the *situtunga,* turned inside out with the hair left on. They were anchored down by stepping on the looped ends or by inserting the toes into them, while the nozzle ends were inserted directly into the tuyere. A layer of ashes lined the hollowed bottom of the furnace. Charcoal was added to a level above the opening of the tuyere and set alight by firebrands. The bellows were worked immediately, and once the charcoal began to glow a few handfuls of ore were placed on it, directly over the vent, and more charcoal added. A blue-green flame was considered a sign that smelting was complete, but to make sure, a stick was inserted through the ventilating hole to test for the presence of molten copper in the hollow. The furnace was then knocked down with a long pole and the charcoal pushed aside. Both slag and charcoal adhered to the liquid copper as it solidified.

A second, similar kiln was built to refine the crude copper. At its base was a clay pot almost filled with ashes. The copper was carefully placed in the center of a glowing pile of charcoal and left to melt into the crucible over a space of about two hours. Once this was accomplished, the kiln was broken down and the metal poured into an anthill mould, except that in the demonstration, this operation failed because the men had not provided themselves with adequate protection for their hands and the metal cooled before they managed to tip the crucible; in earlier days they probably would have had some sort of tongs at hand. The Kaonde, therefore, seem to have smelted in a single operation, without preliminary roasting, and then refined the raw copper. Given the small size of the furnace and consequently of the charge, the amount of metal obtained was modest.[12]

These twentieth-century reenactments are extremely valuable and point up the differences between different regions. There were also clearly differences over time. Yeke furnaces, for example, differed radically from those of the Sanga, their predecessors in eastern Kantanga, who built permanent ovens of clay brick more than twice as large and with four tuyeres instead of three. Why did the Yeke not adopt the more advanced, large-scale technology of their hosts when they arrived in the middle of the nineteenth century? De Hemptinne invokes here, as elsewhere, a law of least effort: Yeke methods required much less work and were sufficient for the seasonal, small-scale character of their metallurgy and the limited market open to them. The permanence and solidity of the Sanga operations, on the other hand, suggest a much greater volume of production to meet the demands of a market not yet in decline; they were, as de Hemptinne remarks, "little factories functioning the entire year."[13] Technology, quite obviously, cannot be divorced from economic and political considerations. There is no point in producing more metal if it cannot be disposed of profitably.

Then, too, mining could be carried on rather simply because of the nature of Katangan ores. These ores all belong to the same geological horizons, the so-called Série des Mines, with the single exception of the Kipushi deposits. Rich pockets of almost pure malachite containing 50 to 55 percent copper lie at or close to the surface and can be recovered for the most part by opencast mining or relatively shallow pits. "The natives dig little round shafts, seldom deeper than 15 or 20 feet," wrote one of the earliest travellers to describe mining in the region in 1886–88. "They have no lateral workings, but when one shaft becomes too deep for them, they leave it and open another."[14] A slight variation was observed at Dikuluwe in 1920: "The diggings consisted of irregular holes in a siliceous dolomite; the natives were mining only the soft ore in small seams and veins in this dolomite. . . . The workings were in the form of inclined openings . . . from 30 to 40 feet deep."[15] Ladders were not even necessary: the baskets of ores could simply be passed from hand to hand along the ramp to the surface. Though both Cornet and de Hemptinne note that underground galleries were occasionally dug, they were clearly unnecessary in many sites. But at Kipushi mineralization follows a deep vein, and extensive underground workings predate European exploitation: at one point the skeleton of an African miner was reportedly found buried under a collapsed drift.[16]

These deeper workings with their more complex technology find an echo to the south in Zambia, Zimbabwe, and the Transvaal. Kansanshi Hill, just across the border from Kipushi, is a roughly circular outcrop, cut by a series of nearly vertical quartz veins running north-south and very rich in malachite. As Bisson describes it,

> there are four main vein systems crossing Kansanshi Hill as well as a wealth of smaller veins, all of which were mined in the past, some to considerable depths. The largest of these systems stretches over 380 meters; it starts near the top of the hill and extends far into the surrounding forest on the lower slopes. Although in places it is over ten meters wide, this particular vein is of special interest because of a very narrow section situated on the side of the hill. The ore from this area was quarried to surprising depths in spite of the fact that the trench here averages only 45 centimeters in width and narrows, in one place, to a mere 27 centimeters.[17]

Bisson excavated a sample portion of one of the trenches, enabling him to reconstruct the techniques used in this section of the workings, subsequently dated by radiocarbon samples of wood and charcoal to the sixteenth or seventeenth century, more than a thousand years after mining began on the hill. Ancient miners, he concludes, removed only the highest grade ore, in this case malachite, and left everything else behind. They used iron picks to dislodge the mineral from its quartz matrix and carried it up ramps made of waste and rubble. Alongside the mine, the ore was cleaned and freed from gangue and other impurities by pounding with iron and stone hammers. Waste heaps line the trenches at Kansanshi and contain many small chips of malachite that were lost in this process of purification. To remove larger blocks of quartzite that frequently blocked access to veins, iron wedges were pounded in along fracture lines. If the exposed vein then proved too poor to exploit, it was simply abandoned. Bisson makes no mention of fire-setting, and timbering would presumably have been unnecessary if trenches rather than underground galleries were used.

Smelting was carried out on the banks of a stream which provided the nearest source of water to Kansanshi Hill. Here an area some 600 meters long and as much as 250 meters wide was found to be littered with the refuse of ancient metallurgy: lumps of slag, ore chips, bits of smelting furnaces, potsherds, and soil darkened by crushed slag and charcoal. The remains of a fifteenth-century smelting furnace suggest a basic similarity with the Yeke model. Circular in shape, its walls were constructed of small termite hills, cemented together with mud, around a shallow depression in the ground. A layer of gray ash lined this depression to keep the molten copper from mixing with dirt. As with Yeke furnaces, it had to be broken down to get at the metal and therefore could be used only for a single smelt.

Mining at Bwana M'Kubwa seems to have followed a similar pattern. There were two main workings, parallel to each other and some 30 feet apart on the northeast slope of a *kopje,* one running unbroken for some 750 yards, the other for about 793 yards. European mining operations disclosed that the more prominent of the two runs was carried to a depth of 160 feet, becoming so narrow that it is difficult to see how the ore was extracted, just as at Kansanshi.[18] By way of contrast, most of the ancient workings in the Hook of the Kafue are mere pits, varying from 10 feet in diameter and 15 feet deep to 50 feet in diameter and 40 feet deep. A few, however, are in the form of narrow trenches, but much less extensive than those at Kansanshi and Bwana M'Kubwa.[19]

In Zimbabwe, Summers has found that essentially the same mining techniques were used for gold and copper, so much so that in some ancient workings where both ores are found it is hard to tell which was sought. Gold reefs tend to run deeper than copper on the average, but the latter were anything but superficial: of seventeen sample stopes dug to extract copper, four were 20 to 40 feet deep, five were 40 to 60 feet, five more were 60 to 100, and a single stope went deeper than 100 feet. Mines were of two main types. The commonest was a narrow, deep trench or "open stope," comparable to those at Kansanshi and Bwana M'Kubwa. In the

Sinoia and Urungwe areas, however, mineralization was such that ore was extracted from enormous open pits, 100 feet wide or more. The second type of mining involved shafts and underground stopes. A shaft was sunk to the depth of the vein, which was then exploited for a radius of several feet in all directions, giving it the shape of a long-necked bottle or gourd in cross-section. Then another shaft was dug nearby and the operation repeated. Backfilling was common, both for safety and for ventilation: if only two shafts were open at any one time, up-down drafts were created to remove noxious vapors, especially those resulting from fire-setting, while if all the shafts were left open, no draft would function.[20]

This type of mining has been described in detail at Umkondo by C. H. Chandler, manager of the mine from 1955 to 1961, who kept careful written and photographic records of the ancient workings before they were destroyed. Chandler reconstructed four basic steps, here presented in somewhat abbreviated form:

1. A small vertical shaft about 18 to 24 inches in diameter was sunk through the soft shale to the pay horizon on the upper surface of the quartzite-shale contact. The shale was soft enough to be dug out, apparently, with sharpened hardwood sticks—a number of these were, in fact, recovered, preserved by impregnation with copper salts.

2. Ore was removed from the pay horizon radially around the bottom of the shaft until the excavation became dangerous; then the shaft was refilled with waste rock and another access shaft commenced. The surface of the ground gradually became a checkerboard studded with these filled shafts, each about 30 feet from its neighbor.

3. A great deal of sorting went on underground. Malachite nodules were easily separated from the soft shale in which they occurred. No evidence of artificial illumination was found, but it has been calculated that with the sun at its meridian in this latitude, there would have been ample light for a miner to see what he was doing for a space of about 20 feet from the base of the shaft. Separation of ore from shale could even have taken place in the dark, according to Chandler. The ore was then hauled to the surface, probably using ropes woven from baobab fiber.

4. Waste rock was stowed away in the stoped excavation to prevent cave-ins and to save hauling it to the surface.

Extensive as this mining operation was, Chandler claims to have found no traces of systematic timbering, in spite of ample supplies of suitable wood in the region, but this is contradicted by other observers. The workings at Umkondo were limited to a depth of 60 to 80 feet by the watertable.[21]

Copperworking seems to have died out in Zimbabwe earlier than in Zambia and Katanga, probably because of the political upheavals of the nineteenth century caused by the Ndebele invasions. As a result, there is no information on smelting techniques, a matter Summers does not touch upon at all, no doubt because of his primary interest in gold, which occurring as it does in simple ores does not require smelting. The evidence must be there, however, if it has not been entirely obliterated.

## SOUTHERN AFRICA

At Lolwe Hill, Phalaborwa, we are blessed with a wealth of information on both mining and smelting, thanks to the careful reconstructions of Van der Merwe and Scully. Fragmentary information gleaned from officials who had seen the old workings in the course of the blasting which destroyed them paint a picture of both bottle shafts like those at Umkondo and shafts with branching horizontal galleries. A working of the latter type was investigated in 1965 and proved to be about 20 feet deep with a 30-foot gallery. It had been back-filled, making examination difficult, but a deposit of charcoal on the gallery floor, left over perhaps from fire-setting, gave a radiocarbon date of A.D. 770 ± 80. The same day's blasting revealed a semicircular trench about 160 feet away from this site, 100 feet long and 70 feet deep in the middle. It, too, had been back-filled and was dated by charcoal sample to A.D. 1000 ± 60. Iron gads and chisels with dolomite hammerstones were used to chip out the ore at Phalaborwa. Though fire-setting was common, there is no specific evidence for timbering. Mountains of tailings at the surface where the ore was sorted and purified testify to the scope of operations.

Phalaborwa was rich in both copper and iron; in fact, iron-smelting furnaces outnumber copper by a large margin. Magnetite pebbles from which iron was obtained were also used as a flux in smelting copper.[22] As at Kansanshi, smelting sites honeycomb the entire area but are rarely found on the *kopjes* themselves. Their location seems to have been dictated by availability of fuel and by demand for the finished metal rather than by proximity to the mines. According to Van der Merwe and Scully, the typical smelting site

> consists of several tons of slag in a circular heap, with a furnace at the center. Copper furnaces are shaped like beehives, about 2–3 ft. in height and in diameter at the base, tapering to a "chimney" hole at the top of about 1–1½ ft. in diameter. A single entrance, about 9 in. in height and in the shape of a gothic arch, occurs at one side. Trumpet-shaped tuyeres of baked clay, with a shaft of 3 in. external and 2 in. internal diameter (length about 18 in.) are

associated with these furnaces. A set of bellows of perishable material (no remains have been found) were presumably connected with a pair of these tuyeres to deliver a continuous air blast. The primary furnace product — which occurs as small ingots of no particular shape, having apparently been cast in the nearest available potsherd or run out into the sand — is remarkably pure copper, indicating a fairly low smelting temperature.

None of these beehive copper furnaces has yet been dated earlier than the previous century, however.[23]

Some forty years before the current investigations of the area began, Schwellnus first identified the characteristic Lowveld furnaces. His type 1 furnace seems to have been intended for smelting iron, except that the dimensions given do not jibe very precisely with later descriptions, while the much rarer type 2, which he called "bowl shaped," seems to correspond with the copper-smelting furnace. His diagram suggests that the metal did not run out the bottom into a potsherd or into the sand but collected at the base within. In that case, the furnace would have to have been broken down after each use, which would account for its rarity. Local tradition, however, implies that this was not so: one informant claimed that the molten metal seeped out through openings in the furnace, another that it was scooped out with an iron ladle shaped like a calabash. Clearly, more work is needed to clear up these discrepancies.[24]

One of the few ancient copper mines still intact was recently discovered at Harmony 24 and 25, also in the Lowveld of the eastern Transvaal. It consists of twenty-five units containing thirty-one shafts and one open stope, with a total length of about 400 meters. A thirteenth-century date was obtained from one of the units, but indications are that some may be older, others more recent. Mining was restricted to the weathered zone where the primary ores encountered were malachite and azurite. Stone tools were used by the miners, including a dimpled variety similar in size and weight to ones found by Baumann far to the west at the Rooiberg tin mines. Ores were dislodged through fire-setting and partially sorted underground. Timbering was used and rubble packed into already mined stopes as a safety measure. Smelting was carried out nearby: the three furnaces excavated conform to the Lowveld type in use at Phalaborwa.[25]

At Messina in the northern Transvaal, just south of the Limpopo, modern workings have all but obliterated traces of ancient mining. Nevertheless, from earlier evidence it appears that mining here followed the pattern observed elsewhere of narrow shafts and underground stopes, both so small it is hard to imagine how they were worked by any but gnomes. Fire-setting and cold water were used to split recalcitrant rock faces, while the basic tool kit of hammerstone and iron gad served to break out the ore. Shafts were dug to a depth of approximately 25 meters. Ore was brought to the surface in baskets or possibly in wooden buckets; Van Warmelo also mentions leather bags.[26]

Stayt has recorded the description given by an elderly Venda informant of the treatment of ore once it reached the surface:

> The copper-ore was first cobbled into small pieces. The kiln for smelting was prepared by making a small circular impression in the ground, about 1½ feet in diameter, and lining it with clay and ashes; on this base a circular clay wall was built up to a height of 1½ feet and reinforced on the outside with stones. A layer of dry leaves of the *mukwiliri* or *mulamvhira* trees was put into the bottom of this kiln to a depth of about 2 inches to help in the kindling, over this was put a thick layer of charcoal and then more leaves. A small hole was made at the base of the kiln to give entrances to the nozzles of the bellows, and the charcoal was fired; as soon as it was red-hot another layer of copper was added and then a final layer of charcoal until all copper was melted, when the worker proceeded to break down the wall of the kiln. All the debris of dirt, charcoal, and ashes was brushed away, leaving the copper in the clay-lined impression in the ground. The copper was left to cool and then again hammered into small cobbles and resmelted in a potsherd about 7 inches in diameter, which was put over the impression in the ground, so that the molten copper could be manipulated easily and poured out into the moulds prepared for it. The usual moulds were made in the ground with a stick about ½ an inch thick.[27]

In the southern Transvaal, the copper mine 47/73 at Olifantspoort, excavated in 1973, consists of open trenches with a retaining wall built to prevent rubble falling in on the miners in the main trench. Between two of the trenches, sorting and crushing tables had been built from boulders of quartz and dolerite.[28] Two types of smelting furnaces have been identified in the region: the beautifully preserved but very small Uitkomst Cave type dated to c. 1640 A.D., which probably could only have taken a charge of several pounds of ore, and the larger domed clay furnace found at Buisport but not dated.[29]

As far as I know, there are no descriptions of ancient mining in Namaqualand, far to the west. Even the unique description of early smelting is open to question. The operation was ostensibly carried out in 1762 at the request of visitors from the Cape, who remarked on the cleverness of the natives in smelting copper: "They . . . built a kind of fireplace of fresh cow-dung, six inches high and about a foot in circumference [diameter?]. On one side of this fireplace they placed two buckhorns each of which had a bellow of skin attached to one end, so arranged that, by opening and closing, the air which was continually passing through the horns was expelled. By this means the glowing charcoals in the fireplace smelted the copper in a short time. They then poured the molten metal into fresh cow-dung in which there were small furrows, about a finger long." Goodwin's skepticism about the whole account stems from his belief that the cow-dung would burn like peat or even explode, while the buckhorns would not have been able to withstand the heat if they were really inserted directly into the fireplace without the intermediary of clay nozzles. He also observes that the rings which were supposed to have been hammered from ingots are described by another source as having no join and hence must have been cast, not smithed. He suspects, therefore, that this was a "demonstration" in which no ore was actually smelted.[30]

Bürg reports that in Namibia, mining was carried to a depth of 7 meters to reach the richest ores, a rather shallow excavation, but that the mineral was then taken to Swakoptal for smelting, where water and wood were more abundant. About Tsumeb we are told only that carbonate ores were smelted with charcoal at some distance from the mines "auf höchst primitive Weise."[31]

## THE NIARI BASIN

For all their eagerness to gain direct control over Angolan deposits, the Portuguese have left almost no accounts of African mining and smelting. Even the rush of books dating from the nineteenth century focus more on the prosperity to be expected from Lusitanian occupation than on the accomplishments and techniques of their predecessors. Monteiro does note, it is true, that Bembe miners dug small round pits, 3 to 4 feet in diameter and 4 to 5 fathoms deep, into the bottom of the valley along its entire length: they did not go straight down but followed an irregular zigzag pattern, with wooden pegs set into the walls to enable the miners to climb in and out. The shafts were not timbered, he claimed, and often caved in, burying workers alive. The only mining tools were hoes, similar to those used in farming, and cheap spear-pointed knives 10 or 11 inches long, obtained from Ambriz traders. Mining occurred only during the dry season and even then could not push below the water table, so that enormous quantities of ore remained untouched. Monteiro does not mention smelting but does insist that malachite itself was brought down to Ambriz in baskets by coastal natives.[32]

French missions to the mineral fields of the Niari Basin are considerably more informative, although there has been no archaeological work at any of the Middle Congo–Angola copperworking sites to supplement the observations of these missions. In 1886–87, Captain Pleigneur made a reconnaissance of the mines at M'Boko Songho, unfortunately in the midst of the rainy season, so that the pits were full of water and mining was suspended until dry weather. In this area, mineralization occurs in a valley along the banks of the Loudima River, a tributary of the Niari, with lead and copper deposits only 1200 to 1500 meters apart. Shallow pits were sunk at the bottom of large open excavations, to mine copper. Pleigneur estimated that teams of twenty miners, aided by other workers raising and lowering the baskets, could extract some 300 to 400 kilograms of malachite ore per day. Still more lead could be dug from quarries and pits on the hillside, but the yield of metal from the quantity of ore was only half that of copper.

There were other differences in the working of the two metals. According to the same source, copper was smelted at leisure during the rainy season, but lead was smelted immediately after it was mined, for reasons he could not learn. In both cases, the furnaces were built of clay in the form of a truncated cone 30 centimeters high and 35 centimeters in diameter at its base but narrowing to 20 centimeters at the top. The walls were about 6 to 8 centimeters thick. A vertical opening the height of the furnace permitted the insertion of a clay crucible to receive the molten metal. The furnace was filled with charcoal and ore, then the opening was blocked up somewhat haphazardly with stones after a clay funnel was put in place to connect the bellows with the interior of the kiln. The smelter added charcoal and ore continually while two children worked the bellows. In the case of copper, a certain amount of previously smelted lead was always added to the charge. The result was a highly malleable metal looking rather like tin. It was then smelted a second time with a new and heavy admixture of copper ore. When this was complete, the vertical opening of the furnace was unplugged and the crucible withdrawn. The molten metal was immediately poured into cylindrical moulds made of wet clay in various sizes. No iron tools were used for any aspect of the operation; the crucible was removed from the furnace by means of green twigs. This second smelt produced a grayish metal with a very faint tint of copper. The ingots were then placed in another crucible pierced with holes and set on a charcoal fire, covered with more charcoal, and heated to a precise color, presumably to eliminate the greater part of the added lead. When the metal was removed from the fire and cooled, it took on a beautiful red copper color.[33]

It may be this rather intricate sequence that gave rise to reports that copper-lead ores were mined as such and that separation took place only during the smelting process. Thus Dupont, writing at almost the same time, claims that ore was broken into small pieces of mixed malachite and cerusite (a lead carbonate) and that the two were separated only by a second smelting.[34] Cholet (1888) also asserts that ingots of mixed copper and lead were produced and that a grilling process using an "assiette percé" (presumably Pleigneur's crucible with holes) was used to separate the lead.[35] Laman, whose investigations took place at a time when native mining and smelting had virtually died out and who may therefore be relying on hearsay, offers a rather odd description of copper smelting, presumably among the Sundi. A forge was constructed of stones brought down from the hills and arranged over a pit in which lead had previously been smelted. "Alternate layers of charcoal and copper are now laid in the lead. The bellows are worked and fresh copper and charcoal are added. When the copper is smelted and begins visibly to shine the fire and stones of the forge [furnace?] are taken away and a pause is made until the copper has settled a bit." While still hot the copper was broken up, heated in a clay crucible and poured into mounds of sand.[36]

The confusion over methods may result from variations on the same basic practice, perhaps adapted to the character of mineralization in adjacent fields. In general, the main metallurgical justification for adding lead to copper during smelting would be to remove the silver which is commonly found in copper ores, though that is not mentioned in these accounts.[37] Such an addition was described, for example, at the Ravenshead and Stanley works in England during the eighteenth century, where small amounts of lead were heated slowly with black copper as part of the refining process, before it was prepared with oil and plunged into water to give it the "japan" finish that was as prized in Europe as the heightened red was in Africa.[38] And of course, leaded copper would be easier to cast, pure copper easier to work cold. Be that as it may, Pleigneur's account seems both the most comprehensive and the most credible and may well be based on firsthand observation, since he includes diagrams and collected specimens at the different stages of the process.[39]

Mining and smelting at Mindouli and elsewhere in the Niari Basin seem to have been essentially similar to M'Boko Songho, but information is more fragmentary. At Mindouli, mining was carried on in shallow pits for both malachite and lead ore (galena). Copper was smelted in three or four stages but with a curious twist, if the lone account is to be trusted: a fixed quantity of virtually pure chalcocite, a simple sulphide of copper, was added to the final stage to remove all traces of oxygen. The smiths would not say whence it came, but it was clear that its use was as a flux, not as a metal-producing ore.[40]

## THE SUDAN AND SOUTHERN SAHARA

At Hufrat en-Nahas, miners apparently found the softer mineralized zones of country rock extending down to more than 50 feet easier to work than the malachite-bearing outcroppings of quartz along the ridges, many of which were left unexploited. Though most of the old diggings had collapsed or been filled in by the time mining came to an end in the late nineteenth century, subsequent surveying indicates that ore had been extracted by sinking shafts or shallow pits close to each other along and across outcrops between the rock walls. As one would be exhausted, it would be filled in with debris, so that new ones could be sunk in the intervening ore without danger of cave-in. An employee of the Nile-Congo-Divide Syndicate, which held mining rights to the area from 1920 to 1925, once crawled through an old tunnel between two recently sunk shafts, showing that driving and cross-cutting had evidently been done to some extent.[41]

Alongside the pits are piles of mining debris and slag heaps, many of them with globules of copper still adhering. According to local information, some of these slags were resmelted at a time after the mines were abandoned, to retrieve some of the globules. By the time of the Sudan Geological Survey, published in 1961, no traces of smelting furnaces were visible at Hufrat,[42] but in the early twenties Christy could report, "Dotted all over the country round about the mine and on both sides of the Umbelasha are to be seen what look like old antheaps devoid of vegetation, but on examination these were found to be the remains of earthen smelting furnaces. In many of these the base of the smelter is still intact."[43] He goes on to relate that the natives in the hills south of Kafia Kengi very reluctantly showed him "antiquated iron hoes and mining tools quite unlike any implements of the sort used today," but he neglects to describe them!

Since copper smelting had long since ceased here as elsewhere, the only description is provided by a reenactment arranged by a mining engineer, A. P. Thompson, and later published by Bower. The operation was supervised by a smelter from Kafia Kengi. The charge consisted of equal parts of sorted copper oxide ore, iron ore from local sources, and old slag shot with copper pellets, mixed with charcoal in a ratio of 1:2. The furnace itself was highly unusual — Bower comments that he has never come across anything like it in the literature. Only the clay hood was visible, the rest being underground. The opening of the hood was covered with lumps of antheap after the furnace was going, except for a hole at the top left for additional charging. The single tuyere was inserted at a diagonal and small pieces of fresh charcoal were fed through it from time to time. The draft was provided by goatskin bellows. Bower suggests that this furnace may have been adapted from a smith's forge, but also suspects from the appearance of old smelter sites in the neighborhood that some other type of furnace may also have been in use in which ore was smelted and slag removed above ground. This would seem to match Christy's observation of the smelter bases. As to the inclusion of iron ore in the charge, it would have served as a flux.[44]

W. G. Browne, the first to refer to the copper of Hufrat though he was not allowed to visit the mines themselves, called attention not only to its fine quality but also to its color. This he said resembled "that of China and appears to contain a portion of zink [sic], being of the same pale hue" — elsewhere he lists it as "white" copper, in fact.[45] Later Baron Russegger, too, would comment on the "light yellowish colour" of Hufrat copper.[46] Gold, not zinc, seems the most likely explanation for this coloring, for the ores of Hufrat carry native gold in a finely disseminated state. The gold, however, never seems to have been separated for its own sake.[47]

At Akjoujt in Mauritania, Mme. Lambert estimates that an area of 400 cubic meters was hollowed out by ancient miners within the Grotte aux Chauves-souris before being partially back-filled with hematite and magnetite rejected by the miners in their search for malachite ore. The ore was broken up with dolomite hammers, sorted, then subjected to a slow roasting with fine charcoal to produce crude copper. Lambert describes this preliminary roasting over an open fire as taking place within the grotto itself, if I read her correctly, which would seem to be a somewhat doubtful undertaking. On the other hand, reduction of the roasted ores, for which a furnace was required, apparently took place away from the mines. Six furnaces were found at Lemdena, sixty kilometers south-southeast of Akjoujt, in a reasonably good state of preservation. All were of thick baked clay and provided with tuyeres. Lying among the slags was an ingot of copper weighing 15.069 grams, with traces of gold. Since copper at Akjoujt has also been found to contain traces of gold, it seems highly probable that Lemdena was a center for refining its ores.[48]

Preliminary work at Azelick/Takedda paints a rather different picture. Bernus and Gouletquer suggest that confusion persisted so long over the location of Takedda precisely because investigators were looking for copper "mines" with their attendant piles of rubble and for smelting sites with slag heaps, when the reality is quite contrary: the evidence turned up in the early campaigns points primarily to the working of native copper gathered from the surface of the ground and refined in small crucibles, presumably in modest refining furnaces. Because of the nature of the mineralization, nodules of native copper embedded in dolomitic rock would have been exposed at ground-level through erosion. There would have been a preliminary sorting out of the most heavily mineralized rock at the quarry site and this would have been taken to foundries, of which three, possibly four, have been identified in the Guélélé-Azelick region. Here the ore would have been more carefully sorted, then pulverized with grindstones and winnowed to separate the particles of rock from the metal. Globules of native copper have been found at these sites.

What followed next was not smelting, which was unnecessary with native copper, but simple melting, to separate the copper from the small amounts of matrix that had not been removed mechanically. This took place in deep little conical crucibles of clay, similar to those found at Marendet, south of Azelick. The small globules of pure, raw copper produced were rarely more than 1.5 centimeters in diameter, judging from the specimens found by the present team in the deeper strata at Azelick and by earlier investigators at neighboring sites. The other by-product of the refining process was a dross in the form of very porous, dark gray fragments which have been found relatively abundantly at certain points in the area.[49]

Still unanswered is the question whether other ores of copper were worked in the Azelick region, especially the oxide and silicates, found in many places, which would have required true smelting and possibly true mining as well. Though it may be that the ore of combined malachite and chrysocolla would have required a complex technology beyond the skills of pre-industrial craftsmen,[50] it is hard to imagine that simpler deposits of malachite and cuprite would not have been worked once the native copper was exhausted — unless the lack of fuel in the area proved an insurmountable obstacle.[51] It takes a great deal more fuel to smelt ores than to refine them, and even the refining process over an extended period may have denuded the area. Undoubtedly work in progress will help greatly to clarify these points.

Unfortunately there is no information on ancient mining and smelting at Nioro.

## SUMMARY

In general, then, African mining was largely opencast. Oxide ores lay near the surface directly under the cap rock and could be extracted by excavating large holes or by sinking a number of small shafts into the ground, or by a combination of the two. In other areas, long, deep, but very narrow trenches were cut along the length of a vein. Underground drives and stopes were considerably rarer; usually only the space immediately surrounding the base of a shaft would be mined out, then backfilled as new shafts were sunk in close proximity. Where tunneling was more extensive, both timbering and rock pillars were used — primarily in Zimbabwe, with its relatively advanced mining technology. Both iron and stone tools were employed until recent times to dislodge and break up ores, and fire-setting was widely resorted to with harder rock faces, especially in Central Africa and the Transvaal. Ore was then brought to the surface in baskets of fiber or animal skins.

The main limits to early mining were those imposed by water accumulation, poor ventilation, and the underground darkness. These restricted both the lengths to which tunnels could be driven and the depths to which ores could be pursued. As far as we know, there were no mechanical means available to remove water or circulate air, although natural drafts were encouraged, as we have seen, by joining two open shafts and filling the rest. In their published account of work at Phalaborwa, Van der Merwe and Scully refer to a partially filled-in "adit," dated to about 1750.[52] Normally the word is used to designate a passage dug in horizontally from the side of a hill at right angles to shafts, to drain water or improve circulation of air, but it may also refer simply to an access tunnel leading to an inclined stope, which is the function Van der Merwe tentatively ascribes to it at Lolwe Hill.[53] Summers has pointed out that with no means of ventilating horizontal galleries, miners could not drive adits into hard rock, since their only technique for breaking it up was fire-setting, which in turn produced gasses which could not be cleared out except in very limited areas.[54] As for illumination, the only sources definitely known are bundles of flaming leaves and pods.

Mining and sorting ores were dry season occupations. Smelting, on the other hand, could take place at any time and was frequently saved for the rainy months. Ores were rarely smelted at the mining sites but were taken elsewhere: to sources of water for washing, to wood, or even to the home village if it was not too far away. Furnaces were rarely as solid as those used to smelt iron, thanks to the lower temperatures and shorter time required for reducing copper ores. In some regions they were built of ant or termite hills, in others of clay. Rickard has noted that the aluminous earth of anthills and termite cones has much the same quality as fireclay, so that it was in no sense an inferior material for smelting furnaces.[55] Because most types of copper-smelting furnaces had to be dismantled to remove the metal, remains are much rarer than in the case of iron, to say nothing of the fact that copper itself is of much rarer occurrence in Africa.

One may wonder why oxide ores, which can be reduced in a single smelting operation, were so frequently subjected to a variety of more complex treatments. At Akjoujt and in Katanga, separated by thousands of miles and as many years, roasting preceded reduction, a procedure usually reserved for the more complex sulphides. In fact, this type of heating in a natural draft, described as early as the twelfth century A.D. by Theophilus, serves to drive off the water content, release some or all of the $CO_2$, and oxidize any residual sulphide, so that the remaining ore is more amenable to reduction and the copper content increased.[56] At M'Boko Songho, in contrast, the roasting which followed several smeltings may have been esthetic in aim: to guarantee the desired color and qualities of the finished metal, thanks in part to the addition of lead.

The use of fluxes to increase the efficiency of smelting seems to have been irregular at best. Cline cites only two references to fluxes in Central Africa: Melland claimed that the northern Kaonde of Zambia added lime to the charcoal (although as we have seen, the modern Kaonde reconstruction did not employ a flux), while Livingstone obliquely referred to craftsmen west of Lake Nyasa using a flux to smelt malachite.[57] In addition, the use of chalcocite was reported at Mindouli, and several early observers asserted that lime must have been used at Messina, judging from its presence in the slags — Trevor even reported the presence of numerous snail and freshwater mussel shells on the heaps.[58] On the other hand, Fripp, who was also familiar with the ancient workings, doubted that fluxes were ever deliberately added, citing the large amounts of metal left unreduced in the slags.[59] Some ores, however, contain natural fluxes, in particular iron oxides. Following information provided by his elderly smelter at Hufrat en-Nahas, Bower speculates that the discovery of iron's value as a flux there may have come about accidentally through the observation of the action of the iron gossan at the surface on the copper ores: as the iron ore decreased with increasing depth there was not enough for fluxing, and the smiths may gradually have learned the proper amount to add from neighboring iron sources.[60] Similarly, the iron oxide magnetite was used at Phalaborwa as a flux, according to Avery and Van der Merwe.[61]

We have noted repeatedly that African miners sought out veins or strata of carbonate ores with an almost obsessive tenacity, and that malachite provided by far the lion's share of the copper produced. Occurrences of native copper have been found at Azelick[62] and possibly north of Mindouli,[63] but it is doubtful that they were ever abundant enough to play an important role. The question of sulphide ores is more complicated. In African ore fields, sulphides are commonly found at lower depths and hence are more difficult and more dangerous to mine. They must also be roasted at subsmelting temperatures in order to remove the sulphur, before they can be reduced. If copper metallurgy reached most of tropical Africa at a relatively late date, about the beginning of the Christian era or slightly earlier, these techniques would long since have been perfected and one would have expected the full repertoire to have been taken over. We have seen, in fact, that a type of roasting was commonly employed, so that the concept was far from alien. Nevertheless, the evidence seems overwhelming that only oxides (and perhaps silicates) of copper were mined and smelted — with one or two possible exceptions.

Near Siracoro, one of the deposits in the Nioro region of northwestern Mali, Mauny states that "two veins of malachite and of sulphides were worked in early times."[64] This information is derived from fairly sketchy geological surveys rather than from archaeological reconnaissance or examination by mining engineers, and must for the moment be set in a sort of limbo, neither proven nor disproven. At the other end of the continent, the controversy centers on Messina and the Lowveld of the eastern Transvaal. Trevor described from personal observation, he claimed, "very large lenses of sulphides" at Messina, worked to a depth of some 80 feet. "The bottom of one working," he declared, "was a mass of almost pure sulphide about 18 feet wide." The working had subsequently been filled in, apparently deliberately. He also claimed that bornite was worked at Wagon Drift at the foot of the Drakensberg escarpment and that sulphides disseminated in pyroxenite were mined and smelted at Phalaborwa. All of these statements were made in an article published in 1930; in an earlier article of 1912, much closer to the time of the observations, this is not specifically mentioned.[65] Nevertheless Trevor's position is supported by Chambers, an early manager at Messina who stated emphatically, "In all the copper occurrences so far reported [from the Messina area] there does not seem to have been found any instance with an oxidized or carbonate zone, the sulphide or zone of secondary enrichment being found at, or quite close to the surface." Then, again, the same Chambers says the country was full of tigers at the time white men first arrived and that since the "Kaffir" was incapable of organizing industry on such a grand scale, the ancient workings throughout the region could not have been of native origin.[66] Louis Thompson, however, reported that an elderly native smelter told him that bornite and chalcocite had formerly been smelted, but not chalcopyrite. Unfortunately, Thompson does not make clear just what area he is referring to and it is difficult to know how much credence to place in the account.[67]

More recent work in the Transvaal casts considerable doubt on these reports. Van der Merwe and Scully state categorically that at Lolwe Hill, the major copper source at Phalaborwa, "all the ancient workings are concentrated in that part of the hill which contains weathered ores — malachite and azurite. The diggings followed the veins with great accuracy." Furthermore smelted copper found at the site was remarkably pure, another indication that it was derived from carbonates rather than sulphide ores.[68]

Messina itself was never studied by archaeologists before the ancient workings were destroyed, but even here Trevor's observations are open to question. Calderwood, a mining engineer who made an early survey of workings in the area, noted that they characteristically ended rather abruptly at a depth of about 80 feet, although much of the richest ore lay below. At Messina mine itself they stopped just above the Bonanza Lode, which was to yield "remarkably high grade massive copper ores of chalcopyrite, bornite, and glance [chalcocite]." His explanation was that "the easily smelted carbonate ores gradually changing to sulphide or copper glance made smelting operations difficult, or it may have been that water level obliged the workers to suspend mining at great depth."[69] Calderwood had no doubts about the presence of carbonate ores in these deposits, and the Geological Survey of 1945 confirms the ubiquity of malachite and azurite in ancient surface workings, with the zone of oxidation commonly reaching down to the water table at a depth of about 80 feet.[70]

"All the reliable observations I know of, including the very useful accounts by old prospectors I have interviewed at length," comments Van der Merwe, "show that 'ancients' occur only in secondary mineralizations of copper at the surface. As soon as the unweathered sulphide ores are encountered (at depths up to 90 feet), mining stops."[71] Friede shares his doubts that sulphides were ever worked, but cautions that "the evidence for coppermining and smelting in Southern Africa is still too meager to make any definite statements."[72]

With these two possible but unlikely exceptions of Nioro and Messina, then, oxide ores and native copper exclusively were worked throughout tropical Africa. In the main, African miners sought out only the richer ores and rejected the rest. Pockets of the Centre Lode at Bwana M'Kubwa (Zambia), for example, averaged 42 percent copper and those at Silver King almost 49 percent.[73] De Hemptinne estimated the copper content of ores smelted by the Yeke at about 40 percent;[74] those at Hufrat en-Nahas were said to yield about 14 percent pure metal.[75] In contrast, Evers and Van den Berg claim that the weathered ores mined at Harmony were not only patchy in distribution but of very low grade: none of the samples contained more than 2.5 percent copper and the majority contained no metal at all,[76] but conceivably this poor showing was the result of the exhaustion of richer ores in this relatively small deposit, since even with careful sorting and concentration it is hard to imagine how ores of such low yield could profitably have been treated under pre-industrial conditions.

Almost invariably, copper obtained by the initial smelting process was reheated in crucibles to refine it further before it was cast into ingots for stockpiling and trade. The final product was a metal of remarkable purity, equal to that of ancient Near Eastern metalsmiths, if one may generalize from the few tests that have been conducted. The smelt at Solwezi, Zambia, conducted by Kaonde smiths, yielded ingots assaying 99.6 copper,[77] while those produced over two thousand years earlier at Akjoujt contained 96.55 percent copper.[78] A copper link chain found at Broederstroom (Transvaal) and dated to the fifth century A.D. was found to be 99 percent copper.[79] Samples from other Southern and Central African objects indicate almost as high levels of purity. There may of course have been exceptions: Dapper declared in the later seventeenth century that copper brought to Loango from "Sondy," that is, from the Niari Basin, was debased by the presence of other metals, and his report was reprinted almost verbatim by Barbot. In this case, however, the mixing of metals, specifically copper and lead, may have been intentional and not the result of a lack of skill as Barbot and Dapper assumed, since their solution was to propose the dispatch of European metallurgists to teach the benighted African![80]

How much copper did the ancient mines and miners of tropical Africa produce? There are estimates aplenty, but can we place confidence in them? Generally they are calculated according to the dimensions of the workings, and obviously this is easier in the case of open stopes than of shaft mines. However, there seems little agreement about the ratio to be used in estimating the amount of metallic copper obtained from a given excavation. Lambert, for example, states that the 400 cubic meters of mineral and rock quarried from the Grotte aux Chauves-souris at Akjoujt would have yielded some 40 tons of copper (presumably using the French ton of 1,000 kilograms).[81] Using the same ratio of 10:1, Sydney Ball estimated native production in the Katangan mines at a global total of about 100,000 tons (presumably English tons, roughly equal to French metric tons).[82] Mauny, in contrast, assumes a ratio of only 1,000:1, so that it would require 1,000 cubic meters of mineral and waste to produce a single ton of smelted metal. On this basis he arrives at an overall output for the nine mines identified in the Nioro region of approximately 100 tons.[83] Other figures are almost pure guesswork. Calderwood judged that the hundreds of excavations pocking the landscape around Messina must have yielded several thousand tons of copper all told, while Trevor's "cautious estimate" for the same deposits escalated the figure to tens of thousands of tons.[84] A Roan Antelope report suggested that native production at Kansanshi and Bwana M'Kubwa in Zambia may have reached as much as several hundred tons per year, "a noteworthy achievement," it added patronizingly, "for a people with little in the way of tools and no technical knowledge."[85]

Marchal approached the problem of outputs differently. He based his calculations on the number of miners working in the mines of the Chefferie Katanga and neighboring regions and the amount paid to free men and slaves as expressed in kilograms of copper. Thus he estimated that in the period immediately preceding Msiri's reign, before 1850, that is, 115,000 kilograms were produced annually in Katanga, about 33,000 in Kiembe, and 6,000 in Poyo. During Msiri's reign, the total for all three areas fell to about 31,000 kilograms, while after his death, exploitation continued only in the Chefferie Katanga and dwindled from a workforce of about ten crews of miners at first to only three or four, producing scarcely

6,000 kilograms by 1903. Marchal's figures are broken down by region, period, and type of worker, conveying a statistical certainty which may be exaggerated, since his figures must be derived secondhand.[86] The same would be true for Pleigneur's much more modest estimates of the amount of ore mined per day at M'Boko Songho by teams of workers—some 300 to 400 kilograms.[87]

In fact, to arrive at reasonably accurate global estimates of copper production in Africa over the centuries, we would have to devise a formula adapted to each area, taking into account the amount of ore and rock dug from the ground, the copper content of the ore, and the efficiency of concentrating and smelting methods, or more simply, a formula based on the volume of slag, the mineral content of the ore, and the recovery rate. Thus Cline claims, for example, that 40 percent of the copper content in Katangan ores was lost because no fluxes were used in the smelting process,[88] but this estimate is apparently based solely on de Hemptinne's account of Yeke smelting rather than on an analysis of slags from a range of sites. More fundamentally still, we would have to have better means for distinguishing copper slags from iron than we have had in the past, so that we would recognize even ancient centers of production.

It is perhaps more illuminating to concede our lack of precise data but to compare the estimates we have with other parts of the world. It has been calculated that the total copper output of ancient Egypt (including Sinai) over fourteen centuries came to about 10,000 tons, while during a span of 1,200 years the Mitterberg mines of Central Europe produced double that amount.[89] Healy estimates the output of the great Rio Tinto mine in Spain at about one ton a day over a period of some 200 years.[90]

The relatively limited scale of production that prevailed not only in Africa but universally during the pre-industrial era is easily forgotten: even in the first decade of the nineteenth century, the annual *world* production of copper, some 18,200 tons, was less than a single month's output of some present-day mines.[91] In Africa, where copper functioned preeminently as a luxury metal, there were only sporadic incentives to increase production and productivity. As long as oxides remained abundant and rich in metallic content, there was no need to tackle the more complex sulphides. Consequently it is largely irrelevant to compare African mining and smelting techniques with those elaborated by, say, Agricola or Biringuccio. In Europe, native copper and oxide ores had been almost entirely depleted centuries before they wrote. Miners had no choice but to follow the trail of enriched ores ever deeper into the ground, into less and less hospitable geological formations. Water accumulation, foul air, darkness, the ever-increasing threat of cave-in, the need to haul large quantities of ore longer and longer distances underground and to the surface—all were problems to tax the engineering genius of Renaissance Europe but scarcely applicable to Africa. In Zimbabwe, as Summers has so brilliantly shown, an essentially simple technology was exploited to the limit to produce significant quantities of gold for export and copper for internal consumption, but this industry reached its peak somewhere around 1500 and then fell off, rather than evolving a more sophisticated technology.

The closest analogies to African mining should, therefore, be sought not in early modern Europe but in antiquity. Unfortunately, few sites have survived, but one that has and that offers interesting points of comparison is Timna, in the Arabah region of Israel—like Central Africa, "a land whose stones are iron-ore and from whose hills you will dig copper." Here Rothenburg and his colleagues have been able to reconstruct the evolution of techniques over some 6,900 years, from the Chalcolithic period to the present.[92] Though Timna operations seem to have become more sophisticated than those in precolonial Africa by about the Ramesside period, yields from African metalworking were much higher, yet another indication that with rich ores readily at hand refinements in technology are unnecessary.

# Smithing, Drawing, Casting, and Alloying

> Phalaborwa where the hammer is heard, the lowing of cattle is not there, the hammer resounds.
>
> — Phalaborwa tradition
> (Van Warmelo)

Copper is the most versatile metal known to man. What it lacks in hardness, it compensates for in malleability and ductility. More protean than silver or gold, its mechanical properties and its appearance change with every treatment: cold-hammering hardens it and makes it brighter and shinier but more brittle; heating softens and darkens. Alloying it with other metals enhances or alters these qualities. The basic techniques of copperworking are known the world over and have been employed in sub-Saharan Africa since the Early Iron Age.

## SMITHING

By cold-hammering and heating, the smith can work a copper ingot or bar into an almost infinite number of forms. The most universal ornament in Africa is the arm or leg bracelet, formed simply by bending a rod into an open or closed ring. This takes little skill if the raw material is a thin bar and the end product an unadorned ring, but it becomes much more demanding and more skilled when more massive materials are used and when the ring is highly decorated. In Burundi, for example, the fabrication of a heavy copper bracelet from an ingot of copper may take eleven hours from start to finish, including engraving and polishing.[1] Brass is even more difficult to smith, since it is a harder metal.

Copper may also be beaten and cut into delicate ribbon, fashioned into chain, twisted into spiral coils and writhing wristlets, flattened into sheets, inlaid into other materials, and beaten into vessels or sheathing for sculpture. The finished products may be adorned with chased, engraved, or punched designs. The Tio, for instance, ornament bracelets and collars of copper with geometric patterns by means of a white-hot engraving burin, plunged into oil to heighten its resistance to heat.[2] The abundance and brilliance of bronze casting at Igbo-Ukwu has tended, understandably but unfairly, to overshadow the quite remarkable skill evident in objects from the same site worked by smithing and chasing: twisted wire, coiled and link chain, knotted wristlets, a profusion of necklaces and anklets. No other archaeological find in Africa has revealed a comparable range of techniques, and this tradition of fine smithing has continued almost to the present in southern Nigeria.

Another aspect of the coppersmith's art that reached its apogee in Nigeria is beaten brasswork. In 1910–14 Leo Frobenius collected quantities of chased "bronzes" (actually brasses) from Nupe for the Leipzig Museum für Völkerkunde and subsequently published a detailed description of them in *The Voice of Africa*.[3] He located the center of the industry in Bida, but noted offshoots in Kano and Katsina which he ascribed to Nupe migration. Since Bida itself was not founded until about 1860 by the Fulani conquerors, the local industry must have been of recent origin, but Göbel argues that it built on an older and geographically more extensive tradition and that brass smiths were attracted to Bida when it became a center of political power. They produced a full panoply of *objets de luxe* for the ruler and his court: weapons, horse trappings, jewelry, and fine brass vessels. But they also made items of everyday use such as food dishes, ewers, kohl boxes, kola cups, and spoons.[4]

Like Frobenius, anyone looking at these pieces is struck by the Near Eastern style of their forms and even more by their decoration, which ranges from purely geometric designs incorporating spirals, double spirals, interlace, zigzags, and triangles to floral and foliate patterns to allusions to animals and birds, using a multiplicity of techniques such as punching, stippling, engraving, and embossing. The oral traditions of the brassworkers, gathered by Frobenius, derive their art from the Benue region, where it was claimed to have been practiced long before the "Kisra-Napata" invasion, although eastern craftsmen later came to dominate the art. The Kisra legend no longer commands the respect it did in Frobenius' day, but it is still plausible to suspect strong influences of Islamic metal arts, less through an influx of foreign workers than of foreign objects, and particularly Persian and Coptic objects, which reached the Niger-Benue region from Egypt or from northern Sudan, itself an area rich in work of hammered brass.[5]

Nupe is not the only region in which a tradition of hammered brasswork has developed: similar or related crafts are also found among the Yoruba and Bini, as well as in Gonja and the Akan regions of modern Ghana. Akan gold dust boxes, sieves, scoops, spoons, and shea butter containers (*forowa*) combine incised, stamped, stippled, and repoussé techniques to produce elaborate decorative patterns on objects of brass and copper. Ross doubts that any of this work dates before the mid-nineteenth century, but

Garrard places the flowering of Akan beaten brass at the end of the eighteenth century and links it to the increasing quantities of sheet brass reaching the coast.[6] Though it may owe stylistic debts to European or Islamic prototypes, the designs are thoroughly Akan, from the repertory of motifs found on goldweights, *kuduo,* and textiles, so that the techniques have been adapted to produce a purely African art form.[7]

We have already touched on another aspect of the smith's art: obtaining the desired color of metal. This can be done not only by alloying but by other treatments. Sundi and Luba smiths reheated refined copper, then plunged it into water, giving it a deep red color. The Bushoong used palm wine for the same purpose.[8] This treatment explains the intense red of Katanga crosses and was no doubt the origin of the "purple" copper of Luanda, prized not only throughout the Congo region but even in the eastern Niger Delta. Probably a similar process produced the rich red copper surrounded by myth in the central Sudan.[9] Lemba smiths in the Transvaal used the juice of a certain plant to give some of their copper wire a fine yellow color, then wove it with flame-red wire in intricate patterns of contrasting colors.[10]

## WIREDRAWING

If indigenous beaten brasswork seems to have been limited to areas of Nigeria and Ghana, wiredrawing is quintessentially a Central and Southern African craft. Here it has been practiced for hundreds of years until very recently, and the techniques have been recorded from a number of localities.

The basic tools for wiredrawing are few — a pincers and a drawplate — and the technique is deceptively simple in appearance. One end of the rod of copper to be drawn is hammered to a point fine enough to be fed into the hole of an iron drawplate and held fast by pincers or a vise. This is usually an iron rod bent double like a sugar tongs with a ring of metal slipped over to make it tight. The pincers is wedged into the fork of a post or tree and the drawplate is pulled against the remaining portion of the copper rod until all of it has passed through in elongated and slimmer form. The process is repeated, over and over, with the hole in the drawplate made smaller each time until the wire is as fine as desired. The wire is constantly reheated and often greased with oil or butter to make it more workable and less inclined to break. Sometimes the process is reversed, and it is the drawplate that is wedged in the fork and the pincers pulled. Either way it is strenuous work, especially in the early pulls, and generally required a team of men to carry it out, as is clear from the scene vividly reported in Livingstone's *Last Journals:* his servants, bringing his body to the coast, came upon a party of Nyamwezi near Lake Bangweolo hauling on a line attached to the wire, singing and dancing to lighten and synchronize their labors.[11]

If the copper to be drawn is in the form of an ingot rather than a thin rod or length of trade wire, it must first be heated and hammered out to manageable size. Zulu smiths reduced ingots to a diameter of about 3 millimeters, then drew them until the wire was about the size of "stout saddler's thread."[12] The same procedure was followed in Katanga, where Capello and Ivens in 1886 marvelled at the "veritable works of art" produced from copper wire drawn till it was as fine as "the strings of a musical instrument in Europe." The wire was used to decorate axe handles and gun barrels, but most of all to manufacture bracelets.[13] Apparently unaware that wiredrawing was a venerable craft in Central Africa, George Grey sought to impress a native smith in Northern Rhodesia with the information that a telegraph was about to be strung requiring two lines of copper wire 15 miles long. Without a moment's hesitation, the smith offered to supply the wire! As it happened, the reverse was more common: wire tended to disappear as fast as it was put up, ending up on the arms and legs of the inhabitants and dealing a mortal blow to the indigenous wiredrawing industry, to the annoyance of a colonial administration already faced with the problem of giraffes.[14]

Recently Steel and his associates at the University of the Witwatersrand tested the wiredrawing techniques described in the ethnographic literature, replicating as closely as possible the tools, materials, and methods used. Though their vise and drawing plate were made of modern steel, they were modeled on those found at Ingombe Ilede and dated to about 1400 A.D., while the copper rods used were cast by the university's department of archaeology. By trial and error, they learned the efficacy of slow annealing to soften the wire after each pull and the value of lubricating the plate hole with fat to minimize shearing. They also gained increased respect for the results achieved by African craftsmen, results they could approximate only crudely because of their lack of experience.[15]

There are numerous regional variants in wiredrawing techniques, none of them apparently significant from an historical point of view. The commonest type of drawplate, for example, is flat and narrow, with one or more holes whose size can be adjusted by forging and reboring with an awl. A conical variety with a single hole is found in certain parts of the lacustrine region and among the Yeke of Katanga (see fig. 6), who, as we have noted, migrated from the east in the mid-nineteenth century. The Yeke also use a lever to draw the wire, as do the Venda and possibly also the Nyamwezi and Lozi.[16] Given the fact that fine wiredrawing requires skill, it is not surprising that it tended to be the specialty of craftsmen within particular groups such as the Kamba, Chagga, and Kikuyu of Kenya; the Longo southwest of Lake Victoria; the Hutu smiths of Burundi; the Bemba north of the Chambezi River; the Nyamwezi and Yeke of Tanzania and Katanga; the Lemba of Zimbabwe and the Transvaal; and the Zulu of Natal.[17]

Any attempt to map the zones of copper wiredrawing in Africa is bound to be unsatisfactory, because the ethnographic literature frequently does not make clear whether the wire in use in an area was actually manufactured there or simply obtained by exchange from near or distant producers. Then, too, some of the information gathered from informants about the past may be open to question. Can we really accept, for example, the statements of de Hemptinne and Ladame, repeated by subsequent writers, that wiredrawing was introduced into Katanga by the Yeke invasions of the nineteenth century, when wire bangles galore have been dug up in cemeteries of the Lake Kisale region, some three hundred kilometers to the north, dating back as early as the ninth century A.D. and certainly common by the thirteenth to fifteenth centuries?[18]

The literature may also fail to make any distinction between wrought and drawn wire. Wrought wire is made by hammering and scraping, and since it is more laborious and produces a less refined end product, we may assume that it was made in areas where drawing was unknown. The same may be true of the manufacture of copper ribbon or strip by cutting narrow bands from thin sheet metal. This has been little documented in the ethnographic literature (the only references uncovered by Cline concern the Ngala of the Upper Congo and perhaps the Mangbetu, although there is also an excellent description by Lichtenstein of Tswana work in the early nineteenth century)[19] but it has come to light in archaeological excavations in Central and Southern Africa. Fragments of copper strip or bangles made from them are common in Iron Age sites discovered by Vogel and others in the Zambezi Valley and elsewhere in Zambia from about the middle of the first millennium A.D. onward. They have also been found at Mapungubwe Hill and, much more rarely, in sites on the Upper and Lower Shire River in Malawi and in the southern Highveld.[20] But even if ribbon and hammered copper wire antedated drawn wire, there were undoubtedly overlaps and discontinuities in different regions, so that one cannot use any single type as a dating device. Nevertheless, it might prove useful if clear descriptions based on microscopic examination of samples were given by archaeologists and ethnographers, in order to plot distribution of the different types of wire and strip more precisely.

In one form or another, then, copper wire has been a staple of the material culture of this part of Africa, both modern and ancient. At Sanga, in southwestern Zaire, it was found spiraled and unspiraled in rings and bracelets as well as worked into chains. One of the most remarkable necklaces consists of fine (0.2 millimeter) copper wire wound spirally into a tube 2 to 3 millimeters in diameter, then wound again to form the necklace itself; another consists of interwoven copper wire.[21] At Ingombe Ilede, bangles of fine copper and copper alloy abound, along with unworked trade wire and bobbins of fine copper, as well as wiredrawing implements.[22] Moreover, all the sites associated with Great Zimbabwe have proven rich in finds of copper and bronze wire, and it is ubiquitous at Mapungubwe Hill.[23] One may infer, therefore, that by the fourteenth or fifteenth century A.D., wiredrawing was a highly developed and widely disseminated skill throughout Central Africa and into the Highveld.

Wire and ribbon could be used in several ways. Short lengths were made into beads by bending, hammering, and annealing. Wire could also be wound spirally around a core of vegetable fiber, hair, or animal sinew to form bangles — a technique Caton-Thompson considers uniquely African.[24] Such bangles have been popular for well over a thousand years, as the archaeological and ethnographic evidence from Rwanda to the Limpopo attests. Raphia and fiber cores are the most common in older sites, but in areas where the craft has been observed in more recent times, animal hair is the preferred material; the Yeke mix the two.[25] Burchell, writing in the 1820s, noted that the northern Tswana made a ring of hair taken from the tail of a giraffe or other creature endowed with a long thick tail and wrapped it with wire of their own manufacture. The resulting bracelet was perfectly pliable, a fact one can verify by handling these wound bracelets in museum collections.[26] The Venda also were famous at this craft: a good Venda artisan, Stayt claimed, could turn out sixty to one hundred bracelets in a single day. Since the extent of a man's affection for his wives was measured by the number of bracelets he gave them, one can imagine a favorite disappearing under masses of wire and cattle hair.[27]

The archaeological evidence is so much spottier in East Africa that it is impossible to say whether the rare early finds are products of native manufacture or of trade, but one suspects that the art did not develop until supplies of copper became more plentiful in the late-eighteenth and nineteenth centuries as a result of extended trading contacts with Katanga and with the Swahili coast.

What of wiredrawing in West Africa? Masses of copper wire anklets are presumed to have come from Igbo Isaiah at Igbo-Ukwu before Shaw began his excavations. In the undisturbed strata themselves wire, some of it very fine, is found attached to iron blades, threaded through beads, or twisted in bracelets and rings, just as wire binding has been found on a hilt at Ifeka Garden Site.[28] However, the heavy coils of wire, reminiscent of Sanga, have no parallel in other West African archaeological findings so far as I am aware, and there is no way of knowing whether the wire was made by native smiths or imported from abroad. The use of coiled and twisted wire at Igbo-Ukwu does suggest a remarkable continuity in the predilection of many Ibo groups in southeastern Nigeria for sheathing their legs in quantities of brass spirals, from ankle to knee and even above. Since the seventeenth century if not earlier, this wire has been made by hammering rather than drawing. As Dapper describes it, the natives of the Calabar River region hammered out trade bars of bright red copper, then divided them in threes and twisted one around the other two like a cable to make bracelets and necklaces.[29] In our own century, Talbot observed wire being made by hammering in southern Nigeria, and one assumes that the excellent twisted wire he ascribes to Ibo smiths was made in the same way.[30] Jewelry of imported brass wire became fashionable at Old Calabar in the nineteenth century and spread inland toward the Benue, but the sources do not specify whether it was hammered fine or simply coiled as it was.[31] The Bafia of neighboring Cameroon hammered and scraped brass trade wire to make a fine thread with which to decorate calabashes and manufacture finger rings.[32] On the Middle Congo, Bentley found blacksmiths hammering out brass wire in the 1880s, "for they knew nothing of wire-drawing," using standard brass trade rods one-seventh of an inch in diameter (about 30 millimeters) and three inches long.[33]

For the present, then, it seems unlikely that copper or brass wire was drawn in West Africa before the colonial period, whatever the case may be with gold and silver. Nevertheless, I cannot accept Denis Williams' proposition that because wiredrawing was not practiced in sub-Saharan West Africa, any wire used or depicted in sculpture must indicate a date after the mid-fifteenth century, that is, after the European arrival on the coast. This totally ignores the centuries of trade across the Sahara, where as Mas Latrie noted long ago, copper was shipped in the form of wire as well as bars, ingots, and sheets,[34] just as it would be after the Discoveries.

## CASTING

The sheer volume of literature on "bronze" casting in tropical Africa tends to obscure how little is actually known about it, particularly about the historical development of regional styles and techniques. We do not know for certain how or when *cire perdue,* lost-wax, casting reached black Africa, assuming that it was not discovered independently. We do not know how Igbo-Ukwu and Ife produced or acquired masterpieces of the caster's art without an antecedent period of technical and artistic experimentation. Even the reliability of the oral tradition that derives the art of Benin from Ife is being seriously questioned. Nor do existing discussions of the subject offer satisfactory interpretations of the so-called Lower Niger industry or of Igala or the Middle Benue, to say nothing of Akan and Cameroon casting, which have been too little appreciated in a Nigeria-centered field.

Perhaps it is best to begin with a reminder that the cire perdue technique is the most complex but not the only nor even the most common method of casting practiced in sub-Saharan Africa. The simplest and most widespread technique is to heat metal in a clay crucible and pour it into open moulds of clay, sand, or stone. Since copper melts at a temperature of 1083° C, however, it must be heated in a furnace with a forced draft, usually similar in design but smaller than a smelting furnace. The melting process also serves to refine the metal: slag separates and floats out, and if the molten metal is "poled" with a green branch, the amount of oxygen and other gases is reduced and there is less of a problem of bubbles and roughness in the finished product.[35] This poling, incidentally, was not limited to Africa; it is still employed in industrial refining of copper in England, for example.[36]

The Yeke described by de Hemptinne do not heat raw copper directly in a crucible but break it up into pieces, using a special hammer of copper, and pile the pieces on the load of charcoal in the furnace. The molten and refined copper then collects in a clay bowl lined with fine cinders at the bottom of the furnace, from which it is poured into ingot moulds made of the ubiquitous anthill (see fig. 7). The Yeke avoid casting in the full sun for fear of blistering, preferring the cool of the evening.[37]

In virtually all copper-producing areas for which information is available, open casting was used to produce ingots for trade and stockpiling (see chapter 8), but it was also used to produce various other objects. The Yeke cast anvils of copper in moulds dug out of earth, since termite hills were too small and difficult to shape.[38] Ornamental casting, however, was far more common. The Kavati of Mayombe, for example, cast copper bracelets in a mould made of damp sand which had been formed to the proper shape by means of a wooden model of the object to be cast.[39] Sand-casting is also documented among the Kuba and Nyamwezi and was no doubt practiced widely in Africa.[40]

Walton is on more speculative ground when he proposes that a soapstone bird with a pronounced ridge down front and back, found at Great Zimbabwe, may have been copied from a bronze original cast in a closed mould.[41] Though soapstone moulds for *open* ingot casting have been found at Zimbabwe,[42] evidence of closed-mould casting is virtually nonexistent in Central Africa until recent times — except where a hole was poked into the ground and metal poured into it or into bamboo stalks or reeds to form rods[43] and except in the case of cire perdue casting, discussed below. Wilson's description of Mtesa's smiths turning out brass drums and bugles and casting brass cartridge cases "wonderfully true and smooth" sounds suspiciously like an art learned from foreign traders,[44] while the cast animals at the royal court of Karagwe, illustrated by Stanley, were probably the work of Arabs, like the iron cows described fifteen years earlier by Speke.[45]

The technique of cire perdue casting consists essentially of translating a form modelled in wax or other modelling medium into metal by direct replacement. If the object to be cast is small, the model is made of solid wax, while larger objects are formed of wax built up on a clay core. In either case the wax is enveloped in several layers of fine clay that follow its contours precisely, and each layer is thoroughly dried before the next is applied. The clay is then baked in a slow fire. This hardens and dries the mould and causes the wax to melt and run out, leaving a hollow which can be taken up by molten metal poured into an opening left in the mould. Once the metal has run in, the mould is removed from the fire and allowed to cool slowly. Next the outer clay investment is broken open, the clay core removed where appropriate, and the cast object polished. Sometimes further decoration is added by engraving or even casting on.[46]

The buildup of gases is a major problem that can ruin a casting by leaving the surface bubbly and irregular. This has been dealt with in Africa in several ways. Sometimes a hole was left in the top of the mould for escaping gases. Benin casters used the more sophisticated method of providing runners not only to channel gases to the outside but also to allow the metal to run into different parts of the mould. In general, however, they and metalsmiths elsewhere in West Africa relied less on vents than on mixing sufficient carboniferous matter with the clay investment to absorb unwanted gases.[47] Bagam casters in Cameroon, for example, mixed chopped grass with the clay,[48] while the Gude of northeastern Nigeria added sifted donkey dung to the fine red clay made from termite hills.[49] Baulé and others used wood ash for the same purpose.[50]

The second problem in casting is to insure an even and ample supply of molten metal so that what is run in first does not begin to cool before the rest has been added, causing unevenness and even breaks in the casting. There were two rather different solutions to this problem. One involved luting the crucible which contained the casting metal directly onto the mould and providing an opening between the two. The combined crucible and mould were heated in a bellows furnace until the metal melted, then inverted so that the metal could run down into the mould. Virtuoso Bamum casters may even tap off some of the molten metal in the luted crucible to fill separate moulds (color illust. 1). This, as far as we can tell, is the technique generally used among the Akan-Baulé and in the brass-casting centers of northeastern Nigeria and Cameroon.[51] While it cannot be used for very large pieces, it is elegantly simple and efficient for ordinary-sized objects such as bracelets, bells, pipe bowls, and the like.

Yoruba, Benin, and Hausa casters, however, do not combine crucible and mould; instead, they heat the casting metal separately in a crucible or crucibles and pour it into the prepared mould. This is what Williams calls the "Cinquecento" method because it was widely used in sixteenth-century Italy, although the relevance of the term and its implications has yet to be demonstrated. In addition, Benin casters used a framework of metal armatures in larger pieces to transmit heat evenly and to burn up the clay core. Ife casters avoided the need for metal armatures by leaving a cavity in the back of the large cast heads so that the inner core and outer mould could be joined. This prevented shifting of the core and facilitated more even heating and cooling. Williams notes that the same technique was used in casting the baseplate figures at Benin.[52]

Two main modelling agents have been used in cire perdue casting in Africa, beeswax and latex, the latter obtained from the *Euphorbia camerounica Pax*. It appears also that the Igala used latex from a species of ficus.[53] Williams associates beeswax with the Cinquecento method of building up the model in layers and keeping crucible and mould separate, while he links latex with the technique of modelling with fine threads on heavier spirals and joining mould and pouring cup into a single unit. He also maintains that latex permits much finer modelling than beeswax, leading him to the assumption that Akan goldweights employed latex.[54] Posnansky has pointed out that this is simply not true: Akan casters used beeswax, not latex, and were able to employ strands less than 0.5 millimeter thick — one-fourth the minimum diameter Williams claims for beeswax.[55] On the other hand, Willett comments that latex is a more solid medium and can be formed into loops that do not collapse during investment with clay, unlike wax, which needs support.[56]

It would, in fact, be very useful to be able to distinguish works modelled in beeswax from those modelled in latex, because the euphorbia tree grows only in the savanna and hence the identification of the agent might help establish the provenance of objects. Works from Igbo-Ikwu and other parts of the Delta, for instance, show very fine modelling (see fig. 8), but with the Akan skill as a cautionary example, it would be unwise to assume that they must have been manufactured in the savanna or have relied on imported latex.[57]

Akan goldweights, being small, were customarily built up of solid wax, with the limbs and other appendages added to the central core. So profi-

8. Shell, presumed from Igbo Isaiah, Nigeria. Leaded bronze

cient did these craftsmen become that they were able to adapt the technique to the direct casting of small organic objects such as fruits and seeds, crustacea, reptile heads and chicken feet, and insects of various kinds (the "lost beetle" process).[58] A variant has been documented in the Middle Congo using a matrix of banana or plantain stem rather than wax or latex. The Ngala cut plantain root into the shape of a leg ring and enclosed it in clay, leaving a small hole. The mould was baked until the root burned to a powder and could be shaken out of the hole and molten brass run in.[59] The Sundi of the Lower Congo employed a similar technique, although it is not clear from Laman's description how they produced the heavy hollow rings that were filled with sand.[60] Wooden models have also been collected from this region,[61] but it would appear that they were used for sandcasting in the manner already described for the Kavati rather than for any type of cire perdue, unless the light wood burned out during the baking.

The brass crucifixes of the Lower Congo are a case apart. Both the forms and the technology were introduced by the Portuguese. The models were apparently provided by early missionaries, but subsequently native artisans learned to make their own, whether in closed moulds or using the lost-wax process. The episode seems to have left barely an echo: by the mid-1930s, when Wannyn was gathering information throughout the region, only the crudest bracelets and crucifixes were being cast with scrap metal in open moulds; the refinements and religious inspiration of the "Mufalengo" period has been entirely forgotten, and in any event, elaborate casting never seems to have been devoted to non-Christian art.[62]

The archaeological evidence summarized by Bisson suggests that open-mould casting, primarily of ingots, began about the end of the first millennium A.D. in the region of the present Zaire-Zambia border.[63] This is consistent with the finger ring of cast copper found at Kamangoza (Zambia) by Vogel and dated to about the tenth century,[64] and with the revised dating of the Sanga sites, where graves rich in copper ingots are no longer ascribed to the eighth or ninth century but to a slightly later period.[65] In spite of the early flowering of copper technology in Central Africa, the art of casting apparently did not develop beyond the open-mould method. True, a bronze spearhead found at Khami by Robinson and considered to be of African manufacture has been examined by several experts who have concluded that it may have been cast by lost wax, but the spearhead was already damaged when found, so that it cannot be accepted as unequivocal proof of the technique.[66]

On the basis of our present knowledge, then, the area of cire perdue casting is limited to West Africa. It extends across the Sudan from the Senegambia to Lake Chad and northern Cameroon and southward into the forest zone. It embraces not only areas where royal patronage played a major role, such as Mossi, Aşante, Ife, Benin, Nupe, the kingdoms of the Niger Benue confluence, and the Bamenda grasslands, but also peoples whose political organization is less centralized: the Dan and Kpelle of Liberia, the Biafadas of Guiné-Bissau, the Senufo, Bambara, Baulé, Bobo, Lobi, Ibo, Tiv, and Hausa.[67] The finds at Igbo-Ukwu seem to reflect a concentration of kingly or priestly power, mirrored in the abundance of metal and beads, though as yet we know nothing more about this civilization.[68] The Sao, south of Lake Chad, remain even more problematical.[69]

Any attempt to date the introduction of cire perdue casting into West Africa or to trace the pattern of its diffusion immediately runs into several obstacles. There are relatively few dated early sites where cast objects have been found and even fewer where the evidence of casting itself has been unearthed. This means that while there is a strong supposition that the objects found in the tumuli of Senegambia and the Middle Niger or at Igbo-Ukwu were cast locally, or at least in sub-Saharan Africa, this cannot be proven. And though crucibles may be found in the inland delta of the Niger and at Begho in northern Ghana, moulds must be broken to get at the casting and hence do not survive to tell us about early technology. Nevertheless a certain amount can be reconstructed from examining the objects themselves, as well as from ethnographic accounts and from oral tradition.

Most of the evidence documenting the wide diffusion of casting in West Africa is recent, dating only from the nineteenth and twentieth centuries. The technique may have reached areas such as Tivland and the Cameroon grassland relatively late.[70] Be that as it may, there is ample reason to believe that the craft was firmly rooted in certain parts of West Africa well before the arrival of the first Europeans on the coast. The systematic excavation of the tumuli of the western Sudan is only just beginning. They reveal a wealth of cuprous objects, including small figurines and highly ornamented bracelets, and appear to date from the period before the spread of Islam, that is, from the later first millennium and the centuries immediately following.[71] And though the precise provenance of the objects cannot be ascertained, they are in a purely African idiom. Sao bronze casting may date from about the same period, but one cannot yet be sure.[72] The abundance of crucibles and crucible fragments — more than 500 — recently found in the Dwinfuor quarter of Begho are a strong indication that casting was carried out by Brong Ahafo smiths, probably under Mande influence, as early as the late-fourteenth and fifteenth centuries, and then spread southward, attentuating their Islamic forms and motifs along the way.[73] It is possible that the Akan began as gold casters and then applied their craft to imported alloys.[74] Probably too much has been made of the bronze copies of Coptic lamps, dated stylistically to the fifth to seventh centuries, found on the Gold Coast: they provide a terminus a quo but no more.[75]

The dating of casting in Nigeria has long been a problem, because until the excavations at Igbo-Ukwu, no major castings had been found in a primary archaeological context. Most were discovered accidentally in construction projects or in sites where they had been reburied; some seem never to have been buried at all. The entire Ife corpus of twenty-seven pieces is so homogeneous in style, however, that Willett argues convincingly that it must have been cast over a short period of time, though not necessarily by the same artist, as Kenneth Murray once speculated. Terra cotta sculpture was produced over a much longer span, but pieces showing stylistic similarities to the castings have been found in undisturbed sites and dated to c. 1100–1450 A.D., the period of the potsherd pavements. Thermoluminescent analysis carried out on the clay cores of a group of Ife and Ife-related castings have an internal consistency but run somewhat later than this.[76] The castings found at Igbo-Ukwu are even earlier than those of Ife and possibly earlier than many of the savanna tumuli, if the ninth-century dates are accepted.

That the earliest evidence of cire perdue casting yet known in sub-Saharan Africa should be found in the region of West Africa most distant from North Africa and the Nile Valley is unsettling for proponents of a diffusionist theory. Nevertheless, diffusion from the north or northeast still seems the most probable explanation, since the technique is complicated and already had a long history in the ancient Near East by the time trading between North Africa and the Sudan intensified in the wake of the Arab conquest of the Maghreb. The case for independent invention such as occurred in the New World would be stronger if there were an identifiable tradition of experimentation with open- and closed-mould casting and if southern Nigeria were provided with its own sources of copper. True, tin is abundant in the Bauchi Plateau and minor copper and copper-lead sources may have been accessible to local artisans, but it seems more likely that cire perdue technology was introduced from the north. Shaw suggests a possible blending of the Arab tradition of filigree and abundant ornamentation with a purely African idiom, to account for what William Fagg has termed the "strange rococo, almost Fabergé-like virtuosity" of the Igbo-Ukwu bronzes.[77]

Both the Ife heads and the Igbo-Ukwu works seem to represent the full flowering of a style that could only have come at the end of a long period of artistic and technological development. Shaw has observed, however, that when casting was introduced it may simply have been adapted to the existing, highly sophisticated canon. In the case of Ife this meant translating terra cottas into metal, while at Igbo-Ukwu a range of objects hitherto made in other media were rendered in copper and bronze: decorative calabashes, pottery, rope, leather, even natural objects such as shells and animal skulls.[78]

Denis Williams has approached the problem of the dating and spread of lost-wax casting rather differently and reached provocatively revisionist but ultimately untenable conclusions. To Williams, the decisive watershed in the history of African casting as in ironworking is the arrival of Europeans on the coast of tropical Africa with their technology and their plentiful supplies of metal. Though he seems to admit an antecedent tradition of casting, probably derived from the north and embodied in the method of luting crucible and mould, he maintains that the true West African bronze age, the period of casting on a significant and monumental scale, began only after A.D. 1500. There is, he claims, no positive evidence of figurative casting before this date. Since the Cinquecento method of casting was introduced by the Europeans, Benin casting did not derive from Ife but developed only under the stimulus of European technology and trade. This is reminiscent of earlier theories that assumed a Portuguese origin for Benin "bronzes," albeit on different grounds. Williams buttresses his late dating with iconographic arguments: the crotal bells represented on the Jebba warrior, on several of the Benin pectoral plaques, and on a piece from Igbo-Ukwu are first mentioned as an import on the Guinea coast in a trading account of 1590; therefore, these works must be after that date. Indeed, he proposes a date after 1640 for the Tada and Jebba warriors, because they also depict drawn wire, which he believes must have been imported from Europe. Conversely, he dates all representation of Portuguese in Benin art to before 1642, when the Portuguese were ousted from the Gold Coast by the Dutch. Iconographic motifs common to the Ife, Benin, and Jebba-Tada works, as well as common technical devices such as internal discs reinforcing potential weak spots in larger figures, lead him, further, to the conclusion that many of these castings were broadly contemporaneous. In consequence, he rejects much of the Benin chronology of Fagg and Dark.[79]

Original and stimulating as many of Williams' hypotheses are, they cannot pass unchallenged. As Posnansky has pointed out, his conclusions suffer from their preoccupation with Nigeria and their ignorance of the antiquity and technology of brass casting elsewhere in Africa.[80] Furthermore, they are seriously weakened by work that was done in the decade preceding his book and of which he takes little account. The findings at Igbo-Ukwu and the dating of Ife casting on the basis of the terra cottas and potsherd pavements both undermine his contention that there was no significant figurative casting before 1500 A.D. Others before him have questioned the authenticity of the oral tradition that derives Benin casting from Ife about the end of the fourteenth century, on the grounds that the tradition is a late one, that at Ife itself there is no surviving memory of brass casting, and that though a few Benin pieces show stylistic affinities with

Ife, most are quite different. There is no evidence at all, however, that the Portuguese introduced brass casting in any form to Benin, nor are there Benin pieces that show stylistic influences from Europe, apart from the representation of the Portuguese with their customary attributes of guns and manillas — in contrast to the Congo crucifixes. Arguing against such an introduction, the report of an early mission to the court of Benin in 1485 describes cast bronze objects as symbols of kingship. Because this report speaks of the oba of Benin receiving them from a powerful lord to the northeast, those who are doubtful of the Ife-Benin link tend to look elsewhere: to Igala, for example, or Nupe, or the Niger-Benue confluence, for the source of Benin's casting tradition, but not to Europe. It is worth noting, on the other hand, that the figure of an *oni* of Ife, found in Benin, has been dated by thermoluminescence to A.D. 1325 ± 60, while a Benin plaque showing similarities to Ife and Tada work has been dated by the same method to A.D. 1420 ± 60.[81]

Williams may well be overemphasizing the importance of technical differences in casting traditions, aside from the fact that so few have been carefully studied by specialists. He insists that the use of wax discs on the larger Ife, Benin, and Tada figures indicates a cultural connection, but it may instead only indicate that casters faced a common problem and solved it independently in the same way. Nor is the Cinquecento method employed at Benin as different from its counterpart as Williams asserts; Bini casters may simply have incorporated technical advances appropriate to larger objects, in a period when casting itself expanded in importance thanks to the greater availability of metals.[82]

As to the use of crotal bells and drawn wire as dating devices, Posnansky has effectively warned against the *argumentum ex silentio*. Because crotals (little spherical bells) are first mentioned by James Welsh in 1590, it does not follow that they could not have been traded earlier, by sea or by land, or even have been cast in Africa, nor that they could not have been added on to the Benin and Tada pieces. And in fact, both crotals and wire are found at Igbo-Ukwu.[83] Nevertheless, Williams is quite justified in challenging the alleged line of descent from Nok to Ife to Benin. Rubin and Neaher have both called attention to the richness of other casting traditions within Nigeria itself and the difficulty of integrating them into this schema. While the magnificent seated figure from Tada shows affinities to Ife sculpture, and others of the so-called Tsoede bronzes bear some similarities to Benin works, there are groups of castings that do not fit easily into the Ife-Benin tradition: "No single Nigerian bronze-working tradition presently known," Rubin points out, "is adequate to explain all the others."[84] He himself has demonstrated the great variety present in the Benue region, extending to the Cameroon border, so far undated and not yet understood in relation to "Sao" casting and other northerly schools.[85] Since casting has died out completely in Nupe, we are also in ignorance of its possible role in mediating technical and artistic influences between north and south; the Nupe themselves deny Hausa or Muslim influences on their art, appearances to the contrary, and claim an Igala source.[86] The possible role of Old Oyo in the development of casting remains equally enigmatic, and the same is true of Owo.[87] Similarly, the "Lower Niger bronze industry" is simply a catch-all for a number of unattributed pieces, some of which hark back to Benin, others of which do not. As Neaher has suggested, the itinerant caster probably played a major role in diffusing both techniques and artistic motifs.[88]

From southern Nigeria and western Cameroon to Zaire there is an enormous vacuum. The casting traditions of the Lower Congo based on the use of plantain fiber rather than wax may be an adaptation of the imported technique responsible for the brass crucifixes, or they may represent an extension of West African casting, transmitted we know not how, but possibly by way of the African crews employed on European ships plying the coast.

## ALLOYS

Different combinations of metals have different physical properties, a fact early noted and early exploited by metallurgists the world over. In Africa, the subject of alloys is of more than metallurgical interest, however. Scholars have hoped that the analysis of metallic content may hold the key to questions of chronology, of the interrelationship of artistic traditions, and of the ultimate source of the metals used.

Alloys of copper and tin — bronze — or of copper and zinc — brass — are much easier to cast than copper alone, all the more so if modest amounts of lead are added. This is so not only because they melt at lower temperatures than copper alone but also because they generate fewer gasses to cause blowholes and porosity in the finished object. Given the difficulties of casting large objects of unalloyed copper in closed moulds, it is all the more remarkable that five of the Ife heads and the magnificent seated figure from Tada (fig. 9) are almost pure copper.[89]

There has been a great deal of confusion in the terminology applied to copper-base metals in Africa. The Benin "bronzes" are a case in point. Already in 1919 Von Luschan demonstrated that a group of them were, in fact, brasses. His findings have been confirmed and extended by Werner and Wolf, who have analyzed more than 250 Benin objects and shown that in the overwhelming majority zinc is the primary metal alloyed with

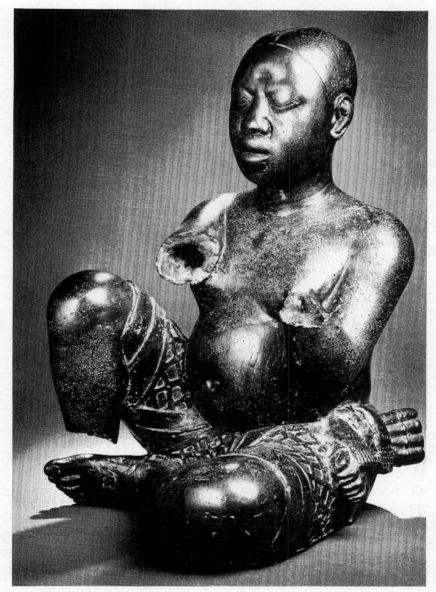

9. Seated figure, Tada, Nigeria. Copper

copper. Only a small number are either bronzes, with low tin content, or virtually pure copper. Zinc is rarely absent and lead is also common. Excluding the five Ife pieces of copper, the rest are also heavily leaded brasses, comparable in zinc and lead content to certain Benin groups. Of related objects, the Wunmonije heads and Ita Yemoo castings are also leaded brasses, although the latter average lower amounts of zinc and lead and contain small amounts of tin. Thus none of the Ife works and very few from Benin qualify as true bronze, if one defines it as an alloy containing at least 5 percent tin as the principal metal combined with copper.[90]

In contrast, the castings from Igbo-Ukwu are of bronze, with additions of lead. As Shaw points out, the craftsmen who produced the Igbo metalwork seem to have been fully aware of the different properties of the metals: they used copper for hammering, twisting, and engraving, and bronze for cire perdue casting.[91] In contrast, it is impossible to say whether Ife smiths cast in copper out of pure bravado or possibly for ritual reasons, or whether they were ignorant of the fine points of alloys — or whether they simply had to use what was at hand. All the more curious in this regard are the so-called Tsoede bronzes, the castings found at Tada, Jebba, and Giragi and linked by oral tradition with the eponymous hero of Nupe. The seated figure, as we have noted, as well as the small, pig-tailed figure, are almost pure copper, suggesting technical affinities with Ife, but the rest of the pieces are of *unleaded* bronze, a very rare alloy indeed in Nigerian casting.[92] Analyses of a large number of Yoruba objects from the collection of the University of California at Los Angeles show them to be largely standard brasses with much lower lead values than in the Ife and Benin pieces published by Werner and Willett.[93]

Alloys outside of southern Nigeria have not been analyzed to a comparable extent. The Lebeufs have published the content of a group of Sao "bronzes" from south of Lake Chad. Here, too, the term *bronze* is a misnomer: a few of the objects are almost pure copper, but most are an *alliage quaternaire,* a rather variable mixture of copper, tin, zinc, and lead, with a high level of impurities such as arsenic, antimony, and iron — in Shaw's words, a "mixed bag."[94] They were probably the result of recycling metals of various sorts rather than of conscious alloying, but since the objects are not linked to a precise archaeological stratum the analyses are not very revealing. Casting has disappeared from the Sao country itself, but a comparison with objects produced in modern times by neighboring Kapsiki (Cameroon) and Lele (Chad) shows that the latter are essentially brasses (11–23 percent zinc), with small amounts of lead and tin.[95]

Analysis of surface metals on crucibles excavated in 1975 at Begho in northern Ghana shows a comparable lack of consistency. The first group of five crucibles "were used for melting copper and possibly bronze, but probably not brass."[96] Here, too, varying amounts of lead were found. A second analysis of nine crucibles from the same source proved all to be brasses, again with a variety of trace elements. Posnansky concludes that it is probable that scrap was being used rather than ingots of any sort. At Dawu, also in northern Ghana and dated to the late-sixteenth and seventeenth centuries, alloys were found to contain about 25 percent zinc, with lead content exceeding 3 percent in only one case.[97] Analysis of objects from two tumuli in southern Senegal show that they, too, are brasses with insignificant tin and lead content.[98]

Were the alloys found in West Africa imported from outside, or might they have been produced by indigenous metalsmiths? Given the absence of appreciable copper sources and the complexity of brass-making (see below), it has generally been assumed that the alloys used were imported. The Lebeufs take exception to this view as far as the Sao are concerned. Following oral tradition, they claim that the copper used was obtained locally and the tin from the Bauchi Plateau and Mount Gara, but they make no attempt to account for the zinc and lead and offer no evidence to confirm the presence of copper deposits in the Waza, Madagli, and Mora areas of the Sao region.[99] Nevertheless, the availability of tin in Nigeria has led to the lingering suspicion that bronze such as that used by the Igbo-Ukwu casters might have been produced in tropical Africa. If so, where would the copper have come from? There may indeed have been minor, unidentified sources within present-day Nigeria: Bernard Fagg was once shown one, but was subsequently unable to locate it again for more careful examination.[100] Otherwise, the closest African sources would be at Azelick, Nioro, Hufrat en-Nahas, or the Niari Basin. Hufrat would seem to be ruled out because no traces of gold were found in the Igbo-Ukwu pieces, while it was a conspicuous constituent of the Hufrat ores.[101] In the Niari Basin, as we have noted, copper occurs in close proximity to lead and was, at least in modern times, smelted with it, which could account for the lead in the bronzes. It is also true that lead is found closer to home in the Benue Valley, where it was produced and traded in the mid-nineteenth century and possibly earlier.[102] Inevitably the question is highly speculative, since we do not even have dates for indigenous tinworking in Nigeria. (The possibility of trade contacts between the Middle Congo and the Niger Delta in the pre-European period will be dealt with more fully in chapter 5.)

Except for the copper-lead of the Niari Basin and Transvaal, copper alloys are much rarer outside of West Africa.[103] The Tervuren Museum has objects of a copper-silver, made in western Angola, according to Maesen, but more detailed information is not available.[104] Although Wannyn's informants claimed that the crucifixes of the Lower Congo were cast of local copper, he found no traditions of alloying, so that it is likely they used imported brass. The analysis he gives, however, could only be a modern brass, that is, nineteenth to twentieth century, and is inconsistent with his earlier dating for the finer pieces.[105] Either the analysis is inaccurate or the dating must be revised.

There have also been a few finds of brass at early sites in Central and Southern Africa: a piece of thin brass wire (Birmingham Wire Gauge No. 29) on the surface of Stratum 2 at the Great Zimbabwe acropolis, and two bangles and a fragment of wire from Bambandyanalo-Mapungubwe (Transvaal). All three are standard brasses.[106] Bronze was much more plentiful at Zimbawe. Indeed, bronze wire bangles were ubiquitous, more common than copper, but bronze beads, sheathing, and spearheads were also uncovered by Caton-Thompson. Earlier, a bronze hoe or axe and an ingot of the familiar *handa* type, matching a soapstone mould from Zimbabwe, were deposited in the Bulawayo Museum. The analyses published are all within the range of true bronzes, with no appreciable amounts of other metals noted. Bronze has also been found at other Zimbabwean ruins and at Ingombe Ilede. Although the brass was certainly an import, the bronze is more enigmatic. Tin slags and lumps of the metal have been found at Dhlo-Dhlo and Khami on the Zimbabwean plateau, but the only ancient tin workings positively identified thus far are at Rooiberg, a considerable distance to the south in the Transvaal. Nevertheless, alluvial tin is present in sizable quantities east of Victoria. Without evidence that it was worked in earlier centuries, Caton-Thompson considers it a moot point whether the tin was African or imported or whether the bronze was imported already alloyed.[107]

Equally moot is the question of bronze-making at Rooiberg in the Transvaal. That tin was indeed smelted there by African craftsmen seems beyond dispute, but we do not know when or for how long.[108] Early in the present century an unformed lump of metal was found at Blaauwbank No. 433, one of the most important of the myriad ancient tin workings in the area. When analyzed, it was found to contain 80 percent copper and 7 percent tin; it also contained "notable amounts" of nickel and arsenic, which was harder to explain. Nevertheless, the find was widely accepted as proof of local manufacture of bronze, in spite of the fact that the "bronze" prills from the smelting site turned out not to be bronze at all but copper or arsenical copper with small amounts of tin.[109] Subsequent analyses of sample tin-copper alloys from the Rooiberg area suggest that smelters did indeed attempt to make bronze, but failed because of the peculiar nature of local ores, which are high in nickel, arsenic, and iron. In this case, the arsenic was probably an impurity in the ore, not an intentional addition. The resulting copper-tin, containing as it did arsenic in the range of 11 to 19 percent, was a useless, brittle bronze. These findings led to a new analysis of the original Blaauwbank ingot, and it was found that the composition published by Trevor in 1912 was completely inaccurate: the tin content was only 1.5 percent, that of arsenic 3 percent, with only minor amounts of other elements besides copper. That leaves only the pellet found by Frobenius at the Smelterskopje site near Rooiberg and claimed by him to contain 74 percent copper, 21 percent tin, and 3.5 percent iron (apparently a reanalysis was not possible). Although the tin content is unusually high, it is the closest to a true bronze yet found at Rooiberg but not enough to confirm the existence of a successful bronze-making industry.[110]

Nevertheless there is evidence that bronze was made elsewhere in the Transvaal, possibly at a later period than the Blaauwbank essays. The account of Jan Van de Capelle, trading at Delagoa Bay in 1724–25, states that the "Machicosjes" (people of Chief Mashakatsi) brought tin and copper to sell but at the same time bought good quality copper "om met hun thin te smelten tot hals en arm-ringen" ("in order to smelt with their tin for neck and arm rings"). In other words, they were exporting their copper, which had too many impurities, and importing copper with which to make bronze.[111] A hundred years later Moffat witnessed a smelt of copper and tin in a crucible, although he mistakenly calls the result brass.[112] A traveller among the Tswana in 1803–5 brought back a massive armlet, worn by the inhabitants, which was found to contain 93 percent copper, 7 percent tin.[113] This also argues for native manufacture, although conceivably the bronze could have reached this remote area by trade from the coast.

The picture regarding indigenous manufacture of bronze is thus hazy and likely to remain so until more archaeological work is done. It is much more certain that brass was not made in sub-Saharan Africa before the nineteenth century, because of the unusual technical problems involved. Since pure zinc does not occur in nature, brass has since Roman times been made from calamine, a collective name for several compounds. This is a complex operation because of the extreme volatility of the metal, so much so that metallic zinc (spelter) was not produced in Europe until the mid-eighteenth century, although it had long been manufactured in China. Before this time, brass was made by smelting calamine in a crucible with refined copper under conditions that prevented the zinc from volatilizing and that cemented it with the copper. Because of the difficulties of controlling the reaction, the ratio of zinc to copper in the finished product could be extremely variable, but it could not exceed one-third. By the eighteenth century, however, the process had become so perfected that the contents could be precisely managed, which may explain why the use of calamine was not superseded by direct alloying of zinc and copper until after 1840, a century after the technology for this was available.[114] Most cala-mines used before this contained lead, albeit in varying amounts, and this lead was carried over into the brass, although it may have been unevenly distributed because of its weight.

Brasses from medieval Europe that have been analyzed show little uniformity,[115] and work is just beginning on the composition of brasses from North Africa and the Near East during the same period. This makes Monod's find of a load of brass rods from a caravan buried in the western Sahara all the more precious. The rods have been dated by the organic matter binding them to the twelfth century A.D. and found by analysis to be a standard brass, containing 80 percent copper and 20 percent zinc, but we do not know where they were made.[116] A recent microscopic examination of one of these rods concludes that the metal was so porous and fissured that it would not have been suitable for drawing or hammering but only for remelting.[117] If such rods were typical, one can understand why casting flourished in West Africa, while wiredrawing did not.

Because of the variations in composition of brasses both inside and outside Africa, attempts to identify the sources of the metal or to use alloys as a dating mechanism have long proved frustrating. Presumably there is some significance in the fact that castings from Igbo-Ukwu, Ife, Benin, and the Tsoede group show distinct differences in metallic composition. Posnansky has argued, for example, that the absence of brass at Igbo-Ukwu tends to confirm the early, pre-European radiocarbon dates — in contrast to a preponderance of brass at Benin, which received ample supplies of the alloy from Europe from the late fifteenth century on. It may be significant that the few finds of bronze by Connah at Benin are in pre-European levels.[118]

In 1970, Otto Werner proposed a Benin chronology based broadly on metallic content:

> Early (16th century or earlier): alloys containing little zinc, i.e., tin bronzes and copper
> Middle (16th–18th century): brasses with high lead and high antimony
> Late (after mid-19th century): objects containing 30–35 percent zinc

Subsequently he has refined this schema, above all by shifting the focus to nickel content and to the lead-zinc ratio rather than absolute percentages of these metals. "The difference in nickel content is so striking," he declares, "that it can be used to date the brasses." Thus European brasses of the eleventh to thirteenth centuries typically have less than 0.1 percent nickel, while more recent ones have more than 0.1 percent. This is the result of the transition in the fourteenth century to the more impure sulphide ores after the exhaustion of secondary deposits. Although Ife and Benin brasses tend to be rather similar in zinc and lead content, all of the former contain less than 0.1 percent nickel — which would seem to lend further support to the view that they are several centuries older than the earliest Benin brasses. The lead-zinc ratio, on the other hand, tells less about dating than about the possible source of the calamine used to make the brass: different German sources, for example, have significantly different ratios.[119] Impressive as this work is, we should not forget that Europe may not have been the only source of African brass, especially in the medieval period.

One further comment about the composition of European brasses. Although the 2:1 ratio was standardized with the perfecting of the calamine process in the eighteenth century, it is important to note that it was (and still is) adjusted according to the uses for which the alloy was intended. Gilding metal, for example, might contain as little as 10 percent zinc.[120] Brass intended for ingots and pins contained somewhat more zinc than that converted into sheets ("latten"). Furthermore, there were recognized differences in quality which affected copper-zinc ratios and resulted in the inclusion of lead and other elements.[121] Consequently, attempts to correlate alloys found in Africa with those produced in Europe and the Muslim world are dogged by the lack of precise information about the metallic content at any one time of the principal forms of copper exported to Africa, namely manillas, rods, and basins of various kinds. To cite only one example: the brass manilla, for centuries a staple of the trade, at some moment entirely ceased being made of brass. When manillas were finally withdrawn from circulation in southeastern Nigeria in 1948, it was found that they consisted of about 60–65 percent copper and 25–30 percent lead, with the rest a miscellany of metals[122] — this in contrast to what was long assumed to be a standard imported manilla, found in Benin and composed of 20 percent zinc and 2 percent lead.[123] Manillas analyzed in 1909 contained about 8 percent tin and "traces of silver and gold"; others analyzed in 1943 contained about 6 percent antimony and traces of iron and arsenic.[124] In his 1866 history of the English brass industry, Aitken claimed that the manillas produced by Bristol, Cheadle, and Birmingham were "cast of a metal composed of copper, with a large proportion of lead as an alloy, and hardened by arsenic," but it is not clear whether zinc was still present.[125] Clearly, the composition was in a state of flux into the present century, perhaps justifying the Bamenda belief that modern brass rods were inferior for casting to the old brass wire anklets,[126] and there is every reason to assume that change was the rule earlier as well.

To add to the difficulties of interpreting the types of alloys, zinc itself was imported into Africa during the nineteenth century, and some smiths learned to make brass directly. Burton noted that the Wajiji had learned from the Arabs on the East African coast to combine one part imported zinc with two parts "fine soft and red copper" from Kazembe's, that is, from Katanga.[127] Ingots of zinc have also been found in the Transvaal, almost certainly the products of trade with the coast; it is even possible that they antedate the import of zinc into East Africa, since the East India Company was shipping the metal from China to Europe in the seventeenth century, though it is not very likely that much of this would have ended up in Southern Africa.[128]

As a postscript to this discussion on alloys and metal sources, a word should be said about the possibility of linking copper itself to a parent ore-body through the identification of trace elements or patterns of elements. For the present, this does not hold out much hope, primarily because ore-bodies are not homogeneous and hence trace elements vary from one part of the lode to another and at different depths; early metals would have been obtained from ore-bodies now depleted. Then, too, some elements are lost in the smelting, while others which are not affected by smelting may be common to so many ores that they have little identifying value. Casting imposes a further difficulty in that different elements do not diffuse evenly through the metal. Samples would therefore have to be taken from several parts of the object, to give representative results.

Copper alloys containing lead hold out more promise to the metallurgical detective. Lead-zinc ratios, as we have seen, may be distinctive enough to identify known sources of calamine used in brass-making. Lead isotope ratios may be even more individual, virtual fingerprints of particular ore bodies. Since so many African alloys contain lead, these ratios could help to shed light on metallic origins if a large enough repertoire can be assembled. The results of lead isotope analysis of a representative sample of Nigerian pieces, in fact, suggests an even greater complexity than has emerged from the analysis of metallic content. The most striking finding is that all the Benin pieces examined have "virtually the same isotopic ratios, in spite of a speculated range of production dates spanning approximately the 15th through 19th centuries," indicating in all likelihood the same source of lead. Interestingly enough, most of the lead deposits in use today were ruled out as sources for these objects. The single Ife piece and the two from Igbo-Ukwu have values different from each other and from the Benin samples, buttressing the hypothesis that Igbo-Ukwu, Ife, and Benin were separate traditions, obtaining their metals from different sources.[129]

For the present, then, all that can be said is that the mosaic of metalworking in sub-Saharan Africa is infinitely more varied than was thought until very recently. If the initial effect of careful scientific study of African metallurgy is to raise more enigmas than it resolves, it is because earlier answers were far too simple. And considering how much has been learned in so short a time, one can hope that many of the pieces will one day fall into place.

# ■ Part II ————
# THE COPPER TRADE

— Chapter 5 ─────────────────────────────────

# Gold for Copper: The Copper Trade before the Period of European Discoveries

A history of metals is almost a history of trading.
— LESLIE AITCHISON

The skeleton of pre-European African history
and archaeology will be reconstructed by the discovery of its trade routes. It now seems likely that
the skeleton will prove to be pan-African.
— GERVASE MATHEW

From the moment that copper was first produced by African metallurgists it entered into the economic life of the continent. With the opening
up of regular trade across the Sahara in the middle centuries of the first
millennium A.D., imported metal also flowed into West Africa, supplement-
ing or replacing the output of sahelian sources. Well before the beginnings
of maritime trade with Europe in the fifteenth century, copper had become the object of extensive commerce, feeding markets ever more distant
from the sources of production in ever greater quantities.

## CENTRAL AND SOUTHERN AFRICA

The copper trade of Central Africa in the Iron Age, as Garlake notes,[1]
has received little attention; that of other areas of the continent is little
better understood. This state of affairs stems on the one hand from a preoccupation with the trade in gold and on the other from the paucity of
direct evidence. Before the late fifteenth century, and in many areas until
the nineteenth century, the evidence for the trading of copper is almost
entirely circumstantial: that is, copper has been found by archaeologists
and prehistorians in places where it cannot have been produced, implying
some sort of commerce or at least exchange. Nevertheless, such finds are
common enough that the decorative use of copper has been proposed as
one of the defining characteristics of the Early Iron Age in Central Africa.[2]

The modest, even tentative nature of trade in the earliest phases of this

103

culture is best illustrated by the pattern of finds in Zambia, where archaeology has advanced farther than in any other country in Africa, with the
possible exception of Nigeria.[3] Mining at both Kansanshi and Chondwe,
as we have seen, dates from the middle of the first millennium A.D. It may
be equally ancient, therefore, in other Central African mines, although
it is also possible that demand and the machinery of trade were so little
developed that more extensive exploitation was not necessary until much
later. Copper objects have been found in most Early Iron Age sites in Zambia: Kumadzulo, Dambwa, Kalundu, Twickenham Road, Chondwe, Kam-
bondo Kumbo. Finds are often fragmentary—primarily bits of bracelets
or bangles made of thin strips of beaten metal wound around a grass or
fiber core—and they are scanty, indicating that the metal was still a rarity.
It also implied wealth, as Vogel points out, since it was used strictly for
decorative purposes.[4] Furthermore, it seems to have been the earliest commodity traded in this part of Africa, or at least the earliest to have survived. Other foreign articles such as glass beads and seashells are even rarer,
and do not appear at all in undisturbed sites until several centuries later
than copper. Bisson quite rightly cautions against postulating "organized
long-distance trading" in copper—even where Early Iron Age sites are far
from deposits as in the case of the Victoria Falls settlements, which are,
in fact, closer to copper sources in the Wankie district of Zimbabwe than
to Zambian ones. It is far more likely that the small quantity of metal involved was bartered for centuries from hand to hand in the form of rough
ingots such as those found at Kumadzulo, or that it was transferred between groups as part of bridewealth payments.[5] Some areas, like Kalambo
Falls in northwestern Zambia, remained too remote from mining districts
and too poor in resources to have been significantly involved in the trade
at all, judging by the meagerness of finds.

As one would expect, copper becomes increasingly abundant in Zambian Later Iron Age sites and strata, that is, after the early centuries of
the present millennium, particularly in the form of bangles made of fine
drawn wire. At Ingombe Ilede, the most spectacular of these sites, literally
thousands of such bangles were found on the arms and legs of skeletons
in the burials. Bobbins of drawn wire and ten ingots of copper and bronze
were also unearthed from several of the graves, in addition to beads and
bracelets of gold. How unusual was the wealth of Ingombe Ilede, however,
is suggested by the contrast with the impoverished burials of the neighboring Tonga. It was a wealth created by a happy combination of factors: fer-
tile soil, tsetse-free grazing lands, an important salt deposit nearby, a stra-
tegic location in the Middle Zambezi Valley. The picture that emerges is,
therefore, of a society firmly grounded in an agricultural base which traded
salt and possibly foodstuffs for copper—perhaps from the Urungwe mines

112 miles south of the Zambezi — as well as for gold from elsewhere on the plateau. Its craftsmen manufactured the raw copper into refined objects that could then be exchanged for ivory, which with gold found a ready sale on the coast for glass beads, shells, and imported cloth, anticipating later patterns of exchange in Zambia.[6]

Ingombe Ilede seems to have occupied, during its brief flowering in the fourteenth and fifteenth centuries, a mediating position between the Iron Age cultures of Zambia and those of Zimbabwe. It may actually be closer to the latter, if one judges not only by pottery types and the predilection for large numbers of wire bangles[7] but also by the presence of bronze and gold. Archaeology in Zimbabwe is still recovering from the devastation caused by treasure hunters in search of King Solomon's mines and biblical Ophir at Great Zimbabwe and other stone ruins. Nevertheless the evidence indicates a pattern generally like that in Zambia: the mining and working of copper along with iron, from the early or mid-first millennium A.D., modest finds of copper bangles in Early Iron Age sites, increasing quantities in Leopard's Kopje settlements, until copper and bronze become abundant at Great Zimbabwe, Khami, Dhlo-Dhlo, and at all the excavated ruins of the plateau.[8] At Inyanga, to be sure, they are somewhat scarce, more plentiful at upland than at lowland sites, but Inyanga appears to have been a backwater, or at least an impoverished culture on the periphery of the great civilizations.[9]

So common are the hoards of copper and bronze at Great Zimbabwe and kindred ruins that they have been taken for granted, while attention focused first on the identity of the builders in stone and then on the role of the gold trade in indigenous state formation. And yet virtually all the scholars seriously concerned with Great Zimbabwe, from Gertrude Caton-Thompson to Peter Garlake, have commented on the apparent anomaly that important as Zimbabwean gold may have been to the Indian Ocean trading system, it played a relatively minor and belated role within African cultures of the region, clearly secondary to that of copper and its alloys.

It is generally agreed that gold mining on the plateau was well under way by the tenth century A.D., when the first written records refer to the export of gold from the coast.[10] Gold, however, does not appear in stratified Early Iron Age sites, including burials; instead, one finds copper and iron. It is not found at any Leopard's Kopje site nor in the lower strata at Great Zimbabwe, but only in levels III and IV, now dated to the period from about the eleventh to the early fifteenth century, as well as at Khami and Dhlo-Dhlo, which are believed to be contemporary with or later than these levels.[11] "It is a remarkable fact," declared Caton-Thompson in the 1971 revision of *The Zimbabwe Culture,* "that these early metal-using peoples, with their iron and copper artifacts and ornaments, the metals for which they were almost certainly mining in the early first millennium A.D. or before, showed little or no interest in gold as a material for beads or other objects of adornment such as mark their successors many years later." [12]

The archaeological record is borne out by documentary evidence from the coast. The Arab writers al-Idrisi (1100–66) and Abu al-Fida (1273–1331) commented that the natives of Sofala valued copper more than gold, a comment echoed in the mid-fourteenth century by al-Wardi. He marvelled at the quantity of native gold found in the country of Sofala and equally that "the natives however employ only ornaments of copper which they prefer to gold." [13] All three writers presumably based their accounts on second-hand information from traders, and their "Sofala" referred to the entire region where gold was obtained. Their reports were confirmed by one of the earliest Portuguese descriptions, that of Figueroa in 1505, which contrasted the Muslim traders of the port, with their fine robes and gold-embellished scimitars, and the local inhabitants whose women loaded their legs with copper bangles. [14] Preliminary excavations at what is believed to be the site of fifteenth-century Sofala suggest that these Africans were a Shona offshoot, very much given to ornaments of bronze but not of gold. [15]

Piecing together the available evidence, Summers concludes that all the known hoards of gold at Zimbabwean Iron Age sites "are likely to be post-fifteenth century" and that the same is true of gold found in burials. [16] This may need to be moved back a little, in view of recent radiocarbon dates, but even then, and allowing as best one can for the predations of Europeans (which Hall estimated at some 2,000 ounces before 1902), the total amount of gold thus far unearthed can be only a fraction of the total output of the goldfields. Summers estimates that whereas before the fifteenth century the entire production was channeled into exports, thereafter possibly as much as 10 percent was absorbed internally. [17]

This radical shift toward local consumption, mirrored in the archaeological record, was accompanied, as he reconstructs it, by a deliberate drop in production, as part of the effort by the centralized inland states to monopolize trade. There is no doubt that production declined once the Portuguese established themselves on the coast and attempted to control gold exports and even gain direct access to the mines. What is less certain, because of the inadequacy of written documentation before 1500 and the scarcity of radiocarbon dates for Later Iron Age sites, is whether this trend toward indigenous consumption of gold, coupled with restriction on production, developed in the fifteenth century or whether it was provoked more specifically by Portuguese policies in the sixteenth. Summers' chronology receives some support from the presence of gold at Ingombe Ilede with its revised dating to about 1400 A.D. It also fits in with the decline of Kilwa, whose fortunes seem to have been so intimately linked with the export of Sofalan gold, though this may have been from other causes, as Summers is well aware. At the same time, the absence of porcelain at Zimbabwe is further evidence of an end to trade with the coast by about the end of the fifteenth century.[18]

In any event, what concerns us here is that only after centuries of production did gold begin to be thesaurized within the indigenous producing and trading culture, to be used for "parade and ostentation." Why did it happen? Ingombe Ilede and the more recent levels of cultures of the Great Zimbabwe type (and the hill burials at Mapungubwe to be discussed below) represent highly stratified societies whose elite proclaimed their status by the possession of rare and valuable foreign imports: Chinese celadon, Indian cottons, glass beads. As this elite incorporated foreign luxuries in its sumptuary system, it also borrowed foreign values. It became increasingly aware of the overweening importance of gold in the Indian Ocean world, the insatiable demand for the metal, and its dazzling role in the courts of South India.[19] The coming of the Portuguese only reinforced this realization of gold's unique value. It did not replace copper and bronze at Ingombe Ilede or Zimbabwe; they retained the material and ritual value they had had since the beginning of the Iron Age — witness the continued profusion of these metals in later sites — but gold joined them as part of the constellation of wealth and status.

The belated valuation of gold by a court elite on the plateau would not in itself have sufficed to account for the decline in the amount of gold available for export, a matter that can only be explained by a more detailed study of the political and economic history of the region. Nor did it alter the fact that copper and iron continued to function as the primary metals in the internal trade of Africa. Indeed, one can argue that the copper trade may have played as decisive a role in state formation as the gold trade. To be sure, Caton-Thompson sounded a note of warning about even the role of gold which has often been lost sight of in subsequent discussions. Disputing the idea of Zimbabwe as a "distributing centre of the gold trade," she observed:

> Gold was melted in tiny crucibles, found sparingly by all excavators, testimony of the reckless exaggeration of the gold yield of the ruins, circulated to "boom" the country. As Schofield and Douslin have pointed out, such gold as has been found has been got mostly from superficial deposits, a fact which diminishes to vanishing point the claim that Zimbabwe was founded as a foreign gold emporium. The proverbial pioneer with his immense bag of gold beads must be classed beside the proverbial fisherman with his immense bag of silver fishes.[20]

Though she errs in contending that there are no gold reefs anywhere in the region, the low values of the only major gold belt would have discouraged ancient miners.[21]

Copper, on the other hand, was found and mined in the immediate vicinity, at the Zimbabwe Copper Mine.[22] Soapstone ingot moulds were found by Bent and Hall in early digging at Zimbabwe and were almost certainly used, Garlake maintains, in copper smelting at the site. These moulds (reproduced by Caton-Thompson) were of "very simple, small, somewhat *H*-shaped ingots, only some 15 cm. long, with shallow rectangular or ellipsoidal cross-sections and without rims," quite different from the larger, rimmed ingots found at Chedzurgwe and Ingombe Ilede with which they have nevertheless been confused (see diagram 2, p. 188).[23]

Portuguese documents of the sixteenth and seventeenth centuries emphasize the difficulty of obtaining gold and at the same time the continuing importance of copper in the plateau economy. In 1512, the clerk of the factory at Mozambique sent the king of Portugal notes he had made on the journey of the *degredado* Antonio Fernandes into the interior of Monomotapa, including a description of the kingdom of Mombara, seven days' journey from the "king of Monomotapa": "In this land there is . . . much copper and it is from there that copper is brought to Monomotapa in loaves [*pais*] like ours, and throughout this other land."[24] Four years later the Captain of Sofala added to the account of Ambar, that is, Mombara, "Here these people, whom I say are whiter than the blacks, come to sell *aspas* of copper and from there they come to the land of Bonapotapa [sic], because this Antonio Fernandes saw them being sold in those fairs and recognizes as being made in the copper rivers of the Manyconguo." Subsequently the Captain recommended that the Crown supply the factory with similar ingots: "The articles from Portugal that would now, Sire, fetch a good price here are *aspas* of copper of eight *arates* and of ten and I assure Your Highness that no matter how great is the quantity that comes here there will be no loss but only gain; if 20,000 *aspas* are worth here fifty and sixty mitical [of gold], Your Highness can guess what they may be worth in the Interior. . . ."[25] In fact, when the Portuguese flooded the market with copper it turned out to be a case of coals to Newcastle, as we shall see; but the point here is the early recognition by Portuguese merchants of the role of copper on the inland market, and specifically, its purchasing power in gold.

As Garlake observes, the very precise specifications given by Almada are close to those of the Chedzurgwe ingots, so that Mombara is probably to be identified with the rich copper-producing region of Urungwe.[26] The region is closer to the Zambezi than Great Zimbabwe, which lay far to the south and about which the Portuguese therefore knew much less.

Evidence from the Transvaal supports this view of the relative importance of copper and gold in the Iron Age economies of Central and Southern Africa. Virtually all early observers were struck by the obvious fact
that ancient miners were more interested in copper than in gold, though
their explanations for the phenomenon differed.[27] The only known ancient gold mines are in the eastern Highveld and escarpment, and probably fed the modest export trade with the Dutch at Delagoa Bay[28] after
our period, since there is no evidence for the use of gold in the pre-European
Transvaal, with the exception of Mapungubwe. It was not offered to Vasco
da Gama along this portion of the coast. In contrast, iron and copper objects are typical of known Iron Age sites from the first millennium A.D.,
some near the mines themselves, as at Harmony and Madjadjies Kraal,
others as far as 60 kilometers from the nearest copper source.[29] The lack
of timber on much of the Highveld, in fact, limited the sites where smelting was possible, making Iron Age communities more dependent on trade
to obtain worked copper. In a recent study of the southern Highveld, Maggs
underscores the quantity and variety of metal ornaments and implements
at sites such as 001 and concludes: "It is evident that the Iron Age societies
[of the southern Highveld] were linked by a more extensive trading network than most historical sources would suggest. Metals, particularly copper, would have been obtained from north of the Vaal. . . ."[30]

Farther north this trading network extended as far as the coast, and when
da Gama anchored in the bay of a "small river" well beyond the Rio do
Infante in 1498 he reported, "In this land there seemed to us to be great
quantities of copper which they wear on the legs, arms and twisted into
their hair."[31] The river on which da Gama bestowed the name Rio do Cobre
(Copper) has not been positively identified; it is generally assumed to be
the mouth of the Limpopo, although this is not a small river.[32] The copper would have come from the eastern Transvaal, probably from Phalaborwa itself. Diagonally southwestward across the continent, da Gama had
found copper greatly prized also by the inhabitants of St. Helena Bay, where
the nearest sources would have been in Namaqualand, several hundred
kilometres to the north.[33]

Where does Mapungubwe fit into the picture? Here again is a site whose
interpretation is rapidly changing in the light of new archaeological findings. Situated in the extreme northern Transvaal on the south bank of the
Limpopo, Mapungubwe ("the hill of the jackals") was originally excavated
in the 1930s, after gold objects were found by a farmer who talked a local
inhabitant into defying the taboos surrounding the hill and showing him
the secret path up the cliff to the hilltop burials.[34] Until recently it was
assumed to be an outpost of Shona culture roughly contemporaneous with
the apogee of Great Zimbabwe. Now the Greefswald sites of which Ma-

pungubwe is a part have been shown to be earlier than Period IV at Great Zimbabwe and an entirely separate cultural development. The earliest sites of this complex are undated, but the lower levels of the village sites of K2 and the Southern Terrace fall between the late tenth and late eleventh centuries. Occupation of the hilltop coincided with slightly later horizons of the Southern Terrace, spanning the period from about the late eleventh century into the early twelfth.

Fouché, who directed the earliest excavations at Mapungubwe, called it one of the wildest and most desolate spots in the Transvaal, and yet it was for several centuries the richest known site in Southern Africa. The inhabitants of the hilltop, in particular, built elaborate daga houses and buried their dead with a lavish accompaniment of copper, gold, and gold-foil objects. Though the economy was grounded in farming and especially cattle-raising, it must have been well above subsistence level. Not only were most of the cattle slaughtered when mature, judging by the faunal remains, but there is evidence of weaving and of fine working in metals and ivory.

The finds of trade beads, together with the ivory-working and weaving, suggest that Mapungubwe was in direct trading contact with the southeast coast. Desolate as the site now is, Fouché pointed out that it may once have occupied a key geographical position astride the routes of major migration from north and west, where the Limpopo is easily fordable throughout most of the year and where trade would have passed easily between the valley and the plateau. And of course, the hilltop would have been impregnable to attack.[35]

In sum, then, while the archaeological and documentary evidence inevitably skews the record in favor of nonperishable elements of culture and gives a disproportionate emphasis to trade at the expense of the pastoral and mixed-farming activities that were of necessity the main occupation of Iron Age societies, it does make clear that copper was an integral part of the exchange economy of Central and Southern Africa. It is well nigh ubiquitous in burials and other excavated sites, becoming increasingly common and more widely traded in the centuries down to 1500. It filled the role of ritual, ornamental, and status metal with almost no hint of utilitarian use — for which more ample supplies of iron were available. One is tempted to postulate a "golden triangle" of Ingombe Ilede, Great Zimbabwe, and Mapungubwe, all of them exporting gold and ivory to the Indian Ocean and thus falling under Arab and Indian influence, but simultaneously immersed in an internal copper trade which may have been of equal or greater importance to their economies: Ingombe Ilede marketing the copper of Urungwe, Zimbabwe of its own and perhaps other deposits, Mapungubwe of Messina. None of these three centers was located near major gold-producing areas, so that the gold must have been obtained through local exchanges.

One cannot calculate with any precision the quantities of copper fed into the Iron Age economy of these regions from the 150-odd ancient mines identified, but Summers reminds us that they lie in far less hospitable zones than the goldworkings, leading him to conclude that "the demand for copper was a keen one when it drove old prospectors into such hot and unpleasant areas as the Sabi valley and the Limpopo lowveld around Messina," to which he could have added Phalaborwa in the steamy eastern Transvaal. Then, too, he notes that whereas gold occurrences were very unevenly exploited, copper deposits were mined to the limit.[36]

Further testimony to the importance of copper in intra-African trade and to the irrelevance of gold where there was no stimulus of foreign demand is offered by the case of Sanga and other sites of the Upemba rift in southeastern Zaire.[37] Since 1957 with the first excavations at Sanga, six sites in the Upemba Depression have been systematically excavated, yielding a total of more than 300 burials. The forty-odd radiocarbon dates, supplemented by several from thermoluminescence, provide a chronology unique in sub-Saharan Africa, extending from the sixth to the seventeenth or eighteenth century A.D. The burials vary considerably in the quantity and lavishness of grave goods, and there appear to be differences between the northern and southern traditions. Copper first appears toward the eighth century in the form of heavy bracelets or anklets and cylindrical beads. Nevertheless the metal remains rare until about the tenth century. Then it becomes so abundant as to be the defining characteristic of the so-called classic Kisalian period, which extended in the north of the Depression to about the fourteenth or fifteenth century. It was used not only for ornamentation but even for utilitarian objects such as needles, fish hooks, nails, small knife blades, and spear points. The Kisalian was succeeded rather than overlapped by what de Maret calls the Kabambian culture (superseding Nenquin's Mulongo and Red Slip), which lasted until the eighteenth century and is marked not only by a distinctive type of pottery but by the presence of copper crosses, as well as jewelry, in the burials. In contrast, only one of the graves definitely identified as Kisalian included copper in ingot form.

Since there are no known deposits in the Upemba-Lake Kisale region it must be assumed that the copper for both ornaments and crosses came from mining areas several hundred kilometers to the south. At first the quantities reaching the area were evidently small and were not traded, it would appear, in ingot form. The Kabambian period, however, saw a "marked expansion of trade" and, de Maret suggests, the development of copper currency, a subject we will deal with at greater length in chapter 8.[38]

The abundant finds of copper far from any source are clear proof of trade in Early and Later Iron Age Katanga and of the accumulation of wealth among a stratum of the population. There are no objects of gold at Sanga or in any of the Lake Kisale-Lake Upemba burials, indeed no evidence of the production or use of gold anywhere in precolonial Katanga. Nevertheless gold is found in Katanga,[39] as it is in so many other parts of Africa, not always in quantities feasible for modern exploitation but easily accessible to pre-industrial metallurgists had they cared to work it. Sanga was essentially isolated from the currents of Indian Ocean trade — only a few beads and seashells made their way to the area — so that the only factors influencing its system of values were those developed within the indigenous exchange economy.

Pellets of copper and wound strip have been found on the Lower Shire in Malawi associated with Kapeni Ware (c. tenth to fourteenth centuries A.D.) and even more rarely, in Early Iron Age sites on the Upper Shire. Recently Cole-King has discovered copper cross ingots in central Malawi similar to those at Ingombe Ilede, whose floruit is compatible with later Kapeni dates, indicating that trade extended into the lake area during the Later Iron Age but probably in very modest dimensions. There has not yet been enough work done, however, to flesh out the map of the copper trade in the Lake Region.[40]

## EAST AFRICA

Copper is almost nonexistent in Iron Age sites of the East African interior. A ringlet was found at a site in the Pare Mountains in northeastern Tanzania and two copper strip beads at Ivuna Salt Pans in the southwestern part of the country, hardly an abundance.[41] No copper has been uncovered in a stratified context at any archaeological site in Uganda, including Bigo, Engaruka, and Mubende Hill.[42] This negative evidence confirms the pre-nineteenth-century isolation of much of this region from the coast as well as from the lands south and west of the Great Lakes.[43]

Chao Ju-Kua, a Chinese writer of the mid-thirteenth century, lists copper among the stuffs imported to "Zanguebar" by Gujerati and Arab merchants. "Zanguebar" is a typically loose appellation for some portion of the East African coast (not simply Zanzibar) where gold and ivory were exported, along with sandalwood and ambergris.[44] Though copper coinage of minute size was minted at Kilwa from about the latter twelfth century A.D., few objects of copper, even coins, have been found at medieval coastal sites, presumably, Chittick speculates, because of their value for reworking. Copper needles and weights and a smattering of rings and bangles were excavated at Kilwa, but the most common finds were of kohl sticks: cylindrical copper rods with incised decoration used to apply kohl as a cosmetic. Similar kohl sticks occur at Gedi and Fort Jesus as well as at medieval sites in Nubia and Fostat; they have in fact been in use up to the modern period, for some thousand years since the earliest specimens at Kilwa. In contrast to the paucity of finished objects, copper crucibles in large numbers were uncovered at Kilwa and more rarely at Mafia during Period II, about the fourteenth century.[45] Copper and brass also figure in the booty seized after the burning of Mombasa in 1505.[46]

Until more information is available, little can be reconstructed about trade in copper on the Swahili Coast; for the present, one is inclined to suspect sources outside of Africa (this would have to be the case with the brass at Mombasa if indeed it is brass) and circulation limited to the coastal culture itself.

## WEST AFRICA

Large areas of equatorial Africa are still blank as far as the economic history of the pre-1500 period is concerned. We may hope that work currently in progress by Volavka and others will remedy this state of affairs to some extent. In the meantime, there is compensation in the fact that the West African copper trade is comparatively well documented. Arab writers, like later Europeans, were keen to find out all they could about the details of a trade so lucrative as that between the two shores of the great desert. Unfortunately, most were second-hand observers, and even the Arab and Berber travellers who crossed the Sahara rarely ventured beyond the cosmopolitan cities of the Sahel, and they knew almost nothing about the indigenous distribution system of the savanna and forest regions to the south.

The importance of copper in the trans-Saharan trade runs like a leitmotif through virtually all the written sources. In 950 al-Husayn noted that at Djarmi in the Fezzan, pure gold was exchanged for copper, which was then traded south to the Sudan.[47] The Jewish traveller Benjamin of Tudela, relying on Egyptian sources, echoed this exchange in the latter twelfth century.[48] Al-Bakri (1067–68) identified a number of copper mines in the Dar'a and Sus Valleys of Morocco, in particular Igli, where copper was worked and then exported to the "land of the pagans," sub-Saharan Africa. Worked copper was traded to the commercial center of Awdaghost in the southern Sahara and to "Kougha," probably a city west of Ghana. At Ghana itself, the king imposed a tax of only five mithqals on each load of copper brought into the country, in contrast to the ten levied on other goods. Rings of copper functioned as currency at Silla in Takrur.[49] According to al-Idrisi a century later, the Huwara of Aghmat, near Marrakesh, had grown rich from travelling to the land of the blacks with "a large number of camels loaded with red and colored copper" and with a variety of textiles, beads, perfumes, and sundry other imports.[50] Copper continued to play a significant role in the trade between Morocco and the Sudan into the sixteenth century, as Leo Africanus' *Description* makes clear.[51]

Al-Bakri and Leo focus particularly on Maghrebian suppliers of copper wares, but copper was also channeled into the trans-Saharan trade from other sources. Genoa and Venice shipped large quantities to North African ports from Ceuta to Egypt for re-export southward throughout the period from the twelfth to the sixteenth century. Mas Latrie writes, "Copper and brass were imported in all forms: in blocks, in bars, in leaves and in wire."[52] By the fifteenth century, Italian merchants, chafing at the barriers thrown in their way by their Muslim competitors, tried to remedy Europe's chronic shortage of gold by participating more directly in the trade. In 1447 the Genoese merchant Antonio Malfante managed to reach the oasis of Tuat in the northern Sahara, whence he sent his letter: "The wares for which there is a demand here are many," he commented. "But the principal articles are copper and salt. . . . The copper of Romania [the Byzantine Empire] which is obtained through Alexandria, is always in great demand throughout the Land of the Blacks."[53] Malfante's initiative had no lasting effect, but Venice continued to supply Djerba, Tunis, and Oran with copper well into the sixteenth century. A Venetian report of 1518, for example, speaks of trade with the "terra de Negri" in a multiplicity of forms of copper rods and wire which the Blacks work into "diverse objects . . . according to their custom."[54] Similarly, a Portuguese letter of 1511 notes the arrival of copper from Venice in Egypt for shipment to the Sudan.[55]

In December 1964 Theodore Monod, pursuing reports of antelope hunters, made a dramatic discovery in Mauritania that confirms the written documentation concerning the amplitude of the trans-Saharan trade in copper. Covering more than 450 miles on foot, leading camels with the food and water indispensable for survival in one of the driest parts of the western desert, he found buried in the sands at Ma'den Ijâfen 2,085 bars of copper, or rather brass, wrapped in matting in semicircular bundles. Each bar was about 29½ inches long and weighed about a pound, and each bundle 100 pounds. A camel probably carried two pairs of bundles, or 400 pounds. The mats and ropes found with the bars, being of organic material, could be dated by radiocarbon to about the twelfth century A.D., when the trade was in full swing. Monod speculates that the hoard may have been buried in the wake of an attack by desert brigands and the theft of the caravan's camels. Probably its owners intended to recover their goods later but were unable to do so, unable perhaps even to find the desolate spot again.[56]

Sahelian sources of copper were clearly insufficient to cut into the mas-

sive imports from North Africa, and they could not be made into brass.
We do not know how much of the copper of Akjoujt filtered into the Sudan.
It may well have fed a local industry, even a Mauritanian "copper age"
on a modest scale, and later made its way to the Senegal Valley. The deposits at Dkra did enter the Sudanese exchange economy if only briefly.
Al-'Umari's account of 1336–38, taking its information from a Cairo jurist
who claimed to be quoting Mansa Musa, Sultan of Mali, declared that
the importation of raw copper from Dkra was an unparalleled source of
taxes for the empire and added: "We send it to the land of the pagan blacks
where we sell it at a rate of one mithqal for two-thirds its weight in gold:
we therefore exchange one hundred mithqals of copper for 66⅔ mithqals
of gold."[57]

Azelick/Takedda, however, is emerging as the most important Sahelian
source of copper. Although exploitation of deposits in the region can now
be documented over a period of more than 3,000 years, there is frustrat-
ingly little information about the quantitites produced or the directions
of trade. Ibn Battuta declared that "copper is carried from there to the
city of Kubar [Gobir] in the land of the unbelievers, to Zaghay and to the
country of Barnu [Bornu] which is at a distance of forty days from Takadda. . . . Copper is also taken from Takadda to Jujuwat and to the land
of the Murtibin and to other places."[58] Gibb suggests that Jujuwat may
be Kawkaw or Kuku, that is, Kuka on Lake Fitri in Wadai or in Bornu,[59]
but Gao would be more likely. Vansina suggests Songhay as the identification for Zaghay.[60] The "land of the Murtibin" remains a mystery. Devisse
has theorized that Mali may for a time have exported copper northward,
especially to Egypt, but this flies in the face of the evidence.[61]

If the main outlines of the trans-Saharan trade in copper are clear from
Arabic and European written sources, the distribution patterns within West
Africa must be inferred from archaeology until supplemented by documentation from the coast for the period after 1450. Archaeological work done
before World War II was carried out primarily by amateurs in what was
often an exasperatingly nonchalant manner: in some cases not only were
the results never published but notes and excavated objects disappeared
completely. Since the war, scientific excavations have been carried out at
a number of places, but scores of tumuli remain untouched from one end
of the Sudan to the other, to say nothing of less obvious sites.

The earliest dated finds of copper in Nigeria come from Daima and Igbo-
Ukwu, almost 800 miles apart, the one in the northern savanna near Lake
Chad, the other deep in the rain forest. Radiocarbon dates at both indicate
that copper and its alloys were being worked before the end of the first
millennium A.D. Bronze disks and bracelets were found at Daima III,[62]
while at Igbo-Ukwu an incomparably richer variety of wrought and cast

copper and bronze was unearthed.[63] The discovery of such a wealth of copper so far from known sources has raised a number of questions, as we have noted. Some scholars have found it impossible to accept the ninth- and tenth-century radiocarbon dates for Igbo-Ukwu on both economic and esthetic grounds, arguing that at this early period it would have been highly unlikely for a society in the forest area so far from trans-Saharan or Sahelian trade routes to have obtained the quantity of metal disclosed.[64] In addition, the objects obviously represent a high level of technical and artistic sophistication which could not have been achieved overnight, even if nothing is yet known of an antecedent tradition. It is true that the radiocarbon dates are not as full as one would like, although they have now been buttressed by new early dates for copper finds at Ke in the Niger Delta,[65] but I have noted elsewhere my reasons for finding the attacks on them unconvincing. If it is assumed that the copper and bronze came from across the Sahara, trade was clearly established by this period — even trade from Takedda is a possibility in the light of recent finds. As to the trade goods that could have been exchanged for metal, ivory and slaves would have served here as elsewhere throughout West Africa; only gold was lacking in Nigeria. Dried fish and sea salt may also have entered into a regional exchange, since the trade could well have been indirect rather than direct.

Almost everyone concerned in the argument about dating has assumed a northern source for the copper, the closest being Takedda, some 675 miles from Igbo-Ukwu. John Fage, however, points out that the copper mines of the Lower Congo are roughly the same distance to the south.[66] Given the increasing evidence for intercoastal trade before the arrival of the Portuguese on the Leeward Coast in the fifteenth century,[67] there is the possibility, remote though it may be, that copper from the Niari Basin or northern Angola reached the Niger Delta, taking advantage of the lagoons, estuaries, and islands along most of this coast north to the Bight of Biafra. The earliest Portuguese reference to the Rio Real describes a people already wearing an abundance of copper, using enormous canoes, and in well-organized trading contact with the inhabitants of the interior. To the south, at Mt. Cameroon, there was also an established demand for copper, which functioned as a currency as well as a commodity.[68] Patterson does not doubt that Africans along the equatorial coast possessed boats capable of carrying on maritime trade: Mpongwe canoes, for example, were made from long, hollowed-out trees and could hold up to eighty men.[69] In the mid-seventeenth century, according to Barbot, they ranged between Cape Lopez and the Cameroon River and perhaps even farther.[70] We will return to this topic in the next chapter.

In view of the large quantities of copper imported across the Sahara, it is not surprising that objects of the metal and its alloys have been found in the tumuli of the Middle Niger as well as those of western Senegal and in the excavations of medieval cities such as Tegdaoust and Kumbi Saleh. Copper jewelry and cast figurines are especially common in the tumuli of the northern Massina region, where the most thorough investigations were carried out early in this century by Desplagnes at Koï Gourey, Killi, and El-Oualadji (figs. 10, 11). Only very limited work has been done at any of these sites, using modern methods, with the result that of all the tumuli, radiocarbon dates are available for only Kouga: c. 1000 A.D. This concurs with what is known about the Islamization of the region, since once converted, the region no longer buried its rulers in pagan mounds. Mauny suggested that ruling dynasties in the region fell largely under the influence of Islam during the eleventh and twelfth centuries, but this may be too early.[71] At Jenne-Jeno, now the best-documented site in the Inland Delta, copper is found in Phase III burials, dated to about 400–900 A.D., but it is comparatively rare and much more crudely worked than at Killi and El-Oualadji, further confirmation of its earlier dating.[72]

The tumuli of the Lower Senegal and Saloum valleys have also yielded a variety of copper objects, particularly rings and bracelets, but also more enigmatic conical and lozenge-shaped pieces whose use was probably ornamental. The growing body of radiocarbon dates show that copper was relatively abundant by the later centuries of the first millennium A.D. The burials at Ndalane, for example, are believed to be eighth- or ninth-century and those at Dioron Boumak possibly earlier, while the Rao sites fall in about the twelfth or thirteenth century.[73]

Copper has been found from roughly the same period at Tegdaoust, the putative site of Awdaghost, and at Kumbi Saleh, tentatively identified as the Muslim city associated with an ancient capital of Ghana, both key entrepôts of the trans-Saharan trade before the Almoravid conquest. At Tegdaoust the copper is in the form of jewelry, primarily rings, beads, amuletic bells, and plaques, while at Kumbi copper currency wires and weights were also found.[74]

Archaeological evidence for the diffusion of copper southward into the savanna and forest is spotty because so many areas have never been investigated. Only modest amounts of copper have been found at the "Tellem" sites in the Bandiagara escarpment of Mali, again evidence of their early date.[75] On the other hand, Labouret found finely cast objects of copper in undated sites in the northern Lobi country of Upper Volta, including a bicephalous serpent, a trident in the form of a tricephalous snake, a fish, and an amuletic pendant.[76] Farther south, excavations at Begho, in northern Ghana on the main route between the Akan goldfields and the Niger Bend, have thus far turned up both objects of copper and crucibles used

10. Lizard, tumuli of Killi, region of Goundam, Mali. Copper alloy

11. Bell, tumuli of Killi, region of Goundam, Mali. Copper alloy

in casting.[77] In a number of Brong and Aṣante towns, large brass basins decorated with Arabic inscriptions in Kufic rather than the later cursive writing are venerated as shrines. A bronze ewer of Richard II found in the palace at Kumasi in 1896 strengthens the argument for the import of these objects about the fourteenth century, although as Posnansky warns, they could have been traded many times over before reaching their final destination.[78] The same is true for the celebrated copies of late antique Coptic lamps found at Attabu in northern Ghana.

Copper jewelry, principally bracelets, has been unearthed at scattered sites such as Wassu (Gambia), Dallol Bosso (Niger), Dawu in northern Ghana, Imperi in Sierra Leone, Songon-Dagbe and Bokabo in Ivory Coast, and at burials uncovered by the rescue archaeology at the Kainji Reservoir area of the Lower Niger.[79] Many of these finds may well be pre-1500, but they are just beginning to be dated. At Benin, however, Connah's excavations have shown that the only copper objects that almost certainly antedate the arrival of the Portuguese are five heavy penannular objects, fifty-six bracelets and three finger rings found in a mass burial in the early phase of Cutting II at the Clerks' Quarter site, dated to about the thirteenth to fourteenth century A.D. All were probably made by smithing rather than casting.[80]

If Benin thus far provides only modest evidence for the extension of the copper trade into southwestern Nigeria, the opposite is true for Ife. Although we have seen that none of the magnificent heads or figures has been found in a stratified context, they are probably to be assigned to the period 1100–1450 A.D. As in the case of Igbo-Ukwu, one must postulate a reliable source of metal over a long enough time to develop the virtuosity the castings display. Indeed, it is one of the supreme anomalies of African economic history that the largest and most sophisticated products of the metalsmith's art were produced in regions farthest from the sources of supply.[81]

By the mid-fifteenth century, therefore, the West African copper trade reached from the Maghreb to southern Nigeria, westward to the estuaries of the Senegal and Saloum rivers and into the savannas and forests of the Akan hinterland. Perhaps the surest sign that it had penetrated through the forest to parts of the Windward and Leeward coasts was the ready demand for copper, for copper in very specific forms, found by the first Europeans as they edged their way along the unknown shores. This was true all along the littoral, not only in the Rio Real and Mt. Cameroon regions already mentioned. Thus well before the European discovery of Africa, *dyula* traders and their counterparts had pioneered the exchange of Saharan and trans-Saharan imports for local products over wide areas of the interior of West Africa. The Portuguese and their competitors were compelled to respond to habits of consumption already well formed, to preexisting demands, and this was as true for copper goods as for textiles and beads.

It is impossible to estimate the global quantities of copper and copper wares traded to West Africa before the discoveries. It is equally impossible to graph fluctuations in the trade or to note different forms of the metal traded to different regions, as we will attempt to do for the maritime trade: bills of lading do not exist for ships of the desert as they do for ships of the sea, and there are no surviving customs records. That is why the caravan found by Monod buried in the desert is of such inestimable importance and offers such a sobering commentary on the state of our knowledge — or ignorance — about the period. This single caravan carried some 2,000 pounds of copper in the form of brass rods. And yet Willett has computed the entire corpus of copper and copper alloys from Igbo-Ukwu at only 155 pounds and that of Ife at about 375 pounds.[82] These are by far the richest pre-European assemblages known, but they only account for a little more than one-fourth of an ordinary caravan load. We must ask, as did early observers of the huge ancient workings of Central and Southern Africa: where has it all gone? A good deal would have been constantly recycled like any scarce, durable material. Most of it, however, must still be underground, hidden under innocuous goatsheds as at Igbo-Ukwu or waiting to be uncovered in gravel pits as at Obalara's Land at Ife.

Incomplete as are the documentary and archaeological sources for the early West African copper trade, they make abundantly clear the demand for the metal and the value accorded it. The bulk of this probably came from across the desert, but the contributions of Akjoujt, Dkra, and especially Azelick/Takedda may have been more significant than first appeared. Just possibly a certain amount found its way into Cameroon and southeastern Nigeria from the Lower Congo. Did Hufrat en-Nahas, too, supply copper to the central Sudan as it would in later times? There is as yet no way of telling, no evidence for the antiquity of mining or of trade from Hufrat.

## COPPER AND GOLD IN WEST AFRICA

West Africa is the land of gold, the *bilad al-tibr* of the Arabs and the principal source of gold for the Mediterranean world during the Middle Ages. Arab descriptions of the courts of Ghana and Mali paint a picture of gold-drenched splendor, just as da Barros' account of early Portuguese negotiations with Caramansa at the future site of São Jorge da Mina marvel at the wealth of gold worn by the sovereign and his entourage. Nevertheless throughout the medieval period the producers of that gold were willing to exchange it for copper, and it was copper, not gold that they principally buried with their chiefs and nobles. With the exception of the single gold earring at Jenne-Jeno, no gold has been found in the tumuli of the Niger, at Igbo-Ukwu, at Ife, at Benin, while copper and copper alloys are ubiquitous in virtually all pre-Islamic and non-Islamic burials thus far investigated.

Indeed, the only pre-1500 archaeological sites in West Africa that have yielded any gold at all are, in addition to Jenne, Tegdaoust, the trading city in Mauritania, where five bars of gold and an assortment of gold jewelry were found under a kitchen floor (the only such cache uncovered during eight seasons of digging), and several of the tumuli in western Senegal. Apropos of the Tegdaoust bars, one of the excavators remarked on the fact that they are "undoubtedly the first ingots [of gold] discovered at a medieval site in West Africa."[83] Of the Senegal tumuli, the most spectacular finds were made by Joire at Rao, near St. Louis, in 1941–42: an ornate pectoral, a quadrilobe pendant, and beads of various sizes and forms, all of gold, along with some jewelry of silver and of course of copper. The Rao tumuli are believed to be twelfth or thirteenth century A.D., shortly before the founding of the Wolof Empire. Though the form of burial is pre-Islamic, the jewelry shows a strong Arabo-Berber influence.[84] A few tubular beads of gold earlier than Rao have been found at Ndalane and at Dioron Boumak, but copper and iron are much more plentiful,[85] suggesting here, too, that copper and iron (and stone beads) were the characteristic grave goods until northern influence made itself felt, with the result that gold, which had been exported for centuries, came to be employed in indigenous societies and to adorn the burial of chiefly figures. The presence of silver jewelry tends to confirm the relatively late date and the North African influence: like the copper, it, too, would have been imported from the north.

Obviously more dates are needed from all these tumuli to confirm the sequence from copper and iron to copper, iron, and gold (and silver) in the transitional period from animism to Islam. The royal burials of Ghana have never been discovered, but if al-Bakri's description is accurate, they should contain quantities of gold, reflecting the centuries of close commercial contact with the north. Unless they differ from virtually all the known pre-Islamic tumuli of the Sahel, however, they should also contain ornaments of copper and weapons of iron.

# Manillas, Neptunes, Rods, and Wire: The Maritime Trade from the Discoveries to c. 1800

> . . . Of the Sorting, this may be observed in
> general; That the Windward and Leeward Parts
> of the Coast are as opposite in their Demands,
> as is their distance.
>
> — ATKINS, *A Voyage to Guinea*
> (1737)

The discovery of maritime routes to sub-Saharan Africa in the mid-fifteenth century did not immediately revolutionize the nature of trade. But with sea transport, the potential existed for a dramatic increase in the quantities of bulky imports such as textiles and metalwares, and this dramatic increase was already manifest by the opening decades of the following century. At the same time, areas that had been on the periphery of older trading systems, particularly in West Africa, could now compete with the older centers of trade for inland markets. The increased demand in Africa, as subsequently in the East and West Indies, put unprecedented pressures on European manufacturers. It is clear that the interaction of the African and European economies is a topic that far transcends the slave trade, yet the slave trade became inextricably interwoven in the fabric of African-European commerce, including the commerce in copper and copper alloys.

One of the ironies of what Marion Johnson has felicitously termed "paleocolonialism,"[1] that is, the far-flung system dominated by European merchant capital between the fifteenth and nineteenth centuries, is the relative simplicity of Europe's demands on the African market but the remarkable complexity of Africa's demands on Europe. The hoary myth that natives could be satisfied by any sort of bauble or trinket has long since been laid to rest. The classic triad, gold, slaves, and ivory, remained constant exports from Africa for some four centuries, along with lesser commodities tied to particular ecological zones, such as gum, dyewood, pepper. While textiles, metalwares, and beads formed a countervailing triad of imports into Africa, supplemented by liquor, tobacco, and the like, the varieties within these general categories covered a bewildering range of

123

goods, subject to change almost overnight and from port to port. "Custom has authorized what fancy began," wrote Matthews in 1788, "in assigning to almost every separate district in Africa a different choice of goods . . . and in affixing different denominations of value to the articles of trade."[2] Woe betide the luckless captain who found himself with an ill-sorted cargo: "You might starve in one place with bales of goods that would purchase kingdoms in another," declared Johnston with only slight exaggeration.[3] He was referring to the Congo in the mid-nineteenth century, but his rueful comment might have applied to any region or any moment during this period.

Not only were African buyers precise in their demands, they also insisted early on that they be presented with an assortment of goods rather than a single type. Hopkins aptly refers to ships putting in at coastal entrepots as "floating supermarkets."[4] Over 150 different items were needed for trade on the Gold Coast at the beginning of the eighteenth century, according to Bosman.[5] By 1870 an "ivory bundle," the goods required to purchase tusks on the Ogowe, numbered more than 60 different articles; in the Gabon estuary it was 140.[6] Success or failure in the African trade, then, depended on having the right goods in the right place at the right time — on the "well sorting and well timing of a Cargo," as Atkins put it. This in turn "depends at several places much on Chance, from the fanciful and various Humours of the Negroes, who make great demands one Voyage for a Commodity, that perhaps they reject next, and is in part to be remedied either by making the things they itch after, to pass off those they have not so much mind to, or by such continual Traffick and Correspondence on the Coast as may furnish the Owner from time to time with quick Intelligence."[7] African fastidiousness was indeed legendary. Sometimes buyers were known to turn out the entire contents of a barrel of manillas and choose a single one, rejecting all the others.[8] The story was often told in the nineteenth century of a certain firm in Birmingham whose manillas were invariably accepted by Africans. Why this was so, no European, least of all the manufacturer, could discover.[9] As a result, the tendency was to make much of "chance," of idiosyncrasy, of irrational whim, when a knowledge of African societies and their internal markets would probably have explained both the particularities of demand and what caused changes when they occurred. This knowledge European traders rarely possessed, although they did in time learn that manillas, for example, might be judged as much by their tone when struck together as by their appearance.[10] And this tone might be as useful a guide to metallic content as an assay.

To turn a profit on the Guinea Coast, Europeans therefore had to divine the "peculiar tastes and fancies" of each district (and its economic hinterland) and at the same time take into account the prime cost of their goods, the price paid for them at the source of supply. The object was to put together an assortment of goods that would mix more profitable with less profitable goods. In 1823, for example, brass pans were regarded as "losing articles of trade" — loss-leaders — but "highly necessary to complete an assorted cargo for Africa."[11] The African role in the trading partnership, in other words, was far from passive; just how influential it was is at last being appreciated.[12] Why the African market should have been so complex is less well understood: it is a question we will consider at greater length in part III.

## THE PORTUGUESE PERIOD, C. 1460–1600

In seeking out sea routes to West Africa, the Portuguese aimed to outflank the Moor economically as well as spiritually and militarily. Navigationally a voyage into the unknown, commercially the way was well worn: the Portuguese simply filled their holds with the same cargoes that had for centuries been carried across the Sahara and that commanded a ready market in black Africa. Indeed, many of them were initially obtained at North African ports, from the same sources that supplied the trans-Saharan trade. Thus the first ships to make regular trading voyages to Arguim Island and points south were well stocked with textiles (which continued to be referred to by corrupted forms of their Arabic names), with beads, and with copperwares: bracelets (manillas), basins, kettles, pots, and rods.[13]

The Portuguese and other Europeans who followed in their wake had to learn the refinements of the coastal trade on their own, however, for while intelligence gained in North Africa prepared them *grosso modo* for the African market, it could not provide a detailed economic geography of the coast, an area that was totally unknown to the Arab world. It could not prepare for the fact, for instance, that while copper and brass were consistently listed, along with bright-colored cloth, as the goods most in demand on the West African coast during the latter fifteenth and sixteenth centuries, not all forms were equally acceptable to all peoples. Furthermore, as imported goods became available in unprecedented quantities and as interior markets were joined to the coast, demand inevitably changed.

To give some examples. At Arguim Island off the Mauritanian coast, brass bowls and pots were in demand in the second half of the fifteenth century, while by 1510 the factor was clamoring for brass rods as indispensable for the gold trade.[14] On the Gold Coast from 1470 to c. 1520, copper was the metal most in demand at São Jorge da Mina,[15] as it was in Benin, in the Rio Real, and on the Cameroon coast. Subsequently, how-

ever, brass bracelets and basins became standard trade goods from the
Gambia to the Gold Coast, while Benin for a time continued to import
both copper and brass manillas. Brass basins were steadily sought after
on the Windward Coast. In 1479 Eustache de la Fosse noted that a slave
and her child could be purchased for one barber's basin and three or four
brass manillas on the Malagueta coast (Liberia).[16] Seventy-five years later,
William Towerson traded "basons," "manelios," and "margarits" (a type
of bead) for pepper and ivory, but commented that "they desired most to
have basons." At Samma, too, the inhabitants were only interested in trading gold for basins, although they reluctantly accepted some cloth. And
yet at Cape Palmas, to the west, "they did little esteeme" anything but manillas and margarits."[17]

Within a few decades, Portuguese activity became concentrated at three
points in West Africa: the Gold Coast (Elmina), Benin, and São Tomé.
For a period, they seem to have had an insatiable market for copperwares.
Between 20 August 1504 and 10 January 1507, for example, the factor at
São Jorge da Mina received 287,813 manillas of copper and brass.[18] Six
years later the inventory listed "302,920 e mea peca manilhas de latam,"
roughly 94½ tons of brass manillas![19] Similarly, the factor at Axim, also
on the Gold Coast, received "67,095 common manillas of brass" over a
seventeen-month period from 1 May 1505 to 30 September 1506.[20] Shipments to Benin were somewhat more modest but not insignificant: during
his twenty months as factor at Ughoton, the port of Benin, Bastiam Fernandez recorded 12,750 manillas.[21] A single shipment in 1518 included
13,000.[22] The captain of São Tomé, for his part, received 16,000 manillas
from the Casa da Mina in Lisbon on 9 December 1510, to carry on trade
with the mainland, along with 1,877 others from the factor at Benin.[23]

Though dwarfed in these years by the flood of manillas, copper and
brass basins were also imported in considerable quantities. These came in
various sizes and shapes: shaving bowls, chamber pots, urinals, kettles,
cauldrons. The accounts of the factor at São Jorge in 1504-7, referred to
above, listed 1,582 shaving bowls, 520 urinals, and 3,192 chamber pots.[24]
Seven years later 5,683 urinals, 722 barbers' basins, and 534 shaving bowls
were listed, along with 25 copper water jugs, 290 copper kettles with covers,
163 copper pots, and 4 large copper basins.[25] The gift of a brass pan was
a common means of initiating trade on the Gold Coast during the sixteenth century.[26] Vogt calculates that at Elmina, manillas and basins combined to account for about 37 percent of Portuguese trade in the period
1480-1540.[27] The ledger book he has published shows that between 10 June
1529 and 31 August 1531, some 216,700 manillas and more than 9,000 brass
and copper vessels accounted for about half of the 3,262.8 marks of gold

(about 7,509 kilograms) purchased at the fort during the period, with cloth a poor second at 25 percent.[28]

Is it possible to calculate the total imports of copper and brass into West Africa during this period? Estimate, yes, calculate precisely, no. Even in the case of Portugal, where the Crown attempted to keep a tight rein on the trade, official records are incomplete, while unofficial sources are handicapped by the obsession with secrecy aimed at keeping information from falling into the hands of competitor nations. The Portuguese failed ultimately in their attempts at monopoly and were faced almost from the first with a series of interlopers for whom precise data is yet scarcer. Nevertheless, Portuguese trading under royal license dominated the trade at its most lucrative points for some sixty years, from 1480 to 1540, so that figures for this period provide a reasonably solid base for the opening phase of European contact.

Portugal did not mine copper or produce finished wares herself. Instead she imported massive quantities from abroad, primarily from Flanders, to a much lesser extent from Venice and Morocco. Godinho estimates that from the late-fifteenth to the mid-sixteenth century an average of about 10,000 cwt. (600 tons, based on the Portuguese quintal of 120 pounds) of raw and wrought copper was imported into Lisbon annually, ranging from a minimum of about 6,000 cwt. in off-years to a maximum of more than 20,000 cwt. in 1515–16.[29] Some of this copper stayed in the country for coinage, ordnance, and other domestic uses. After 1500, sizable amounts departed annually with the Carreira da India, where it took its place with silver as an essential lubricant of the spice trade.[30] A large portion, however, was reexported to Africa through the Casa da Mina e Guiné. Orderly records for the Casa do not begin until the reign of Manuel I (1495–1521), the high point of Portuguese activity in West Africa. Typically, triennial contracts let by royal agents in Flanders provisioned the Guinea trade. In 1494–95, for example, the Portuguese factor supplied 71,000 manillas of which Vogt estimates some 80 percent would have gone to Elmina alone.[31] Twenty years later the Casa da Mina received 6,394 quintals of copper (384 tons) to be directed to Africa.[32] Goris' figures suggest that for Manuel's twenty-five-year reign, some 1,250 tons of manillas and basins were exported from Flanders to Portugal and thence to Africa.[33]

In 1548 when the trade was beginning to decline somewhat, the Crown nevertheless signed a contract with the Fugger agent in Antwerp to supply "for the Negroes of Guinea" 6,750 quintals of brass rings for the commerce of São Jorge da Mina, 750 quintals of rings for the rest of the Guinea trade, 24,000 brass urinals, 1,800 large-rimmed basins, 4,500 barbers' basins, and 10,500 brass kettles with handles, all to be delivered within three years.

The contract is unique in its specificity. The brasswares — and in this case
it seems to be entirely brasswares, not copper — were to be

> well laureated and filed and of the metals suited to the said trade of Mina
> and Guinea, of such size and sorts and perfection as has always been the custom
> for the said trades and which correspond to the accustomed weight which
> is: the manillas of Mina, 160 in each 100 arrates [the Portuguese pound] just
> about, and with smooth and well-filed heads which are called *tacoais*; and
> those of Guinea of 190 or 200 manillas in each 100 arrates; and the urinals,
> 58 pieces in 100 arrates, which is two pounds per basin more or less, and the
> shaving bowls of which there are twenty-five in each 100 arrates, one more
> or less, each piece being four pounds; and the kettles which are fourteen, one
> more or less, in each 100 arrates, each weighing seven pounds, more or less.
>      These manillas, basins, pots and kettles will conform to the models the
> aforesaid factor now gives to the said Christoff [the Fugger agent] and of
> the type and perfection that the other contractors customarily have for the
> said trade of Mina and Guinea.[34]

The Mina manillas were therefore slightly heavier than the "Guinea"
manillas, presumably those destined for Benin, São Tomé, or other points
outside the Gold Coast. Earlier sources are not as precise as the Fugger
contract, but it is intriguing that a Portuguese document of 1439, more
than a century earlier, specified that manillas manufactured for the Crown
in Venice be "muyto bem acabados as cabecas e limadas" — "with heads
or ends well finished and filed."[35]

Evidence from Antwerp and Lisbon, supplemented by factors' accounts
from the Gold Coast and to a lesser extent from other centers of trade,
show that sales of copper- and brasswares peaked at Mina in 1520–21. This
is altogether consistent with Godinho's conclusion that global imports of
copper into Portugal peaked five years earlier, stabilized for a few years,
then fell off during the 1520s.[36] Vogt has tabulated a series of figures on
the sale of hardware at São Jorge and at Axim, the principal Portuguese
comptoirs on the Gold Coast, between 1504 and 1531 — hardware at this
time meaning almost exclusively copper and brass manillas and various
vessels.[37] In the years for which data are available, copper imports ranged
from a low of 40 tons annually in 1529–31 to a high of 57 tons in 1519–22.
It is not clear how the same author, presumably using these same figures,
arrives elsewhere at an annual estimate of 8,000–9,000 quintals (480–540
tons) for the Portuguese trade with Mina in the 1520s — figures equal to
the entire annual import into Portugal from Antwerp at this period.[38] Tim
Garrard, basing his estimates on the two sets of factors' accounts from
Elmina (1504–7) and Axim (1505–6) cited above, and on Vogt's ledger
book for Elmina 1529–31, puts brass and copper imports into the Gold

Coast at 35–45 tons per year (based on the British or long ton of 2,240 pounds rather than the U.S. ton of 2,000 pounds used here).[39]

Figures from the point of sale are undoubtedly more reliable than receipts of copper at the Casa da Mina or contracts let in Antwerp, since these latter would probably represent stockpiling and the provisioning of all the African trade, not simply the Gold Coast which is the best documented. Then, too, some of the copper from the Casa da Mina may in fact have been diverted to non-African destinations.[40] Be that as it may, figures for the first half of the sixteenth century are consistent enough to project imports of copper- and brasswares to the Gold Coast at about 45 tons per year throughout this fifty-year period, a total of 2,250 tons. To this must be added Portuguese imports to Arguim, Senegambia, Upper Guinea, Benin, and São Tomé, as well as those of interlopers who defied Portuguese claims to monopoly. During the brief period of Castilian activity in West Africa, 1474–80, for example, a single fleet of thirty-five caravels sailed from Seville to Mina loaded with "old Clothes, shells, mortars and manillas of brass." They returned laden with gold, all of which was captured by the Portuguese. One can assume that brasswares would have accounted for between one-third and one-half of the gold purchases, but without knowing how much these amounted to we cannot calculate the metal carried by the Castilians.[41] French and English interlopers did not become a serious threat until the middle decades of the century, the Dutch not until the 1590s.

What Elmina was to the Atlantic gold trade Sofala was to that of the Indian Ocean. With the successful opening up of the sea route to East Africa and India in 1497–98, the Portuguese determined to divert the gold of Monomotapa to Lisbon just as, they believed, they had succeeded in diverting the golden trade of the Moors in West Africa. They assumed they were dealing with the same sort of market and deluged the factor at Sofala with manillas, "piss pots," barbers' basins—the standard Gold Coast assortment—intended to pay for the basic needs of the fort and for gold from the interior.[42] The local inhabitants were willing to accept a modest number of brasswares, it appears, but they disdained the thick manillas in favor at Elmina, preferring bangles of thin wire typical of Southern Africa. Soon, in fact, they refused payment in brass altogether, so that in 1506 gold had to be used to buy food for the garrison.[43] Needless to say there was no demand for imported copper inland; as yet brass does not seem to have competed with locally produced copper as it would subsequently in the Congo Basin, for example. Eventually copper was exported to India from Mozambique, but in the first decades of contact, the Portuguese trade in metals at Sofala was, as Lobato puts it, "um autentico fracasso," a real fiasco.[44]

The Sofala miscalculation aside, trade in copperwares on the scale that obtained in the period 1480–1550 had profound implications for both the importer and the exporter. Copper and brass were suddenly abundant in areas where they could not be produced indigenously and where they had previously been scarce luxuries, making their way from sahelian entrepôts and ultimately, for the most part, from North Africa. Carrying Tim Garrard's stimulating observation one step farther,[45] one might almost suggest that gold was being used by Gold Coast smiths *faute de mieux* when the first Europeans arrived; Africans gladly traded it for copper and brass, and the industry "took off," if one is allowed to borrow a Rostowian model.

Copper imports clearly did not all stay on the coast. Coastal societies could neither have absorbed the quantities traded nor supplied the goods for which the metal was exchanged, so that it was immediately fed into inland distribution systems. This was most obvious in regions where such systems antedated the European arrival: the Senegambia and Gold Coast. Pacheco (c. 1505) was well aware that the Senegal led to the interior markets of "Tambucutu [Timbuktu] and Janyh [Jenne]," saying that "tin and copper are greatly prized there."[46] Similarly, the gold reaching Elmina was obtained "from the negro merchants who bring it thither from distant lands," and who took back textiles and brass bracelets.[47] Indeed, it was to carry on this trade with the interior that slaves were from the first imported into the Gold Coast to serve as porters through the forest. By the 1530s Portuguese merchandise was being sold at markets several hundred miles into the hinterland.[48]

The almost insatiable demand for copper goods until about 1550 is a good indicator that the trade from the north had been inadequate to satisfy the market or to stimulate maximum production of gold. But what are we to make of the steep drop in the quantities of copper and brass reaching the coast, particularly the Gold Coast, after the mid-century? Had the African market reached a point of saturation, at least temporarily? Was the Atlantic system running up against the trans-Saharan system? Or were a number of factors at work, reflecting a more complex convergence on both the European and African sides of the trading equation?

The gold trade of West Africa and the spice trade of the East Indies were intimately linked with the expansion of the south German copper industry and the rise of Antwerp. By 1500 Antwerp had usurped the earlier dominance of Venice and Bruges as chief suppliers to the Portuguese Crown. Until the political upheavals of the 1560s, raw copper from the mines of Thuringia, Saxony, Tirol, and Hungary and worked copper and brass from Dinant, Aachen, and Nürnberg poured into the port. In his celebrated description of the city in 1567 Guicciardini wrote: "Ci inviano per terra li arienti sodi & li arienti vivi, i rami crudi & raffinati in quantità incredibile."[49] Incredible quantities indeed (and by sea as well as land):

in 1527 the Fugger stockpiles amounted to some 34,202 quintals (roughly 1,850 tons, based on the Antwerp cwt. of about 108 pounds), worth approximately 205,215 Rhenish gulden.[50]

Not coincidentally, the great merchant princes of early sixteenth century Antwerp sprang primarily from the traditional centers of copper and calamine production in Belgium and the Lower Rhine. Erasmus Schetz, for example, held a monopoly of the calamine deposits of German Limburg, controlled the extraction of copper in Westphalia, and oversaw the production of finished brass- and copperwares on a grand scale. Schetz's brass manillas were considered the most beautiful in the world and served as the standard of perfection against which all others were measured. De Haro, Pruynen, Vleminickx, van Rechtergem — all were closely tied to the copper trade.[51] This indigenous commercial aristocracy was soon eclipsed, however, by the rising power of the Fugger of Augsburg. In 1494, the year the Fugger-Thurzo combine gained outright ownership of the rich Neusohl mines in Hungary, they made their first deliveries of copper to the Portuguese factor in Antwerp. For the most part they supplied raw metal rather than finished products, but this was not always the case. Thus when the Crown contract with Erasmus Schetz lapsed at the end of 1547 because Schetz refused to lower his prices, the Portuguese factor, Juan Rebello, signed the famous contract already cited for the same sorts of goods from the Fuggergesellschaft.[52]

Vogt estimates that up until about 1530 Portuguese profits in the Mina trade were greater from metalwares than from cloth. Manillas, for example, cost 10 reis apiece in Flanders and were sold for 120 reis worth of gold at São Jorge. Basins also brought a profit/cost ratio of between 10:1 and 12:1, allowing for breakage. Or, manillas might be traded at the rate of 50 for a slave, which would then purchase 9,000–18,000 reis of gold at Elmina, theoretically an even more profitable transaction, except that slaves had to be fed and transported and many died or were rejected by African merchants. The prime cost of cloth, on the other hand, was higher and a greater quantity was lost through spoilage.[53]

The profitability of copperwares, however, was largely a result of the tremendously expanded output of Central European and Swedish mines, which reached a peak about 1515. The market then stagnated, thanks to a leveling off of demand. In an effort to counter the effects of overproduction and to maintain prices, the Fugger tried to create a cartel of major suppliers, an effort in which they were partially successful. Nevertheless in 1546, Anton Fugger decided against renewing leases to the Neusohl mines in Hungary, more, it has been suggested, because of apprehension over the Turkish threat than because of the unprofitability of copper mining.[54] Meanwhile, Swedish production had declined drastically as a result of catastrophic cave-ins and did not revive until the late century.[55]

A combination of economic and political factors led to the doubling of copper prices in Europe between 1546 and 1566 and a second doubling several decades later,[56] just at the time the Portuguese were facing a definitive challenge to their trading hegemony in West Africa. Even earlier, however, there had been a dramatic inflation in the cost of slaves and gold. Near the Rio Cestos on the Grain Coast, for example, at the turn of the century, the price of a slave jumped from two barbers' basins to four or five in a few years' time.[57] In Benin and the Slave Rivers of the Niger Delta, the price escalated from 12 to 15 manillas in the opening years of the sixteenth century to about 57 in 1517. King Manuel I tried to set a ceiling of 40 manillas but soon had to raise it to 50.[58] Similarly, the Crown ordered that damaged goods be returned to Lisbon rather than sold below the market price. Nevertheless, factors at Elmina found it increasingly necessary to give extra gifts as a means of circumventing the prohibition against lowering prices.[59]

Once the French and English became regular visitors to the coast after 1550, the buying power of European goods plunged. On his second voyage to the Gold Coast in 1556 William Towerson was willing to pay 80 manillas for an ounce of gold, double the price fixed by the Portuguese.[60] These interlopers obtained their metalwares from the same suppliers as the Portuguese, but their costs were considerably lower, trading as individual entrepreneurs rather than as agents of a cumbersome bureaucracy with expensive establishments. Though records are missing for much of the second half of the sixteenth century, it appears then that Portuguese trade declined precipitously because of a variety of factors: the loss of Safi (Morocco) in 1541 and the closing of the Antwerp factory eight years later, which seriously curtailed supplies of cloth and metalwares; fierce competition from European interlopers and serious losses to pirates; higher prime costs for trade goods and reduced purchasing power in African markets.[61]

When in 1604 two Portuguese ships reached Elmina with 15,000 manillas (along with cloth and cowries), they were the first manillas landed in several decades. Thirty-three years later the Portuguese commander urgently requested 4,000 manillas, and they did indeed arrive two years later.[62] It seems therefore that manillas were still in demand but that the Portuguese were less and less able to keep the factory supplied and totally unable any longer to dictate prices, a sign of Lisbon's diminished place in the world as well as in the African economy.

## THE SEVENTEENTH CENTURY

During the seventeenth century the Dutch wrested supremacy in the seaborne commerce of Africa and Asia from Portugal, while Amsterdam replaced Antwerp as the great emporium of northern Europe. A century later, the succession passed to Great Britain. Like those of the Casa da Mina, the records of the Dutch West India Company for Africa are grossly incomplete, so that for much of the seventeenth century, invoices from individual voyages, along with first-hand accounts by traders or second-hand compilations from often unacknowledged (and undated) sources, must supply most of the documentation. Here again, to give a proper context to the data, we would need to know more than is possible at present about the history of the coast and its hinterland and about the factors influencing European trading activity. Nevertheless the picture that emerges is consistent with what went before, suggesting, however, a commercial evolution of remarkable proportions.

In 1635 Samuel Blommaert, a director of the Dutch West India Company, estimated that among them the Dutch, English, French, and other Europeans annually shipped some 1,000,000 to 1,400,000 pounds of copperwares to West Africa.[63] Based on the Dutch pound of 1.09 pounds avoirdupois, this amounts to 545 to 763 tons a year, more than a tenfold increase over the peak Portuguese imports of a century earlier. Is this a credible estimate? According to de Marees, about 20 tons of copper and brass basins and other hardware were being sent to Guinea by the Dutch within fifteen years of their first expedition to the coast in 1593.[64] This would have expanded greatly with the formation of the chartered company in 1621, but it is doubtful whether the seventeenth-century brass industry was able to supply anything like such quantities. The only other quantitative data going beyond invoices for single voyages were compiled by Davies from the invoice book of the Royal African Company for 1673–1704 (see table 1). His compilation distinguishes only between copper bars and brasswares, leaving other copperwares in limbo, but it is very valuable nonetheless. Exports varied wildly, and one can assume that this would have been equally true for the Dutch West India Company and the chartered companies of other nations, to say nothing of individual traders. In terms of sheer quantity, 1680–85 were the peak years for RAC brass exports. During the 1690s the company concentrated its activities on the Gold Coast, which is no doubt reflected in the very low exports of copper in relation to brass.[65]

In the eighteenth century we will be on firmer ground with English customs data, but the seventeenth-century evidence indicates such variability from year to year that it would be risky to project totals for the entire century. Conditions of war and peace in both Europe and Africa were bound to affect the trade. Intermittent war between Holland and Portugal and later between France and England brought swarms of warships and privateers to African waters. In wartime, as Davies has noted, the trade of the chartered companies was primarily castle-based for defensive reasons, while

**THE ROYAL AFRICAN COMPANY:**

*Table 1*         **EXPORTS OF COPPER AND BRASS, 1673–1704**

| | Copper Bars | | | Brassware | |
|---|---|---|---|---|---|
| | Weight | | Value | Weight | Value |
| | tons | cwt. | £ | cwt. | £ |
| 1673 from 15 Nov. | 1 | 0 | 132 | 6 | 36 |
| 1674 | 23 | 16 | 3251 | 216 | 986 |
| 1675 | 26 | 0 | 3890 | 179 | 1860 |
| 1676 to 15 Nov. | 11 | 14 | 1733 | 89 | 465 |
| 1680 | 12 | 7 | 1553 | 377 | 2952 |
| 1681 | 20 | 6 | 2704 | 443 | 2900 |
| 1682 | 27 | 4 | 3595 | 404 | 2578 |
| 1683 | 10 | 5 | 1346 | 423 | 2722 |
| 1684 | 12 | 16 | 1661 | 143 | 1019 |
| 1685 | 17 | 16 | 2349 | 533 | 3242 |
| 1688 | 8 | 5 | 1054 | 217 | 1431 |
| 1689 | 1 | 12 | 197 | 71 | 485 |
| 1690 | 4 | 0 | 477 | 86 | 686 |
| 1691 | 1 | 10 | 214 | 90 | 634 |
| 1692 | 1 | 12 | 218 | 278 | 1913 |
| 1693 | 3 | 6 | 455 | 263 | 1929 |
| 1694 | 4 | 19 | 675 | 123 | 769 |
| 1695 | — | — | — | 100 | 892 |
| 1696 | — | — | — | 113 | 985 |
| 1697 | — | — | — | 89 | 754 |
| 1698 | 0 | 11 | 100 | 295 | 2473 |
| 1701 | 3 | 18 | 652 | 351 | 2944 |
| 1702 | 3 | 12 | 534 | 465 | 3762 |
| 1703 | 0 | 12 | 96 | 69 | 533 |
| 1704 | — | — | — | 298 | 2508 |
| Total, tons | 198.26 | | | 320.38 | |

Source: K. G. Davies, *The Royal African Company* (London, 1957), app. 1, p. 351

in peace it could be mixed castle and ship trade.[66] In the same way, wars in the hinterland of Senegambia or the Gold Coast influenced the flow of exports to the coast and of imports to the interior: if they increased the eventual flow of slaves for sale, the gold trade often came to a dead halt in times of particular turmoil.[67]

Much as traders tried to provision themselves with goods produced in their own countries to reduce costs, this was not always possible.[68] While England and France manufactured some copperwares, most had to be purchased in Amsterdam or Hamburg. Copper was particularly vulnerable to price fluctuations, as it still is. The first quarter of the seventeenth century, the period of early Dutch enterprise, coincided with steadily mounting prices that resulted from an increasing demand for foreign trade, for shipbuilding and war materials, but even more specifically from the Spanish switchover in 1599 to an all-copper currency. When Spain returned to silver in 1626 and Japanese copper began reaching the Netherlands as ballast in East Indiamen, prices fell. There was some slight recovery after 1631 but no significant rise until the late 1650s.[69] The period of Blommaert's estimate, 1635, therefore marks a moment of relatively plentiful and inexpensive supplies of copper goods, thanks especially to Swedish production, which was booming in spite of the ravages of the Thirty Years' War.[70]

The mammoth increases in copper imports into Africa demonstrate a remarkable capacity for expansion on the part of African and European entrepreneurs. During the period of WIC monopoly on the Gold Coast in the first half of the century, the going rate was 35 pounds of copper for 2 ounces of gold. When the market was opened up to the English and French, they were willing to offer 40 pounds.[71] It is obviously much easier to transport 2 ounces of gold through the forest than 35 or 40 pounds of copper, and one realizes the complexity of organizing the inland trading economy, especially since the other goods imported (textiles, iron, beads, liquor) were also bulkier and heavier than most of those exported. The same is true for other parts of the coast that furnished mostly slaves and ivory.

In the course of the century, too, the tendency of different areas of the coast to demand different forms of metalwares was accentuated, hence the importance of such authors as de Marees, "D. R.," Dapper, and Barbot, who like their late-fifteenth- and sixteenth-century predecessors offer a rundown of what was saleable where. The difficulty is that they often mix information from a variety of sources and periods. Given the changing tastes of the African buyer, this leads to occasional contradictions, even though on the whole the information is undoubtedly more reliable than that on other aspects of Africa. In general these authors point up several trends, confirmed by other sources. First of all, in the later sixteenth century and throughout the seventeenth, iron overtook copper and brass as the major metal imported. Candice Goucher argues cogently that the import of large quantities of iron into Africa reflects not the superiority of the European product—there is ample evidence that African iron was often of higher quality—but environmental deterioration in Africa and above all the depletion of fuel supplies.[72] It also reflects the ability of Europe for the first time to produce surpluses of iron: Aitchison points out that iron production did not overtake copper until early in the fifteenth century.[73] The expansion of both copper and iron production in Europe brought its own ecological devastation, from which the industries were rescued only by the adaptation of coal and coke to processes that had previously depended on charcoal. In many areas of West Africa, on the other hand, ironworking became, like copperworking, an industry relying primarily on imported metals.

Although of far less importance overall, pewter also began to be imported in this period. But just as the sources are often imprecise in distinguishing copper from brass, so there is imprecision about other metals. Towerson, for example, refers already in 1556–57 to the sale of "Wite basons." These may be the same as the "pots of coarse tinne" traded on his next voyage a year later, or they may be pewter (an alloy of tin and lead) or even heavily tinned brass.[74] There is the same uncertainty in identifying the "blancke akers" (white pails) listed with metalwares in the inventory of the Dutch factor at Elmina in 1645.[75] Fortunately, English sources of the seventeenth century tend to be clearer that pewter was indeed exported in considerable quantities to the Gold Coast, Gambia, Benin, and New Calabar. Just why this should be so remains a minor mystery. Possibly it was cheaper, yet still acceptable. Perhaps, too, it will show up when more metal analyses of indigenous castings have been made in the form of higher tin or lead content. One small clue is provided by Richard Brew, who in a letter of 1771 emphasized that pewter was a peculiarly Aşante taste, so that when war cut off trade with Aşante, the metal was "not called for."[76]

Pans, basins, and kettles of brass and copper were in almost universal demand from Senegambia to Angola during the seventeenth century. They were sold by weight, but since the specifications of the various sorts are often very precise, it seems doubtful that they were simply bought for their metal content, to be melted down or reworked by local smiths and casters. Some were put to use. At Fetu, for example, large and expensive copper wash basins served the well-to-do for their daily ablutions.[77] The greater part, however, were probably employed in less mundane spheres, as we shall see in part III.

Beyond this, each region had its peculiar preferences. Thus according to Barbot, brass kettles, chains, bells, bracelets, and trumpets were traded on the Senegal coast, but upriver the demand was for kettles and basins ("satalas") of very precise sizes.[78] On the Gambia, tin (or possibly pewter) rings sold along with those of copper and brass.[79] The Ivory Coast was little developed, but locally produced *quaqua* cloth obtained with brass manillas and beads fueled the coastal trade.[80] Not surprisingly, the Gold Coast, as the most highly evolved trading area on the West African littoral, was also the most demanding. Dutch accounts list a half-dozen varieties of copper and brass vessels (see table 2), including the familiar barbers' basins and cooking pots, but by now the lion's share belongs to "large and small neptunes." A factor's account of 1645 includes 10,915 large neptunes and 1,500 small ones traded for gold.[81] On the other hand, manillas almost totally disappear from bills of lading to the Gold Coast by the mid-century. And yet Daaku notes that suddenly in 1645 there was a great demand for copper bracelets,[82] while Dapper still lists them among trade goods in 1676, probably a sign of obsolete information, although possibly there may have been another ephemeral burst of popularity.[83] Conversely, even brass kettles were unsalable on the Gold Coast at the time of Phillips' visit in 1693–94, along with other goods that usually commanded a ready market.[84] It may be still another case of sending the wrong article. Thirty years earlier English merchants at Coromantin had complained that they had large stocks of unsold brass vessels because the vessels were too heavy. "What brasse you send," they pleaded, "pray let it bee as light as you can procure and well coloured."[85] If these wares were mostly being sent inland, one can well understand the preference for lighter weight.

On the Slave Coast, where trade had been virtually nonexistent earlier, the standard assortment of trading goods included brass neptunes by the second half of the seventeenth century. An RAC invoice dated 1678 in "Arda" lists "Brass pans of all Sorts," "Ditto large to wash their Bodies in," and brass kettles.[86] In his account of trade at Whydah, Phillips noted that next to cowries, the items most in demand were "brass neptunes or basons, very large, thin and flat," and that half a trading cargo must be made up of brass and cowries. This was clearly disadvantageous to Europeans, who preferred a larger proportion of cheaper wares, but, Phillips said, "without the cowries and brass they will take none of the [other] goods."[87]

Manillas, both copper and brass, continued in strong demand in Benin and the Delta.[88] Farther to the east, copper rods became the standard currency. Dapper describes them as one and a quarter pounds in weight and one and a quarter ells in length.[89] In Old Calabar, James Barbot found them still the unit of account in 1698 although overshadowed by the iron bar, which was worth four of the copper.[90] What is striking is the continuing preference for copper in the eastern Delta and Calabar, in contrast to brass farther west. True, Dapper notes a demand at Calabar River for "graeuwe kopere armringen," which probably indicates a lead alloy, but Barbot also underscores the eagerness of the inhabitants of Old Calabar and Rio del Rey for purple copper armlets from Luanda.[91]

Beyond Old Calabar, trade was rather insignificant in this century, with only an occasional ship putting in along the Cameroon coast or at Cape Lopez. Here too, however, the demand was for copper rods, bracelets, and pots and brass basins.[92] Farther south, in the area nebulously referred to as Angola (which included Loango and Cabinda as well as Angola proper), copper and brass manillas, basins, and chains were imported by Portuguese and Dutch traders, although as we shall see, the region was also an exporter of copper.[93] Still farther south, the Khoikhoi at the Cape were renowned for their eagerness for copper. To their ultimate injury, they exchanged cattle and sheep for copper beads and flat copper discs in order to fashion jewelry resembling that which they had made from the trickle of copper which earlier had reached them from distant sources in Namibia and Botswana. As European supplies became more regular and more plentiful, the peoples near the Dutch East India settlement at Table Bay established trading networks with the interior which intersected with preexisting ones supplying copper from Khoi chiefdoms of the Orange River and possibly with Tswana sources as well.[94] The same pattern was followed by the Xhosa of the eastern Cape and Natal. The Journal of the *São Alberto,* wrecked west of the Infante River in 1593, notes, "They value the most necessary metals, as iron and copper, and for very small pieces of either they will barter cattle, which is what they esteem most. . . ." In fact, the Nguni were so avid for copper and iron from the survivors of shipwrecks along the coast that a source of 1686 warned that they gave "inducement to the murder of those that have them."[95] Every two or three years during the mid-seventeenth century East India Company traders put in to Delagoa Bay for more formal trading contacts. There they sold "ould Copper or Brasse which hath been used in Potts etc. & broken to pieces whereof they make Shackles [i.e., ornaments such as an armlet or anklet]."[96]

By the end of the seventeenth century, then, the European copper trade stretched the length of the west coast of Africa, albeit discontinuously, from the Senegal River to Table Bay and beyond. In 1653 the adventurous Buckeridge even sold copper and iron at Pate, north of Malindi, a voyage that seems to have been without immediate sequel.[97] Perhaps the best single glimpse of the trade is provided by the Vijf Dagregisters of the Dutch West India Company (WIC) for the period 1645–47. Table 2 describes the main copperwares traded by the WIC, their prime cost in Europe, and their purchasing power in West Africa. The cost of copper pots was almost double that of rods, with neptunes about halfway between. A slave bought in the eastern Delta or at Calabar for copper rods was slightly cheaper than one bought for brass bracelets, and considerably cheaper than one bought for neptunes, basins, pots, or kettles. The European trader had little room to substitute, but he could refuse to buy slaves on the Gold Coast, for example, if the price was too high, and could sail on to Calabar. The difficulty, of course, was that it might prolong the voyage and increase the rate of mortality among both Europeans and African slaves, to say nothing of the fact that slaves from the Bight were considered much less desirable than those from the Gold Coast—Barbot paints a lurid picture of their sup-

*Table 2*    DUTCH COPPER AND BRASS EXPORTS TO WEST AFRICA, FIRST HALF OF THE SEVENTEENTH CENTURY

| | Prime Cost | Purchasing Power | Area of Circulation | Characteristics |
|---|---|---|---|---|
| Brass bracelets | 56 gulden/100 lb. | no exchange for gold but 3 rings = 1 Benin cloth = 4 gulden gold on Gold Coast<br>Calabar: 120 rings/M slave, 100 rings/F slave<br>4 rings = 1 copper rod; 15 rings = 1 iron rod | Grain Coast<br>Arbo (Benin)<br>Bight<br>Cameroon | c. 1½ oz., furnished in bundles of 500. Cf. Dapper: wt. 5½ oz. |
| Barber's basins (Copper) | 68–70 gulden/100 lb. | 100–130 gulden/100 lb. | | |
| Copper pots | 95 gulden/100 lb. | 130 gulden/100 lb. (gold)<br>25 lb./1 M slave 23 lb./1 F slave worth 23½ and 21½ gulden resp. = rather expensive | | 7″–10″ deep, w/small rims tinned |
| Copper kettles | 68–70 gulden/100 lb. | 100–35 gulden (for gold) | | very large, some with cross-sections of 1 ell or more. |
| Copper rods | 50 gulden/100 lb. | not traded for gold, mainly traded for slaves in Bight:<br>23 rods/1 M slave, 18 rods/1 F slave = 11½ and 9 gulden resp. | | red copper, rods = 1 lb., or heavier ones = 1½ lb.<br>length = c. 1½ ell (= c. 1 yard) |
| Neptunes | 70 gulden/100 lb. | 100–35 gulden/100 lb. (for gold) VERY POPULAR | | shallow copper pans in different sizes: small = for palm oil, large = for shrines on graves.<br>Most common size = ¾ ell measured on both sides, wt. = 5 lb. |

Source: K. Ratelband, ed., *Vijf dagregisters von het kasteel São Jorge da Mina (Elmina) aan de Goudkust (1645-1647)* (The Hague, 1953), introduction

posedly "cruel and bloody . . . temper" — and were apt to fetch a lower price in the New World.[98] In fact, since the purchase of African commodities required an assortment of goods which varied from region to region and was expressed in different units of account, it is difficult to isolate the profitability or unprofitability of copperwares. What is undeniable is their indispensability if trade was to be conducted at all.

## AFRICAN COPPER EXPORTS

In two regions of the West African littoral, European traders found copper available for export: northern Angola and Loango, north of the Congo mouth. So readily was this channeled into trade with Guinea that it again raises the suspicion of a preexisting commerce which the Portuguese appropriated to their own advantage, very much on the model of the coastal trade between Benin and the Gold Coast or in Upper Guinea, albeit with less spectacular success.[99]

In 1506 the King of Kongo, Don Afonso, sent 500 manillas of copper to King Manuel I of Portugal, the first of a series of gifts intended to cement the alliance between the two kings. Although most of these gifts seem to have been diverted by unscrupulous Portuguese intermediaries, Manuel I quickly recognized the wealth of his brother monarch and its potential value to the Portuguese economy. In 1516 he sent an emissary to learn more about such local trade goods as copper, ivory, and slaves and to estimate how much could be expected on an annual basis. Two years later, 2,300 copper manillas were exported from the Congo mouth. In 1526 a French ship tried to buy some as well.[100] By the next decade relatively large quantities were being shipped north to the Guinea coast,[101] probably to Benin in particular, which clung to its preference for copper manillas. The linchpin in this regional trading system was the island of São Tomé.

Portuguese sources do not tell us the origin of these exports, no doubt because they did not know it. Later in the century mines farther south, just inland from Benguela, were feeding "very fine copper" into the trade, as Andrew Battell noted.[102] The Portuguese in fact founded the colony of Benguela in 1617 to develop the copper trade.[103] A report of the Dutch West India Company, probably dating from 1645, estimates Angolan exports at some 20,000 pounds of red copper per annum.[104] The "purple copper armlets, or arm-rings" made at Luanda were particularly valued at Calabar and the Rio del Rey during the mid-seventeenth century.[105]

Not content with a simple trading relationship, however, the Portuguese Crown was convinced almost from the start that production could be expanded with European "technical assistance." Ruy Mendez and a team of smelters were dispatched to make their way to the copper mines in 1536. Their objective may have been Bembe, or since Manuel Pacheco's account mentions that they were also looking for sources of lead, it may have been Mindouli.[106] This reconnaissance, like others that followed over the next century, was a failure, but it marked the beginning of a protracted struggle to bring Congolese copper mines, which were real, as well as those of silver and gold, which were not, under direct Portuguese control.[107] The struggle led finally to a bitter war in which the Portuguese defeated and decapitated the Kongo king, D. Antonio I (1665). What had begun as a trading partnership had long since been deformed by the pursuit of elusive riches in gold and silver and by the tangled conflicts between Kongo and its former vassal Angola on the one hand and Portugal and Holland on the other. Even with their victory, the Portuguese were unable to occupy the mines at Bembe, and production seems to have ceased until revived fleetingly in the mid-nineteenth century.[108] Benguela, too, and the other copper sources mentioned in Portuguese documents, no longer supplied copper for export after the later seventeenth century, although both Dutch and English sources of the early 1670s indicate an interest in the trade.[109]

There is a curious echo of these events on the other side of the continent. Just as a succession of writers were memorializing the Portuguese crown to play a more active role in exploiting the mineral resources of Kongo-Angola in the early decades of the seventeenth century, so it became a common refrain by the 1620s to urge the export of copper from the Zambezi as ballast to India, where it was sorely needed to cast artillery. Supposedly the ruler of Monomotapa had publicly ceded all of his mines to the king of Portugal in 1607 in return for Portuguese military support to save his kingdom. Like his Kongo counterpart, however, the Monomotapa never let the Portuguese find out where the mines were. In fact, transport costs would have been far too high to export copper on any scale, so that what Zambezian copper did enter the Indian Ocean trade was primarily in the form of debased gold: pure gold arriving from the rivers was mixed with as much as 35 percent copper by the captain and residents of Mozambique before it was sent on to Goa.[110]

European sources first mention the availability of copper for export from the Loango coast, north of the Congo mouth, in the late sixteenth century. Andrew Battell found an abundance of merchandise, including "molangos" (bracelets) of copper.[111] Broecke's account of his visit in 1607 described these bracelets as made of "beautiful red copper, weighing anywhere from one-and-a-half to fourteen pounds." On his next voyage out, he brought back some of this copper for his employer, the Dutch East India Company,[112] and within a few years the Dutch were shipping large quantities of Loango copper to Brazil and Amsterdam. In 1642, for example, a trader found 22,050 pounds of copper ready to be laded, while the agent at Sonyo estimated that the port of Loango could supply 70,000 to 80,000 pounds of copper and ivory annually.[113]

This figure becomes impressive when we realize that the copper in question came to the coast by head porterage from beyond the Mayombe Mountains, from the metal-bearing region of the Niari Basin known in contemporary accounts as "Sondy" (Nsundi). The mountains are not particularly high, but they are rugged — "accidentées" is the standard epithet in French writings on the area.[114] Dapper, presumably drawing on Dutch information when the trade was at its height in the 1640s, describes the annual caravans from the Kingdom of Loango:

> Towards September many smiths from different regions gather to go to Sondy to smelt copper which the people living there let them dig out of the mines and cast in the forms in which it is brought back. These smiths stay in Sondy until May and then return from there, since the dry season brings many wars to the country. The quality of the copper is debased thanks to the ineptitude of the inhabitants who smelt all the ores together.[115]

Since both Broecke and Brun earlier extolled the red copper of Loango from firsthand knowledge, we may be properly skeptical of Dapper's last statement. The mixing of metals in the Niari Basin where copper and lead are found in close association was probably intentional, as Pleigneur reported more than two centuries later (see above, chapter 3). The deliberate admixture of lead produced a rather malleable alloy looking somewhat like tin; the addition of more copper to this alloy yielded a grayish metal which was cast into bars. This was certainly the source of the "graeuwe kopere armringen" which Dapper says were made in Luanda of copper from "songo" for shipment to Calabar and Rio del Rey.[116] On the other hand, a final roasting of this gray metal on a perforated plate yielded the "schoon roodt copper" more widely exported.[117]

As Phyllis Martin has pointed out, the Vili of Loango had originally organized caravans into the interior to feed a purely inter-African copper trade. The king, or *maloango,* played an active part in promoting and regulating trade generally, stocking the major goods such as copper, ivory, and palm cloth, presumably to control the quantities reaching the market and hence their value. All three of these items had an extensive market within Africa and were not dependent on European demand as it developed in the late sixteenth and especially the seventeenth century. The Vili themselves wore large amounts of fine copper jewelry and probably provided the rings worn at least as far to the north as Cape Lopez.[118] As I have suggested earlier, it is not out of the question that copper from the Niari Basin had been reaching the Eastern Delta well before it entered into the European *cabotage* — before the Europeans took over much of the coastal trade within Africa.[119] This hypothesis is supported on the one hand by the evidence of such highly developed entrepreneurial systems as that of the Vili, which clearly were not European-inspired and which could have supplied ample amounts of copper for export, and on the other hand by the well-established taste for copper among the coastal peoples from the Eastern Delta to Mt. Cameroon to the Gaboon estuary, a taste noted by the earliest Portuguese sources. If Niari copper was reaching these areas it was probably indirectly, through a series of intermediaries such as the Mpongwe, Orungu, and Benga, plying the lagoons and estuaries and perhaps even using the islands in the Gulf of Guinea as stepping stones.[120] In the absence of written sources and in view of the unreliability of oral tradition for this time span, metal analysis, especially lead isotope analysis, may offer the only means of testing the hypothesis.

The Dutch had been attracted to Loango because of the weak Portuguese presence there, but they soon found themselves caught up in a fierce trade rivalry, part of the larger struggle for hegemony on the West African coast. Unable to dislodge the Dutch, the Portuguese in the 1620s tried to undermine their position by diverting both the copper and ivory trade of Mindouli from Loango to Portuguese posts in Kakongo, north of the Congo mouth. The Portuguese Crown authorized the purchase to 5,000 cruzados of copper annually, which was transferred to Luanda and thence shipped to Bahia for the manufacture of artillery to defend the Portuguese in Angola and Brazil against the Dutch.[121] By the latter half of the century, the picture was still further complicated by the arrival of the English and French and by the growing preoccupation of all the Europeans with the slave trade. The maloango had tried to resist this traffic, but by the late years of the century, slaves far overshadowed the traditional exports of copper, ivory, and redwood from the Loango coast.[122] A century later, Degrandpré, while noting that the inhabitants of Mayombe, north of Loango, had access to large quantities of copper which they used with avidity, fails to mention any export of the metal.[123] When Richard Burton visited Loango in the 1860s, the copper mines of the interior had ceased entirely to send their produce to the coast.[124]

A third region that seemed for a time to promise exports of copper was Delagoa Bay on the southeastern coast. Though a Portuguese expedition of 1544 had found copper to be available in abundance to the north at the mouth of the Limpopo, the first significant supplies apparently began reaching the bay area in the second half of the seventeenth century. In the 1680s, English traders set themselves up on an offshore island and were manufacturing copper bracelets, not indeed for export but to trade with local peoples.[125] In 1721, the Dutch East India Company established a factory at the bay and attempted to exploit the mineral wealth of the interior more systematically. Jan Van de Capelle sent samples of both copper and tin to his employers, noting that "the copper is very handsome in color."[126] In some years, quantities obtained were significant: 223 kilograms in 1722 and 136 in 1725. Gold, too, was worked by inland peoples, but its export was tightly restricted. "Paraotte," which Van de Capelle's informants gave as the source of the copper, is undoubtedly Phalaborwa in the eastern Transvaal. The trade may already have been in the hands of Venda middlemen.[127]

The Dutch were ultimately less successful in profiting from the trade than the English. Operating out of Bombay, they founded a trading factory, sent boats into the rivers emptying into the bay, and once again began manufacturing copper bracelets from indigenous metal. In 1777, however, Delagoa Bay was occupied by the Austrian Asiatic Company of Trieste and then by the Portuguese, who had found themselves unable to compete during much of the century.[128] At Delagoa Bay during the seventeenth century, then, copper but especially brass from Europe converged on copper from the interior; copper was both an import and an export. This is less confusing when we realize the complexity of internal trading networks from the eastern Transvaal, their vulnerability to local politics, and the thirst for copper and brass not only among the inhabitants of the bay area but throughout Natal to the south. Ronga traders were successful in keeping the Dutch and other Europeans from penetrating into the interior, but in their efforts to maintain a monopoly of trade to and from the bay they tended to discourage trade altogether.[129] No doubt that is why thriving enterprises such as the English manufacture of copper bracelets on the spot were so sporadic. And while the interior could supply copper and tin, imported copper seemed better suited to bronze-making. This bronze probably entered into trade alongside imported brass. Already in the seventeenth and eighteenth centuries, it was the fine quality of English brass that, according to Smith, gave the English their edge over Portuguese, and then Dutch, traders.[130]

In any event, it is impossible to estimate the quantity of copper that may have been shipped from Delagoa Bay or the amount that may have been used in the bracelets manufactured *in situ* by the English, but it seems doubtful that it was ever more than ancillary to the primary object of trade in these parts, ivory.

## THE EIGHTEENTH CENTURY

The history of the chartered companies, so much a fixture of the seventeenth-century African trade, is a history of unprofitability. They were as unsuccessful in excluding private traders as the Portuguese Crown had been, and found it hard to compete with the flexibility and lower costs of interlopers. Gradually their monopoly powers were whittled away and the African trade became a free-for-all.[131] Paradoxically, however, this greater freedom to trade abroad was accompanied by the erection of tariff walls at home, in England particularly, which in turn affected the forms in which copper was available for export to Africa. This was especially true in the first half of the eighteenth century before Great Britain was able to supply most of her own copper and brass.

English Customs House data on exports to Africa (see charts 1–3, tables 3–6) provide a much more comprehensive picture of the trade than earlier ones from the Royal African Company or than anything surviving from Dutch sources.[132] Even the customs figures represent a minimum, however, since ships stocking up on brasswares in Holland might sail directly to Africa, leaving no hint in the English records. "Unwrot" includes copper bars and rods, while "battery" refers to kettles or pans "with the visible mark of the hammer," that is, made by hammering.[133] "Metal prepared" is the stage of manufacture before battery: kettles or pans not having the mark of the hammer.[134] The different forms of metal were subject to different amounts of import duty, so that importers tried to evade charges by declaring them at the lowest rate.[135] This shows up in the Customs House data, where between 1700 and 1717 there are no reexports of metal pre-

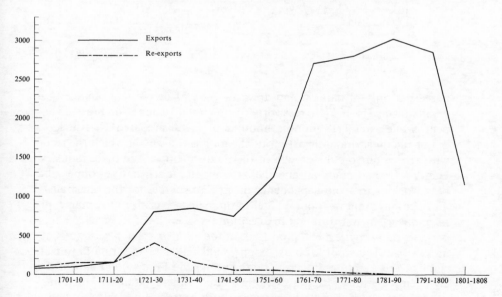

Chart 1. English copper and brass exports and reexports to Africa, totals by decade, 1701–1808. Source: PRO/CUST 3 and CUST 17

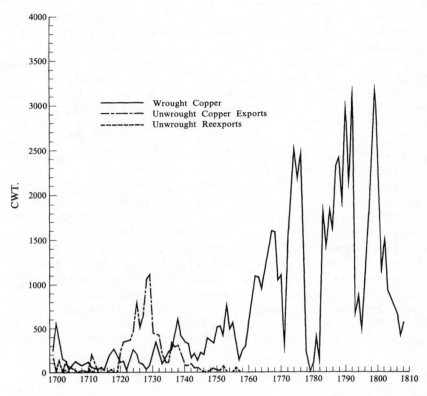

Chart 2. English copper exports and reexports to Africa, 1700–1808. Source: PRO/CUST
    3 and CUST 17

pared but only of battery, and down to 1710, of unwrought metal. With
a shift in tariffs in 1711, reexports of unwrought copper or brass disappear, while after 1718 modest amounts of metal prepared are listed.

But the most dramatic aspect of the data is the way in which the trade
with Africa mirrors the growth of the English copper and brass industry.
Henry VIII had made an abortive attempt to launch native copper and
brassworking to avoid dependence on foreign sources for the raw materials of coinage and weaponry. Later in the sixteenth century German capital and workers were brought in to exploit the deposits of Keswick in Cum-
berland. To keep the metal produced for the home market, a series of statutes forbade the export of brass, copper, and bell metal (a form of bronze),
some of these statutes lingering on the books until the second half of the
eighteenth century. Often overregulated and undercapitalized, the industry did not thrive. Even into the eighteenth century English brass had a

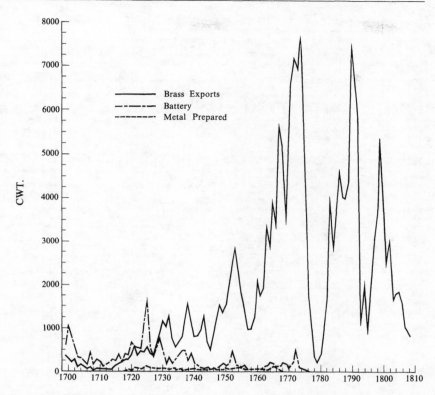

Chart 3. English brass exports and reexports to Africa, 1700–1808. Source: PRO/CUST 3 and CUST 17

reputation, probably deserved, for being inferior to foreign-made brass. Most of the metal consumed at home and shipped abroad was therefore imported from Sweden, Germany, Hungary, and even Morocco. A contract of 1685, for example, calls for Peter Joye to supply the Royal African Company with copper bars bought on the continent to be delivered the following year at the rate of £6 5d per cwt., not to exceed a total of 40,000.[136]

A series of developments late in the seventeenth century provided the impetus that led with surprising rapidity to the worldwide dominance of British copper and brass. Some of the developments were technological: the successful use of coal in smelting copper, improvements in reverberating furnaces, the reclaiming of copper ores associated with tin deep in Cornish mines, ores that had previously been discarded as too impure. Others were regulatory, opening up mining by removing royal and monopoly controls, repealing Tudor restrictions on the export of home-produced

*Table 3*    **ENGLISH COPPER AND BRASS EXPORTS TO AFRICA, 1699–1808**

| | Wrought Copper | Wrought Brass | Unwrought Copper | Other | Total |
|---|---|---|---|---|---|
| 1699–1700 | 837.11 | 656.95 | 1.25 | 0 | 1495.31 CWT = 83.74 TONS |
| 1701–10 | 1222.82 | 946.01 | 24.54 | 0 | 2217.91 CWT = 124.20 TONS |
| 1711–20 | 1059.43 | 1407.01 | 464.06 | 0 | 2930.50 CWT = 164.11 TONS |
| 1721–30 | 1240.28 | 5597.59 | 6120.37 | 3.05 | 12961.29 CWT = 725.83 TONS |
| 1731–40 | 3190.94 | 9362.94 | 2476.42 | 1.50 | 15031.80 CWT = 841.78 TONS |
| 1741–50 | 2853.75 | 10,254.10 | 376.50 | 26.54 | 13510.89 CWT = 756.61 TONS |
| 1751–60 | 4299.02 | 17,662.73 | 136 | 558.55 | 22656.30 CWT = 1268.75 TONS |
| 1761–70 | 11,999.44 | 36,406.19 | 0 | 0 | 48405.63 CWT = 2710.72 TONS |
| 1771–80 | 12,238.82 | 38,202.69 | 0 | 0 | 50441.51 CWT = 2824.72 TONS |
| 1781–90 | 16,946.57 | 37,185.64 | 0 | 0 | 54132.21 CWT = 3031.40 TONS |
| 1791–1800 | 17,835.27 | 33,234.54 | 0 | 0 | 51069.81 CWT = 2859.91 TONS |
| 1801–8 | 6896.97 | 13,765.33 | 0 | 0 | 20662.30 CWT = 1157.09 TONS |
| | | | | | 16,548.86 TONS |

Source: English Customs House PRO/CUST 3 and CUST 17

copper, and ending the monopoly privileges enjoyed by the Royal African Company. English manufacturers continued to complain about competition from Swedish and Barbary copper, agitating for steeper import duties on imported metalwares, while those engaged in the African trade of course wanted the duties lowered. After the 1730s, the supremacy of the British brass industry and the precipitous decline of copper mining in Sweden made protectionism less urgent. Japanese copper, too, no longer competed on the Amsterdam market; indeed, it no longer sufficed for the Asian market and had to be supplemented by British exports. By 1780 at least 40 percent of the national production of some 30,000 tons was exported: to the Continent as well as to Africa, the West Indies, and Asia.[137]

So great was the demand for brass late in the eighteenth century and so inadequate was the production of British copper that prices skyrocketed. Amidst charges of monopoly and price-fixing, a parliamentary inquiry was

Table 4  **ENGLISH COPPER AND BRASS REEXPORTS TO AFRICA, 1699–1808**

|  | Battery | Metal Prepared | Unwrought | Other | Total |
|---|---|---|---|---|---|
| 1699–1700 | 1657.98 | 0 | 173.32 | 3.15 | 1834.45 CWT = 102.73 TONS |
| 1701–10 | 3206.17 | 0 | 363.57 | 7.94 | 3577.68 CWT = 200.35 TONS |
| 1711–20 | 2888.02 | 37.50 | 0 | 1.41 | 2926.93 CWT = 163.91 TONS |
| 1721–30 | 6994.41 | 681.96 | 0 | 4.87 | 7681.24 CWT = 430.15 TONS |
| 1731–40 | 2941.14 | 290.54 | 0 | 0 | 3231.68 CWT = 180.97 TONS |
| 1741–50 | 775.26 | 153.87 | 0 | .50 | 929.63 CWT = 52.06 TONS |
| 1751–60 | 1137.42 | 285.12 | 0 | .27 | 1422.81 CWT = 79.68 TONS |
| 1761–70 | 1114.53 | 183.37 | 0 | 0 | 1297.90 CWT = 72.68 TONS |
| 1771–80 | 731.16 | 12.37 | 0 | 2.98 | 746.51 CWT = 41.80 TONS |
| 1781–90 | 0 | 0 | 0 | 0 | 0 |
| 1791–1800 | 0 | 0 | 0 | 0 | 0 |
| 1800–1808 | 0 | 0 | 0 | 0 | 0 |
|  |  |  |  |  | 1324.33 TONS |

Source: English Customs House PRO/CUST 3 and CUST 17

held in 1799 which puts the African trade in a comparative framework.[138] By this time, it should be noted, English exports to France had been curbed because of hostilities between the two countries, which in turn forced France to accelerate the growth of her own industry. The inquiry brought out the conflicts between the various segments of the industry: the need of mine owners for protection against wild fluctuations in prices of raw copper, the desire of brass manufacturers for inexpensive and abundant supplies of good quality metal, the concern of slave traders and other merchants for wares that would be both acceptable and profitable.

The growth of Bristol as a major producer of brass and a leading slaving port for much of the century cannot have been entirely fortuitous.[139] Bristol, which wrested its manufacturing position from London, would in turn be replaced by Birmingham as a center for finished brasswares. Initially, however, a number of separate works produced goods for the African trade. From the late 1720s, for example, Robert Morris manufactured manillas and possibly rods at Landone. He used a "hard metal" that combined one-half cwt. lead with a ton of copper: since lead cost only

*Table 5*     **ENGLISH EXPORTS OF BRASS AND PLATED GOODS, 1790–92**

|  | 1790 | | | 1791 | | | 1792 | | |
|---|---|---|---|---|---|---|---|---|---|
|  | cwt. | grs. | lbs. | cwt. | grs. | lbs. | cwt. | grs. | lbs. |
| West Indies | 4,570 | 0 | 24 | 10,295 | 3 | 0 | 15,181 | 3 | 2 |
| Asia | 6,993 | 1 | 0 | 8,105 | 0 | 0 | 14,405 | 0 | 0 |
| Africa | 7,519 | 0 | 0 | 6,580 | 0 | 0 | 5,631 | 0 | 23 |
| Total production | 38,295 | 1 | 9 | 46,482 | 0 | 11 | 62,770 | 2 | 22 |
| African exports represent | £32,849 of a total £171,338 | | | £29,610 of a total £209,769 | | | £25,340 of a total £282,469 | | |

Source: *Report of the Select Committee on the State of the Copper Trade,* 1799, app. 33

half as much as fine copper, this was cheaper than either copper or brass manillas and evidently already acceptable on the African market at this early date.[140] Several decades later the Cheadle Company established a copper works at Greenfield for "plating and rolling copper . . . and for the making and finishing copper rods such as are usually sold to the guinea merchants." Soon there was a branch at Warrington to make manillas.[141] William Champion's 1767 compilation of the stock on hand of the Warmley Company included copper wares such as Guinea manillas and rods and brass kettles, pans, neptunes, latten, and wire.[142] The Forest Copper Works in Swansea, Thomas Williams' Holywell Works in Flintshire—all churned out goods for the African trade.[143] The Minute Books for the Cheadle Brass Wire Company contain an entry in 1790 having to do with the erection of a "Manilla House and Assay Office." A year later they record an "enquiry about the probability of being supplied with materials for manillas"; if a supply can be had "with certainty" they recommend "that this manufacture be increased."[144] So closely were copper rods associated with the African market that they came to be called "Negroes."[145]

Already in 1713 and 1722 government papers underscore the dependence of the Bristol copper industry on exports to Africa, just as the development of its offshoots in Lancaster was influenced by the growth of Liverpool as a slave-trading port. By the later eighteenth century, copper and brass were second only to iron and textiles (or occasionally beads) as a constituent of English cargoes. The records of the Cheadle, Warrington, and Macclesfield companies show that the manufacture of specialized goods for the trade was indeed an attractive enterprise. In 1788 Thomas Williams, the "Copper King," and his partners declared that the slave trade in particular had led them to invest heavily in the copper industry.[146] Liverpool alone exported 134½ tons of wrought brass to Africa in 1770, along with 672 cwt. of wrought copper.[147]

Table 6   ENGLISH EXPORTS OF WROUGHT COPPER TO AFRICA, 1790–98

|  | Cwt. | Value (nominal) |
| --- | --- | --- |
| 1790 | 3,079 | £16,318 |
| 1791 | 2,073 | 10,989 |
| 1792 | 3,240 | 17,172 |
| 1793 | 634 | 2,860 |
| 1794 | 872 | 4,603 |
| 1795 | 446 | 2,363 |
| 1796 | 1,147 | 6,083 |
| 1797 | 1,710 | 9,065 |
| 1798 | 2,127 | 11,273 |

Source: *Report of the Select Committee on the State of the Copper Trade,* 1799, app. 34

How all of this was translated into day-to-day trade can best be seen in ships' invoices. Donnan has published some, and a few unpublished ones remain in the Bristol Archives and probably in other port cities, but they are scarce before 1750. For the period 1758–1806 Richardson has located 93 such invoices.[148] "Hardware" (which includes copper, brass, and pewter, that is, nonferrous metals) is most conspicuous in ships bound for Sierra Leone, the Windward Coast, Benin, Old Calabar, and Cameroon. Demand was only modest at Annamabo and the Slave Coast and insignificant on the Gambia — British traders were barred from Senegal by the French. Interregional variations in types of hardware were as pronounced as ever. Copper rods continued to be peculiar to Calabar and manillas to Bonny, while brass pans and kettles were the staples of trade to Sierra Leone and the Windward Coast as well as to Cameroon and Gabon.[149] Earlier, Atkins had insisted on the indispensability of such goods as "Brass-mounted Cutlasses" if one wished to trade on the Windward Coast.[150]

At Benin, manillas had almost entirely lost their value by the opening decades of the century. They were replaced by neptunes, ranging from the small "Spanish" neptunes a foot or less in diameter to pans 2 or 3 feet across weighing as much as 8 pounds. Between 1715 and 1717, the Dutch factor sold all but 419 pounds of his stock of over 2 tons of neptunes, and when he departed, his underclerk requested another 10,000 pounds.[151] Indeed, the reign of Eresonyen, about the 1730s, is remembered as a time when brass was plentiful and when the brass stool (*erhe*) was made.[152] By Landolphe's visits in the later century, trade had fallen off but basins were still in demand: they even functioned as display cases for the rest of the merchandise.[153] The penchant on the Gold Coast was also for "very large brass pans" at this time.[154] Some were, in fact, enormous — hence the point of the demand that the Aşante fill one with gold for their then-overlord, the King of Denkyira.[155] Still more impressive would have been the 50-

and 77-pound kettles included as part of the "sorting" for the purchase
of slaves at Sierra Leone, according to Atkins, although it may be that
we are meant to read it as seven kettles weighing 77 pounds and seven
weighing 50 pounds altogether.[156]

Richardson has attempted to construct sterling exchange rates for various
goods used in the slave trade at various points on the coast at different
moments in the century from 1721 to 1797. By and large, he finds, "brass
pans, copper kettles, and 'neptunes' . . . tended to be rather poor trade
goods as far as the English were concerned." Their prime cost in sterling
was relatively high and stayed that way even into the nineteenth century.
As at the time of the Vijf Dagregisters (1645–47), copper rods and manillas were considerably cheaper: less than half the cost of neptunes at both
New Calabar and Bonny.[157] Inikori's calculations from a single voyage di-
verge somewhat from Richardson's. Analyzing the relative values of the
goods traded on the Windward Coast in 1787 by the *Fly*, he finds that
brass kettles and pans fall in the middle between guns and textiles as far
as profitability is concerned:[158]

| £1 sterling | textiles | 4.0 bars on the coast |
|---|---|---|
| | guns | 13.0 |
| | kettles | 8.5 |
| | pans | 8.3 |

For the same year and the same region, Richardson gives the prime cost
in shillings per unit of account as:

| brass kettles | 2.3 bars |
|---|---|
| brass pans | 2.0 |

Of course, all of these calculations are illustrative rather than definitive:
conditions at both ends of the system could change from one voyage to
the next. But they do serve to underscore the complexity of the trade and
the difficulties of computing returns from specific goods and categories
of goods. And whatever the fluctuations, it seems consistently true that
rods and manillas had a greater purchasing power relative to prime cost,
which helps to explain the eastward shift of the slave trade.

If the English sources are the most abundant and give the clearest picture of the copper trade, it should not obscure the fact that there were also
Frenchmen, Danes, Brandenburgers, Swedes, Dutch, and Portuguese on
the African coast during the seventeenth and eighteenth centuries. What
material is available would appear to confirm the patterns we have already
noted. Although Hamburg and Holland continued to supply copper utensils, the continent became increasingly dependent on British brass, plated
goods, and wrought copper.[159] Nevertheless, much like Bristol, the fore-

most French slaving port, Nantes, also became a center of manufacture for brasswares destined for Africa.[160]

French sources are fullest for Senegal, their primary comptoir in West Africa. Here there was a steady demand for *quincaillerie,* the catch-all term for hardware.[161] Pruneau de Pommegorge observed that copper basins were often given as presents to Moorish gum traders. These basins were also part of the assortment in trade with the Wolofs on the right bank of the river, but it was the neighboring Serer who were the most avid for copper — and here he is specific about the preference for red copper rather than brass — which they used to make a variety of ornaments.[162] On the other hand, brasswares did not form a significant portion of mid-eighteenth-century French slavers' cargoes, if Van Alstein is typical. For the various voyages for which Rinchon has found data, quincaillerie, which included knives and iron bars as well as brass basins, generally accounted for only 1 to 2 percent of the value of the cargo. Van Alstein traded primarily with the Slave Coast and occasionally with the Congo region, so that this seems to bear out the shift in demand in these areas, in fact the lack of a market for copper and brass goods.[163]

By the eighteenth century it had long ceased to be a curiosity that one could buy a human being for brass manillas or barter copper for gold. The copper trade had become enmeshed in the slave trade to an extent never dreamed of by fifteenth-century merchant adventurers. In the nineteenth century it would face the challenge of adapting to legitimate trade and to the protocolonial economy.

— Chapter 7 ——————————————————————

# The Copper Economy
# in the Nineteenth Century

> Ships went out to Africa with holds full of brass
> idols and rings, while cabins were occupied by
> missionaries, an edifying example of a material
> good in competition with an immaterial one.
>
> — HENRY HAMILTON, *History of
> the English Brass and Copper
> Industries*

The copper trade in the nineteenth century elaborates themes from the past and introduces new ones. Sheet metal, now produced on an industrial scale in steam-powered rolling mills, manillas and rods turned out by the ton in Birmingham brass foundries, all flooded African markets, continuing longstanding patterns of consumption. But new areas were brought into the sphere of European brass and copper imports as old ones dropped out: above all, the Congo Basin and East Africa. The extension of coastal distribution systems farther and farther inland reached peoples previously untouched, and brought European metalwares into direct competition with indigenously produced metal just at a time when this production, after a period of expansion, suffered from the twin blows of political upheaval and ecological impoverishment. By a variant of Gresham's law, trade brass drove out African copper in almost all the arenas where the two met head on. These themes have their roots in the pre-1800 world and extend into the twentieth century, but our focus will be primarily on the period down to the eve of colonial occupation.

## INTERNAL TRADE

Information on local and regional trade in copper from African mines is so scanty compared to that on imported metal that it is virtually impossible to write its pre-nineteenth-century history in any detail. In some areas, this history is little more than the description of an industry in decline or an obituary pure and simple.

The primary focus must be on Central Africa: the great copperbelt of Katanga and Zambia, and the less extensive but historically only slightly

154

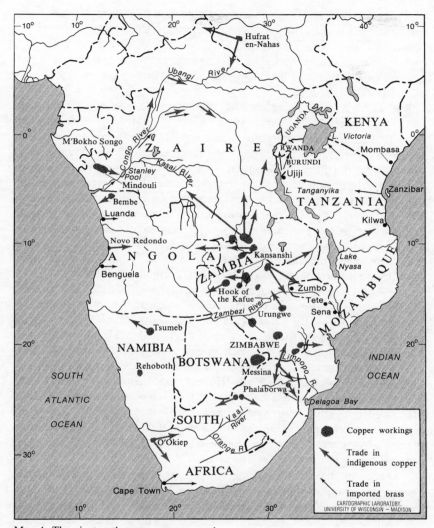

Map 4. The nineteenth-century copper trade

less important metalliferous zones of the Lower Congo. As we have noted in chapter 1, the first indisputable written references to Katangan copper date only from the closing years of the eighteenth century. However, the sheer size of the workings, the wealth of copper objects found in well-dated Iron Age sites in the Upemba Depression several hundred kilometers to the north, and the early radiocarbon dates obtained for copper mining at Kansanshi — all argue for an early exploitation of Katangan copper and for its diffusion over a wide area of eastern Zaire during close to a millennium. The quantity of copper found in the graves excavated in the Upemba region increased over time, illustrating, as de Maret notes, "the progressive development of inter-regional trade,"[1] since Katanga would have been the closest source.

Reefe's remarkable reconstruction of Luba history supplements the archaeological record. He describes the gradual creation of a trading network that linked the copper-producing regions with the southern fringes of the rain forest, passing through the Luba Empire to the Songye kingdoms on its northwestern frontier. This Shaba-Kasai trade, as he terms it, became significant between the fifteenth and eighteenth centuries, reaching its full extension around 1800. Interestingly enough, it came into being without benefit of specialized trading groups or a state monopoly. Instead, "villagers organized themselves for a single trip into ad hoc groups, under a designated leader, and after having solicited the protection of spirits, they travelled to near or distant regions to trade," bands of adult males accompanied by women who carried and cooked the food.

The route to the western copper-mining districts of Mwilu and Kanzenze lay through the Samba kingdom, a client state of the Luba, about 300 kilometers south of the Luba heartland and 200 kilometers north of the mines. So closely were the Samba linked to the flow of copper northwards that "the kingdom . . . was popularly known as *Samba ya Myambo* ('Samba of the Copper Crosses')" because of the abundance of copper crosses, *myambo,* sent to the Luba courts as tribute. Nevertheless Reefe stresses the dangers inherent in these trading expeditions, especially in periods of political conflict. They were "symbolized in a song, sung at the end of the circumcision ceremony at Samba, in which an individual's successful completion of this *rite de passage* was described in terms of a villager's safe return from a journey to the copperbelt."[2]

Just how much farther Katangan copper was going before the nineteenth century, however, remains problematical. Vansina believes that the first imports reached the Kuba only in the eighteenth century and did not become voluminous until the nineteenth.[3] Miller, on the other hand, assumes that copper from Katanga was being traded in Mbundu, considerably farther to the northwest, by the seventeenth century.[4] Is it not more likely that Mbundu obtained its copper from the much closer Bembe mines at this period? By 1770, however, the Bembe mines were "en pleine décadence" — "all those who know how to work the metal are dead," according to a Portuguese missionary report. Only in the region of Novo Redondo was some copper still being produced in Angola.[5]

And yet copper jewelry was worn in profusion in the interior, as Portuguese officials were becoming increasingly aware. In 1799, the governor learned that "it was coming from the Moluas [Lunda] but [he said] we cannot identify the precise sources in spite of all our inquiries."[6] No doubt some copper had been making its way westward before the Lunda Empire expanded into the copper-producing areas, but the growth of empire paralleled the growth of the copper trade. As in the case of the Luba, this trade was initially an extension of the tribute system: new subjects and subsidiary Lunda rulers such as Kazembe were required to send tribute to the Mwata Yamvo, and this included large quantities of copper, especially in the form of crosses. A portion of these were then traded as they were or were drawn into fine wire bangles, wrapped around elephant hairs, by Lunda craftsmen.[7] Both copper and salt found a ready market at Kasanje on the Kwango, and it was here that goods from the Atlantic met those from Katanga. In the opening years of the nineteenth century the Portuguese at Luanda tried to encourage the Lunda to establish a regular export of copper to the west coast, and, in fact, 55 ingots — "bars of copper in extravagant form" — were re-exported to Rio in 1808, harbingers, it was hoped, of things to come. A Lunda caravan reached Luanda in 1812.[8] Though the trade does not seem ever to have matched Portuguese expectations, it continued for several decades; by the time of Livingstone's trans-African journey in 1855, it was already in decline because of growing insecurity of the interior regions.[9]

Lunda expansion similarly affected the eastward flow of copper from Katanga. Kazembe, the Lunda chief who had pushed all the way to the Luapula River, gained control of much of the copper production of eastern Katanga. The two *pombeiros* who crossed Katanga in 1806 and spent four years in Kazembe before continuing on to the Zambezi provide the first eye-witness account of the crucial position the ruler had carved out for himself in the east-west trade of the southern savanna. The Bisa seem to have been indispensable to Kazembe's rise, serving as middlemen in the exchange of cloth and beads for copper ingots and malachite, along with ivory and other products, which they traded to northern Zambia and to the Portuguese settlements of Tete and Sena on the Zambezi.[10] It is intriguing that all of the early accounts of the trade specify that not only copper cast in ingots but also green stones — unsmelted malachite — were in demand.[11] Apparently they were used for ornaments,[12] but malachite powder was also widely used in Central Africa for the treatment of wounds.[13]

While some of the trade from Kazembe went south to the Zambezi, much of it, as Livingstone noted, "crosses Nyassa and the Shire, on its way to the Arab port, Kilwa, and the Portuguese ports of Iboe and Mosambique."[14] A more northerly route, in addition, led to the Maniema country of eastern Zaire or crossed Lake Tanganyika at Ujiji. Most of it was undoubtedly fed into regional trade to obtain the food needed for the ever-growing caravans plying their way between the coast and the interior, to purchase the ivory and slaves that were the primary objects of the caravans, or simply to win the goodwill and protection of local chiefs.[15] In 1870, for example, Livingstone found that "for a copper bracelet three large fowls are given, and three and a half baskets of maize."[16] An Arab caravan he met travelling east from Katanga was transporting five tons of copper on the backs of its slaves.[17]

From the eastern Congo, Katangan copper could be redirected to the interlacustrine kingdoms. Katoke believes that Nyamwezi and Sumbwa traders brought copper to Karagwe, west of Lake Victoria, by the end of the eighteenth or early nineteenth century well before Arab traders appeared in the land.[18] Rwanda and Burundi pose more severe dating problems. Célis and Nzikobanyanka argue that since enormous quantities of the metal were worn in the form of heavy bracelets and packets of copper wire, and since coppersmiths had an important social status as furnishers of royal regalia, there must have been a thriving precolonial trade. According to traditions, it came from markets located between Burundi and Buha, in Tanzania.[19] But what was its ultimate origin, the East Coast or Katanga? Probably Katangan copper preceded or overlapped with European or Indian brass, but when the trade began is impossible to say. In neighboring Rwanda the grave of Cyirima II Rugugira, the Tutsi king who is supposed to have died in 1708 or 1768, contains a number of copper and brass objects. This might seem to be proof that the trade goes back at least to the 1700s—indeed the grave goods have been postulated to be eighteenth century.[20] However the body was kept in a mummified state for some two centuries before being buried in 1931 or 1932, and the presence of brass is suspect: while copper from Katanga could certainly have reached Rwanda in the eighteenth century, the brass would have had to come from the coast at this period, and it is highly unlikely that it would have penetrated this far so early. Campbell, incidentally, recorded a "current legend that many of the early kings of Uganda were buried in copper coffins made from Katangan copper,"[21] but this, too, may well be an anachronism. The oral traditions of the Ganda record that some coastal goods began filtering into the kingdom during the reign of Kabaka Kyabagu in the latter half of the eighteenth century and that his son Semakokiro amassed great quantities of copper and cowrie shells.[22] The copper probably came from the coast, however, along with the shells.

At its peak, then, "the great Central African copper market" of Katanga embraced the southern savanna from Angola to Nyasaland, Tanganyika, and Zanzibar, the Congo Basin from Kasai to Stanley Falls, and the interlacustrine kingdoms. But the groups that transformed its relatively decentralized productive and trading economy and engineered its prodigious expansion in the nineteenth century also sowed the seeds of its disintegration by undermining the fragile political equilibrium of the area. This is not to say that all was peaceful until the Arab-Swahili and Nyamwezi merchant-princes appeared on the scene. The Lunda Kazembes had imposed themselves on the chiefs of eastern Katanga by force — already in 1831 Gamitto was lamenting that the prospects for trade with the Portuguese were dim because the despotic Kazembe "had ruined, through his wars, the lands from which [ivory, copper and green stone] come."[23] At the outset, too, the Swahili and Nyamwezi came as peaceful traders, offering considerable advantages not just to rulers such as Kazembe but also to local economies whose goods they purchased and to whom they brought hitherto unobtainable commodities. By the second half of the century, however, Swahili captains such as Juma Merikani and Tippu Tip were powerful enough to rival traditional authority over a large area of Central Africa. Their large private armies equipped with firearms enabled them to overrun weaker societies and to intervene in strong ones, taking advantage especially of institutionalized succession struggles.[24]

The Nyamwezi and neighboring groups in northwestern Tanzania were also attracted by Katangan copper in the early decades of the nineteenth century. According to information gathered by Burton in the 1850s, the "white" Indian copper coming through from the coast was much less valued in this area than the "red" copper of Katanga[25] — and Katanga crosses can be very red indeed — but just what is meant by "white" copper Burton does not make clear. It could simply be a form of brass or even zinc itself, which he also notes was being imported at this time; as far as I know, other sources do not refer to this type of copper. In any event, a group of Sumbwa Nyamwezi established trading links with copper producers, including Chief Katanga, around 1850. In 1856 the son of one of these traders, the future Msiri, settled in Katanga with a motley band of followers who became known collectively as Yeke, "hunters," because the pursuit of a wounded elephant by hunters had supposedly first led them to the copper.[26] Msiri married into local royalty and established close ties with the Sanga chief Mpande, who controlled the mines in the region of Kambove.

Unlike his Swahili contemporaries, Msiri moved from trade to direct intervention in the production of copper. He brought in blacksmiths from his homeland, who were taught the art of smelting copper by Sanga craftsmen. The *fours volants* that became a feature of Yeke smelting were, in de Hemptinne's view, symptomatic of the period: they were no more efficient than larger permanent furnaces, but they did permit more rapid and more generalized production by enabling more workers to take part in a campaign without the need for a permanent installation. Furthermore, permanent furnaces were more vulnerable to destruction in troubled times, while *fours volants* were knocked down anyway after smelting.[27]

It is generally believed that Msiri also altered the relations of production, imposing a levy on output and eventually shifting to forced labor and a monopoly of the trade, although there is some difference of opinion about this.[28] Certainly as Msiri consolidated his political position, he felt freer to alter customary rights of access to resources and to direct trade as suited his interests, particularly his insatiable need for guns and powder. Thus when trade with the east began to dry up, he sought new markets in the Luena-Lovale country to the southwest, ultimately linking up with caravan routes to the Atlantic coast at Benguela.[29] By this time, however, copper, which had been the lodestone that drew him to Katanga, had dwindled in importance in Msiri's trading empire, for reasons that are not quite clear. Reichard visited two mines in his domains in 1884, noting, "They are exceedingly rich, but are not being worked at present."[30] In 1891–92, the geologist Jules Cornet surveyed seven of the most important ore bodies. "At the time of our visit," he observed, "the country had just been profoundly troubled by long wars; work in the copper mines had everywhere been suspended and seemed to have been for several years."[31] Indeed, the Sanga had revolted in the very heart of the empire. Though Cornet does not mention it, Msiri himself had just been killed in an altercation with Europeans who in their turn would take advantage of the turmoil he had helped to create.[32]

The northern counterpart to the Katanga copper trade was the distribution of copper from the Niari Basin via Stanley Pool in what Sautter has called the "great Congo commerce." Although there is very little information about the details of this vast trading network before the second half of the nineteenth century (except for its extension to the Atlantic coast, discussed in the preceding chapter), there is no doubt about its antiquity; Harms believes that copper and camwood were the earliest goods to have been traded over long distances in the Central Zaire Basin. Porters carried the metal from the mines of Mindouli and M'Boko Songho to the Pool, where it passed from one medium-distance circuit to another until an ever-diminishing amount reached the upper river. There were subsidiary circuits up the major tributaries such as the Alima, Sangha, and Ubangi, and possibly north to the Upper Ogowe as well.[33] Stanley's account of the five-year odyssey of a barrel of European gunpowder from the coast to Ngala country is probably typical also of centuries of exchanges of copper: the powder passed "from district to district, market to market, and hand to hand" through a series of different ethnic groups after leaving the Pool and before reaching the Yanzi. The Yanzi carried it to Irebu, whence it wended its way to Ikengo and finally came into the hands of the Ngala, who brought it to Upoto, the farthest extension of the trade in the 1870s.[34] Even with the advantage of water transport over the main arteries, the presence of so many middlemen inevitably added greatly to the cost. De Brazza had a graphic illustration of this simple economic truth when he noticed that the copper bullets fired at him on the Alima were much smaller than those at Mpio a Bwaani, which was closer to the Pool.[35]

Dupont, one of the first Europeans to visit the Niari Basin, describes the crowds returning from the "famous market in copper" at M'Boko Songho, "which takes place every four days in the middle of the plain."[36] According to Stanley, several hundredweights of copper bars changed hands at the Manianga market, and these became the lubricant of the entire commerce: ". . . at Stanley Pool and on the Congo, texts contemporary with the colonial penetration speak only of copper."[37] As elsewhere, it was used in local exchanges, but also to obtain ivory and slaves to feed international trade. Stanley recorded that in the mid-1880s the Yanzi were selling ivory to the Teke for eleven copper bars per pound.[38] More than a half-century later, Sautter found Teke who still remembered when a male slave could be bought for 40 to 80 bars.[39]

By the 1870s, the zone supplied with copper from the Lower Congo must have come close to meeting that supplied by Katanga, at least in some areas. Similarly, if copper from the Lower Congo was reaching the Uele, a tributary of the Ubangi, as Dupont believed,[40] it may well have complemented that diffused south from Hufrat en-Nahas. The material on Hufrat, however, is so scattered and so fragmented that it is worth going into disproportionate detail.[41]

Hufrat is one of the most remote spots in Africa. Set in a vast plain which turns into swamp during the rainy season, it is infested with malaria and sleeping sickness.[42] The mines were abandoned about 1897, and the depopulation that followed may have brought an increase in tsetse. Supposedly the fame of the mines was the reason for Mehmet Ali's annexation of Darfur.[43] In 1838–39 he sent Burgrath Russegger, an Austrian mining authority, to make a feasibility study, but it appears that Russegger never actually reached the mines, basing his report on information and samples gathered in Kordofan.[44] In the 1850s a Ja'ali Arab, al-Zubayr, settled in the Bahr al-Ghazal and like Msiri in Katanga gradually built up a trade monopoly in alliance with local leaders. He was given a free hand by the Egyptian government and by the Zande chiefs to the south, in return for respecting their authority. In 1869, however, a Moroccan adventurer appeared on the scene whose claim to ownership of the copper mines was backed by the governor of the Sudan. In the conflict that followed, al-Zubayr emerged victorious, and now felt strong enough to subdue the northern Zande chiefs, build up a private army of Zande troops, and eventually, in 1874, conquer Darfur itself. At the same time, he opened up trade with King Munza of the western Mangbetu on the upper Uele, who furnished him with ivory in return for a monopoly of the extremely profitable copper trade. The alliance was short-lived and a power struggle broke out in Mangbetu. Determined to regain control of the region, the Egyptian government sent a force under Gessi Pasha which defeated al-Zubayr's son Sulayman in 1879, but the Mahdist uprising followed almost immediately.[45]

Against this background of chronic violence, the economic history of the area is a complex one. The main trading routes from Hufrat led northward to Darfur and thence east to the Nile Valley, but more especially westward to Wadai, Bornu, and the Hausa states. Barth is the primary source for the trade to the central Sudan: ". . . a considerable supply of this useful and handsome metal [copper] is also imported every year by the Jallaba of Nimro in Waday, who bring it from the celebrated copper-mine, 'el-hofra,' situated to the south of Dar-Fur." Barth estimated the total value of copper imports to Kano, including that from Tripoli (discussed below), at about 15 to 20 million cowries.[46] In a footnote, he added that the Jallaba stood to make a 100 percent profit even when, as was generally the case, they bought the copper in Darfur rather than at the mines: they purchased a kantar (about 50 kilograms) of copper for a young slave, which was equivalent in value to one kantar of ivory, then sold it in Kukawa for 4,000 rotls, equal to two kantars of ivory. The price was about the same in Kano. In the appendix to his *Travels,* Barth again stressed the high return on copper brought to Bornu from Hufrat.[47]

While this copper supplied a thriving local industry in Kano, "only the smaller part of it remain[ed] in the country."[48] The rest was exported throughout the region. In fact, two curious passages in Horneman's *Journal* of 1797–98 may refer to this reexport of Hufrat copper: "copper is imported in great quantity" to Murzuk, he claimed, the trade being in the hands of the Tibbu of Bilma. Then, later, he declared, "The best natural production of Burnu is copper, which is said to be found in small native pieces. That which is gold in Tombouctou and Haussa, is answered by copper in Burnu; the value of all their commodities is fixed by pounds of this metal."[49] Horneman's information was gathered in the Fezzan, for he had died before reaching the Sudan. He was right that the currency of Bornu was based on the rotl, or pound of copper — a fact that may argue for the antiquity of the trade from Hufrat — but was misinformed about the source of the copper.

A number of nineteenth-century travellers refer to a trade down the Benue which may have come ultimately from Hufrat. MacGregor Laird, remarking on the many bronze-casting workshops in Panda just northeast of the

Niger-Benue confluence, noted that the "ore came down the Shary [Benue] from the eastwards."[50] The sphere of Hausa copper- and brassworking extended throughout the Upper Benue as far as Hamaruwa and even Adamawa by mid-century, and possibly earlier.[51] Hutchinson obtained samples of copper from al-Haqi, a Kano smith in Hamaruwa, which al-Haqi said had been brought to Kano by Arabs. Since the copper was in rings, the customary form in which it was traded from Hufrat, this may well have been the source,[52] as it may have been for copper reaching the Cameroon grassfields from the north.[53] Colonists from the Bornu region also settled near Hufrat in the nineteenth century, as the pilgrim route from the central Sudan to Egypt shifted southward for reasons of security.[54]

The intricacies of the market are underscored, however, by the fact that at the same time that copper from Hufrat was reaching the central Sudan it was also competing with or complementing copper coming to Kano from Tripoli and from Egypt, via the ancient Forty Days Road to Darfur. Barth estimated that about fifty loads of copper were imported from Tripoli to Kano in the 1850s.[55] This is confirmed by the Mircher report of 1862,[56] and indeed the trade goes back at least to the seventeenth century. Lavers cites the case of one Muhammad Saqizli, who as soon as he had secured himself in power in Tripoli, "realizing the great profits made by those engaged in businesses with Borno . . . resolved to draw all the trade to himself alone. For this purpose he wrote to the Prince of Fezzan and to Mahi Hamour . . . offering to supply them with large quantities of copper in sheets, paper, Venetian beads and cloth, but he declared that none of his Tripolitanian subjects should have any part of this trade without his consent."[57]

The copper trade from Egypt to the Sudan is of comparable or greater antiquity but took different routes at different periods. As we have noted earlier in chapter 5, Malfante found that it was channeled through Tuat to the western Sudan in the mid-fifteenth century. With the expansion of trade to Bornu, however, the Fezzan became the logical juncture for routes from both Tripoli and Lower Egypt. The Forty Days Road, which had been in eclipse for much of the medieval period, seems only to have been revived in the eighteenth century.[58] Darfur then became the entrepôt not only for copper from Hufrat but also for metal coming from Egypt which might earlier have taken more northerly routes to the central Sudan. Thus at the same time that W. G. Browne included copper among the exports to Asyut in Upper Egypt, he noted that "Jelabs" brought to Darfur from Egypt copper facepieces for horses, a few copper cooking pots, and "old copper for melting and re-working," along with brass and iron wire.[59] Three years later, in 1796, "old copper" ranked second in value only to a particular cotton among exports from Egypt to Darfur.[60] The Arab traveller 'Umar al-Tunisi, who followed the Forty Days Road himself early in the next century, confirmed that great quantities of old copper were being exported to Darfur, where they were melted down with small amounts of zinc to make brass bracelets. Four of these bracelets plus one rotl of salt sufficed to buy a slave. For men of rank, it was indispensable to have their horses' heads adorned with brass plaques, but the most lucrative article of all in Darfur and Wadai, he declared, was "red copper; it is sold at the price of gold." Next in value were zinc, Maria Theresa thaler, and brass sheet.[61] Al-Tunisi simply noted that these metals were imported by "djellab" traders without distinguishing one from another, but certainly both "old copper" from Egypt and "new copper" from Hufrat were part of the commerce.

This becomes much clearer from Schweinfurth's account in the 1870s. He described the penetration of the "Khartoomers" into the northern Congo watershed. Arab caravans opening up trade in ivory with the "Niam-niam" (Zande) carried "huge bars of copper and beads of every description." English copper was most in repute, "but not infrequently," he said, "they make use of the lumps of copper which they obtain from the mines to the south of Darfoor."[62] Elsewhere, he refers to the copper from Hufrat as in the form of rings or "long oval cakes," which are presumably the lumps referred to.[63] Just as in the regions served by Katangan copper, smiths would make up rings of various sizes from the large bars for "small change." Even a finger ring was enough to buy a chicken.[64] The Niam-niam, wrote Schweinfurth, "are an acquisitive people, and never lose an opportunity to increase their store of copper, attaching comparatively little importance to any other wealth." The Mangbetu were, if anything, even more eager for it. The Khartoumers had to supply large quantities of the "red ringing metal" to buy ivory or to gain permission to travel beyond King Munza's realm.[65] So drenched in copper was the court of this king that it is hard to believe the trade was of recent date, although Schweinfurth is probably right in suspecting that before the era of the Khartoumers, the copper could have come from the "Congo region" as well as from Hufrat.[66]

It seems somewhat surprising that old copper from Tripoli could be competitive in Bornu and Hausaland with that from Hufrat—and even more so that English copper shipped to Alexandria could vie with it for the Mangbetu trade. The most obvious explanation is that Hufrat simply could not produce or distribute enough copper to satisfy the demand. Another is that the copper from various sources differed in key ways. Both Browne and Russegger comment on the light color of copper from Hufrat. Browne writes that it "is of the finest quality, in colour resembling that of China, and appears to contain a portion of zink [sic], being of the same pale hue."[67] Or Russegger: "This copper is of a light yellowish colour, extremely fine and pliable."[68] He was unable to detect traces of other minerals in it, but

later geologists have found the malachite ore laced with finely disseminated gold. Christy observes that "the native workmen either failed to realize that the ore contained anything but copper, or knew no way of separating the metals successfully."[69] These traces of gold may have detracted
from the value of the copper by diminishing its redness. As we have seen,
al-Tunisi underscored the particular penchant for red copper in Darfur
and Waday, while Schweinfurth was struck by the redness of Mangbetu
copper.[70]

Hufrat, the Lower Congo, and Katanga were the primary areas feeding
copper into the internal trading systems of sub-Saharan Africa up to the
late nineteenth century, but they were not the only ones. The modern bound-
ary separating Katanga from Zambia is of course artificial: the copperbelt
is continuous between the two countries, and undoubtedly metal from mines
in present-day Zambia was part of the same trade. Nevertheless, with the
exception of Bwana M'Kubwa, most of the deposits in Zambia had been
abandoned before the arrival of Europeans, because the oxide ores closer
to the surface had been exhausted and native smiths were unable to smelt
the remaining sulphides. The zone of oxidation ranged from a few inches
to about one hundred feet, so that in some cases this could indicate a long
history of exploitation.[71] Bisson's excavations, for example, have shown
that mining, which began at Kansanshi about the fourth century A.D., continued until the nineteenth.[72] Roberts believes that production in the Bwana
M'Kubwa area may have expanded gradually until it reached its full efflo-
rescence in the last century.[73] As far as mines in the Kafue region are concerned, some near Mumbwa were still being worked in 1898.[74] While at
Naliele on the Upper Zambezi, Livingstone was told that traders called
"Balokolue" came from the east bringing large quantities of copper for
sale. These traders have been identified as Lukolwe, living south of the
Dongwe in Mankoya District. The copper probably came from Mankoya
itself or one of the other mines in the area.[75] In 1863, African agents in
the employ of the Portuguese at Tete found a cosmopolitan horde at the
court of Sekeletu in Barotseland: Englishmen from Natal, Portuguese from
Benguela, Yao and Swahili from Zanzibar. They were trading for ivory and
some copper, but the reference is too vague to pinpoint the source of the
copper.[76]

Zambian copper was certainly reaching Zambezi markets in the eighteenth century. Portuguese sources are primarily concerned with the fair
at Zumbo, founded in the early years of that century to exploit the prime
geographical location at the confluence of the Luangwa and Zambezi
rivers.[77] An anonymous Portuguese report of 1762 notes that traders from
"Urenje come every year to Zumbo to trade in ivory and in copper, which
they bring ready smelted in great bars, and of which there is great abun-

dance."[78] There has been a good deal of speculation about the identification of "Urenje." It is generally thought that they were ancestors of the present Lenje, living west-northwest of Zumbo and in relatively close proximity to the copper-producing areas of the Hook of the Kafue.[79] Alpers considers that they might even have been Bisa, who after the accession of Kazembe III (c. 1760) became the primary carriers of ivory and copper from his kingdom to the Zambezi markets and the east coast.[80] Conceivably, however, "Urenje" could also be Urungwe, which Garlake has proposed as the source of copper referred to in Portuguese documents of the early sixteenth century. Indeed, documents of the mid-seventeenth century continue to refer to copper from this region of "Ambara" as well as that brought by the Uringi.[81] The cause of all this confusion may therefore be that copper was coming to Zumbo from a number of sources: the Kafue, the plateau country immediately south of the Zambezi, and Katanga. Especially in boom periods there would have been every incentive to increase production and improve distribution, and the 1760s seem to have been such a period. The 1762 report estimates the copper traded annually in the "Rivers" at about two to three tons, most of it coming from Zumbo, though, as Sutherland-Harris points out, in some years no copper came at all.[82]

Some of this copper was undoubtedly recirculated in the regional economy to buy ivory or foodstuffs, but some of it was also exported: "For its quality it is preferred in India to that which comes from Europe," declared the anonymous report-writer of 1762. And yet he admits that the Portuguese traders, obsessed with gold, "never exert themselves for these two commodities [ivory and copper], except when the gold supply fails or to use up spare trade goods,"[83] so that there seems to have been little energy expended in developing copper exports to India. Nevertheless, this is a tantalizingly mysterious subject which deserves to be pursued.

Aside from the possibility that some copper from the Urungwe district may have been traded at Zumbo in the eighteenth century, there is a frustrating lack of information about the production and distribution of copper in the Shona kingdoms after the early sixteenth century. Excavations at Khami and Dhlo Dhlo confirm the continuing predilection for copper anklets and leglets.[84] Sutherland-Harris assumes that the metal was part of the tribute reaching the Rozwi court[85] and it may have been traded by itinerant merchants circulating within the state,[86] but in fact there are precious few references in the written sources, and Beach seems to have found little in the oral traditions. Lancaster and Pohorilenko trace the lack of Portuguese interest to the fact that copper would have been primarily absorbed into the domestic economy, especially if it did not enter into the ivory-slave exchange system as it did in the north.[87] A Portuguese source of 1788 mentions that copper was traded to Manicaland by the Duma of the Sabi Valley.[88] Some mining continued into the nineteenth century, according to an account by Ferão, Captain of Sena,[89] but it is likely that the turmoil in the country, beginning with the Ngoni invasions of the 1830s, took its toll here as in all other spheres.

The output of South African mines also fed an almost exclusively internal market until the late nineteenth century. Even the export trade to English and Dutch stations at Delagoa Bay, as we have noted, was partially redirected to African consumers. Trading networks must have been extensive, since copper ornaments were ubiquitous over much of the interior. While some European copper would have filtered through from the Cape or Delagoa Bay, to be vastly augmented by brass in the nineteenth century, most of it can only be accounted for by the workings of the Transvaal and Namaqualand. As Elphick describes the early trade of the Khoikhoi, there were no markets and no professional traders.[90] By the eighteenth century, however, traders insured the circulation of copper over large areas of the High- and Lowveld, the plateau north of the Limpopo, and the coastal regions of Natal and southern Mozambique. Traditions gathered by Van Warmelo speak of a "constant stream of travellers going to and coming from the copper mines at Messina." Because of the unusual degree of specialization there—both men and women were occupied full-time in the various aspects of mining—everything had to be purchased. Venda, Sotho, Pedi brought cattle and grain; the Tsonga of Mofumo bartered the black plaid cloth that was especially prized at Messina.[91]

Copper from the mines of Little Namaqualand seems also to have been extensively traded. Delesse, who surveyed these mines in the 1850s, believed that they were the source of the ornaments worn throughout the entire Orange River region: "For a long time," he wrote, "it has been noticed that the copper rings worn by the Tswana, the Sotho and the tribes that live along the banks of the Orange River, do not have the color of pure copper." His analysis showed in fact that they contained a proportion of gold, which gave them a yellowish color and which corresponded to that found in ore samples from Namaqualand.[92] Nevertheless, early travellers' accounts also suggest that some Tswana peoples were themselves mining and smelting copper closer to home. Wikar was impressed by the ornaments of copper he found worn by the Khoikhoi on the Orange, and was told that they were made by the "Bliqua" (Tlhaping), who dug their own ore.[93] Later travellers insisted, however, that though the Tlaping made ornaments and tools, they did not smelt metals, but obtained them from the Hurutse.[94] Lichtenstein, on the other hand, pinpointed the source as the "Macquini," a subtribe of the Kwena, living beyond the Hurutse: "It is from these people that the other Caffe [sic] tribes receive their metals: they are reported to be dug out of a vast mountain, one side of which yields iron, the other copper."[95] If we add these tidbits of hearsay evidence to Livingstone's actual observation of the extensive mining operations in the Mabotsa and Kolobeng regions (see chapter 1), it seems clear that considerable quantities of copper were being produced in the border areas between modern Botswana and the western Transvaal and possibly in the Magaliesberg area as well.[96]

As so many other places, mining in the Transvaal seems to have been virtually extinct by the later nineteenth century, but it was still a living memory at both Messina and Phalaborwa.[97] Zulu legend has it that Shaka led an expedition to Messina for copper, and it is recorded that a Venda elder told Trevor that the mines had been filled in for fear of Zulu incursions.[98] But according to the tradition published by Van Warmelo, Messina was the victim of a series of attacks culminating in a massacre by the Ndebele. The reason given was that the Messina miners had become "swollen with pride," insolent and inhospitable to those who came to trade.[99] Whatever may have been their sins of hubris, surely the root cause was the breakdown of traditional political systems as a result of the political upheavals of the *mfecane* and then of the influx of European settlers.

The mines of Little Namaqualand were overtaken by a fever of European mining speculation beginning in 1846 and continuing for several decades.[100] This copper fever extended north of the Orange River in Namibia as well. In 1792 Pieter Brand had discovered that the Bergdamas beyond the Rhenius Mountains were smelting copper, which they exchanged with nomadic Namas for cattle. He was followed by a succession of explorers, lured into this inhospitable land by tales of the red metal.[101] Still farther to the north, Galton and Andersson found that ore was being dug by "Bushmen," who brought it to the Ovambo to be smelted and worked.[102] In many areas, the overlordship of deposits was disputed by indigenous chiefs, so that throughout southwest Africa European intrusion into mining exacerbated old enmities; squabbling among themselves, African leaders were oblivious of the subjugation that awaited them.[103]

One of the earliest copper mines to come to European attention enjoyed a brief resurrection in the nineteenth century. Production at Bembe in northern Angola had died out, as we have seen, during the seventeenth and eighteenth centuries, apparently as a result of Portuguese attempts to bring it under their direct control and probably, too, because of the political disruptions following the disintegration of the Kongo Kingdom. During the 1820s and 1830s, however, both American and English traders discovered that malachite ore "of the richest quality" could be had at the port of Ambriz, brought down from the mountains in baskets on the shoulders of porters.[104] Brooks quotes an anecdote about a Yankee captain who supposedly recognized the green stone, gulled the ignorant natives into believing that he was interested in it only as ballast, and shipped several hundred tons before they or his fellow traders caught on.[105] By now the evidence against such credulity should be obvious!

As the involvement of Liverpool trading houses increased during the 1840s, the British hatched a scheme to exploit the Bembe deposits themselves on a large scale. The Portuguese occupation of Ambriz in 1855 forestalled this. Roads were built into the interior and the mines themselves seized soon afterward. Almost immediately the Brazilian slave dealer who had masterminded the occupation ceded mining rights to the Western Africa Malachite Copper Mines Company Ltd., an enterprise financed with English capital. Ultimately history repeated itself at Bembe. Of the first contingent of twelve miners and a Cornish mining captain whom the English engineer Monteiro took out to develop the mines, eight died within nine months, while the mining captain declared that there was no malachite in the area at all—"where the natives for years previously had extracted from 200–300 tons every dry season!"[106]

In the decade 1857–67 some 1,095 tons of malachite ore were shipped from Ambriz, according to official Portuguese figures.[107] How much was exported from Ambrizette, where the British moved to avoid Portuguese duties, is not known, but the value of British malachite from that port in 1854–55 was put at £50,000.[108] Nevertheless, this was not enough to recoup earlier losses, the country was remote and inhospitable, and once again the mines were gradually abandoned. In 1872 the governor recalled the last garrison that had been stationed in Bembe to protect the company's operations.[109]

## THE EXTERNAL TRADE

Copper and brass continued to be imported into Africa in large quantities during the nineteenth century, showing the regional preferences we have already noted. At the same time, the trade expanded into areas that had been marginal, such as the Ivory Coast and equatorial Africa, or in the case of East Africa, totally undeveloped.

The *Report of the Select Committee on the West Coast of Africa* in 1842 confirmed the accounts of individual traders. In the fifteen-year period 1827–41, British exports of copper and brass were insignificant to Senegal and the Windward Coast, substantial to Sierra Leone, the Gold Coast, and the vast expanse simply designated "Rio Volta to the Cape of Good Hope." To Cape Coast Castle and the Gold Coast, imports increased more than tenfold in these years, from a mere 21 cwt. to 2,423 cwt. Over the entire coast, the report found a 500 percent increase in both weight and value of copper and brass exports.[110] The absence of exports to Senegal is not surprising, since this was French territory. But even Bouët-Willaumez, the most authoritative French source, notes that in 1840 the value of copper sheet and rods shipped to Senegal came to only about 10,000 francs.[111] The French, however, tended to lump all metal imports under the heading "quincaillerie," as the British were later to use the all-purpose "hardware."

Basins of various sizes and sorts as well as rods continued to be part of the standard trade package. From Cape Mount to Cape Palmas, brass pans were necessary to the ivory trade, with neptunes especially prized, as they were also at Cape Lahu.[112] Brass pans, neptunes, manillas, and copper rods all went to make up the Benin "pawn," the unit of account. Nor had copper lost its preeminence in the eastern Delta. At Bonny, neptunes were in particular demand for salt-making, while at Old Calabar copper rods served not only as a money of account but also as an actual item of trade, successfully making the transition from the traffic in slaves to palm oil.[113]

The coast between the Cameroon estuary and Cape Lopez came into its own essentially in the eighteenth and nineteenth centuries, as an important supplier of slaves and ivory and later of rubber. Here, too, copper and brass bars, rings, and basins held their own as an indispensable part of the "round" or "bundle" trade down to the colonial period. As explorers and trading companies pushed their way up the Gaboon and Ogowe rivers, they discovered new markets for their wares. Du Chaillu found the Fang eager to trade ivory for "brass, copper kettles, looking-glasses, flints, fire-steels, and beads. . . . Of all these, however, they set the greatest value on copper and brass,"[114] a taste probably already formed by indigenous traders from the Lower Congo. Even as late as 1883 Brazza was able to purchase an entire sheep for a single brass bell on the Upper Ogowe.[115] The increase in trade brought a rapid rise in the price of African products, just as it had in the early days of trade on the Gold Coast and at Benin.

In contrast to earlier periods, however, Europeans were no longer content to sit in their comptoirs and hulks on the coast, leaving contact with interior markets to African entrepreneurs. The missions up the Niger and Benue to develop inland markets during the middle decades of the century had their counterparts in the French expeditions in equatorial Africa, exploring the Upper Ogowe, the Alima, and the Congo itself.[116] As in West Africa, they ran into stiff resistance from local peoples who benefited from their own monopoly position as intermediaries and who were threatened by both European penetration and the attempts of other ethnic groups to bypass them and make direct contact with European traders. What had not changed, on the other hand, was the complexity of putting together an acceptable assortment of goods. The bells that had been so profitable on the Ogowe found no market at all at other points on Brazza's itinerary.[117] In addition to the differences in the goods demanded, the explorer had to anticipate different currencies of account: during Brazza's 1883–85 mission, for example, this meant pieces of cotton on the Loango Coast, neptunes on the Ogowe, blue beads in Manianga, then copper and brass bars throughout the Congo Basin. He carried 21 cases of manillas of four different sorts, each containing 125 dozen; 20 cases of various types of copper neptunes, assorted bells, bracelets, and chains; not to speak of the textiles, iron goods, etc.[118] On his first mission in 1875 he had astutely included under "articles de Paris" 12 dozen "anneaux pour bras contenant du plomb pour faire du bruit," again a recognition that more than appearance counted when it came to bracelets.[119] Could it also have reflected a knowledge that bracelets manufactured in the Niari Basin, which had long circulated in the same zone, had also been made with a deliberate mixture of lead? "Hoping to surprise and satisfy his clientele," he also had the foresight to stock copper and brass wire in rolls which could be cut to the desired lengths for bracelets and necklaces and fastened with little rivets.[120] This was standard practice in East Africa, as we shall see.

Though imports of both copper and brass now entered trade circuits that had been dominated almost entirely by indigenously produced copper, it was brass that quickly won a preeminence throughout most of the vast Congo Basin. Some groups such as the Teke of the Alima continued to be eager for copper wire to ornament their guns, lances, and knives,[121] but by and large, brass wire, ribbon, bars, basins, nails, and staples flooded the market. It did not spread evenly, however: Johnston noted that the peoples of the Mfimi River had an abundance of brass rods at a time when those living around Lake Leopold II had none.[122] They were still unknown on the Upper Congo before Stanley's arrival in the 1870s, but in the course of the 1880s the imported brass *mitako* rapidly superseded its prototype, the copper *ngiele* from the Niari Basin, as the commercial currency of the region[123] — a tangible symbol of the "opening up" of the continent to waves of explorers, missionaries and traders.

A variant of this phenomenon seems also to have occurred in Southern and East Africa. At both the Cape of Good Hope and Delagoa Bay, the European imports that provided a modest addition to indigenously produced metal were primarily in the form of copper before the late eighteenth century, just as copper, along with iron, was the metal most eagerly sought from the survivors of shipwrecks along the Natal coast.[124] Sheet copper was especially popular at the Cape, where sailors at first snipped small thin squares from kettles and pans to trade with the Khoikhoi.[125] In 1797 Barrow observed that copper sheets were also a staple of trade with the Xhosa, a fact confirmed by Alberti. By this time, nevertheless, brass wire was also in demand.[126] A few years later Burchell stocked both brass rings and brass wire, together with sheets of copper and tin, for his journey into the interior from Cape Town.[127] The same shift seems to have occurred at Delagoa Bay. From the reign of Dingiswayo on, Zulu monarchs encouraged Tonga traders to bring large quantities of brass from the Portuguese at the Bay to meet an apparently insatiable demand.[128] In 1835 Dingane offered to transfer the bulk of this trade to Port Natal if the English could supply as much brass as the Portuguese.[129]

Already by the early decades of the century brass had reached the Highveld. Brass wire was among the trade goods coming regularly into Lesotho at mid-century, and by this time was probably widely dispersed through the interior and beyond the Orange River.[130] In the 1860s brass rods and wire were a standard part of the outfit taken by travelers to the goldfields of the northern Transvaal, Zimbabwe, and Botswana.[131]

Far more massive, however, were the imports of brass wire into East Africa. Though it is possible, as we have noted, that some copper and brass from the Indian Ocean was filtering into the interior before the nineteenth century, it could only have been the merest trickle, given the absence of organized commercial contacts. What exchanges there were would have passed from hand to hand: coastal traders did not reach Lake Victoria, for example, until 1850, and areas to the south only a few years earlier.[132] While the opening up of East Africa is linked to the establishment of the Omani dynasty at Zanzibar, its commercial successes were built on a foundation already laid by the Nyamwezi and other African trading groups who had pioneered caravan routes between the coast and the deep interior, routes intimately related initially to the exchange of indigenously produced metals — copper and iron.

In contrast to other parts of the continent, European copper and brass were imported almost exclusively in the form of wire. To be sure, an occasional copper cauldron would be in demand or copper ornaments would be given as gifts, but Burton makes plain that the requirements of the market were very specific:

> After piece goods and beads, the principal articles of traffic, especially on the northern lines and the western portion of the central route, are masango . . . or brass wires, called by the Arabs hajulah. Nos. 4 or 5 are preferred. They are purchased in Zanzibar, when cheap, for 12 dollars, and when dear for 16 dollars per frasilah [a unit of weight equal to about 30 lb.]. When imported up country the frasilah is divided into three or four large coils, called by the Arabs daur, and by the Africans khata, for the convenience of attachment to the banghy-pole. Arrived at Unyanyembe they are converted by artisans into the kitindi, or coil-bracelets, described in the preceding pages. Each daur forms two or three of these bulky ornaments, of which there are about

11 to the frasilah, and the weight is thus upwards of three pounds. The charge
for the cutting, cleaning, and twisting into shape is about 1 doti of domestics
for 50 kitindis. . . . Thus, the kitindi, worth one dollar each — when cheap,
nine are bought for ten dollars — in Zanzibar, rises to five dollars in the lake
regions. . . . They also import from the coast Nos. 22 to 25 [gauge wire] and
employ them for a variety of decorative purposes. . . . The average price of
this small wire at Zanzibar is 12 dollars per frasilah.[133]

Just how closely intertwined this trade was with its Katangan counterpart
and antecedent is apparent from a number of points. First of all, Burton
observes that the wire was destined particularly for the northern and western parts of the trading area, and it was the experience of many travellers
that it was not until they were well into the interior that they began using
their stocks of copper and brass.[134] And just as Katanga copper had to
be worked for local markets in the eastern Congo, so trade wire from the
coast had to be made up into bracelets by Nyamwezi smiths "to suit the
tastes" of the people. Then, too, there is Burton's suggestive comment that
"the East Africans have learned to draw fine wire, which they call uzi wa
shaba," an apparent allusion to the Nyamwezi apprenticeship to Katangan
copperworkers.[135]

The typical caravan from the coast therefore included a contingent of
porters carrying coils of wire "lashed to both ends of a pole, which is generally the large midrib of a palm-frond, with a fork cut in its depth at one
extremity to form a base for the load when stacked, and provided at the
point of junction with a Kitambara or pad of grass, rag, or leather." Surprisingly, "wire is the lightest, as ivory is the heaviest, of loads."[136] Speke's
expedition of one hundred Nyamwezi porters carried ten frasilahs of brass
wire and nine and a half of copper, making in all thirteen loads;[137] Thomson took a total of forty-four loads of brass, copper, and iron wire.[138] The
coil bracelets made up at Unyanyembe and which Burton labels a "peculiarly African decoration" consisted of a "system of concentric circles extending from the wrist to the elbow; at both extremities it is made to bulge
out for grace and for allowing the joints to play; and the elasticity of the
wire keeps it in its place." Women of some tribes would wear four of these
coils for a total of about twelve pounds on their arms and legs. At Unyam-
nyembe each bracelet was valued at 2 to 4 shukkah, but at Ujiji it would
sell for 4 to 5. Thus with proper timing one could turn a profit of 100
percent.[139] "Wire for native adornment" continued to be a regular item
in Tanganyika customs records well into the twentieth century.[140]

To some extent, therefore, the pattern of the nineteenth-century copper
trade can be seen as a series of intersecting circles. Copper from one
domestic source was distributed over larger areas until it met that from
other zones of production. This may well have happened earlier in some

cases — for example, copper from northern Angola and the Lower Congo may have converged at the Pool in the fifteenth and sixteenth centuries — but it is most apparent in the Congo Basin in the last decades of the pre-colonial period. Because output does not seem to have matched demand, these distributive systems were likely to have been complementary rather than competitive. This was even true of the different mining areas of Katanga that produced for distinct markets. Imports of European copper and brass into equatorial and East Africa may originally have also complemented native metals; indeed, an interesting parallel with the Atlantic and trans-Saharan trades in West Africa is suggested.

At one time it was axiomatic that the discovery of maritime routes to West Africa sounded the death knell for the trans-Saharan trade. If a further *coup de grâce* had been needed, it was provided by the Moroccan invasion of Songhay in 1591. This view was challenged as early as 1965 by J. C. Anene in a paper entitled "Liaison and Competition between Sea and Land Routes in International Trade from the Fifteenth Century." Anene drew his evidence primarily from southwestern Nigeria to show that where trade with the north declined, the reasons were political more than economic. "It does appear," he concluded, "that the development of the sea route notwithstanding, the trans-Saharan routes continued to perform their function to their greatest capacity up to the nineteenth century." The increase in the slave trade to the coast, for example, he explains as an increase in totals, not a diversion, since there were natural limits to the carrying capacity of the desert trade.[141] At about the same time, Newbury's study of the trade of North Africa and the Sudan in the nineteenth century argued equally for revision of the standard view, in the light of his findings that the trans-Saharan trade, so far from being in decline, actually increased before the period of partition.[142]

Leo Africanus, describing the trade as he knew it in the early years of the sixteenth century, noted the great value of Moroccan "vases de cuivre" in the land of the blacks.[143] These and other Islamic vessels of beaten copper and brass served as prototypes for Akan work. Some came directly from North Africa and the Middle East, while others were fashioned in Mali from imported metal. Tradition underscores the high reputation of metalworkers from the north, especially craftsmen from Bono Manso and Dagomba who held honored positions in Aşante.[144] The difficulty comes in identifying the point of transition, when the raw materials and finished products came from the south rather than the north; more likely there were periods of overlap or alternation just as in the case of gold, which sometimes was channeled to the coast and sometimes to the markets of the Niger Bend. In some cases copperwares brought overland from the north seem to have acquired a special cachet: Wilhelm Mueller, a resident of the Gold

Coast in the 1660s, describes "large copper washpans or kettles skillfully punched. These are worth a high price because they are reputed to come from a land far beyond Accania. On occasions I have seen such kettles which have been valued at a pound of gold." Garrard estimates that a pound of gold would have represented no less than twelve years' labor by an Akan gold digger.[145]

Sundström believes that much of the Sudanese interior continued to be supplied from the north down to the nineteenth century. "It can be assumed," he declares, "that copper and brass goods traditionally imported to West Guinea (e.g. Portuguese Guinea, Sierra Leone, Liberia) did not pass beyond the consumers of the Coast and its immediate hinterland. Whether the supply to the Senegal-Niger area from the North was of a sufficient volume to make imports from the West and South superfluous, or whether the latter were never sufficient to supply the demand beyond the coastal fringe cannot be ascertained."[146] However, he seems to overstate the importance of brass and copper in the western branch of the trans-Saharan trade in the nineteenth century: Miège's work has shown that it no longer played a significant part.[147] By this time demand for these goods seems hardly to have existed at Timbuktu and Jenne,[148] while Mossi and Senufo artisans were being supplied with copper and brass rods from the coast via such trading centers as Salaga, Kong, and Bondouko.[149]

How, then, do we explain the continuing imports of brass and copper from Tripoli and Alexandria to the central and eastern Sudan, in the face of the ever more aggressive European imports added to the competition from Hufrat en-Nahas? According to Staudinger (1889), the brass and copper used by Hausa smiths came from both the Arabs and the English: "Bent copper and brass rods have a constant value," he declared, adding that the finished metalwork was so cheap that European goods could scarcely compete.[150] If this was true in the 1880s, it was certainly more so earlier, for Bornu and the Hausa cities had long supplied such wares to a vast hinterland, as we have seen. Landolphe's eighteenth-century account of traders from "Ayeaux" coming to Benin may in fact refer not to Oyos but to Hausa, in Ryder's view. "Whoever these men were," he comments, "they afford one of the few glimpses available of Benin's commercial and political relations with the states of the interior which were always more important than its dealings with Europeans."[151] Benin, Oyo, Nupe—all were for several centuries in a pivotal position analogous to that of the markets of northern Ghana between the trading systems of north and south, east and west.[152] Lest we overestimate the area of diffusion of European goods before the mid-nineteenth century, it is worth reflecting on observations such as Allen and Thomson's that even in 1840 few European goods— except guns and powder—were to be found in the Idah market, the most important one in the *atta*'s kingdom on the Lower Niger.[153] Were the brass ornaments offered for sale there still products of the northern trade?

## BRASS VERSUS COPPER

By the late nineteenth century, indigenous copper mining in Africa was almost extinct. In the Congo Basin, in southern and eastern Africa, it had not survived the flood of imported metal, especially of Birmingham brass. Aitken's history of the Birmingham and Midland brass industry shows that orders for the "guinea rods" that circulated inland from Calabar frequently amounted to 5 to 20 tons each. The demand for tubular rings was on the same scale: "Some idea will be gathered of the extent of Birmingham orders for this commodity," he comments, "from the fact that some three years ago [1862] one order executed in this town extended to 20,000 dozen or 240,000 rings, 3½″ diameter, the weight of brass consumed in their manufacture amounting to nearly 23½ tons."[154] Different regions continued to have their preferences for rods, manillas, coils, basins, and the like. Copper did not disappear entirely from the market: Thomson noted that the Chagga, for example, preferred pure copper to brass in the mid-nineteenth century, and in Burundi copper continued to be appreciated more than brass down to the present.[155] Generally speaking, however, brass took over the market.[156]

The shift from copper to brass had taken place in a number of areas served by the maritime trade well before the nineteenth century. On the Gold Coast, Vogt believes that it was almost complete by 1530: he has found that in subsequent decades copper manillas and basins were rarely offered for sale in any quantity.[157] At the Cape of Good Hope there was a fad for brass early in the seventeenth century. Elphick suggests that the hardness and shininess of brass may have been behind it, as well as the fact that brass may have more closely resembled the yellowish copper the Khoikhoi had been accustomed to receive from Little Namaqualand. He notes, however, that sailors at the time blamed the change on a particular Khoikhoi who had been carried off to England and who served as trading intermediary on his return, instigating his fellow countrymen to drive harder bargains than they had been wont to do. They now insisted on "brass Kettels which must be verie bright," and many more of them for their sheep and oxen.[158] Since the bulk of imports mentioned in subsequent company records seem to have been of copper, this may have been a passing fancy.

Torday explained the immense value of brass among the Bushoong in terms of its rarity. Copper had come earlier from Katanga, but when brass appeared from the west, it "was so rare that it had a value equal to our gold and the king alone was allowed to possess or use it." [159] In the Rubunga region of the Upper Congo, Stanley found that "copper was despised, but brass wire was gold — anything became purchasable with it except canoes." [160] Brass would still have been a novelty in 1877 at the time of Stanley's passage, which may or may not explain this preference. Schweinfurth noted that among the Dyor of the Upper Nile, brass had "about thrice the value of copper" even though it had been imported long before the arrival of the Khartoumers. [161] There were of course practical reasons for choosing one metal over the other. Brass casts more easily than copper — and yet Benin was conspicuous in the sixteenth century for continuing to prefer copper over brass from the Europeans. Brass is also more resonant, and we have seen repeated references to the sonority demanded of trade metals: Vogt comments that Gold Coast inhabitants became adept at testing alloys by striking two pieces together and gauging the tone. [162] Copper, on the other hand, is easier to work with a hammer.

On the European side, brass was cheaper to produce than copper. In Speke's accounting of the trade goods he took to East Africa, 10 frasilahs of brass wire cost 90 dollars, while 9½ frasilahs of copper wire cost 130 dollars, some 50 percent more. [163] Nevertheless, cost of manufacture in Europe was not always related to purchasing power in Africa — trade assortments still had to include more and less profitable goods — and, in any case, European traders had only a limited sphere in which to maneuver. In the end, they had to accommodate to African taste, and taste in copperwares could be almost as elusive as taste in textiles and beads. This is a question to which we will return in part III.

Questions of preference aside, there are other factors that were weakening the position of the indigenous copper industry entirely apart from the competition of imports. We have frequently referred to the political upheavals that undermined traditional economic structures in the region of Hufrat, in Katanga, in the Transvaal, and in Zimbabwe. Even without these disruptions, many mines would have been abandoned because the oxide ores were worked out or because miners had reached the water table. Virtually no attention has been paid to the ecological effects of copper mining in Africa, and yet they must have been far-reaching. One has only to recall Dupont's description of the total deforestation in the area of M'Boko Songho in 1887 (see p. 20) to form some picture of the long-term devastation wrought by mining — Brouin's comment on the "rareté du combustible" around Azelick would seem to be a classic of understatement. [164]

If, as Vansina says, copper from the mines of the Lower Congo "could apparently no longer match the price of brass" in the 1880s, [165] could this not perhaps have been the result of a dwindling supply of proper fuel for smelting and casting? Goucher has shown that the West African iron industry declined because of environmental changes, and in particular because of widespread deforestation and consequent "scarcity of combustibles." [166] The case of copper may have been parallel, with the deforestation begun at Azelick and Akjoujt ending at M'Boko Songho.

# Totals: Toward Quantification

Ci inviano . . . i rami crudi & raffinati in quantità incredibile.

—GUICCIARDINI (1567)

African miners excavating giant open stopes or boring narrow shafts to extract ores to be smelted into copper; camels laden with brass and copper wares plying the Sahara; caravels outward bound to African ports with cargoes of manillas, rods, and neptunes. What does it all add up to? What kind of global figures are implied in the data for indigenous production and for the importation of copper and copper alloys into sub-Saharan Africa?

No one has yet had the temerity to try to estimate total African production up to the late nineteenth century, but there have been figures galore for individual mines and mining areas, as we have seen. Ball estimated native production in Katanga, for example, at a grand figure of 100,000 tons.[1] Output at Kansanshi and Bwana M'Kubwa in Zambia may have reached several hundred tons per year, according to Roan Antelope sources, that of the Messina mines perhaps 10,000 tons during the centuries of African exploitation.[2] Lambert puts the yield of the Grotte aux Chauves-souris at Akjoujt at some 40 tons.[3]

These figures represent informed guesses based on the size of ancient workings. Fripp warns against putting too much stock in such estimates. Ancient workings were often filled in to hide their existence or to keep livestock from falling down the holes; they tended to collapse under ordinary conditions of weathering. Refuse dumps consisting of finely broken up debris were absorbed into the landscape when they were not used to fill in shafts and stopes.[4] Even if the volume of material removed were accurately measurable, there would have to be an acceptable formula for reckoning the metallic yield from a given quantity of ore. This in turn would depend on its richness and the efficiency of local technology. For example, the malachite ores worked by the Yeke had a copper content of more than 40 percent so that 50 kilograms of washed and sorted ore should have produced about 20 kilograms of metal.[5] In the absence of fluxes, a good deal of metal was commonly lost in slags, however. In fact, calculations based on the volume of slag are preferable to those based on extent of mine workings in many cases. Warnier and Fowler have demonstrated the validity of this approach in quantifying nineteenth-century iron production on the Ndop Plain in western Cameroon.[6] Copper slags would have their own ratios of slag to metal, and would have to have escaped being swamped by modern workings.

The problem has also been approached from another angle: the output of individual miners and teams of miners. At M'Boko Songho, Pleigneur believed that a force of twenty miners could extract 300 to 400 kilograms of malachite per day.[7] In Katanga, Marchal compiled figures for miners in the different chefferies immediately before, during, and after Msiri, arriving at a grand total of some 80,000 kilograms of finished copper per year or about 90 short tons.[8] De Hemptinne's figures for the same period and for the entire central mining area of Katanga are considerably higher. Based on oral traditions relating to output per smelter, he claims that about 700 (long) tons of copper were produced from 1850 to the arrival of the Union Minière at the end of the century.[9] In 1871 Livingstone met an Arab-Swahili merchant whose ten slaves allegedly had produced 3,500 pounds of copper in three months' work at mines in southern Katanga.[10] But we must remember that mining was a dry-season occupation, limited to several months of the year, and that political difficulties, natural disasters, and supernatural interventions could all affect productivity.

We have at least the illusion of greater certainty when it comes to imported metalwares, because there are written documents. And yet as far as the trans-Saharan trade is concerned, it is only an illusion. The camel caravan buried at Ma'den Ijâfen carried about a ton of brass rods. How many such caravans were there annually? How many others did not make it? Over how many years or centuries? Noting the large numbers of cuprous bowls and basins that reached the Akan from the north, Garrard has suggested that they probably amounted to 2 to 3 tons per year, equal to 10 to 15 camel loads, 45 to 70 donkey loads from the Niger to the forest, and 80 to 120 headloads into the forest.[11] This is a graphic way to breathe life into figures, but here, too, we run into the problem of time span. Nor can we safely take averages and simply multiply them by the number of years postulated for the trade, since this does not allow for periods of disruption along the route and at either end or for the host of other factors that affected such commercial contacts. Thus Barth's estimate that 50 loads of copper were shipped annually from Tripoli to Kano in the mid-nineteenth century assumes peace and relative prosperity—hardly characteristics of Sudanese history.[12]

The same is true for the maritime trade. The wild fluctuations in English exports of copper and brass to Africa year by year through the eighteenth century would disappear if we took only decennial averages or a single total for the entire century, and yet each of the fluctuations tells us something about the societies in question (or will if we are able to decipher them fully): about production, demand, profitability, communications, conflict, human fallibility.

What *do* we know, then, about quantities of copper reaching Africa by sea? We know that in the first fifty years of the sixteenth century, the Portuguese shipped about 45 tons of copper and brasswares annually to the Gold Coast, a total of about 2,250 tons.[13] This does not include exports to other parts of the coast nor exports by other European nations. These high levels were not maintained throughout the century but did resume in the period of Dutch activity, in Africa. Whether the 1635 estimate of Dutch shipments of 545 to 763 tons per year is credible or not, there seems little doubt that the trade was in full expansion. This expansion was dwarfed in its turn by the explosion of British exports in the eighteenth century.

English Customs House data are the solidest quantitative documentation we are ever likely to have about the copper trade, and yet even they have their limitations. Most important, they only record shipments to Africa from English ports. Since a great deal of battery was purchased directly in the Netherlands and carried directly to West Africa, it does not show up in customs figures. Hence they are minimum rather than complete records. And of course they are limited to English shipping—we need comparable data from other trading nations, especially France. Nevertheless, when we add up all the exports and reexports from 1699 to 1808, it comes to a total of 17,886.85 short tons of copper and brass in their various forms.

Evidence contained in Parliamentary Reports of 1842 and 1865 shows that British exports continued at high levels in the nineteenth century. Between 1827 and 1841, 1273.6 tons of brass- and copperwares were exported to African ports from the Senegambia to the Cape of Good Hope, an average of some 85 tons per year, although here, too, there were tremendous fluctuations from year to year and from region to region. By 1865 the picture is blurred, because copper and brass are lumped under the general rubric "Hardware." But Aitken assures us that Birmingham manufacturers frequently received orders for 5 to 20 tons of brasswares; one order, in 1862, consisted of rings totalling almost 23½ tons of brass.[14] A minimum base estimate of English brass and copper exports to Africa from 1699 to 1865 would therefore come to about 20,000 tons.

From this base a *very* conservative calculation of all quantities of copper and brass ending up in sub-Saharan Africa from the beginnings of copperworking in Aïr in the second millennium B.C. to the later nineteenth century A.D. would total some 50,000 tons. If Ball's estimate of Katanga production or Blommaert's of Dutch exports in 1635 should turn out to be anywhere near the mark, we would have to much more than double this figure.

It is next to impossible to visualize such amounts. Fifty thousand tons would equal 100 million of the rods traded in the Bight during the seventeenth century or 20 million neptunes. It would equal about 300 million of Dapper's brass bracelets. The 2,464 tons of metal redeemed in the course of Operation Manilla themselves represented 32,354 manillas of three varieties.[15] Still harder to imagine is what has become of it all. Willett has commented that the entire Ife and Igbo-Ukwu finds of metal amount to only about 530 pounds.[16] These, together with the discoveries at Sanga, in the Senegambia, on the Zimbabwean Plateau, are surely only the tip of the iceberg. Fynn noted in his *Diary* that after Shaka's assassination, several tons of brass, beads, and other valuables were collected for burial with the dead ruler.[17] Later in the century and across the continent, a British expedition in Aro country discovered caves in which several tons of brass and copper rods had been hidden away with guns and other weapons.[18]

One is tempted to suggest that the soil of Africa may be red not only with lateritic earth but with the tons of copper and brass buried beneath.

# Part III

# COPPER IN TRADITIONAL AFRICAN SOCIETY

## Chapter 8

# Copper as a Medium of Exchange

> There is a copper mine outside Takadda. The
> people dig for it in the earth, bring it to the town,
> and smelt it in their houses. . . . They make it into
> rods about the length of a span and a half: some
> are of fine gauge and some thick. . . . It is their
> means of exchange.
>
> — IBN BATTUTA, *Travels*

One of the primary uses of copper in Africa has been as currency. Currency is generally defined as anything that is widely accepted for goods or in discharge of other kinds of business obligations — that has "undifferentiated purchasing power" — and that possesses the property of being expressed in units.[1] It might be just as well to delete the word *business* lest it suggest too narrow a role for currency, since copper, like other African currencies, entered into the social and prestige sphere as much as into the market economy.

Goods functioning as currency can actually change hands or they can be "invisible," a recognized standard against which the items that do change hands are evaluated. Most, if not all, invisible currencies were at one time circulating mediums, replaced when they were no longer required or available as tangible goods, or when demand assumed the form of an assortment of goods rather than a single commodity.[2] When appropriate, too, copper, in common with other currencies, could be withdrawn from circulation and transformed into objects serving other purposes, but never losing the connotations of value on which its initial role as money had been predicated.

There has been considerable and sometimes heated debate about whether general purpose money even existed in traditional African economies. The distinction between general and special purpose money may be unnecessarily rigid, just as the distinction between barter and currency exchange can be a fine one even today. As Allen has pointed out apropos of trade in the ancient Mediterranean, "when precious metals changed hands in the course . . . of trade . . . their status was that of any commodity," whether they were in the form of coins or not. Indeed, the greatest trading nation of all, Carthage, came late to minting coins.[3] Similarly, in precolonial Africa copper was always a commodity at the same time that it was a standard of value, and the many forms in which it was traded are to be ex-

185

plained partly by the exigencies of transport, partly by the ultimate uses for which it was intended. It circulated in the form of lumps, ingots, rods, bars, wire, rings, basins, knives, bullets, "top hats" (*musuku*), and "golf clubs" (*marale*), but virtually never as coins.

## THE INGOT ZONES OF CENTRAL AND SOUTH AFRICA

The evidence for the copper currencies of Central Africa comes primarily from finds of both ingots and ingot moulds, many of them undated, and from travel and ethnographic accounts. Thanks to the work of Bisson, Garlake, and de Maret, much of the earlier confusion in typologies has been untangled. The picture that now emerges suggests the beginnings of standardization at Kipushi in the period between the ninth and twelfth centuries A.D., with the very gradual diffusion of copper currencies over a wider area, so that by about 1400 A.D. there were at least two well-defined types of currency.[4]

The first of these have been found in the extensive grave sites of the Upemba Depression in southeastern Zaire. All are unflanged *H*-shaped crosses, but they vary considerably in size. The smallest range from 5 to 15 millimeters, the next from 16 to 35 millimeters, the medium from 36 to 70 millimeters, and the large from 71 to 150 millimeters. In addition, 2 crosses exceeding 150 millimeters were found in separate burials at one site. Of the 1,215-odd crosses or *croisettes* unearthed thus far, the greatest number are of the smallest variety:

| | |
|---|---|
| 648 | very small |
| 493 | small |
| 62 | medium |
| 8 | large |
| 2 | very large |

This classification, it should be remembered, is based on length, not weight, and in the absence of precise measurements by his predecessors, de Maret was forced to extrapolate for the whole of the corpus from the 221 that could be measured with precision.[5]

The second type of ingot is that associated by Garlake with the Ingombe Ilede-Chedzurgwe culture complex. More than sixty of these have been identified, all similar in form to those found at Ingombe Ilede in the Middle Zambezi Valley and at Chedzurgwe in the Urungwe District of Zimbabwe. They are in the shape of a St. Andrew's cross, with long arms in relation to the mid-section, trapezoidal in cross-section, and a distinct flange on the bottom edge. They are about 30 to 33 centimeters long on the diagonal but of varying thicknesses and hence of varying weights. Of the eight found at Ingombe Ilede, six weighed 4 to 4.5 kilograms, two weighed 2.3 and 2.6 kilograms respectively. The two ingots from Chedzurgwe weighed 3.1 and 3.5 kilograms.[6] One ingot of this type has turned up at Chumnunga, southwest of Great Zimbabwe, well beyond the ordinary range of circulation. The ingots produced at Great Zimbabwe itself were evidently of a very different sort: simpler, smaller, rimless, to judge by the moulds or mould fragments found by Bent and Hall.[7] (Diagram 2 illustrates the variety of ingot design.)

The very small croisettes found at Sanga et al. and derived presumably from Katangan mines to the south date principally from the fifteenth through the eighteenth centuries, according to de Maret's revisions, although a few have been found in somewhat earlier graves. The much larger crosses from Ingombe Ilede and the Zimbabwe Highveld have been dated to the fifteenth and sixteenth centuries, so that the two zones are very roughly contemporary. Both obviously served as units of value, since they were of uniform shape with gradations in size, but what are we to make of the extreme difference in size between the two areas? Bisson argues that the Ingombe Ilede ingots "cannot be viewed as anything but a limited purpose currency. Their size, scarcity and association in the burials with ceremonial items (hoes) and emblems of status (gongs) place them strictly within the prestige sphere." If they were to have functioned as general purpose currency it could only have been through conversion into smaller units, most especially into the copper bangles found so abundantly not only at Ingombe Ilede but throughout Later Iron Age sites on the plateau.[8] Bocarro used such bangles in his travels northeast from the Zambezi in 1616, and it was, as we have seen, standard practice in the nineteenth century to transform the bars and crosses from Katanga as well as the coils of brass wire from the coast into bracelets, to provide an all-purpose currency. Large ingots would certainly also have been the raw material of the little copper bars, about one-half span in length and two fingers in width, that dos Santos mentions as a currency for small purchases in the "Rivers" (the Lower Zambezi) in the late sixteenth century.[9]

De Maret explains the small size of the Sanga croisettes as part of his provocative reconstruction of the monetary history of central Shaba, a reconstruction based on the unique evidence of 300 excavated graves covering a thousand years. He notes that although there is a profusion of copper in the graves of the classic Kisalian period from about the tenth to the fourteenth centuries, nothing about the objects suggests a uniformity or standardization "other than that imposed by the constraints of the metal." The only case in which one might question whether the largest and thickest rings might have functioned as objects of value as well as objects of

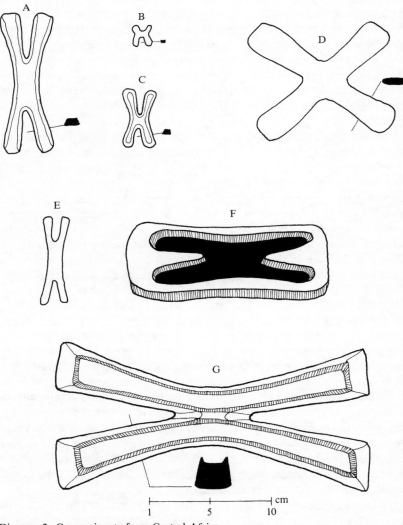

Diagram 2.  Copper ingots from Central Africa.
          A–C.  Crosses from Sanga, showing three typical sizes (after Bisson, 1975)
          D.  "Handa" ingot from Northwestern Zambia (after Bisson, 1975)
          E–F.  Ingot and ingot-mould from Great Zimbabwe (after Caton-Thompson, 1970)
          G.  Flanged ingot like those from Ingombe Ilede/Chedzurgwe (after Garlake, 1970)

adornment is that of a newborn baby buried with twenty-two copper rings having a mean diameter of 55 millimeters and a cross-section of 4 millimeters: "Piled on the pelvis, these rings clearly were not worn by the infant." Their ritual function may have been the dominant one here, however. None of these Kisalian graves or the related Katotian sites contain any sort of ingot. Either copper was not reaching the region in ingot form, or ingots had not yet acquired a symbolic function that would have dictated their inclusion in burials.

When the crosses at last make their appearance in the succeeding Kabambian A and B periods (fourteenth to eighteenth centuries), de Maret finds a clear evolution from larger to smaller. He also finds a number of other intriguing changes which he summarizes in terms of a sixfold process:

1. An increasing standardization of the format of the croisettes
2. A diminution in their size
3. A rise in the total number of croisettes
4. An increase, followed in the Kabambian B by a drastic decrease, in the total weight represented by the croisettes
5. An increase, then probably a decrease, in the number of croisettes in each burial
6. A shift in placement of the croisettes from the thorax to the hips and hands

What this suggests to him is that the earliest (and largest) ingots were limited in circulation to the prestige sphere, which may well have included matrimonial exchanges. The diminution in size and the accompanying increase in numbers probably indicates, as Bisson proposed, the gradual transformation of the croisettes into a commercial currency, or what de Maret prefers to call *monnaie polyvalente*. This in turn would have been intimately connected with the expansion of the market economy of the Luba state, which would have heightened the demand for copper to be employed as currency, especially if it was constantly being withdrawn from circulation for burials and other forms of thesaurization. Radiocarbon dating becomes much less accurate the closer ones moves toward the present, but it is striking that the croisettes disappear almost completely from the graves that are considered the most recent: "having become too numerous, they finally lost all value" and were replaced in the nineteenth century by beads in this region, although in other areas fed by Katangan copper various forms of crosses continued to circulate, as we will see, until much later. Inevitably, attempts to write the history of currency from burial sites rather than market places carries dangers, but it is a tribute to the creativity of archaeologists that they are beginning to break through the impasses of the older economic anthropology.[10] One would need a great many more dated ingots to know when Central African casters were able to achieve the precision of Akan brass casters, for example. When Arnot visited copper mines of the "Garenganze" kingdom in Katanga in the mid-1880s, he was struck by the uniformity of the finished product:

> This business is handed down from father to son, and the instructions of forefathers are followed with the greatest accuracy. At one place the copper is cast in the form of a capital H, and the angles of the figure are perfect. At other mines it is cast in the form of a Maltese cross, the mould being made in the sand by the workers, with their fingers; and out of twenty casts from such a mould scarcely a fourth or an eighth of an inch difference is discernible.[11]

Uniformity of shape is, to be sure, less surprising than uniformity of weight, which Arnot does not specifically address and which would have been a matter of thickness.

But the account is interesting also for a number of other points. As Katangan copper expanded its market currency role, it was cast and traded in increasingly diverse forms. Whereas the Kipushi mines turned out these croisettes during Phase I (ninth to twelfth centuries), in the succeeding phase (fourteenth to sixteenth centuries), they produced larger ingots identical to the Ingombe Ilede model. Presumably these were not traded northwest to the Luba sphere, where they have not been found, but south to Zumbo and the Zambezi network. They may also have gone more directly eastward, bypassing the Zambezi: the hoard of eight copper ingots found at Chombe in Malawi is undated, but they, too, are similar in shape and length to the Ingombe Ilede type, although somewhat lighter.[12] By the time of Livingstone, Arnot, et al., the different mining areas within Katanga were casting currencies in a multiplicity of forms. The largest ingots were those produced in the central zone by the Sanga predecessors of the Yeke: the *mukuba wa matwi* or "copper with ears," a bar some 90 centimeters long and 6 to 7 centimeters wide which terminated in two transverse extremities, the "ears." It weighed 50 kilograms and was normally fixed to a stick and carried by two men. A medium-sized version weighed 12 kilograms, so that two would make up a single porter's load. According to de Hemptinne, the largest represented the purchase price of a female slave; if she had been exceptional, an extra small cross would have been added.[13] He acknowledges that he never actually saw a mukuba wa matwi, but Livingstone saw variants: "large bars shaped like the capital 'I.' They may be met with of from 50 pounds to 100 pounds weight all over the country and the inhabitants draw the copper into wire to form armlets and leglets."[14] At Chinsamba's, near Lake Nyasa, he had been offered a bar four feet long.[15]

The classic currency associated with Katanga is the $X$-shaped cross, the *handa* (color illust. 2). This was produced in the western zone for the markets of the Lomami and Kasai, and eventually reached as far as Angola and the Atlantic coast. Some forms had a raised rib running along the center of the arms.[16] Unfortunately, not enough of them have been studied to know what the primary units were, and the literature is apt to use the word *cross* or even the designation *St. Andrew's cross* indiscriminately, without making a clear distinction between the different types. All of them are referred to as handa and the weights given range from about a half-pound to 2 kilos.[17]

The large crosses and bars represented a convenient way to transport copper where demand was heavy. They could easily be stockpiled for fashioning bracelets or thesaurized in royal treasuries. The Bisa of Zambia still keep such a store of ingots on Cisi Island in Lake Bangweulu.[18] By the mid-nineteenth century, however, the use of copper currencies was so generalized that the Yeke added a number of refinements. They cast ingots of 2 to 3 kilos which were apparently a unit of account but not a circulating medium. From these they made three types of goods: wire, bullets, and hoes. About 15 meters of heavy gauge wire could be produced from a single ingot, and it was this caliber of wire which was reproduced in Europe for trade with the interior from Zanzibar to make the familiar heavy bracelets. The Yeke also took the wire a stage farther, drawing it much finer until it was only half a millimeter in diameter. They would then wind it around a vegetable fiber mixed with goat and animal hair to produce the *mutaga,* the most common currency within the Yeke sphere. These bracelets and the bullets both had a higher value per unit weight than the ingots, but since de Hemptinne does not tell us how many could be made from an ingot, we cannot calculate the relative values with any accuracy. Curiously enough, he suggests that even lumps of unrefined copper seem to have had a standardized size and value.[19]

There seems little question, then, that copper came to function as a general currency in the wide area supplied by Katangan sources, but we are left with a host of unanswered questions. When was this evolution accomplished — did it wait on the integration of the area in East Coast networks or was it achieved without any outside stimulus whatsoever? Was there any standardization, by weight or size, of the different currency forms produced by the various mining areas of Katanga, so that they could be exchanged for one another, be mutually convertible? If so, what would have served as the basic units of measurement? Why is there so little evidence for the use of copper currency in Zimbabwe after the seventeenth century and virtually none at all in Zambia, aside from Ingombe Ilede and the presumptive evidence of copper bangles in grave sites?

There are even more questions surrounding the copper currencies of the

Transvaal. Here copper was cast in a variety of ingot forms also—blocks, hemispherical buns, nails, musuku and marale—but only the last two are known to have served as currency. No examples of the cross or *I* currencies have been found south of the Limpopo,[20] nor have the Transvaal ingots been found to the north;[21] they seem to have been entirely separate currency zones.

The musuku has a highly unusual shape which has been likened, *faute de mieux,* to a top hat (diagram 3). Fripp describes them as "ancient ingots of copper, rectangular but with many finger-like protrusions on the lower side. The whole ingots were each roughly eight inches long, four inches wide, and four inches deep. They were slightly tapered towards the bottom. The projections on the lower side seemed as if they had been produced by the impress of a slender finger up to the first joint in the bottom of the mould. The depth of these imprints . . . would vary from about half an inch to about an inch and a quarter."[22] Louis Thompson's wife interviewed a number of elderly informants in their own language about the

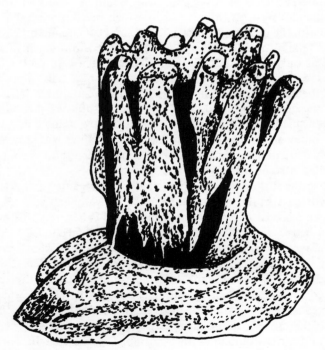

Diagram 3. Musuku (after Stayt, *BaVenda*)

musuku, one of whom claimed to be a descendant of the head man in charge of the Messina mines when they were closed by the Venda chief in the 1860s. She was told that the word is derived from Karanga *tsuku,* meaning red, and refers to two ingots of similar form, the one commercial, the other ceremonial.

The commercial ingots, already extremely rare by the 1930s when the interviews took place, varied in shape: the smaller ones were cylindrical, the larger ones rectangular. The top was decorated with studs set in rows equidistant from each other, with the number of studs indicating the amount of copper in the ingot — roughly a quarter of a pound of copper per stud. Thus Thompson's sample of ingots gave the following weights:

| studs on top in 3 rows (base missing) | lbs. | ozs. |
|---|---|---|
| 13 | 3 | 2 |
| 15 | 3 | 5 |
| 28 | 6 | 14 |
| 38 | 10 | 3 |
| 40 | 10 | |

He claims that the largest one took two men to lift, but he does not say how much it weighed.

The ceremonial musuku differed in that the studs on the top were larger, the interior of the body hollow or filled with sand, and the bases much broader. They varied slightly in size and in the complement of studs.[23] Informants refused to discuss the uses of these musuku. Thompson was content simply to label them ceremonial, but others have speculated that they were intended for ancestral or fertility rituals. Dicke, for example, concluded that they served religious purposes "or purposes in connection with the sacrifices made by the natives," suggesting that the form imitated a now extinct, insect-eating cactus which was a sacred symbol of the ancestors.[24] Stow was even more imaginative in declaring that the musuku "appears to have been a *madula,* a phallic charm."[25] Plumping for the other sex, Trevor offered a mamillary interpretation of the projections.[26]

At the same time, there has been controversy as to whether the studs were actually remnants of long rods that would have provided the raw material for wire and bangles, with the rest of the object serving as carrier or a head to force the molten metal into the moulds during sand-casting. This might explain, too, why the core could have been left hollow or filled with sand or stone. However Steel, who has not only studied specimens of musuku but also made experimental castings employing traditional techniques, doubts that copper rods were ever an essential part of the musuku. In fact, he sees the ridge-stud pattern on the top not as a signifier of weight and hence of value but as "probably just an ornamental feature whose meaning is unknown to us."[27]

The musuku have been associated specifically with the Lemba, whom some traditions identify as the principal copper miners at Messina, rather than the so-called "Musina." The marale (sing. *lerale*) are equally linked to the Sotho-speaking metalworkers of Phalaborwa. They are straight rods about 49 centimeters long, with a diameter of 13 millimeters and weighing about 900 grams. At one end is a head in the form of a flattened cone attached at a slant to the rod. Small rootlike bars project from the basal end of the cone, in most cases (diagram 4).[28] It has sometimes been assumed that the rod is the essential portion of the ingot, with the flattened cone simply the funnel into which the copper was run down during casting, but, as Lindblom points out, the rootlike bars must have been a deliberate addition "possessing some special meaning." Indeed, the extreme reluctance of their owners to part with them reinforces the theory that their value was more than monetary.[29] As a consequence, examples are extremely rare: only about fifteen are known in private or museum collections.[30]

By 1930 every musuku, like every lerale, was a sacred object. Even when they had been turned into bracelets and charms, they were still considered to possess "some of the spiritual power of the wearer's ancestors."[31] Nevertheless, informants were unanimous in agreeing that the solid musuku and the marale had once been mediums of exchange, either whole or in the converted form of bracelets. One Lemba source put the value of a musuku with four studs at one cow or twenty bracelets or ten anklets.[32] As for the marale, Hemsworth claims that in the middle of the nineteenth century, a single lerale would have fetched about ten cows, a value that seems doubtful.[33] Van der Merwe and Scully's informants are more credible in suggesting that thirty marale or fifty-five iron hoes were equivalent to one ivory tusk or about eight to ten head of cattle.[34] Obviously, prices would have fluctuated, but these estimates lead one to believe that in their whole form, both types of currency could only have been used in major transactions and in bridewealth payments;[35] for smaller purchases, they would have been subdivided.

This said, we are once again faced with the problem of historical depth.

Diagram 4. Lerale (after Haddon, "Copper Rod Currency from the Transvaal," *Man*, no. 65, 1908)

It seems clear enough that these ingots functioned at least to some extent as currencies as well as means of storing wealth, within the memory of informants during the early decades of this century, but this takes us back no farther than the middle years of the nineteenth century. They have not yet turned up in datable archaeological sites, nor do the scanty written records dealing with trade in indigenous copper at Delagoa Bay mention anything unusual about the form in which the metal was traded, which may only mean that different types of ingots were cast for different markets.

## COPPER ROD CURRENCIES OF WESTERN AFRICA

Copper and brass rod currencies have circulated over large areas of Africa for many centuries. Ibn Battuta's account of the copper currency of Takedda speaks of thick and thin red copper rods "a span and a half" long. "The thick are sold at the rate of four hundred rods for a *mithqal* of gold, the fine for six or seven hundred to the *mithqal*. . . . They buy meat and firewood with the fine rods: they buy male and female slaves, millet, ghee, and wheat with the thick."[36] The standardization of the rods and the "minting" of two different sizes adapted to cheaper and more expensive purchases would seem to bear out his description of the rods as a true means of exchange, not simply ingots for barter. The difficulty comes in reconciling the values given in terms of gold: the copper would seem to be grossly undervalued in the light of other contemporary sources. A span is usually defined as the distance between the thumb and little finger when the hand is extended to its maximum — about 9 inches or 22 to 24 centimeters — or, exceptionally, the distance from the thumb to the forefinger.[37] The fault could be an error in transcription, or it could be, as Mauny and Bucaille suggest, an imprecision in the Arabic word *cheber,* which may not have had the meaning "span" or "empan," as it is usually translated, but could equally have been "palm" a smaller but rather indeterminate measure.[38]

On the other hand, the values may refer to wire rather than to rods or bars. Some two hundred well-preserved copper wires were collected at Azelick by Thomas, Prautois and Mauny. They measured about 50 to 70 millimeters when unbroken, though they were often bent, twisted, or folded.[39] The more recent and extensive work of Bernus and Gouletquer has also yielded a quantity of wire. Some have an average diameter of less than 1 millimeter, while a second type is as thick as 2 millimeters. Except for very short fragments, they are generally bent back on themselves like worms. In addition to the wires, these investigators also found copper in the form of "tongues" and plaques, the latter frequently pierced with holes. All of these are small but sufficiently uniform to suggest that they too might have been forms of currency. None of them matches Ibn Battuta's description, which is perhaps not surprising: given the early dates recently obtained for copper smelting at Azelick, they may represent a very different period.[40] More than twenty years ago, Raymond Mauny called attention to the similarities between the thinner rods described by Ibn Battuta and the fine copper wire found at the medieval site of Kumbi Saleh. These "fils à double tête" fall into two types which differ not in diameter but in length. One is about 38 millimeters long, the other 18 millimeters or approximately half the length of the first. The gold equivalents given by Ibn Battuta would be more plausible for these wires of a span and a half or about 35 millimeters.[41]

Mauny also pointed to similarities with the "petites barres de cuivre pointues" which were the standard currency in much of the Congo Basin during the nineteenth century. Some of these last, he claimed, even had values close to those recorded by the Arab traveller.[42] Mauny might have extended his comparison to the rod currencies of Old Calabar and the Cross River as well; the finds of copper wire at Igbo-Ukwu suggest that copper in this form may have had at least some attributes of currency as early as the end of the first millennium A.D.

The first documentary evidence for the use of copper rods as currency in the Calabar-Rio del Rey littoral comes in the 1660s. This has prompted some historians to assume that they were introduced from outside with the expansion of the slave trade, but Latham has argued convincingly for a much greater antiquity. It is hard to imagine that they would have caught on so readily had their use not already been well established: "What is far more likely is that the Europeans utilized and copied the existing domestic currency,"[43] as in fact they had done consistently in West Africa. This currency could have been derived from the north, from the copper rods of Takedda or the trans-Saharan trade, or it could be a link with the copper economy of the Lower Congo.

In any event, Dapper leaves no doubt that from the beginning, European rods had to meet very precise specifications. They had to be "red and smooth . . . for the smoothest pass there as the best."[44] Before long it also became standard practice among English manufacturers to beat them with hammers in the belief that they would be more highly prized if they showed the mark of the hammer.[45] In Dapper's time they were an "ell and a quarter long" and weighed about one and a quarter pounds. Fourteen or fifteen represented the price of a good slave. But they did not circulate only in their original form. Local smiths would beat them out until they were long and thin, resembling drawn wire, then divide them into three strands and braid them like a cable to be made into bracelets and necklaces. These may have served for smaller purchases, along with the gray copper arm-rings, which he also mentions as currency at Old Calabar. By the nineteenth century, however, the problem of providing a domestic currency had been solved by splitting the imported rods into a number of wires about 18 to 24 inches long, bent like a hairpin. These were the so-called "black coppers," and it was largely in this form that the currency entered local markets.[46]

In some areas of the Eastern Delta, rods had become primarily a money of account by the nineteenth century, but in others they continued to be a medium of exchange as well. Bold noted that at "Egbosherry," a major palm oil market near Old Calabar, traders would accept nothing but copper rods. The Calabar people therefore had to convert the goods received from the ships into rods in order to buy oil. If rods were scarce, they had difficulty obtaining any oil at all. At the time of Bold's writing (1822), the rods had not been imported for some time, with the result that, in his words, "you may get a copper and a half for each rod, particularly if new."[47] Naturally traders were not long in cashing in on such profits, and the market was soon flooded with coppers, leading to a fall in their value—"Calabar imported inflation," as Latham puts it. The situation was further complicated by the changeover to brass rods in the 1840s and 1850s. Interestingly enough, Latham's figures show that the value of the wires fluctuated independently of the rods, with their main decline coming after 1875 rather than at mid-century.[48] So much had they come to symbolize money, however, that the sign for wealth in the Ekoi *nsibidi* syllabary is a series of concentric half-circles, an evocation of the bent copper wires, the *obubit oku*.[49]

Copper and then brass rod currencies spread along the main routes to the interior. By the later nineteenth century their sphere included not only the Efik but also the Tiv, Ibibio, some Ibo groups, and even the Igala.[50] Here, too, rods were adapted to specific markets. For example, the "Udam" rod was about 3 feet long, while the "Wukari" rod was only about 10 to 12 inches long and functioned particularly in the salt trade. Both were convertible into cloth strips.[51] At Nsukka, on the fringe of the cowrie currency areas, brass rods were used for larger purchases, but cowries rather than wires were used for very small ones.[52]

The copper bar currencies that circulated throughout the Congo Basin had their origin, as we have noted, in the mining areas of the Niari-Kwilu. Since the earliest written documentation dates only from the second half of the nineteenth century when these currencies were already competing with imported brass rods, there is often a good deal of confusion as to the type of currency in question. For clarity, we will use the original Tio designation *ngiele* for the copper currency and *mitako* for the brass rods. Ngiele were small ingots cast in or near the mining areas.[53] Bentley de-

scribes them as about the size of a finger.[54] Other writers put their length
at anywhere from 2 to 9 centimeters.[55] Laman's information gathered during his years as a missionary in the Lower Congo from 1891 to 1919 is the
most complete, if from a slightly peripheral area. He found that the Sundi
had traditionally made four kinds of sand moulds for casting ingots. The
first was two finger joints in length, counting from the tip of the finger;
the next reached to half the third joint; the third was measured from the
middle of the breast to the nipple (a rather imprecise standard!), or, in
a variant form, from the left to the right nipple; the smallest was only the
length to the first finger joint. In fact, the moulds, although they used
the finger as a measurement of length, were narrower than the average
finger.[56] Among the Bobangi and Tio, the basic ingot was 3 inches long,
half an inch in diameter and bent at the ends.[57]

Just how complex the local adaptations of this basic currency could become is superbly illustrated by Obenga's discussion of the monies circulating among the Mbochi of the Lower Alima. He shows the particular
forms employed by each subgroup and whether shells or beads were also
in use as secondary currencies (see table 7). Since copper currencies were
the only one used by all Mbochi groups, he concludes that they were the
oldest in the region. The presence or absence of a type in individual subgroups is an indicator of commercial circuits—who was trading with whom
—just as language also provides clues to such relationships. Unfortunately,
however, Obenga uses the term *monnaies en cuivre* without distinguishing
between copper and brass. Are the *lengyele* in fact copper and the *okyenge*
brass, or what is the difference, if any, between them? This information,
too, would point to trading connections and the period in which certain
groups entered long-distance networks.

These copper currencies had their recognized units, equivalences, and
values in goods. Thus among the Akwa Opa (Mbochi):

> *ondzongo konga:* simple *ondzongo*
> *ndzongo okombo:* double *ondzongo,* larger
> *eduma:* simple, flat
> *eduma okombo:* double *eduma*
> 1 *ondzongo konga* = 10 *eduma* = 1 goat
> 5 *ondzongo okombo* = 1 male elephant tusk
> 2 *eduma* = 1 *ondzongo* (simple)

Whatever the local variations, Obenga believes that the standard for the
copper currency among the Mbochi was the eduma, the copper rod bent
in the form of an open bracelet and weighing between 3 and 4 kilograms.[58]

Congo groups on the copper standard thus had systems which could
accommodate local differences and coexist with other, noncopper curren-

*Table 7* **MBOCHI CURRENCIES**

| Group | Metal (copper) | Shells | Beads |
|---|---|---|---|
| Olee | lɛngyɛlɛ ngyɛlɛ | ndzyi<br>ndzyi loni<br>1,000 ndzyi | — |
| Ngilima | ɔkyɛngɔ | ndzyi | — |
| Tsambitso | ɔkyɛngɔ | ndzyi | — |
| Mbondzi | indzɛyi (= ɔkyɛngɔ) | | ɔngɔmɔ |
| Obaa | tɛndɛlɛ (= ɔkyɛngɔ)<br>ebanga<br>ngyɛrɛ | tyi | — |
| Koyo | ɔkɛngɔ, ɔkyɛngɔ<br>ngyɛrɛ<br>ebanga ya lɛndzɔkɔ | tyi | — |
| Ebɔyi | ɔkyɛngɔ | tyi, letyi | — |
| Akwa Mbangi | ngɛdɛ, ngyɛrɛ<br>tɛndɛlɛ | otsi, tsyi | |
| Akwa Epede | ngyɛrɛ<br>tɛndɛlɛ | ndzyi | — |
| Akwa Opa | ɔndzɔngɔ<br>eduma | tyi, otyi<br>Okamɛnɛ<br>    400 tyi<br>olone<br>    1,000 tyi | — |
| Ngare (Asi Bvua) | receive copper money<br>from the Akwa and Koyo<br>in exchange for ivory | ndzyi | angyɛsi |
| Ngare (Asi Ngare) | ɔbdzɔkɔ<br>elima (= eduma) | | angyɛsi<br>angyɛsi |
| Mboko | ɔndzɔkɔ<br>elima (eduma) | | angyɛsi |

After Obenga, *Cuvette Congolaise*, pp. 105–6

cies. The overlapping systems must inevitably have invited speculation, though this is most evident in the period of intense European commerce. Once the brass mitako had come in, for example, traders could take advantage of the fact that the rate of exchange was six ngiele for one mitako at Gandchou, four at Stanley Pool.[59]

Another means of making money from money was cutting down the bars, comparable to clipping the coins in European monetary history. This was particularly well attested in the case of the mitako, which were apt to become smaller and smaller as they worked their way up the Congo from the coast. Speaking of the Ngombe Lutete district, Weeks declared that where the brass rod had once been twenty-seven inches long, "now it is scarcely five inches. Those who came into possession of a number of brass rods cut a half-inch off each, so as to procure for nothing the brass for his or her ornaments, and then passed the shortened rods into circulation, and others cut off pieces for the same purpose. Suddenly they awoke to the fact that there was not so much brass in their rods — that they were short; but there were so many in circulation that they agreed to take the short rods by giving and receiving an increased number for the cloth or goats . . . for sale."[60]

Clipping was not the only reason for the rapid devaluation of the rods, whose lengths incidentally were probably never as standardized to begin with as Weeks implies.[61] "Hundreds, if not thousands, of tons of the brass wire" were poured into the region by European traders and by the French Congo and Independent Congo authorities, who used them to pay local labor and who tried to manipulate their value.[62] Later, these authorities attempted to substitute colonial coinage for copper and brass currencies but met with obdurate resistance, a good proof of their serviceability.[63] For, as Vansina observes, the brass rod "had become the one item that served currently for both calculating value and making payment, just because the value per unit was neither too low nor too high."[64]

## MANILLA CURRENCIES OF SOUTHEASTERN NIGERIA

Ring currencies are associated preeminently with West Africa and especially with areas of the Niger Delta, but as we have seen, wherever copper currencies existed they were an actual or potential unit: bars, crosses, wire could always be transformed into rings, which in turn could continue to be used as money or withdrawn from circulation.[65] In the western Sudan they were a medium of exchange at least as early as the eleventh century A.D.[66] Rings and heavy knotted wristlets have been found at Igbo-Ukwu, while at Benin Connah excavated "five heavy penannular" objects in a cutting dated to the thirteenth century A.D.[67] It seems reasonable to suspect that peoples on the Gold Coast and at Benin, and perhaps those farther east as well, were eager to accept rings as both a money of account and an actual currency, in the early decades of European trade, precisely because their contacts with the north had already made rings thoroughly familiar.

Manillas were the most common form of copper-ring currency along the west coast from the period of the Discoveries into the twentieth century, but it is remarkable how little is actually known about them: most authors simply repeat the same handful of sources and fall back on the fascinating but very inadequate data provided by "Operation Manilla," the withdrawal of manillas from the Nigerian economy in 1948–49. The word *manilla* itself simply refers to a ring of metal, but in practice the manilla is generally defined as an open bracelet in the form of a horseshoe with lozenge-shaped ends, measuring about 2¼ inches across and weighing about 3 ounces.[68] This is the form that became standardized at some undetermined date, probably in the late eighteenth or early nineteenth century; it is certainly not the same manilla traded by the Portuguese or Dutch, and it has had a number of variant forms even in the last phase of its existence.

For the past, we know little about manillas besides their weight and some details about their finishing. We do not know for sure if they were always open bracelets. While Vogt states that the brass manilla traded by the Portuguese at Elmina in 1529 weighed about 0.6 kilogram, or about 1⅓ pounds,[69] the Fugger contract of 1548 (see chapter 6) specifies the weight of the Mina manillas as 160 for each 100 arates, that of the Guinea manillas as 190 per 100 arates, or about 10 and 8½ ounces respectively. In most factors' accounts they are simply labelled brass (*latam*) or copper (*cobre*), but the Fugger contract refers to manillas "de letan fusalera," which seems to mean fusible or good casting brass. Unfortunately it assumes that the manufacturers already knew "the metals suited to the said trade" and the "size and sorts and perfection as has always been the custom."[70] The "geele ringe" listed in the *Vijf dagregisters* a century later were certainly brass manillas, and Ratelband puts their weight at 1½ present-day Dutch ounces or about 150 grams (about 5⅓ ounces avoirdupois).[71]

Once the English became the primary suppliers of manillas, one would expect to find industrial records giving precise specifications for the Africa trade, but a search of Birmingham brass industry archives has turned up very little. As Grant-Francis has observed, "copper Manufacturers of the present day are often said to keep close the secrets of the Trade; if so it appears to be an old practice amongst them."[72] Aitken's histories of the Birmingham brass industry would inspire more confidence if he were not so muddled in his African geography and so condescending toward the "belles on the banks of the distant Zambesi."[73] He does, however, describe two types of ring sent to the "Gold Coast." One was made of solid brass wire about ⁷⁄₁₆ of an inch thick with a ring diameter of 3¼ inches; the other was of tubular bars, varying in size from 1¾ to 3½ or 4 inches in internal diameter. Each weighed 2½ to 4 ounces. These last were not soldered at the joint, so that they could easily be opened and fitted to the arm or leg of the wearer. In addition, a fine gauge brass wire, little thicker than ordinary pin wire, was exported to Africa, as well as the heavier wire sent to Zanzibar.

None of these does he qualify as "manillas," which he discusses separately as "a species of money . . . at one time produced in Birmingham by casting. It was exported to the Spanish [sic] settlements on the New and Old Calabar, and the Bonny Rivers in Africa." He makes it clear that these were, in fact, not brass but copper-lead hardened with arsenic.[74] This composition was confirmed by the analysis of sample manillas at the time of Operation Manilla.[75] As Morton has discovered, the addition of lead to manillas goes back at least to the late 1720s, when Robert Morris began combining one-half hundredweight of lead with a ton of copper,[76] but this is a far cry from the 25 to 30 percent lead of later years. If we are ever able to date manillas, it will be crucial to pinpoint when the changeover from brass to copper-lead took place in the common currency manilla and what other types of manilla continued to be made of brass.

Aitken claims that Birmingham was only just getting back into the maret at the time he was writing (1865–66), because of the unscrupulous trader who tried to pass off cast-iron manillas electroplated with copper. This was immediately detected by African buyers, and the counterfeit manillas were left lying "builked up by the side of the African river where they were disembarked," a reminder of European cupidity as well as naiveté.[77] Nevertheless, there are strong indications that some iron may have been desirable in certain types of manillas. Although no thorough analyses have been carried out, several knowledgeable sources have suggested that manillas used primarily in ritual contexts—especially the so-called king and queen manillas—have a higher iron content than the traces found in the common currency manilla.[78] The Pitt-Rivers Museum in Oxford has an example of an iron manilla for trade with the Ibo that was manufactured in Birmingham "after the pattern of the country." It was part of a shipment bound for New Calabar which was wrecked on the coast of County Cork in Ireland. As Elechi comments, the contents of manillas, not just their size, form, and decoration, may have been related to their value and function.[79] At the same time, it appears that there were "some slight differences in manillas which were in common use in differing areas of Southern Nigeria," those in the Delta area of Warri, Sapele, Koko, and Benin having a higher brass content than those circulating in the Rivers area (Abonnema, Abua, Nembe, Akassa).[80] The term manilla has thus come to embrace a variety of rings made of brass wire, cast brass, copper-lead, and iron, and since contemporary sources often use the terms *copper* and *brass* indiscriminately, we are a long way from sorting things out.

In the mid-nineteenth century, the manilla zone was centered on the Bonny-Brass region of the Niger Delta. The standard of value was the "bar" which was equal to 20 "copper" manillas valued at 3 pence each but circulating in five different styles. "Although the casual observer could scarcely discriminate between them," wrote Consul Hutchinson in his report of 1856, "the practiced eye of the natives does it at once and cannot be deceived. The *Antony Manilla* is good in all interior markets; the *Congo Singolo* or *bottle necked* is good only at Opungo market; the *Onadoo* is best for the Eboe country between Bonny and New Calabar; *Finniman Faidfilla* is passable in Juju-Town and Qua market; but it is only half the worth of the *Antony;* and the *Culla Antony* is valued by the people at Umballa (Ahombele)."[81] The casual observer continued to have such difficulty distinguishing between the different types that at the time of withdrawal in 1948 when only three were still widely used as currency, there was still confusion about which was which (see diagram 5)—a matter of importance, since they were reimbursed at very different rates. By that time the most common manilla was the *okpoko,* which derived its name from the Efik word for brass.[82]

In international commerce, manilla currencies made the transition from the slave to the palm-oil trade with ease. Perhaps the best contemporary description comes not from Nigeria but from the Ivory Coast, where the "native coinage equivalent" was also the manilla. "The native traders," wrote Mary Kingsley, "deal with the captains of the English sailing vessels and the French factories, buying palm oil and kernels from the bush people with merchandise, and selling it to the native or foreign shippers. They get paid in manillas, which they can, when they wish, get changed again into merchandise either at the factory or on the trading ship. The manilla is, therefore, a kind of bank for the black trader, a something he can put his wealth into when he wants to store it for a time." The Ivory Coast manilla was worth from 20 to 25 centimes and made in Birmingham and Nantes, she thought, of "an alloy of copper and pewter," a rather dubious suggestion.[83] A slightly later account explains that "for small purchases, the [Ivory Coast] natives carry manillas on their arms since the opening enables one to put the wrist through"—either these were slightly larger than the Nigerian okpoho or the natives had very slender wrists—"while for large ones they tie them up in packets of twenty and put twenty of these

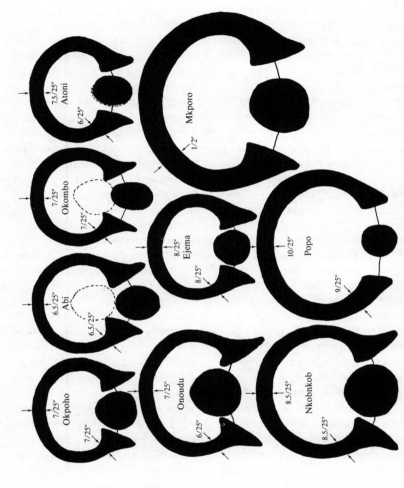

Diagram 5. Manillas (after Sven-Olof Johansson, *Nigerian Currencies*, 1967)

in a sack which then weighs about 60 kilos and is worth 80 fr., all of which makes transport difficult and costly."[84] The equivalent load in Nigeria for an able-bodied man was about 400 manillas, worth only 5 pounds.[85]

In spite of this cumbersomeness, manillas had become thoroughly integrated in the domestic economy of southeastern Nigeria. They were used to purchase food and palm wine, to compensate diviners, to satisfy court claims, to contract for a wife, and to be buried with.[86] If they died out early in areas such as Benin and Onitsha and gradually ceased to function as currency even in the old heartland of Degema, Brass, and Bonny, in other regions, right down to 1948, they resisted government efforts to supplant them with English coinage: in parts of Calabar Province west of the Cross River, Aba and Bende divisions of the Owerri Province, and Ahoada and Ogoni divisions of the Rivers Province.[87] Here their very tenacity made them a mark for speculators, who would buy them up when they were relatively cheap, in order to make a killing when their value rose. This would happen at the time that palm oil and kernels came to market, in the spring and early summer, since producers demanded payment largely in manillas. Even salaried employees and laborers and those, like them, not directly involved in the trade were affected by this seasonal rise in the price of manillas, because although they were paid in West African currency, they had to buy food in the local market with manillas. The problem was compounded by the habit some chiefs had of holding large quantities of manillas in reserve for long periods, seeing them, like Mary Kingsley's traders, as a kind of bank account, but diminishing the number in circulation, inasmuch as none had been imported since the 1890s.[88]

## MISCELLANEOUS COPPER CURRENCIES

Copper served as currency in a host of other forms, from buttons and beads to daggers, ceremonial knives, and axes.[89] The fragments of copper mentioned by al-'Umari as a currency in Kanem in the fourteenth century, as well as the somewhat amorphous lumps and cakes of copper cast at Hufrat, were probably all based on the rotl, a weight of copper equal to about 375 grams or 1 pound. For centuries the rotl served as the principal currency of Bornu, continuing as a standard of account long after it ceased to circulate.[90] And while the Portuguese sought with limited success to introduce copper coinage into Angola, United States copper pennies enjoyed an inflated value in the coffee trade with São Tomé in the 1830s and 1840s.[91] Far more widespread than any of these were the copper and brass basins, especially the neptunes, that came to form part of the trading assortment on many parts of the coast and were standardized by size and weight.

They were undoubtedly a form of currency as well as in some cases a commodity. An aide of de Brazza, for example, paid his Adouma paddlers in neptunes, and in 1893 they became the "monnaie obligatoire" of the factories of the Société du Haut Ogowé.[92] Nevertheless they seem to have been reserved most particularly for bridewealth payments, at least in equatorial Africa.[93]

In trying to assess the often ambiguous data on African copper currencies, we need to remind ourselves that ingots are not necessarily the same thing as currency. Any long-continued standardization in weight or form, however, implies, as Bisson says, "a uniform system of values operating at least at their place of manufacture."[94] Unfortunately we know the base units for hardly any of the indigenous ingot forms. Laman's information that three of the Sundi ingots were based on the human finger seems credible: after all, our own system of inches, palms, spans, and ells uses the human hand and arm as natural modules. But it will require a good deal of measuring of many specimens to accomplish for these currency forms what Garrard has achieved for Akan goldweights.

A striking feature of the copper ingot currencies produced within Africa is their small size. True, the Ingombe Ilede crosses were about 30 to 33 centimeters long, but ingots from Takedda, Sanga, and the Lower Congo were almost minute. Presumably this was an indicator of the scarcity and value of the metal—gold coins have also been small. Such value would inevitably confine their use to the prestige sphere, and the tendency to thesaurization in regalia, jewelry, and burials would limit still more the amount available.

By the nineteenth century, in contrast, enormous quantities of copper, both indigenously produced and imported, were in circulation, and it is at this point that the evidence becomes conclusive that at least in certain areas copper currencies came close to being general-purpose money with which "both provisions and status-conferring offices could be bought"— and people, that is, slaves.[95] By this time, too, either the currencies themselves had declined in value to the point where they could be used for small purchases, or they could easily be subdivided to do so. Nonetheless, even if they filled the usual definition of universal or general currencies, they were rarely *exclusive* ones: they usually functioned alongside other forms of exchange such as cowries, cloth strips, beads, and ingots of other metals. This was already true in the Rivers during the late sixteenth century when small copper bars, small ingots of tin, colored beads, various types of cloth, and gold all served as currencies.[96] Across the continent and several centuries later, Talbot's table of currencies in use in southern Nigeria in the early twentieth century is bewildering for the multiplicity of monies identified with each group or even subgroup.[97] The same diversity obtained in the Congo Basin, so that Weeks' photograph of a Sunday church collection in the Lower Congo could just as well illustrate Cotterell's memoirs of the early years of St. Clement's Church in Bonny. Weeks itemizes "20 boxes of matches; 2 eggs; 200 gun-caps; 1 umbrella; 1 tin of gunpowder; 1 calabash of gunpowder; 2 pieces of cloth; 1 bottle of kerosine; 15 francs (cash); and 3373 short brass rods. The whole represents 8931 brass rods (Congo money), or £2 19s 6d English money."[98] Cotterell's collection included "manillas, heads of tobacco, cotton cloths, etc. etc."[99]

All these currencies had to be convertible, or potentially so. And yet, as Vansina points out, money changers at the Pool, for example, could make a living only because "the different currencies did not buy the same goods. They were perhaps theoretically universal standards of value but restricted means of payment." In practice, other goods would be demanded for certain commodities.[100] Similarly, although prices for slaves and oil might be settled between Aro traders and coastal merchants in manilla currencies at Bonny or brass and copper rods at Calabar, the traders preferred goods to actual currency because they could control the price more easily.[101]

When the transfer of a major Delta market was negotiated from Bende to Usuakoli in 1896, the chiefs of the latter town gave the Aro council 2,800 brass rods, 1 cow, 1 ram, 1 goat, 1 cock, 4 stone jars of gin, 16 yams, and 4 kola nuts. Each Aro chief received a slave, while other members of the council were given presents of 100 to 150 manillas and a bottle of gin. A portion of the 2,800 brass rods went toward preparing the market charm.[102] We have been concerned in this chapter essentially with the currency functions of manillas, rods, crosses and ingots of various sorts, but in Africa as elsewhere there was no hard and fast line separating the economic from the social, political, and ritual spheres, a topic we will deal with more fully in succeeding chapters.

# Copper as a Medium of Art

They put copper rings on their hands and in
the ears of their women.

—AL MAS'UDI (late tenth–early
eleventh century)

Their women weare a Ring of Copper about
their Neckes, which weigheth fifteen pound at
least, about their armes little Rings of Copper that
reach to their elbowes, about their middles a cloth
of the Insandie Tree . . . on their legs Rings of
Copper, that reach to the calves of their legs.

—ANDREW BATTELL (late sixteenth
century)

I frequently saw whole caravans, every individual of which wore ornaments, rings, buttons, etc.,
nay, even weapons entirely made of [copper].

—G. TAMS (1845)

Almost all the ornaments worn by the Monbut-
too are made of copper. . . . One of the most frequent uses to which it is applied is that of making
flat wires, many yards long, to wind round the
handles of knives and scimitars, or round the
shafts of lances and bows. Copper, as well as iron,
is used for the clasps which are attached to the
shields, partly for ornament, and partly to prevent them from splitting. Copper necklaces are
in continual wear, and copper fastenings are attached to the rings of buffalo-hide and to the thick
thongs of the girdles. The little bars inserted
through the ear are tipped with the same metal;
in fact there is hardly an ornament that fails in
an adjunct of copper in some form or other.

—G. SCHWEINFURTH (1873)

The variety of cuprous objects in sub-Saharan Africa is almost infinite.
To poke through the reserves of any major museum collection of African
art is to be overwhelmed with the multiplicity of forms, decorative motifs,

and applications. Every type of object has a range of variations, often within a single society, and there were undoubtedly variations over time which we will be fortunate if we can document in a handful of cases. With extremely common objects such as bracelets we may never be able to establish hard and fast typologies, because records of provenance are so unreliable and because such objects were traded or exchanged over large areas, the product of centers known for their craftsmanship or of itinerant smiths.

What is striking, however, is how rarely copper and copper alloys were used for utilitarian objects in the usual sense of the word, if we exclude their role as currency. The main exceptions were provided by the copper and brass basins traded so extensively along the west coast. They were widely used by the indigenous salt-making industry in the Niger Delta and along the Gabon coast as far as Loango, providing an important commodity for inland trade.[1] Small neptunes were used for palm oil, while the great Scottish pans, whose diameter exceeded an ell, served instead of tubs "om een schaep of verken in te slaghten, en schoon ten maken," for slaughtering a sheep or pig and making it clean.[2] Basins were also employed for washing and shaving, and sometimes for cooking.[3] At Tete on the Zambezi, little copper pots were used to boil down juice from sugar cane.[4] Proyart describes how in the Loango-Congo region "vases de cuivre" were used to prepare an especially acidic kind of manioc whose juice was poisonous and had to be expressed. The acid kept the pans from ever discoloring through oxidation.[5] Brass pans and basins might of course be considered utilitarian, too, in that they provided a source of sheet metal for native working.[6]

For the Gold Coast, Garrard quotes a Dutch description of 1697 concerning the use of a copper sieve in Akanni gold diggings, but a half century later Dutch prospecting in the Egwira district was thwarted by the refusal to use such sieves, on the grounds that "it is fetish to use copper in seeking for gold."[7] Presumably it was never "fetish" to mix brass filings with gold dust, a common practice in Butua on the Zimbabwe Plateau as well as on the Gold Coast.[8] Though one might assume that items such as the copper hoes forged by Yeke smiths were used primarily for currency or in ritual, de Hemptinne claims that they were actually employed in farming in the Dikuluwe region until about 1910, when they were gradually replaced by imported iron hoes.[9]

There were of course many other objects that were undoubtedly utilitarian, from Tuareg brass tongs and locks to Bamum pipes to copper bullets to Akan brassweights. I will argue, however, that more than utility was generally involved in the choice of material. Or, to put it another way, the use of copper in many or most contexts was part of a language of materials expressing values or beliefs integral to the culture in which the object was employed. In this chapter I propose to offer an overview of the myriad forms of use in African societies, and in the next to suggest an interpretive framework.

## THE HUMAN BODY AS A WORK OF ART

What we are in essence talking about therefore is copper as an artistic medium, and as with any discussion of art in Africa, the starting point must be the human body. Copper adorned the human body from head to foot and laterally to the tips of the fingers: hair ornaments, earrings, collars and necklaces, pendants, girdles and cache-sexes, bracelets, anklets, rings, bells, amulets, crowns (figs. 12–17, 30, 35, 37, 38; color illusts. 3, 4). Copper ornamentation is, or has been, quasi-universal in African societies. Scarcely a modern ethnographic survey or traveller's account from the past that is at all specific in describing jewelry does not mention such objects as worn by at least some fraction of a given population. As we have seen, they turn up in virtually all Iron Age archaeological sites south of the Sahara. Since they do not always fit western definitions of the fine arts, they are consigned by the hundreds to oblivion in museum storage drawers. And yet in themselves and even more as part of a human whole, they frequently combine esthetic and technical qualities of the highest order.

Aside from the evidence of archaeology (see chapter 5), documentary sources testify to the antiquity of copper and brass jewelry in Africa. Herodotus describes the Adyrmachidae, a people living near Egypt: "They dress like the rest of the Libyans. Their women wear a bronze ring in each leg." [10] According to Strabo, the same was true of Nubian women. [11] Idrisi, writing of the arid regions west of medieval Ghana, notes that the people "deck themselves out with ornaments of copper." [12] This was still true when Pedro de Anhaia landed on the Mauritanian coast at the beginning of the sixteenth century and found the blacks unclothed but prizing beads, "brass bangles or like ornaments which they use in those parts." [13] Echoing this are accounts such as that of Pacheco (1505–8) concerning the Ijos of the Niger Delta who go all naked except for thick copper necklaces [14] or of Conçeicão (1696) describing the territories on the northern Zimbabwe plateau where the people are "all naked, and only on their legs do the women wear some bracelets of copper." [15] At the far end of the continent, Pieter van Meerhoff, the first European known to have reached Namaqualand, wondered at the magnificence of Nama ornamentation:

> Their dress consists of all kinds of beautifully prepared skins . . . gorgeously ornamented with copper beads. . . . Their locks they thread with copper

12. Earrings, Songhay, Mali. Copper?

13. Bracelets, Mali. Copper and brass

212

14. Bracelet, Mali. Brass

beads, covering their heads all over. Around their necks they have chains, slung round them 15 or 16 times. Many have round copper plates suspended from these chains. On their arms they have chains of copper or iron beads which go round their bodies 30 or 40 times. Their legs are encased in plaited skins, ornamented with beads.[16]

What particularly struck many travellers was the sheer massiveness of copper and brass jewelry in many regions. Richard Eden's account of John Lok's voyage to Elmina in 1554–55 referred to the "great shackles of bright copper" worn by the local women on their legs.[17] Later in the same century Paludanus remarked on the penchant of women at Cape Lopez for "great iron or red copper or tin rings on their legs . . . which often weigh three or four pounds."[18] Clearly this was no passing fad, for by the mid-nineteenth century Mpongwe women were loading their legs with an ever

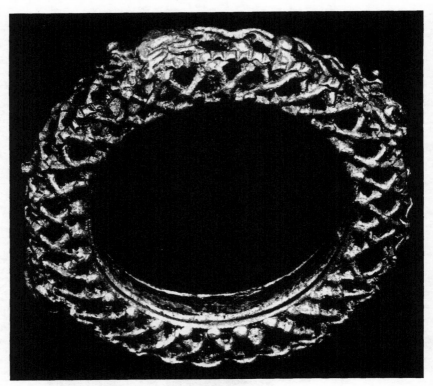

15. Open-work bracelet, grasslands, Cameroon. Brass

greater weight of metal: Du Chaillu claimed they were wearing 25 to 30 pounds on each ankle, an estimate scaled down only slightly by Richard Burton. "It is the pride of a Mpongwe wife," he wrote, "to cover the lower limb between knee and ankle with an armour of metal rings, which are also worn upon the wrists; the custom is not modern and travellers of the seventeenth century allude to them. The rich affect copper. . . . The native smiths make the circles, and the weight of a full set of forty varies from fifteen to nineteen pounds." [19]

On the Middle Congo and Ubangui, the preference was for enormously heavy collars. Bentley and Johnston put the Bobangi collars at anywhere from 20 to 30 pounds,[20] but Coquilhat declared that the "monstrous" collars he found at Wangata weighed 15 to 25 *kilograms:* "In short, the well-turned woman of the world wears day and night a weight equal to the pack of a Belgian infantryman in the field." [21] These collars had to be fitted by a blacksmith, who pounded the opening shut with the wearer lying on the

16. Greave-type bracelet, Dahomey. Brass

floor, one end of the collar resting on an anvil. To get it off, a metal wedge
was pounded into the opening to force the ends apart.[22] Just how much
variety one might find within a single group is brought out by Gutersohn's
account of the Mongo. Using the copper provided by *mitako (ngiele?),*
the local smith produced eight different types of collars, bracelets, and
leglets, ranging from the neckring that weighed about 10 kilograms to spiral
leg rings that covered the entire lower leg, to simple light arm rings.[23]

17. Necklace, Bamum, Cameroon. Brass

The Mpongwe, Bobangi, and Mongo may have represented an extreme, but many other areas shared their fondness for heavy pieces or for large quantities of smaller ones. Among the Gogo, Masai, and other East African peoples, this took the form of continuous coils of brass and iron wire encircling the neck or enveloping the arms and legs.[24] In Burundi, bracelets weighing as much as 5½ pounds and often beautifully chased with simple geometric designs would be worn three or four to an arm.[25] Elsewhere women might wear four to five hundred finer bracelets at one time twisted around zebra hair or fibre on their arms and legs.[26]

Nor were heavy bracelets limited to Equatorial and East Africa. Heavy, solid or hollow, cast or wrought, closed or open, twisted or smooth — such bracelets and anklets were formerly to be found from the Cameroon grasslands across the Sudan to Liberia and Sierra Leone. In 1600 de Marees noted that the women of Benin wore 3 or 4 pounds of red copper and

1. Brass casting, Fumban, Cameroon. The caster is pouring molten metal from a luted crucible into a ring mould

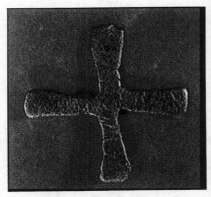

2. Currency cross, Katanga, Zaire. Copper

3. Spherical ornament, Verre, Cameroon. Brass, copper

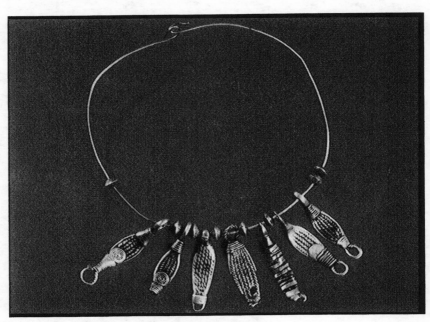

4. Cache-sexe pendants, Kapsiki, Cameroon. Copper, brass

5. Pipe, Fumban, Cameroon. Brass

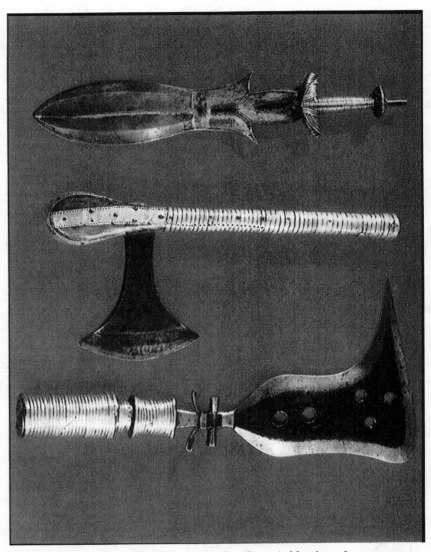

6. Ceremonial weapons, Zaire: Kuba, Zappo Zap (Songye), Mangbetu. Iron, copper

tin rings on their arms and legs, often so tight that it was hard to imagine how they had put them on.[27] Among Ibo groups in southeastern Nigeria, long spirals of brass were worn by girls up to the time of their marriage: they stretched from the ankle to the knee and sometimes halfway up the thigh, like leggings. Even more striking were the enormous brass anklets known as *adalà,* which were beaten out of a solid brass bar and then fixed on the leg by the blacksmith. They not only sheathed the leg but had a flat disk that projected out at right angles as much as 6 inches (fig. 37, p. 269). "Once hammered on," wrote Basden, "they are permanent evidences of deluded vanity, and from that hour the wearer can never again stand, sit or lie in a normal position." In walking, one leg had to be swung clear of the other to manage the weight and to avoid tripping.[28] Much more restrained greave-type anklets and bracelets, often beautifully decorated, are characteristic of the Verre and neighboring peoples of Adamawa and the Middle Benue.[29] One writer has referred to the massive collars and bracelets, which were on virtually for life, as "véritable carcans, instruments de torture," and this verdict has been echoed by other observers.[30] Only Livingstone drew the obvious parallel with his own culture, likening the heavy anklets that blistered the skin of Makololo women to the rigid lacing and tight shoes of Victorian England.[31]

In contrast, fine wire bangles have been characteristic of Central and Southern Africa for hundreds of years. In West Africa they seem to have been limited to southeastern Nigeria and its hinterland. Dapper, as we have noted, described their manufacture in the seventeenth century, and they appear to go back to the Igbo-Ukwu culture.[32] The Tiv and other peoples of the Middle Benue also use wire and chain, but less as a primary material than to provide elaborate decoration, particularly for cast armlets and other objects.[33] In parts of Uganda, necklaces were made of fine wire bound around a core of goat hair and looped about the neck. A Madi variant consisted of flattened brass decorated with a fringe of tiny bells.[34]

Copper and brass earrings are almost as universal as bracelets and neckrings. The most common type from Egypt and the central Sudan to Southern Africa is the double spiral of brass joined by a band or coil of wire, for which Arkell has pointed out analogues in the ancient Near East.[35] Elsewhere in the Sudan, brass earrings frequently imitate the spectacular twisted ones of gold worn by well-to-do Fulani women in the region of Timbuktu. In Southern Africa, there is a remarkable continuity in two types of earrings illustrated by travellers to the southern Tswana in the early nineteenth century and those found in Iron Age burials of the southern Highveld. One is an almost rectangular sheet of copper with a rounded base put through a single ear; the other consists of a wire hook in the shape of a question mark which is put through a hole in the lobe and joined to a shank, made either of straight wire or wire that has been doubled back on itself, often wrapped in a spiral. The Tlhaping often wore more than one of these at a time, even as many as six.[36] In West Africa, too, it is not uncommon to pierce the ears with a number of rings. The Bororo, for example, may wear six or seven in an ear, the Bambara and Dogon, three or four.[37] The Masai penchant for heavy coils of wire around the neck and limbs is matched by a predilection also for extravagant earrings which often incorporate heavy coils or rings of brass hanging from painstakingly stretched earlobes, a predilection shared by the Pokot of northern Kenya.[38]

Nor is it surprising that various forms of copper were used to ornament the forehead and hair. The Kurumba of Upper Volta, for example, adorned themselves with hairpins of all sorts, "some finely worked and decorated."[39] The same was true of a number of Congo peoples, especially the Tetela.[40] In Gabon, the Fang and "Osyeba" were fond of working copper wire or rings into the hair.[41] The Nguru, inland from Zanzibar, "dressed their hair in long ringlets adorned with penticles of copper or white or red beads," according to Stanley, while the Vinza of the eastern Congo fastened "small shot-like balls" to their hair.[42] Early descriptions of the Khoikhoi all remark on their fondness for decorating the hair with copper and brass: beads, buttons, coins, plaques, indeed almost any form of the metal.[43] But the most extravagant coiffure is that described by Barth at Doré, northwest of Say on the Niger:

> Copper is worn by the inhabitants by way of ornament to a large extent, and I was greatly amused on observing that some of the young girls wore in the long plaits of their hair a very remarkable ornament made of that metal, representing a warrior on horseback with a drawn sword in his hand and a pipe in his mouth.[44]

## SCULPTURE

The line between ornamentation of the human body and sculpture is an invisible and even false one. Just as horsemen might be worn in the hair, human heads or chameleons or serpents could be cast onto bracelets or metal masks worn as pendants on breast or hip. Conversely, metal jewelry, real or represented, turns up frequently on sculptured forms, no matter what the medium. It has often been remarked that African art frequently reconciles abstraction and a lack of interest in anatomical detail with a love of naturalism in all that concerns decoration. The most obvious examples are the Ife and Jebba figures and Benin heads and plaques (fig. 18),

18. Plaque, Benin, Nigeria. Brass

which are extremely precise as to dress, beads, bracelets and scarification; but one could just as well cite the Kuba *ndop,* some of which are bedecked with real neck rings in the same way that Chokwe statues may be adorned with copper bracelets, anklets, and earrings, or Bambara antelope masks with metal earrings.[45] By the same token, what is ostensibly jewelry may never have been meant to be worn, functioning instead much more like sculpture: thus, for instance, the large cast bracelets of the Senufo representing Fo the python,[46] or the so-called king and queen manillas and torques found in Lower Niger shrines.[47]

Here we will be concerned primarily with two forms of copper art, sculpture in the narrow sense and masks. The former is preeminently the product of the lost-wax casting process and hence is limited essentially to West Africa. The exception is that region of the Kongo where Europeans introduced lost-wax casting to provide the cult objects for the spread of Christianity. Even here, Wannyn's observation that the process was never used for "fetishes," only for Christian art, is very revealing.[48] The most spectacular development of the caster's art occurred, of course, in southern Nigeria. The corpus of Ife, Benin, and "Tsoede" "bronzes" is too well known to need description, but at the same time we should never forget just how atypical these heads, plaques, and full- or almost full-sized figures are within the totality of African metal art.

For whatever reasons—technical, economic, cultural—small figures of animals and humans are much more characteristic, for the most part different from those cast onto jewelry or worn as pendants only in that they are free standing. The oldest known thus far would appear to be the little lizards, caiman, and birds found in the tumuli of the Middle Niger and believed to predate the spread of Islam into the region (fig. 19; figs. 10, 11).[49] Figures such as the Jukun hippopotamus in the Art Institute of Chicago may also be old, but the date of 1500 A.D. assigned to it is purely speculative. The Dan and Guere have cast female and mother-and-child figures.[50] In northern Ghana pieces such as the Janus figures of Nsawkaw have been connected with myths of origin.[51]

The best-known brass sculpture outside of Nigeria, however, is that of the royal casters of Dahomey, of the Senufo, Akan, and grasslands people of Cameroon. The Dahomean capital of Abomey became a particular center of brass casting, specializing in single figures and more recently in tableaux. Herskovits was told that the emphasis was on animals in earlier times because they represented totems in ancestral rites. In the court art, these animals symbolized the monarchs themselves. Although tradition claimed that the kings of Dahomey had storehouses full of such figures, there does not seem to be much firm evidence for dating this art form.[52]

Fortunately we are on surer ground with the Akan goldweights, thanks to Garrard. He has shown how these evolved in two stylistic traditions,

19. Ibis, tumuli of Killi, region of Goundam, Mali. Copper alloy

the one geometric, the other figurative (figs. 20, 21). Both became more ornate in the course of time and more numerous with the burgeoning of trade. By the Late Period (c. 1700–1900) there is a virtual explosion in the figurative weights—almost everything in Akan society ends up being represented, directly or symbolically and metaphorically. Garrard comes up with the astonishing estimate that as many as three million brass goldweights may have been cast over the five centuries between 1400 and 1900 in the area embracing modern Ghana and Ivory Coast, with two-thirds

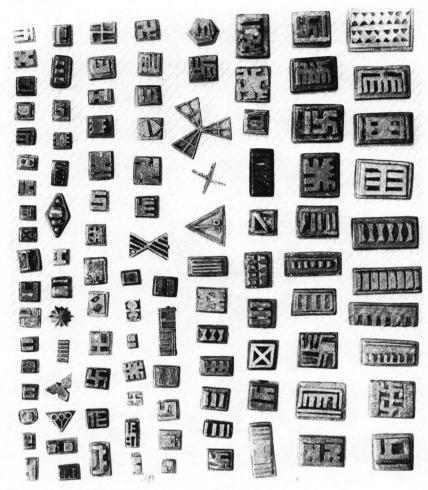

20. Geometric goldweights, Akan, Ghana. Brass

of them dating from the Late Period.[53] Like the goldweights, Senufo charms and divinatory sculptures are small. The stunning brass face masks as well as the male, female, and equestrian figures are primarily translations of wooden forms, and dating is problematical.[54] Casting in the Cameroon grasslands is first documented in the late nineteenth century and was probably not of great antiquity, given the isolation of the region from regular supplies of copper and brass.[55] It is largely an art of masks and of ornamentation, of sculpted figures on brass vessels, pipes, horns, and thrones, and as such belongs more appropriately in the next section.

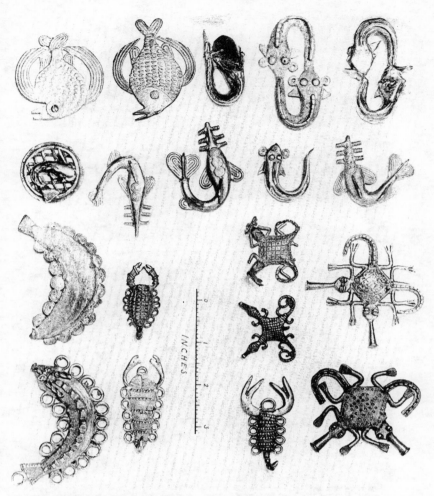

21. Figurative goldweights, Akan, Ghana. Brass

Cast metalwork was only one of many ways in which copper and brass entered the realm of sculpture. Just as common was the addition of metal to objects made of other materials. As Thompson notes, "the taste for mixing the main medium of the sculpture (wood, bone, brass) with a minor medium of beads, brass, or iron is very African."[56] So it is that the magnificent *nimba* masks of the Baga and Nalu are often decorated with brass rosettes and studs (fig. 22), that Fang statues have brass eyes, or Bambara, Guere, and Dan sculpture is patterned with strips, plates, and studs of copper and brass (fig. 23; fig. 36, p. 268). Often these additions are difficult

22. *Nimba* mask, Baga, Guinea. Wood, brass, fiber

to see from a distance, especially if the metal is darkly patinated. Such is the case with Bamum and Kom royal sculptures, for example, where the brass sheet covering the head or the entire figure has come to look much like the wood it sheaths.[57] A Bobo *Do* mask in the Detroit Institute of Arts has copper plates and coins on the upper side, so that when the mask is danced they would only be visible from above, presumably to the non-human world.

The most striking of the many styles that add copper and brass to wood are those of the Marka, Songye, Salampasu, and Kota. Marka masks seem

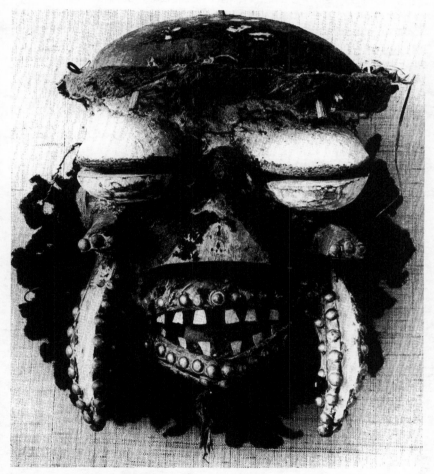

23. Mask, Guere-Wobe, Ivory Coast. Wood, brass, iron, fiber

almost to embody a machine esthetic, the face characteristically coming to a point at the chin, overlaid with sheets or leaves of copper and brass in punched and stamped designs that give them a robot-like quality. Some of these may be very recent; in any case, those that add aluminum can only date from the very late nineteenth or twentieth century.[58]

The predilection of the Songye for metallic decoration on wood statuary is attributed by Olbrechts to the fact that they, and especially their subgroup, the Zappo Zap, are among the most skillful smiths in Zaire if not in all of Africa.[59] A wooden figure surmounting a raffia skirt in the Brooklyn Museum has strips of copper sheet on the face and breast and a plaque of copper on the navel. Other pieces commonly are adorned with diagonal or crossed bands of copper and add studs, sometimes in what seem to imitate scarification patterns (fig. 24). Cornet notes that the copper nails embedded in Songye heads are forged by hand.[60] Both the Chokwe and the Dan also make extensive use of brass studs, and the Salampasu of the left bank of the Lulua River cover their masks with hand-worked copper, in strips or more commonly in thin sheets ornamented with large brass nailheads.[61] Indeed, the use of decorative studs goes back to some of the Sanga sites, especially Katoto.

Far more familiar are the *bwété,* the copper-covered reliquaries of the various Kota and Kota-related groups of eastern Gabon (fig. 25). With the publication of the Chaffin catalogue we can now appreciate the tremendous diversity of substyles, from the extremely austere, concave heads covered with ribbons or wire of copper and brass to the ornate, sheet-enveloped crested figures.[62] These sculptures were first mentioned by travellers in the 1870s and 1880s, but Perrois has proposed that some may date back to the middle of the nineteenth century, a remarkable longevity for wood sculpture in sub-Saharan Africa and one that can be explained by both the extremely resistant wood used and the preservative action of the copper sheathing.[63]

Several rare masks are made entirely of hammered copper or brass. The *ngongo munene* of the Kongo of northeastern Angola was described by Baumann and subsequently documented more extensively by Bastin. The mask is of red copper, almost without relief except for the thin, straight nose and the slight ridges outlining eyes and nose.[64] To my knowledge, the closest parallel is offered by the sheet brass Alakoro masks of the Yoruba. These, however, are much more rounded, often with large, open eyes and more fully formed nose and mouth, so that they do not convey the deathlike calm of the Kongo masks. They were apparently created by the priests of the thundergod at the time of the Fulani invasions, as an invocation to Shango and as a means to frighten and mislead the enemy.[65]

## THE ORNATE IMPLEMENT

Tamara Northern's elegantly simple term can be extended well beyond the knives, swords, axes, and adzes in her Dartmouth exhibition to encompass the whole range of objects which are neither human bodies nor sculpture in the narrow sense but which become works of art in precisely the same way as both. When Stanley wrote of the Vinza in the eastern Congo, "Copper appeared to be abundant. . . . It was used wound around their spear-staffs and encircled the lower limbs and arms, the handles of their knives [and] walking-staffs, and hung from their necks in beads, and small shot-like balls of it were fastened to their hair," his alternation between man and object was altogether appropriate, confusing as it may seem at first glance.[66] He was simply recognizing, consciously or unconsciously, the esthetic unity that met his eyes.

For the most part, implements fall into two categories: those intended for utilitarian purposes but decorated in ways or made of materials not dictated purely by utility, and those which although structurally similar to utilitarian implements have, in Northern's words, "undergone a morphological modification and elaboration" which allows them to function in a different sphere.[67] In both cases they convey a complex statement about their cultures analogous to the decorated human body and sculptured form.

Stanley's description goes on to note that the Vinza used brass tacks to decorate the edges of their stools. This is a practice shared by many Congo peoples and beyond—it has been carried over into the New World in Surinam decorative art—but it reached its apogee among the Chokwe, who ornament not only sculpture but all manner of stools and thrones with brass studs. In West Africa, the counterpart of the Chokwe throne is the *asipim* chair of the Akan, which may be decorated with both studs and sheet metal. Studs also decorated Chokwe snuff containers and tobacco pipes. Along the same lines, a Kuba wooden cup in the Brooklyn Museum is a sculpture in miniature: the face on the side opposite the handle has brass studs across the forehead, a stud between the eyes, and one in front of each ear.

In Southern Africa, finely drawn wire is widely used on gourds and pipes. Where animal horns are used to drink out of, as in the Cameroon grassland or among the Binji east of the Kuba, copper and brass wire frequently ornaments the pointed end. Grasslands pipes have in fact become an art form in themselves: not only are they ornamented with wire, but the bowls are often elaborately cast as hollow figurines, some taking on baroque dimensions and elaboration (color illust. 5) Vessels and containers are indeed a natural invitation to embellishment. Akan *forowa*, made of beaten

24. Fetish figure, Songye, Zaire. Wood, copper, brass, iron, fiber

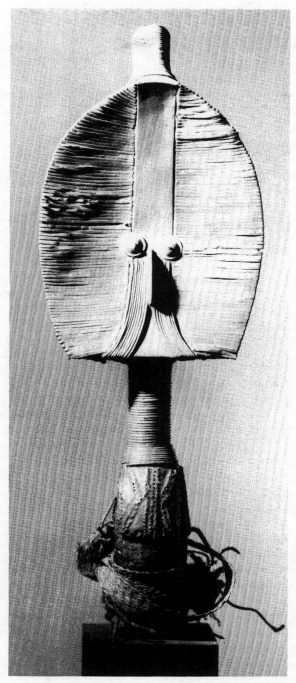

25. *Bwété* reliquary figure, Kota-Mahongwe, Gabon. Wood, covered with copper and brass

brass and used to store shea butter, are frequently works of decorative art. The same is even more true of the cast brass *kuduo* of the Aṣante or of Tikar palm wine containers, cast in the form of a large calabash and ornamented with a riot of drunken figures. One need only think of the exquisite bowls and calabash handles from Igbo-Ukwu to be reminded that the ornate vessel has a long history in Africa.

But the most spectacular forms of decorated implements are staffs and, even more, weapons. Here, too, the finds at Igbo-Ukwu offer a historical perspective. The elaborate staff heads from Igbo Isaiah, for example, have later parallels in Guiné "Sonos" and in Yoruba, Benin, Tiv, or Senufo staffs in wood or metal topped with cast human or animal figures (fig. 26). The bronze scabbards and hilts are forerunners of brass hilts of the Bata or of the Senegal scabbard described by Barbot "all covered with a thin-copper plate,"[68] or even of the brass knob and bands on the Gold Coast sword collected by Weickman in the seventeenth century and now in the Ulm museum.[69]

To be sure, there is nothing particularly African about such decoration: copper and bronze have been used to decorate iron weapons in pre-Roman Britain, by the Vikings, in Japan, India, and Sarawak, throughout the Near East, in the ceremonial arms of Europe.[70] In many cases, it can even be argued that such additions serve a practical purpose. Morgen, for instance, claimed that the copper or iron rings attached to the end of Wute bamboo spears provided for "bessern Durchschlagskraft," a greater ability to pierce.[71] Lienhardt believed that the coils of copper or aluminum wire decorating the shafts of Dinka spears serve to "strengthen and balance them."[72] In the case of Mangbetu shields, the copper shields were also intended to prevent them from splitting.[73] Copper wire wound around the handle of a throwing knife may have replaced fiber and helped to weight the knife as well as offer a secure grip.[74] So widespread is the custom of decorating African weapons with copper and brass in every conceivable form — wire, ribbon, bands, plaques, incrustations, rivets, disks, and studs — that utility alone cannot be an adequate explanation, however.

Furthermore, when European guns came in, they, too, were highly decorated with copper and brass. Where the barrels were banded with strips of metal, this may have helped to prevent them from exploding, but where the stock was covered with studs and nails or coils of copper wire as it so often was from the Rio Grande to Angola, the pattern is altogether similar to that of hand arms.[75] Ryder reports that an invoice of 1715 for the Benin trade includes fifty fine flintlocks with copper mountings, while Sundström states that guns with trimmings of brass or silver (in demand by peoples of the Sahel) could command double the price of plain guns, if not more.[76] Certain types of weapons, too, were made entirely of cop-

26. Royal messenger's staff, Benin, Nigeria (detail). Brass

per or brass rather than iron, indicating by the choice of materials a different function, no matter how similar their form might be.

What is equally important is that where copper and brass were added to weapons, it was often in intricate and beautiful patterns. In the western Sudan the pommels of swords or knives were frequently cast in brass. Hausa swords, for example, are shaped somewhat like a cutlass, gracefully curved with leather fringes and ridge patterns that may be repeated in the rounded or pyramidal metal knobs of the pommel. Tuareg arms, on the other hand, apply lozenge-shaped plaques of copper on the top of the pommel or decorate the shank of spears with inlaid brass or bands of copper or brass. Some specimens of Tuareg arm daggers have brass sheet covering the sheath. In Gabon, Fang and Kota knives are reminiscent of the reliquaries from the same area, as Siroto has noted, in that the handles of knives may be wrapped in combinations of fine copper wire and heavier ribbon of brass or copper. Siroto also illustrates a knife from the Middle Ogowé whose sheet-brass scabbard is decorated with repoussé motifs like the sheet-covered, "foliate" reliquary figures.[77] And yet this also has echoes in Galton's nineteenth-century description of Ovambo "dagger-knives" far to the south. These, he wrote, "were creditably made, and very pretty. The knife was set into a wooden handle, and fitted into a wooden sheath; but both handle and sheath were in part covered with copper plating, and in part wound round with copper wire beaten square."[78]

Though such wrappings of copper, brass, and iron wire are found on arms in virtually all parts of sub-Saharan Africa, there are distinct regional variations which will undoubtedly become clearer when more work is done in the field and in museums. Thus in Malawi and Zambia, very fine brass wire may be woven into extremely intricate patterns covering the entire shaft, while the Lemba of the northern Transvaal may apply their wire-drawing skills to decorating spears "filigranartig," as Mauch put it.[79] Kuba knife handles, too, may be covered with plaited copper wire. Indeed, many of the most beautiful arms come from equatorial Africa—in particular knives, throwing knives, and axes (figs. 27, 28; color illust. 6). Stanley observed that in the Ikengo region near the confluence of the Ubangui and Congo Rivers, "every weapon [they] possess is decorated with fine brass wire and brass tacks. Their knives are beautiful weapons, of a bill-hook pattern, the handles of which are also profusely decorated with an amount of brasswork and skill that places them very high among the clever tribes."[80] Less grudging in his admiration, Lemaire referred to the "splendid arms" of the Songye with their "axes incrusted with copper and handles spangled with red or yellow."[81] Foliate, spatulate, hooked, or gracefully curving, open or solid, there is an almost infinite variation on the basic theme of blade and handle—nor is it surprising, then, that the Bobangi decorated their

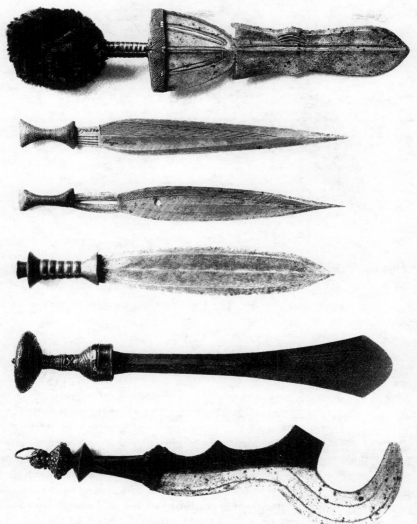

27. Ceremonial knives, Zaire. Iron, copper, brass, wood

233

28. Throwing knife, Kuta, Zaire. Iron, brass

oars with copper and that the Tio king brought back such an oar as a trophy of war.[82]

## SOUNDING BRASS

Thus far we have looked at copper as a medium of visual art, but it also served as a medium of aural art: drums, trumpets, rattles, bells.

Drums have long been part of the panoply of royalty. Leo Africanus wrote of the "drums of copper" of the king of Fez in the form of large basins. Each was carried by a horse, which had to be counterweighted on the other side because it was so heavy. They made such a terrific din that horses and men trembled at the sound.[83] Such drums may have been ancestral to the copper drums which according to al-Tunisi accompanied the sultan of Darfur;[84] the post of chamberlain at the court of the dynasty of Darfur was literally titled "malik en nahas," "king of copper," in reference to the state drums.[85] Tubiana has described a ceremony among the Turrti of northern Darfur in which a copper drum arrives on the back of an unaccompanied camel [sic]. Such drums are also used by the Zaghawa

(Chad), who call both the metal and the instrument *naas,* clearly a loan word from Arabic, although the drums are used in rites of fertility that obviously antedate Islam in the region.[86] Copper drums also figured at the royal court of Buganda. One of them was called *wango-tabuka,* "the kabaka is like a leopard." Another was made of copper over wood, and beaten with the hands rather than with sticks.[87]

The Ganda drums were undoubtedly modern, probably nineteenth-century. By contrast, when the Portuguese sacked the court of the Mwene Mutapa on the northern Zimbabwe plateau in 1629, they found "an immense copper drum, covered with rich silk cloths and lion skins," the sacred *ngoma.*[88] In West Africa, de Marees (1600) found copper basins used as drums: "Others," he wrote of the Gold Coast, "have instruments whereon they play, as some Copper Basons whereon they strike with wooden sticks." On the occasion of deaths, too, women would beat basins as they danced around the house and approached the corpse.[89] Palisot de Beauvais (1787) noted that copper cauldrons were employed as drums in the yam festival celebrated at Benin.[90] Similarly, the "huge copper dishes" presented to the Mangbetu king by Khartoum merchants were not relegated to the kitchen but were "employed for the far more dignified office of furnishing music for the royal halls."[91] Indeed, Armstrong has suggested that the splendid roped pot cast in bronze found at Igbo-Ukwu (fig. 29) may have been a sort of idiophone, a model of a sacred instrument, like the more recent globular pots in a nest of cord tied to a thick circular base of braided rope. These are struck across the mouth with flat, fanlike implements of cowhide, and the rope nesting enables them to reverberate somewhat like a double bass.[92]

Copper and brass trumpets and bugles are found primarily in the Sudan, associated with court ceremonials heavily influenced by Islam. Baghirmi tradition claims that the first king arrived from Yemen with one hundred wooden trumpets and one of copper, which only the hunter Lubadko had the right to blow on behalf of the ruler.[93] Part of the investiture ceremony of the Bariba kings at Nikki includes the blowing of the "famous royal trumpets of copper which evoke with each of their blasts one of the kings of the dynasty."[94] According to the *Kano Chronicle,* Rumfa (c. 1463–99) was the first *sarki* of Kano to have *kakati,* or long trumpets, blown before him, and long trumpets are still the insignia of kings throughout northern Nigeria.[95] They have also spread southward to enter the regalia of Nupe, Oyo, and Igala.[96] In Dahomey, King Glele had a trumpet in copper and brass in the form of a hunting horn,[97] while Mtesa of Uganda created a sort of military band which included brass bugles, one of them made by his own smith.[98]

The Tiv were expert at casting mouth whistles. The oldest types con-

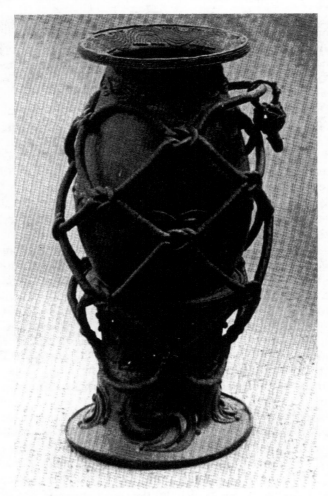

29. Roped pot, Igbo-Ukwu, Nigeria. Leaded bronze

sisted of human arm or leg bones to which a modeled or cast head was attached. Later the bone was replaced by hollow cast tubes with heads added in the same way; most recently the entire tube has been cast in human form.[99] Musina traditions in the Transvaal contain a curious reference to a "brass flute" which was given to Tshishonga and his people "to blow, so that his enemy might fall asleep and lack strength, and they could break into their town." The Venda text seems to use the word *musuku*, which Van Warmelo translates "brass," but one wonders if it could not just as well be copper. Unfortunately, there is nothing in the passage to make clear where the flute came from or what it looked like.[100]

Copper and brass rattles were also a fixture in the musical repertoire of many societies. They are depicted on Benin sculpture, and they have crossed the Atlantic as *here* or *chechere,* the copper rattles shaken in Shango ceremonies in Bahia, Brazil.[101] A rattle effect could be achieved by the frequent practice of attaching bits of copper to drums, as Matthews (1788) describes in Sierra Leone,[102] or copper rings to various stringed instruments.[103] Dapper refers to copper cymbals in seventeenth-century Loango,[104] and Phillips, later in the same century, describes the local musicians entertaining the Dutch at Axim and Whydah by "beating a hollow piece of brass with a stick."[105] Perhaps the most exotic instrumental use of copper is that employed in the Songhay "culte des génies." A single-stringed violin made of a horsehair stretched taut over a half-calabash covered with iguana skin is played with a bow of horsehairs attached to an arc of copper.[106]

But as with other forms of art, we also find the human being as musical instrument in Africa. Writing of the lavish use of beaded and metallic dangles and loose metal anklets among the Turkana, Samburu, and Pokot of northern Kenya, Herbert Cole declares, "All of these produce clinking, clanging sounds which are of course magnified in dances, when the entire ensemble of dress and decoration comes alive. *Much jewelry, in fact, seems to have been designed so as to dramatize the sounds and motions of dancing.*"[107] Lembezat makes the same point when, describing the dancing of the Toupouri of the Logone River in northern Cameroon, he notes that the iron and copper bracelets, and especially the anklets which may cover the entire leg, "become for the moment instruments of music, the Toupouri synchronizing the rhythm of the dances with the metallic sounds of their jangling anklets."[108] The copper bracelets of Lemba in the Lower Congo also resonate beautifully when struck together. Janzen was told that the "Ko-Ko-Ko" of Lemba songs, in fact, is the chiming of the rings.[109] Achebe's *Things Fall Apart* has the unforgettable scene of an Ibo marriage feast where at night the girls come to dance, last of all the bride herself: "Her brass anklets rattled as she danced and her body gleamed with cam wood in the soft yellow light."[110]

To intensify the sound of jewelry, bells were frequently added to bracelets and anklets and waist bands. One thinks of the incredible rhythmic intensity of Zulu dancing, but the custom is widespread. In 1600 women of the Gold Coast "put Rings with many bells [on their legs]," that they might sound when they danced.[111] Wilson and Felkin described a spectacular Shilluk dance at Fashoda in the mid-1870s performed by warriors decked out in leopard skins, sheep tails, and grass streamers on their head bands: "The ankles and forearms were adorned with rings of copper or brass, and small bits of metal of all shapes were fastened just below the knee, and in some instances bells were tied above the right elbow." [112]

Nor do bells figure as personal adornment only in the dance. They are often attached to children's bracelets in particular. [113] In the Oil Rivers, Clough found young girls eligible for marriage wearing clusters of little brass harness bells hanging from waists and ankles, while pregnant women wore small bells suspended on leather thongs over their navels. [114] Ornate bells are represented on Benin brass sculptures and on the so-called Tsoede bronzes, and have continued to be worn throughout wide areas of Nigeria and Cameroon by men of rank or their retainers. [115] Similarly, Degrandpré described rich "Angolans" in the eighteenth century wearing cat-skin skirts decorated with "crotals and small bells that they wear over their private parts." [116] The inhabitants of the Gabon coast also had a fondness for tinkling bells on their loin cloths. [117]

Bells are not only depicted on sculptures, they are also attached to them. The best known are the often frightening masks of the Poro Society from the Dan and Guere with their rings of bells around the face. Ekwe figures, too, were formerly decorated with oval bells. [118] In the same way, bells adorned objects of ritual use such as the *Kimbi* knife illustrated by Meek or the hunting prophylacteries of the Mpongwe. [119] Or they augmented musical instruments like the *bata* drums used in the Shango cult or the marriage calabashes common among the riverain peoples of the Middle Niger. [120] In Ghana, ceremonial stools customarily have bells of cast iron and brass attached to them, the number of bells indicating the status of the chief to whom the stool belongs. [121] The Golden Stool itself has several bells on it. Rattray recorded differing traditions about these bells: one claims that there were already two bells on it when it descended from heaven, the other that the priest Anotchi instructed Osei Tutu to make four bells, two of gold and two of brass, to hang one on each side of it. [122] One of the bells now hanging on the Stool is of a copper alloy and is known as *donkesse,* the great bell, which has the power to cause people to gather whenever it is rung. [123]

Many bells, however, are free-standing works of art, sculpture in their own right, attached neither to human beings nor to objects. These may include bells of European manufacture, but the finest are those cast in Africa itself. Here again the variety is prodigious, and precisely because they were often traded over long distances or produced by itinerant craftsmen such as the Awka, it is extremely difficult to classify them. [124] Many of the finest, however, can be linked to the traditional centers of brass casting: Benin, Igbo-Ukwu and other areas of southeastern Nigeria, the Benue Valley–Adamawa region, and the Cameroon grassfields. While some are clapperless, many are clappered. They may be cast onto bracelets or have figures cast onto the bells. Tikar/Bamum bells, for example, are often ornamented with anteaters, lizards, and human figures. The bell itself may be elaborately decorated with human faces or geometric patterns; it may be rounded, cylindrical, squared, conical, or in the shape of a double gong.

When African art burst upon the Paris scene in the early years of the present century, it caught the mood of an avant-garde proclaiming the primacy of pure form. Juan Gris made a maquette of a Mahongwe reliquary figure, evidently delighting in its abstract two-dimensionality; Derain was captivated by a geometric Kuba head. The arts of Africa can indeed be appreciated for their purely formal qualities and for their sheer exoticism, but to do so is in a sense to acquiesce in a continued intellectual imperialism, to show a disregard for the meaning of the object in its own society, for the language of which it is a part. It is not simply in the guise of musical instruments that it speaks—as "sounding brass." The object is the sum of its form and materials but a great deal more, for it is deeply embedded in a living, changing web of beliefs and values.

# Copper as a Medium of Power

To the wearer of *Sapuli* [brass wire],
We pay due fealty,
For well we know that she must be
The wife of Royalty.

—Yao song

When [Sambanza] had finished his long ora-
tion he rose up, and in going off was obliged by
such large bundles of copper rings on his ankles
to adopt quite a straddling walk. When I laughed
at the absurd appearance he made, the people
remarked, *"That is lordship in these parts."*

— LIVINGSTONE, *African Journal*

Thousands of tons of cuprous metal were absorbed by African cultures
over almost two millennia and were transformed into a bewildering array
of objects. So much is clear. The more difficult question is why? With
the variety of materials at hand, why choose copper or its alloys?

On a superficial level, one need not look far for the answer. These metals were easy to work and durable, and scarce enough to have the value
attached to any material available in limited quantities — and until the nineteenth century quantities *were* limited in most areas by technological constraints and the difficulties of transport. On another level, however, the
answer or answers can only be suggested in this chapter and the next. For
the distant past we are reduced to arguing by present or recent analogy,
and even for later periods we depend for our interpretation on the kind
of deep investigation that is still extremely rare. "It is quite clear," observes
Daniel Biebuyck, "that a single art object does occur in different rites, events
and circumstances. The objects are multivalent in usage and function; and
as symbols, they can express many meanings."[1] The artist's work in giving
form to a particular material (or cluster of materials) is only the beginning. The form and material contain a core meaning which is constantly
augmented, qualified, extended, even contradicted by the context. A static
object is an incomplete statement. To arrive at a more complete statement
one must, as Biebuyck asserts, observe and participate in the various ritual
uses to which a single art object or a particular set of art works is put;
and even these particular uses must be part of still larger units of observa-

240

tion, so that one is faced with an almost impossible ideal, especially if one adds the dimension of time and change to the cultural equation.

On the other hand, a comparative study, even when it must be based on uneven data and on observation that usually falls far short of Biebuyck's ideal, has the advantage of pointing to patterns of signification that transcend individual contexts and cultures. True, there is the very real danger of submerging the nuances of the particular and the unique in an over-facile invocation of universality, but there is also the possibility of elucidating the unique by reference to broader usages.

One premise which is fundamental to the argument that follows needs to be made clear at the outset. This is the belief that the choice of materials for objects that in any sense make a social statement is not a random or purely personal matter. We have spoken earlier of the role of taste and fashion in the history of trading contacts between Africa and Europe. To merchants who faced bankruptcy when the taste changed from one type of textile or bead or metal bracelet to another, this no doubt seemed explicable only as some sort of irrational whim, and in most cases we cannot account for it with certainty. But if we had sufficient information we probably could, and it would involve not only the opening and closing of inland markets, unknown to coastal traders, but also a complex interplay of the personal within a framework peculiar to the larger society. That is, African societies, like pre-industrial societies everywhere, set limits within which individual choice had to operate. Materials and the form given them were part of a language accepted by the society and which one had to speak properly, as it were. All materials, including metals, had inherent properties which dictated and circumscribed their use, just as the spheres within a society required objects that could embody their ideologies. This language of materials can be seen most clearly as it applies to personal ornamentation. "The choice of personal ornaments," Denise Paulme emphasizes, though it may seem to be a matter of "spontaneous coquettry . . . is in most cases nothing of the sort. A coherent body of interdictions and restrictions and of properties which must be observed limit their use. In many African societies, as in Oceania or among the American Indians, jewelry and body marking constitute a veritable system of signs which amount almost to a language. . . . It is rare that these ornaments do not have a social significance which prescribes the wearing of certain ones and the prohibition of others."[2] This applies equally to the range of objects whose role is in any sense significant.

Does this mean then that one could not simply adorn oneself or one's belongings with copper or some other material just because it was pleasing? Certainly in more recent times this has been increasingly the case, but in earlier periods the notion of what was pleasing seems to have been tied so closely to the values attached to the materials and their forms that we may be imposing an alien dichotomy. Even now, concepts of the esthetic in African societies (and in our own) often cannot really be divorced from social statements. Speaking of Senufo notions of beauty, Glaze writes:

> Another Senufo term of aesthetic valuation is *tana* (or *tahama*). *Tana* may be translated as "ornamental" or "decorative" and is invariably employed in a context that implies personal show, pride, prestige, and even ostentatious display. Children's bracelets . . . , for example, were described as *tahama*. Mothers who could afford the costly brasscaster's fees would traditionally purchase a set of shiny brass bracelets for their children as an expression of parental pride, to encourage rhythmic response to sound patterns, and to amuse the child with their jangling sound.[3]

Similarly, Gubert suggests that the copper and brass banding and nailheads common on Songye wood sculpture create an esthetically pleasing contrast between the play of sunlight on the metal and the almost black wood, but this does not preclude the metal from making a statement about power and wealth at the same time.[4]

In precolonial African societies as a whole, copper was a signifier of status: status in the sense of wealth, prestige, rank, and authority, but also status in regard to gender, age, and the stages of human life. It was also used in a variety of other ritual contexts which are harder to categorize. The common denominator in its myriad uses, I will argue, is, or was, the connotation of power, understood not just in our narrower sense of political power—although this is a crucial part of its role—but power defined within a view of the world that assumes the interpenetration of the political, religious, social, economic, and esthetic spheres. To speak of these spheres as if they existed separately is to do violence to the contextual integrity, but it will sometimes be unavoidable. For the purposes of our discussion, we will deal briefly with copper as a symbol of wealth, more fully with the status significations of the metal and its role in ritual, and in the following chapter suggest the ideational associations that may underlie all of these usages.

## COPPER AS WEALTH

Since copper served so widely in Africa as a standard of value, it goes without saying that the wearing of copper ornaments has always been an indicator of wealth—the more jewelry or the larger its dimensions, the greater the wealth. Few accounts are as explicit as that of Gutersohn, which ascribes a precise value in mitako to the various copper ornaments of the Mongo,[5] but presumably it was not difficult for the well-informed to reckon up the worth of the enormous quantities of copper rings and necklaces described in so much of the literature. In the same manner, copper and brass often formed part not only of bridewealth payments to the family of the bride but also of gifts to the bride herself as proof that her husband could keep her properly. In Burundi, for example, the ideal of any self-respecting man was to be able to offer his wife enough copper wire bracelets to cover her leg from ankle to knee.[6]

Characteristically, in fact, the most massive amounts of jewelry were worn by women rather than men, representing a sort of double thesaurization: wives, daughters, even slave women and their ornaments served as tangible symbols of their husbands', fathers', and owners' wealth. As Wannyn comments, when a Kongo woman carried a dozen kilograms of copper on her person, this was more than an indicator of her rank, and probably actually represented the wealth of the clan chief.[7]

Such manifestations of wealth had by-products beyond the economic realm. Though Livingstone remarks in several instances on the encumbered walk of Lunda chiefs, this was more typical of the wives of notables and rulers. Loyer (1714) claimed that the well-to-do women of Assinie began accustoming their children to wearing heavy bracelets on their feet and wrists while they were still babies.[8] Foreigners might deplore such heavy loads of jewelry as a fettering of women and ridicule the waddle that resulted as duck-like or bovine. But this missed the point completely. Such a stately walk conveyed the message that the wearer was above manual labor, and it was the ultimate in dignity. The heavy freight of bracelets and anklets, note Célis and Nzikobanyanka of the pastoral Burundi, "had the inestimable advantage . . . of giving women a gait suggesting the most admirable walk of the cow."[9] Herero women, bedecked with brass rings, scorned European women whose bustle betrayed their lack of status, their ignorance of what it was to be mistress of a household.[10] And Livingstone noticed that in Kazembe's country those whose status did not entitle them to load their legs with rings imitated the walk of those who did.[11]

In Khoikhoi society, too, copper was a sign of wealth, and men were accustomed to pass on to women many of the ornaments obtained from the Dutch in trade. It is generally acknowledged that the sale of cattle for copper and tobacco seriously undermined the traditional structures of Khoikhoi society, but Elphick makes an interesting distinction between men's and women's roles in this process. Although chiefs and wealthy men saw copper as "at once a prestigious and easily defensible form of wealth," it supplemented rather than replaced cattle. Women, on the other hand, were likely to sell much more extensively because they could inherit and pass on ornaments but not cattle unless they had no brothers, and thus their measures of value would have been reversed.[12]

Ostentation is obviously one of the prime requisites of wealth, as the Senufo recognize, and copper was and is highly visible. This has not been an unmixed blessing. In the massacre of the Hereros by Jonker Afrikander in 1850, women's hands and feet were hacked off to obtain their copper bangles more speedily.[13] Moffat describes a similar scene of carnage when the "Mantatee" warriors severed the heads and arms of their enemies to obtain copper rings.[14] Coquilhat claims the same thing happened to the wife with the heaviest brass collar when a chief at Wangata died, and Stanley has a comparable tale about recovering such collars when any of Chumbiri's wives died. But both of these sources are less-immediately credible than the accounts of war — even in the case of Chumbiri who boasted that his forty wives carried a total of some 800 pounds of brass between them.[15]

## COPPER AND POLITICAL POWER

So far we have spoken of copper as a primary signifier of wealth, but we need to explore more deeply the interconnections of wealth and status. Nadel defines status as a more or less fixed position on the social ladder which is determined by birth or promotion.[16] Chavannes, for example, makes this distinction between wealth and status explicit in his observation that in the Lower Congo "the number and size of the [brass] anklets which a woman is entitled to wear depend not only on the prosperity of her husband but also on his rank and birth."[17] Prestige entails a more fluid form of social recognition, gained by service, deeds, or wealth. Nonetheless, status is closely linked to wealth, that is, to the means of obtaining it and disbursing it to preserve one's position.

Copper, naturally enough, figured widely in the gift-giving between rulers and between subjects and rulers. In Dahomey, emissaries to the king were given brass castings to take back to their lords, since of all the neighboring states, say the Herskovitses, only Dahomey produced these figures.[18] At Great Ardra in the seventeenth century, tribute was paid in "great" brass rings.[19] Among the Beti it took the form of cylindrical anklets, among the Igala, brass rods.[20] Edo chiefs were required by political etiquette to bring kola and other offerings to the oba in *ori-evbee,* wooden boxes often richly decorated with brass-studded designs.[21] Reciprocally, copper could be given by a ruler as a mark of special recognition. Among the Zulu, until the reign of Cetshwayo, the privilege of wearing the heavy brass armlet called *ingxota* was conferred by the king as a badge of distinction.[22] A comparable medal for bravery among the Ovambo was a "quite small knife in a large, decorative, triangular sheath of shiny copper." In an Ovambo sub-group, the Ondonga, this took the form of a miniature knife of copper.[23]

But it is primarily with copper as an emblem of leadership itself that we will be concerned here, for this has been the most conspicuous use of the metal and its alloys in all parts of the continent for many centuries. The references to copper and brass attributes of authority are legion, and they have taken virtually all the forms given to these metals: bracelets and anklets, collars (fig. 30), crowns, pendants and bells, stools and thrones, staffs and weapons, ornate vessels, masks and statues. The literature is replete with references to rulers and their families being laden with copper and brass, some of them so heavily that their arms had to be supported by attendants.[24] It would be tedious to catalogue all the variations on this theme, so that we will limit the discussion to representative examples or interesting extensions.

Frequently all we are told is that a ruler was recognizable by having more of something of value than his subjects, but where information is available, it usually turns out that there is a prescriptive aspect, some sort of sumptuary restriction in force: the king-chief-notable is he who is entitled to possess certain objects, including those in copper and brass, that are forbidden to other people. When Sultan Njoya "democratized" the use of these

30. Chief's collar, Teke, Congo Republic. Brass

metals, allowing anyone to smoke from cast brass pipes and all Bamum women to wear copper rings, he was opening up what had heretofore been strictly the prerogative of the court and king.[25] Throughout the Cameroon grassfield chiefdoms, copper and brass in the form of double gongs and bells, anklets, pipes, drinking horns, and sheathed masks and stools were until this century tied closely to royal power (fig. 31, color illust. 5).[26]

In Benin, cast brass was even more narrowly the prerogative of the king (although chiefs were apparently allowed objects of beaten brass), and in Nupe and Dahomey, casting was also a court art—in all three, the royal residence was, as Tardits has described the palace of Bamum, a "vitrine d'exposition du royaume," where the choicest works in copper and brass, along with other luxury crafts, were reserved for those in power.[27] Earlier, this may also have been true of Ife or of the Jukun capital of Kororafa, both of which obviously had a close identification of brass casting with kingship.[28] Perhaps Igbo-Ukwu should also be included: it may be that kingship as such never existed in this area, but ritual authority seems clearly implied, and this has always been an aspect of African kingship and its material embodiments.[29]

Outside of the areas of cire-perdue casting, copper and brass were also the privilege of kingship. Among the Yao, chiefs kept tight control over trade goods, especially foreign goods from the coast, reserving brass wire for their own personal use and that of their king.[30] As late as 1880, it was reported that only chiefs could wear ornaments of red copper among the Bende, Nyamwezi, and Gogo of Tanzania.[31] Lemba smiths of the Transvaal were at first prohibited from making copper ornaments for any but the Venda royal family and themselves.[32] Robinson suggests an interesting parallel between the hoard of iron and bronze spears and the axe-head with a copper disk implanted in its blade, found at Khami Hill, and the royal spears of the Venda. Possession of the Venda spears meant possession of the chieftainship, inasmuch as they represented male ancestors in the chiefly line. Since the Venda are thought to have migrated from the north and to have been linked historically with the Rozwi, similarities in emblems of kingship would be altogether plausible.[33] In Katanga, it was the chiefly right to cast copper ingots that was at issue: when the Lunda conquered the territory of Musonoi, they left the former rulers certain traditional privileges such as the exclusive right to cast copper croisettes, and when the mines were ultimately ceded to the Union Minière du Haut-Katanga early in the colonial period, the company in its turn agreed to continue furnishing these rulers with the copper necessary to cast the croisettes.[34]

Among the Kuba, "brass . . . symbolizes the refusal to be or become a subject" and as such was an emblem of the supreme authority of Kuba kings over tributary chiefs. There is even a tale about a war that broke

31. Cast horns and bell, grasslands, Cameroon. Brass or wood with copper and brass

out between Bushoong and Bokila when King Mboong aLeeng heard that the Bokila chief had the audacity to wear brass. Vansina believes the story may be anachronistic, since it refers to a time before brass would have reached the Kuba kingdom and been incorporated into the regalia, but it underscores the importance the metal would acquire.[35] Torday noted at the time of his visit early in this century that only members of the royal family and representatives of the smiths were allowed hatpins of brass.[36] Through Kuba influence, perhaps, brass had in fact become a sort of touchstone of kingship among the neighboring Lele: "Katera's village," writes Torday, "was so big that we thought he might be the paramount chief, but I offered him, as a test, some brass, and he would not even touch it, so I knew he was not; this metal is the monopoly of Goma N'Vula and Nyimi Lele, as it used to be that of the Nyimi of Bushongo."[37]

According to Burundi tradition, the first blacksmith king, Ntare Rushatsi, had a hammer in copper "in order to display his superiority: all that belonged to him must be different from that which others possessed." Each subsequent king as he ascends the throne is given this hammer, with the words, "Here is the hammer which the *mwami* gives to men to make them true men." It is always kept at the head of his bed, while a second hammer, larger than an ordinary one, stays with the royal drum. The association of kingship and smithing makes these symbols especially appropriate, but they are reinforced by the lances of copper which the mwami had forged — also different from those of his subjects, "as a sign of grandeur, power and wealth." In like manner, the copper and bronze bracelets fashioned by court jewelers for members of the royal family are different from those made for commoners.[38]

The Burundi case is typical. Conventional objects such as hammers, axes, and weapons are transformed into elements of regalia by making them more ornate, by adding copper or brass, or by making them entirely out of these metals rather than iron; they become ceremonial and ritual rather than functional. Schweinfurth gives a stunning description of the ceremonial arms of the royal hall of the Mangbetu king (fig. 32):

> Posts were driven into the ground, and long poles were fastened horizontally across them: then against this extemporized scaffolding were laid, or supported crosswise, hundreds of ornamental lances and spears, all of pure copper, and of every variety of form and shape. The gleam of the red metal caught the rays of the tropical noontide sun, and in the symmetry of their arrangement the rows of dazzling lance-heads shone with the glow of flaming torches, making a background to the royal throne that was really magnificent. This display of wealth, which according to Central African tradition was incalculable, was truly regal, and surpassed anything of the kind that I had conceived possible.[39]

32. King Munsa of Mangbetu in his court

Of course much more than wealth was being invoked: the dazzling luminosity and color of the metal were themselves quintessential "signs of grandeur and power."

And, as in Burundi, oral tradition and especially genesis myths may offer explanations of the association of copper with kingship. In the central myth which Reefe uses to explicate the political structures of the Luba Empire, "Kipuku wa Mbuyu ('Big Water Rat'), the chief of the villages in the vicinity of the confluence of the Luguvu and Lomami rivers, ferried Nkongolo [Rainbow] across both rivers so Nkongolo could escape Kalala Ilunga. . . . Nkongolo bestowed upon Kipuku wa Mbuyu the title *mwadi* and gave as symbols of his attachment . . . a copper bracelet, an axe with a copper blade, and a finely carved paddle that contained the images of two birds and was covered with copper strips." Kalala Ilunga later put in his own people as hereditary titleholders of the crossing and this lineage became the possessors of the bracelet, axe, and paddle. He also gave Chief Kapese the same type of insignia that Kipuku wa Mbuyu had received from Nkongolo. The Chief was designated a royal ferryman across the Lomami, and his insignia were periodically anointed with human blood. As elsewhere, possession of such insignia was more than symbolic. It legitimated claims to office and constituted tangible representation of the permanency of the bonds between client states and the Luba royal dynasty.[40]

The Tsoede legends offer a similar attempt to explain the insignia of Nupe kingship and their connection with the creation of the kingdom. Nadel places Tsoede's birth about the middle of the fifteenth century, at a time when Nupe consisted only of a collection of small chieftainships united under the chief of Nku, a village near the confluence of the Niger and the Kaduna; but the dating is not very secure. In any event, the Nupe villages were tributary to the *atta* of Igala at Idah. A son of the atta fell in love with a daughter of the Nku chief and had a son by her who was Tsoede. At the age of thirty he was sent as a slave to the atta, as custom demanded. By this time it was his father who was atta, and Tsoede in due time was recognized and won favor through his bravery. This made his half-brothers intensely jealous, and when the atta felt death approaching he advised Tsoede to flee and to carry back to Nupe the rule which was his parting gift. He also gave him riches and the various insignia of office: "a bronze canoe 'as only kings have,' manned with twelve Nupe slaves; the bronze *kakati,* the long trumpets which are still the insignia of kings in northern Nigeria; state drums hung with brass bells; and the heavy iron chains and fetters which, endowed with strong magic, have become the emblems of the king's judicial power, and are known today as egba Tsoede, Chain of Tsoede."

Pursued by his half-brothers, Tsoede made his way up the Niger till he reached the Kaduna. There he turned into a creek called Ega, where he lay in hiding until his brothers gave up the search and went home. Tsoede and his men then sank the canoe in the river, and the people of Ega still perform an annual sacrifice on the spot where tradition has it that the canoe was sunk: "At these ceremonies they are able, you are told, to see the bright bronze of the canoe glitter in the water." Next Tsoede went to a nearby village, killed the chief, and took power himself. He then conquered Nku and made himself ruler of the confederacy, assuming the title *etsu,* king. The twelve companions of his struggles he made chiefs of the twelve towns and bestowed on them the sacred emblems of chieftainship, brass bangles and magic chains, which still serve as insignia for their descendants.[41]

Apart from the royal insignia and emblems of magic, Tsoede is also supposed to have introduced to Nupe hitherto unknown techniques, including cire-perdue casting. Nevertheless, the appellation "Tsoede bronzes" given to the collection of ten cast figures found at Tada, Jebba, and Giragi is now generally considered to be unacceptable. Although Nupe has a highly developed tradition of brassworking it may be relatively recent, and in any case there is no evidence that it ever included casting large figures such as these—five of them are more than 3 feet high, the largest bronzes found anywhere in Africa.[42] Furthermore, the pieces are stylistically heterogeneous. While the beautiful seated figure is close to Ife sculptures in both metal and terra cotta, the provenance of the others has been hotly debated: Benin, Idah, Owo, Oyo-Ile, or some possibly unknown center in southwestern Nigeria.[43] How they got to their present somewhat obscure sites is a mystery, but once there, it is not surprising that local traditions assimilated such striking objects to the legends of Tsoede.

Given the central role of brass in Benin regalia, it is also not surprising that Bini traditions discuss its origins. According to Chief Egharevba, "Oba Oguola [the fifth king] wished to introduce brass-casting into Benin so as to produce works of art similar to those sent him from Ife. He therefore sent to the Oni of Ife for a brass-smith and Igueghae was sent to him."[44] This derivation has been questioned as part of the general reassessment of the Ife-Benin connection. Paula Ben-Amos has suggested that the connection may have been invoked initially in the first half of the eighteenth century as part of the revival of kingly power after a period of turmoil—a rewriting of history to legitimate the present.[45] Such a link is not mentioned earlier in European accounts of Benin, and seems even to be denied by the celebrated account of the Portuguese embassy of 1485 which describes a tributary relationship with a monarch called Ogane, stated clearly to be located to the east of Benin—although the distance, twenty moons' journey, may be fanciful:

> In accordance with a very ancient custom, the Kings of Beny, on ascending the throne, sent ambassadors to him with rich gifts to inform him that by the decease of their predecessor they had succeeded to the Kingdom of Beny, and to request him to confirm them in the same. As a sign of confirmation this Prince Ogane sent them a staff and a headpiece, fashioned like a Spanish helmet, made all of shining brass, in place of a sceptre and crown. He also

sent a cross, of the same brass, and shaped like those worn by the Commen-
dadores, to be worn round the neck like something religious and holy. Without these emblems the people would consider that they did not reign lawfully,
nor could they call themselves true kings.

The details of this regalia, reported so precisely, are also unknown in Ife
art — especially the cross motif, which recurs in smaller form as an insignia
for royal ambassadors. And unlike Ife, brass continued to play a crucial
role in Benin down to the present.[46]
    Benin plaques and heads show an evolving iconography of kingship (fig.
18 and fig. 40, p. 291).[47] The process of change can be followed in other
cultures as well. The descriptions left by successive visitors to the Ganda
court show how readily these kings adopted paraphernalia made available
by the rapid expansion of trading and diplomatic contacts. Each new European traveller in the latter half of the nineteenth century found Kabaka
Mtesa wearing a different garb and surrounded by different insignia. It
was during this period that copper drums and bugles were added to the
regalia; the copper lances and "grapnels" and the copper embossed shields
that now adorn the Kasubi tombs outside Kampala are all ascribed to the
last five kabakas, reflecting the relatively late date that copper reached this
region.[48] Similarly, Ndagara I (c. 1820 to 1853 or 1855) is the Karagwe ruler
credited with putting together the nucleus of the remarkable collection of
iron and copper objects which ultimately numbered 120. When Speke visited the kingdom at the time of Rumanyika, Ndagara's successor, he found
"a large assortment of spears . . . brass-headed with iron handles, and iron-
headed with wooden ones . . . , a number of brass grapnels and small models of cows, made in iron."[49] By the time of Stanley's passage, the royal
treasury had expanded to include sixteen "rude brass figures of ducks with
copper wings," ten "curious things of the same metal meant to represent
elands," and ten "headless cows of copper," plus massive copper trays, the
gifts of Arab traders.[50] The king himself was known as Bugororoka rwa
Kakindo Biringa bya Bihogo, "the upright one of Kakindo's house, the
wearer of the copper bangles, of Bihogo."[51]
    What Speke and Grant described as grapnels are in fact anvils, in the
opinion of Sassoon, and have parallels in the regalia of Rwanda, Ankole,
and Buganda. In Rwanda they are actually iron anvils with horns, called
*nyarushara,* a name similar to the Ankole name for a bull with downturned
horns. In both Karagwe and Buganda they became ceremonial anvils in
copper, again an evocation of the intimate association of smithing and
kingship such as we have already seen in Burundi.[52]
    Implicit in the evolution of many insignia of kingship seems to be the
shift from iron to copper. This may account for conflicting versions of

what is the same core story in the Kuba legend of the "hammers and anvils." The tale constitutes, in Vansina's words, "a genuine political charter of kingship," offering a historical justification of the primacy of the Bushoong, but some of the versions refer to copper objects which the rivals had to make float in the water, others to iron.[53] The bracelets that are important insignia of chieftaincy among many Central African groups reflect some of the same sort of interchangeability. The prototype for these bracelets is the Lunda *rukan,* the metal bracelet wrapped in human sinew which in the Lunda genesis myth was given to Chibind Yirung as a symbol of the transfer of royal authority to him. The term was borrowed by neighboring Luba groups, who changed it to *lukano* and also gave it a mythological anchor as an insignia of kingship.[54] Among the Kongo west of São Salvador, the *chef couronné* takes off his own iron bracelets and gives one to each newly elected chief as part of the investiture ceremony.[55] Mertens, however, reported that among the eastern Kongo, influenced by "coutumes BaMfunuka" (by which he presumably means the Fumu subgroup of northwestern Bantu),[56] chiefs no longer wear iron bracelets. Instead, they wear a single bracelet of red copper in the form of an undecorated spiral on the left arm.[57] In the Lower Congo and Lower Kwilu and among the Mbochi of Congo-Brazzaville, copper bracelets are a common emblem of kingship, but because they are close to sources of copper, their use may be more ancient than in areas that are more distant.[58]

Even in societies without centralized political institutions, copper and brass carried connotations of political authority. We have already seen that masks of the Poro Society, one of whose primary functions is to maintain social and political control, are often made with brass bells and strips of metal. In the title societies of southern Nigeria and the Lemba society of the Lower Congo, however, the role of copper and brass is even more closely analogous to its role in emblems of kingship. Ibo groups vary considerably in social organization, but most of them seem never to have had chiefs or kings comparable to those west of the Niger. They do commonly have *ozo* or title-taking societies, and these offer a means of acquiring prestige not by birth but by achievement. The details vary from town to town — some have more degrees than others or higher fees — but essentially every grade is open to any free man who can afford the progressively steeper initiation fees. In return, he obtains status and the right to the emblems of his particular rank. Brassbound iron staffs and spears are a part of the insignia of the different grades. At the Ajalija stage, for example, when the fees begin to get high, the insignia include an iron staff 9 feet long, forked at the top end and spear-pointed at the bottom, with brass bindings at top, bottom, and in the middle, and the insignia include copper anklets 3 or 4 inches wide, as well. At the time of Basden's writing (1921), few men aspired to climb higher, since the attainment of this grade marked an honorable and influential position in the community.[59]

Among the northern Ibo, bells were an integral part of ozo society insignia, the specific kinds depending on the rank. The upper ranks wore them attached to special goatskin or cowhide bags, especially the most prestigious bell, the *odu*. Neaher points out that the tubular bells found at the fifteenth-century site of Ezira are identical to modern odu, and bells found at Igbo-Ukwu suggest that their use in such contexts may be even older.[60] Brasses are also common to other title societies, such as the Pere in the northwestern Niger Delta[61] and the Ekpe of Old Calabar and the Cross River. In the mid-nineteenth century the latter had eleven grades, the next to the highest being the "brass" or *okpoko* (that is, manilla). At this stage, the initiate's body was daubed all over with a yellow dye to simulate brass. Brass ekpe was responsible for law enforcement, an especially important function in an area where so many different peoples were drawn together by commerce. The "sacred yellow band" of ekpe was attached to property sealed by the society, and when the yellow flag of brass ekpe was raised, everyone of inferior grade had to remain indoors.[62]

## COPPER AND RITUAL POWER

Given the ritual authority embodied in kingship and the political implications of priesthood, we would expect to find many of the same symbols in both. This is particularly obvious in such cults as Lemba and Ogboni, but the parallels extend to many other ritual functions.

Like Ekpe, Lemba facilitated trading contracts by means of a supranational organization that helped to compensate for the lack of large-scale political units in the area immediately north of the lower Zaire River. The organization was centered on the copper-mining area from Mindouli to M'Boko Songho but extended from Mpumu and Teke country as far as the coast. Its initiation fees were highest at the site of the mines, so that it was closely connected with the industry—Janzen terms it a "market + commerce + alliance = building association."[63] Lemba priests played a judicial role in resolving market and intervillage disputes. More fundamentally, Lemba channeled "the aspirations to power of client groups into a common corporate ritual."[64]

But Lemba had other aspects that do not seem to have been part of title-taking societies. These concerned marriage and healing. As a marriage cult, it sanctioned alliances between clans but apparently consecrated relationships between individuals in a particular way. Deleval writes: "When a notable really loves one of his wives and feels himself loved by her, they make a second marriage before the *lemba* fetish. This marriage is very expensive; it joins the spouses for life." Their house is decorated with the lemba plant and becomes a sort of shrine to the order.[65] Deleval may well over-emphasize the element of romance at the expense of other implications of the ritual such as the remarriage necessary after the initiation of the neophyte priest and the consecration of the bracelets.

Typical of many healing cults, Lemba recruited from those who were called to the priesthood by first being afflicted with sickness, provided of course that they could afford the substantial fees which in practice maintained its elite membership. It did, however, admit women as well as men, and members of slave clans could gain access through patronage from a "Lemba Father." The primary insignia of Lemba was the copper bracelet worn by the priests and their spouses. Although the bracelets were made in sand moulds, some of them have remarkably ornate human figures and decorative motifs sculpted in relief. In Lemba ritual they are invoked as the symbols not only of the society itself but of its promises of health, material prosperity, and marital well-being with its implications of fertility and survival of the clan. They are also protective and fear-provoking: the Lemba priest "is greatly feared as he travels in villages lacking Lemba. He will carry only a staff and a copper bracelet on his arm."[66]

The Yoruba Ogboni combines a number of the same functions, but unlike Lemba it has apparently coexisted with stronger institutions of kingship for centuries. Ogboni members are titled elderly men whose age and high status are assumed to place them above petty ambition and also exempt them from many of the rules of ordinary behavior: as Thompson observes, "the inversion of propriety . . . is the soul of Ogboni custom."[67] Whereas brass is only one element in Yoruba kingship, it is the primary material used by Ogboni for its insignia and shrine furniture. Upon initiation, each member receives a pair of male and female figures, usually cast in brass, and joined by a chain of iron or copper, the *edan ogboni* (fig. 33). They are often worn around the neck as pendants. In addition, larger edan may belong to the society as a whole. Ogboni ceremonial swords or "cutlasses" in brass are also commonly decorated with ornate patterns and human or animal forms.

While some writers have stressed the twin-ness of Ogboni symbolism, the pairing of male and female, heaven and earth, Thompson has insisted on its "three-ness." "This is the number of the essential support of mankind by the earth, bulwark of morality, without which civilization falls." Like the three stones under the cooking pot of the Yoruba woman's outdoor hearth, threeness is the tripod of the social order. At the same time the Earth, to whose cult Ogboni is dedicated, is not simply a benevolent mother. There are implications, as elsewhere in Yoruba ritual, of "a hor-

33. *Edan ogboni,* Yoruba, Nigeria. Brass

rific maternal force watching humanity from the depths of the earth."
Roache has defined five functions of the edan: (1) judicial; (2) oracular:
predicting the life span of a member and even offering the means of adding to it through appropriate sacrifice; (3) healing; (4) protective; and
(5) magic communication and surveillance: the power of the edan to travel
on its own in the guise of a bird. Small wonder that, as we have noted
in chapter 2, such powerful objects are supposed to be cast only by men
past the age of fathering children.[68]

Within Akan society political authority has been symbolized first and
foremost by gold. Nevertheless, important ritual functions are served by
brass and especially by brass vessels. These rituals seem to have had their
origin in northern Ghana, in the core Akan area of Bono. Bono is generally considered to be the oldest centralized Akan state and the source of
major art forms.[69] It was also a trading polity, flourishing on the trade
in gold with the north, and the earliest vessels found throughout the area
are imports, primarily from Muslim North Africa and the Near East.
Though some of them have been dated — the earliest to the thirteenth century A.D., others to the fifteenth and sixteenth — this only provides a *terminus a quo*. They are made of sheet brass and were intended to be used
for ablutions, but among the Akan they have become sacred objects associated in a number of places with genesis myths and central to continuing
ritual observances.[70]

At Attebubu and Nsawkaw in Brong Ahafo, and Ejisu and Amoaman
in Aṣante, the basins are very large, some several feet across. They bear
Arabic inscriptions in Kufic script and are venerated as fetishes thought
to have come down from heaven.[71] An Ndenye myth recounts the descent
from heaven on a chain of a copper basin, still visible at Apibweso, containing a stool and two ceremonial swords,[72] while a Brong variant describes a brass basin that came "from the skies" suspended on a chain and
full of water.[73] At least ten sites with bowls linked to creation myths are
known in the Brong area or to the south. According to tradition, Ayewaso,
the old up-country capital of Accra, abandoned in 1680, means "place of
the brass bowl."[74]

In some cases traditions relate how bowls were brought to Aṣante with
the decline of the northern commercial towns and the conquest of Tekyiman. The large bronze ewer dated to the fourteenth century and found
at the sack of Kumasi where it served as "the great war fetish of the Ashanti
Nation" may have been such a spoil of battle.[75] According to a tradition
recorded by Meyerowitz, the Denkyira-Aṣante war of 1700–1701 was provoked when the *denkyirahene* sent an enormous brass basin, decorated
with toads and so heavy it took four men to carry it, to the *kwamanhene*
at Kumasi, demanding that it be returned filled to the brim with gold, a
demand followed by a request for the wives and daughters of the Aṣante

chiefs. Meyerowitz was also told that in the aftermath of the Begho-Nsawkaw civil war between pagans and Muslims, the two groups joined forces and killed a neighboring king. His skull was buried under a tree and is still marked by a large brass bowl with the Arabic inscription "Allah the Victorious." According to the elders of Nsawkaw, the bowl was captured from the Muslims along with other brass work: jugs, vessels, spoons, ceremonial spears, and the like.[76]

The two most important categories of Bono shrines, writes Warren, "are those whose spirits are from the forest and those whose spirits manifested themselves to man at the source of the Tano River. This river is the font for all Akan Tano (Taa) deities, which are those kept in brass-pan shrines." The paramount shrine, that of Taa Kora, is at a rock altar in a cave nearby. At least once a year, envoys from other Akan states come to Tanoboase to offer sacrifices to the deity and to collect water from the source of the river to purify their own ancestral stools and national deities.[77] When Meyerowitz visited the temple in 1944, "Taa Kora's shrine — i.e. the brass basin with the sacred water (it was wrapped up) — stood on the top of the altar which was covered with a silken cloth, and against it leaned a number of white and gold-hilted *Afena* swords, symbols of Taa Kora's authority."[78] The close association of religion and political life, of priest and chief, is underscored by this extension of the emblems of power to major shrines.[79] Silverman has suggested that the intimate connection of many of these vessels with water — some of them are supposed to have descended from heaven during rain, others are ritually filled with water, still others belonged to the queen mother in her capacity as rainmaker — may be a memory of their original use in Islamic ablutions.[80] Possibly, but the association of copper and brass with water is widespread, as we will see.

In Aşante itself, brass basins were integral to a host of fundamental ceremonies. Indeed, the basic Aşante altar was a forked branch with a basin or pot on it. "It is hardly an exaggeration," declared Rattray, "to say that every compound in Ashanti contains an altar to the Sky God, in the shape of a forked branch cut from a certain tree. . . . Between the branches which are cut short, is placed a basin, or perhaps a pot" filled with medicines and a celt.[81] Rattray describes a number of rituals that use brass pans, rituals involved with the birth of twins, with driving away evil spirits, with sacrifice, with commemoration of the dead. In *abosom* shrines, as in the Atano shrines generally, the brass pan "upon certain definite occasions, becomes the temporary dwelling, or resting-place, of a non-human spirit or spirits." For reasons he was never able to learn, widows of men of the Eknona clan wear small brass basins on their heads during the mourning period.[82]

Formerly, a great brass basin stood in front of the entrance to the royal

Aşante mausoleum at Bantama near the spot where victims were sacrificed for royal funerals, but Rattray denies that it was ever used to collect blood. Basins are frequently involved in funeral rites, however, not only in the royal ceremonies for the dead that were part of the annual "yam custom," but even in the burial of ordinary citizens: "Occasionally a brass pan is placed beneath the head and later is buried in this position, in order to receive the head when it drops off. Instead of the hands being folded . . . they are sometimes allowed to rest with the fingers inside one of the metal vessels called *kuduo* which contain gold dust."[83] This is a modern counterpart to the grave, probably of a priestess, excavated east of Kumasi and dated to the seventeenth century. Here the body was buried with its arms spread out, each hand lying in a brass dish.[84] Even earlier, de Marees mentioned that "the greater sort" of basins were "set in the graves of the dead" on the Gold Coast,[85] while Landolphe describes the use of copper basins in the rites of sacrifice accompanying the burial of the oba of Benin.[86]

The brass kuduo were a particular type of ritual vessel, made of cast brass rather than sheet metal (fig. 34). Nevertheless they recall, as Delange remarks, the "coffers of hammered copper in the Aşante royal mausoleum which contain the treasures of the king and the hexagonal caskets of lesser dimension in which the royal skeletons respose, dressed in rich clothing, and adorned with jewels of gold, their bones joined together with gold wire." Like the various basins and bowls, the kuduo undoubtedly had Near Eastern antecedents, but they evolved into a distinctly Akan art form:

> The periphery of these receptacles is decorated with figures in the round and with a fine geometric pattern, engraved or in relief. The cover is usually topped with a group of figurines similar to those of the proverb-weights. The *kuduo* is associated with private family cults, those of ordinary people as well as those of royal blood. It is the material support of the *ntoro,* the masculine principal inherited from the father, transmitted by men alone. As a result it intervenes at every essential moment of the life of an individual.[87]

Kuduo are used in ceremonies such as that of "washing the ntoro," and when a man dies, his kuduo is buried with him, ideally filled with gold dust and aggrey beads.[88] The royal kuduo are, next to the stools, among the most sacred objects of Aşante kingship, linking the ruler to both God and the ancestors. Rattray also describes a ceremony in the sacred grove where the queen mother places small pieces of meat from a sacrificial sheep in a kuduo, then, using a brass spoon, transfers them a spoonful at a time from the kuduo to each of eight pots representing the eight primordial ancestors, plus one in a hole and on the "truthful" stone.[89]

34. *Kuduo,* Aṣante, Ghana. Brass

Clearly a good measure of the veneration accorded basins and other vessels stemmed from their exotic origins and their rarity and even from the Arabic inscriptions on many of them, as well as from the fact that they were useful for carrying anything from Tano water to the "king's fetish."[90] But it is hard to believe that there was no sacralization of the metal itself when one sees how bound up these objects became in many of the key rituals of Akan life.

Although brass vessels have in fact had a historical role in a number of West African societies,[91] the finds at Igbo-Ukwu, different as they are stylistically, suggest the most striking parallel to their centrality in Akan ritual life. Under the rubric "receptacles," Shaw lists a total of 26 major and 161 minor pieces from the three sites. In addition to the cast bowls and the roped pot, there are a host of bronze calabash handles and conical spiral bosses which would have ornamented the calabashes. Calabashes themselves almost certainly provided the inspiration for both the large and the small bowls. Shaw notes that there is still preserved at Idah a ceremonial calabash which is also decorated with brass or copper ornaments. It belongs to the *atebo,* one of the senior priests, and is used to hold water for washing the kola nuts that are offered at the shrine of Otutubatu, an ancestral staff of the royal clan in Igala.[92] If the calabash is the prototype for the Igbo-Ukwu vessels, in contrast to the foreign models of the Akan, it reinforces still further the view that the art forms found at Igbo-Ukwu were of purely African inspiration.

We have no direct information about the ritual context in which these bowls and calabashes were used, but Shaw has pointed out interesting parallels between the objects found in the burial chamber at Igbo Richard and the regalia of the Ibo *eze nri.* The eze nri is a priestly official whose functions are not directly political but whose authority is recognized over large areas of Ibo-land. He is chosen from the Umundri clan, and his coronation begins with a ritual death, burial, and resurrection. Copper anklets are put on his legs, although his feet remain bare, to give him insulation from the earth. He carries "the special sacred *ofo* . . . which has copper bound round it, and the special *alo* which is an iron spear with bands of copper on it." He wears brass bells slung over his left shoulder and around his neck a brass casting of a human face. Shaw writes, "Just as the *Eze* is virtually buried at his coronation, so at his burial he is clad in his coronation robes." A particular type of manilla is put on his right wrist, he is swathed in beads, and a crown is set upon his head. Finally he is placed upright on his stool in a corner of a wood-paneled grave which is roofed over and piled up with dirt. Allowing for the inevitable changes over time, one can imagine the eze nri as a lineal descendant of the figure buried in Igbo Richard and the materials stored at Igbo Isaiah as ancestral to those used by the eze nri in the exercise of his priestly office.[93]

Divination and magic represent still another aspect of priestly power. Copper and brass figure in the paraphernalia or emblems of the diviner in some societies but more commonly in the amulets and charms they prescribe. Yoruba Ifa diviners, for example, sometimes use a chain of circular brass links joining together eight halves of seed shells as an alternative to palm nuts: although less reliable, this method is a good deal quicker.

Somewhat more rarely, they will even use a chain of copper markers shaped like seeds, and one sees carry-overs of this in Cuba as well. One verse of Ifa refers to a brass tray, also mentioned in myth, but more recently the trays of Ifa divination are almost exclusively of wood.[94]

The copper chain crops up in a number of rituals and myths, and seems to be related at least tangentially to divination and clairvoyance in a remarkable purification rite witnessed by Jean Rouch among the Songhay. In this rite, the Sohantye magician performed a dance holding the emblematic sabre of his clan "whose copper handle represents the head of a vulture." At the climax of the dance, the magician is seized with violent trembling and vomits a small, fine chain of copper, "which balances like a minute serpent in front of his face. Then he sees things more clearly than usual. He sees evil in all four directions, he stabs the *tyarkaw* [evil spirits] which are taken by surprise. For these few seconds, he is the dangerous master of all the bush and all the villages. Then doubling over on his heels, he painfully swallows the small, shiny chain again. He does not say a word or make a sign, but at the sight of the chain, all those in attendance are seized with intense emotion." Rouch comments that it was one of the most beautiful and moving ceremonies he had ever seen in Africa, but exactly what was represented by the chain we are unlikely ever to understand fully.[95]

In Burundi, certain diviners use a small lance made entirely of copper, which they plant on the ground in front of their house. It is supposed to take its form from one used by a great woman chief and diviner. Some also employ small conical, clapperless bells.[96] Jeannest describes a diviner in northern Angola who wore a band of copper in his hair, which sounds a little like the copper frontlet of the Galla diviner.[97] The Mossi *bâton magique,* on the other hand, is a variant of the staff: a rod fringed with copper, iron, and cowries.[98] In an interesting footnote to Samori's encouragement of native metallurgy to serve his military needs, Person describes how the Malinke leader also employed Syagha-Bori, a member of the Kante clan, to cast figurines in bronze to be used in divination. After Samori's capture in 1898, Syagha-Bori settled in Siguiri, where his descendants continue to be distinguished casters, although their work now feeds the tourist trade.[99]

It is in Senufo divination, however, that brass is most prominent and the casters of Siguiri were undoubtedly influenced by Senufo forms. The system of *Sando* divination, as Glaze describes it, is closely tied to Senufo social structure and supernatural beliefs: "It is a ritual form of diagnosis and a technique for determining the supernatural cause of any misfortune and for actively soliciting supernatural aid in order to obtain a desired result, such as good hunting, successful pregnancy, or a good harvest." Since the bush spirits are both the chief source of Sando's power and the chief cause of misfortunes, it is to them that the diviner directs her actions — for Sando is a woman's organization, although not exclusively so. Even if the troubles turn out to be caused by witches or ancestors rather than bush spirits, it is up to the diviner to discover this, so that she exercises considerable power in Senufo society.

The core objects essential to Senufo divination are of two sorts: the signs thrown for each reading and the figurative sculpture set up on display in the diviner's quarters. The beauty of form and detail of the display sculpture is a reflection of the diviner's prestige and powers, in that only a successful diviner can afford the best sculptors and the more expensive materials such as brass and iron. At the same time, since the bush spirits respond to esthetic stimuli just as do humans, the more beautiful the decoration, personal adornment, and equipment, the more she can count on pleasing them and bending them to her purposes. In essence, "the degree of expert craftsmanship and artistic merit appreciably enhances the power of the ornament to fulfill its religious function." This is an oversimplification of Glaze's marvelously subtle discussion, but it is the framework in which she describes the brass objects that may be part of Sando: the python bracelet, which is the indispensable prop, the equestrian figures, the miniatures of divination paraphernalia used as signs, the various human and animal figures. All of these except the python bracelet may be in wood, brass, or iron, but metal augments their prestige. The bushcow rings sometimes linked with divination are in fact the insignia not of Sando but of the society of healing specialists (fig. 35).[100]

All of the ornaments used in divination fall under the heading *yawiige,* literally "thing worn as protective medicine," and may be prescribed for a client by the diviner. A mother of twins will wear cast-brass rings, bracelets, and amulets bearing twin motifs, because of the tremendous and fearful power associated with twins; men will wear brass chameleon rings reflecting the identification of the animal with "supernatural powers of transformation, sorcery, and primal knowledge"; children will wear extremely small cast charms which will later take their place on the household altar. Even the cast-brass python bracelets can be worn as expiation for broken taboos.[101]

The wearing of charms and amulets seems almost universal in Africa as in much of the rest of the world. They may be provided or prescribed by the diviner, healer, blacksmith, or in Islamized areas, the marabout. Although many statues have functions that are amuletic in nature, we will be concerned here primarily with personal amulets, the variety of objects worn to protect an individual against danger and disease and to attract good fortune. Denise Paulme has commented that protection is simply the other face of ornamentation, whether on a statue or a living model:

35. Bush cow ring belonging to an association of healers, Senufo, Ivory Coast. Brass

"In a general way, jewelry . . . responds to a double concern—adorn, protect."[102] Frequently, sculptures simply adapt amulets worn by people; for
example the Ibo *Ikenga* figure in the Pitt-Rivers Museum in Oxford, which
has horns sticking out of two brass rings set on cowries and an upside
down manilla on the front, or Akan terra cotta figures of priests, which
are adorned with a protective ring of copper on their right wrists.[103] Similarly, a Tikar figure in wood and brass intended to control leprosy represents an old woman with a brass bell around her waist of the type worn
by lepers to warn of their coming.[104] Paulme also observes that body openings are considered particularly in need of protection, hence the frequency
of lip ornaments and earrings, both of which are frequently of copper or
brass. Presumably this same reasoning might also apply to the Kapsiki use
of copper and brass in cache-sexes, for example, and the cast ornaments

worn by women in a fringe over the genitals.[105] (See color illust. 3, and fig. 38, p. 272).

Copper and brass rings are an even commoner form of amulet. The Mande marabout may prescribe copper bracelets to protect against witches[106] or the Kongo *féticheur* furnish *lukanu* bracelets of brass for success in judicial proceedings.[107] The copper anklets of the eze nri, as we have seen, insulate him from the dangers of the earth. Among the Moors and Tuareg copper rings on the toe or finger "protect against rheumatisms, restrain the malefic influences of the 'Kel Esouf' (the People of the Void) or the 'Ehel Belhamar' (the Son of the Devil) transmitted by the coldness of the earth, or simply cure the stiffness recurring from old wounds." It is interesting that the Moors call this ring by the global term for all magic coming from their Wolof neighbors to the south.[108] Copper and silver anklets are also worn in Mauritania to protect against the bites of scorpions, tarantulas, and snakes.[109] Among the Ijebu Yoruba, "nearly every person wears a copper or brass ring on one of his fingers." Once energized by appropriate medicines, these imbue wearers with more than normal physical force and protect them against the powers of their enemies.[110]

Hunters as the takers of lives are in a particularly parlous condition. In the Sudan, the initiate of the supraethnic hunters' society replaces his own descent group with that of the mother-son pair Sanin and Kontron, who embody both the ideal relationship and supernatural force. This mythical pair is represented in statuettes of copper or iron, which are venerated in hunting rituals; at the same time, copper bracelets figure in the armory of hunting prophylacteries.[111] A "medicinal" copper bracelet from the Sara (Chad) has a related function. When a man has killed big game or another human being, either by his own force or by magic, he may be troubled by headaches or blinded by the "blood of the dead animal or person." As a remedy, he commissions a particularly adept smith to make him special copper bracelets which must be boiled up with the roots and leaves of the *kuga*. Each day for about a month, the "patient" washes his head with the medicinal water and drinks some of it, all the while wearing the bracelets. Anyone having such bracelets is feared and respected.[112]

For obvious and probably universal reasons, bells are a ubiquitous form of amulet, for hunters, children, camels, and horses—to say nothing of kings and priests. They act, as Neaher says, both to summon sacred forces and to repel inimical ones.[113] Two other types of amulet may be more localized within western Africa: the "pince-amulette," or tongs, and the fetters. Again, these are prescribed by diviners for very particular needs, but there is very little information on this aspect. Among the Bozo, the most expensive and presumably the most effective tong-amulets are made in copper by a smith working at night, naked, in the presence of his client. Pinces may also be part of the equipment of the Kono diviner, or function as a miniature shrine within an ordinary house.[114] The fetter or leg-iron charms probably have a range of metaphoric associations like the tongs, but one of the commonest uses seems to be to "tie children down," to keep them on earth, understandable enough in a world of high infant mortality. Twins and other children considered especially prone to return to the spirit world are decked out by the Yoruba in the whole panoply of charms: rings, tongs, shackles, staples, and chains.[115]

## COPPER AND THE STAGES OF LIFE

The use of copper and brass to signify the stages of life brings together many of the elements we have already been discussing. Rites of passage are also rituals of empowerment and protection, and the symbols that accompany them serve these ends. Essentially, the rites and the signifiers of social status aim at the enhancement of procreative power and the control of ancestral power. Under the first rubric we could lump puberty rites, bridewealth payments, and marriage itself, under the second, burial and funeral ceremonies and the veneration of ancestral spirits. While the objects in question continue to make statements about wealth and authority, there are added dimensions bound up with notions of fertility and vitality.

Many forms of ornamentation are gender-specific, and since puberty marks the acquisition of a sexual identity, it seems to be at this moment that the differentiation takes place. Careful descriptions will generally note what types of objects are common to both sexes, which can be worn only by one or the other, and at what stages of their lives the ornaments can be worn. Schweinfurth illustrates, for example, copper ornaments worn by the Bongo in their noses, lips, and ears, commenting on which are particular to men or to women.[116] In the Lower Congo the "anneau de chef" was distinguished from the bracelets worn by women by its masculine decorative motifs: rectangles with two diagonals and two medians, lozenges, small triangles, cross-hatchings, and striations.[117] Similarly, the young Masai warrior wears on his upper left arm a bracelet consisting of a boat-shaped ring of hide whose ends are bound to lengths of brass and copper wire connected by an iron chain.[118] But when he later marries, both he and his wife put on earrings made of a double disk of spiral copper wire which hangs down from the distended lobe.[119]

Signifiers of male and female extend into the world of statuary as well, not simply in the depiction of sexual characteristics but in ornamentation. According to Imperato, the gender of Bambara and Wassalunke *sogoni koun,* or antelope masks (related to but distinct from the *tjiwara* headdresses), is established in a number of ways: in size and number of horns, but also in "added decorative elements such as strings of beads and shiny metal bits (indicating femininity) and tufts of goat hair and silver or brass earrings (indicating masculinity)" (compare fig. 36 where metal may also imply gender). [120] Toma *bakorogi* masks are always in couples. The male mask has round eyes, made by punching two holes, or by inserting two cylinders of wood encircled with metal, or especially by inserting two copper tubes. [121] In the Mbari houses built for the worship of Ala, Mother of Earth, in southern Iboland around Owerri, the mud figure of Mother Earth usually has her legs painted in spirals like the brass rings worn at puberty which we will be discussing below. [122]

Sometimes copper figures in boys' puberty rites as part of the ornamentation of the initiate or in the copper knife that may be reserved exclusively for circumcision. [123] More frequently, it is the girls who don particular jewelry to indicate that they are nubile, and later, that they are married. Among Ibo groups the accumulation of spiral brass leglets begins even earlier, but not until girls reach puberty can they extend the spirals above the knee. Basden illustrates "three stages of girlhood": the youngest has only a single brass ring on her ankles, the next has the graduated spirals almost to her knees as her breasts begin to grow, the third, fully mature, has the spirals over the knees. The last are added for the final festivities after the girl has been secluded for several months in the fattening house, then emerges with her body adorned with paint and cloth, tiny brass bells around her waist, and bits of brass or pearl in her hair. Once she marries, she no longer wears the spirals; instead, if she is wealthy enough, she would in the past have exchanged them for the *adalà*, the spectacular cylindrical beaten brass ornaments with projecting plates (fig. 37). [124]

One can find parallels in many other cultures, not only among the neighboring Ibibio, Ijo, and Efik, [125] but much farther afield. In the 1770s Sparrman, while remarking on the predilection of the Khoikhoi for brass rings, noted that girls were not allowed to wear them until they reached a marriageable age and went through the appropriate ceremonies. [126] Rundi girls wear small bracelets from infancy, but only on reaching puberty do they receive their first pair of large copper ones. [127] In the region of the Lower Congo–Kwilu, young women cover their forearms and calves with rings of copper or iron wire, but when they marry they substitute enormous heavy bracelets and anklets of brass. [128] Already in 1600 de Marees recognized the prescriptive nature of much of the jewelry to be seen. Speaking of the Gold Coast, he wrote:

Women weare eare rings of Copper or Tin and Copper bracelets about their armes, and some of Ivorie, and upon their legs also they weare many red and

36. *Tjiwara* headpiece, Bambara, Mali. Wood, brass

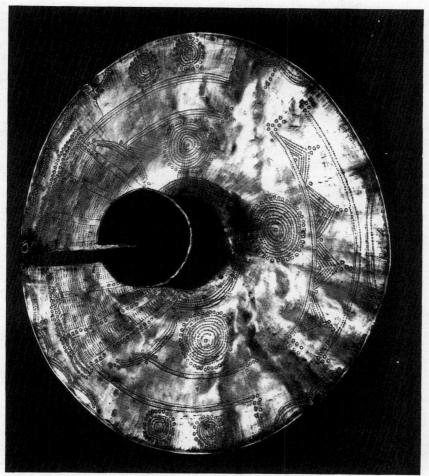

37. *Adalà* anklets, Ibo, Nigeria. Brass

yellow Copper Rings. But a yong maid that is unmarried weareth many Iron Rings about her armes, sometimes thirty or forty upon one arme: a Whore . . . oftentimes weares Copper Rings upon her legs, with bels hanging at them, which she goes ringing through the streets.[129]

In many contexts there is little doubt about copper's connotations of fertility. Dupire brings this out superbly in her study of Bororo proprietary marks. Describing the significance of the copper earrings worn by the Bororo and other pastoralists, she comments:

Among many nomadic tribes, men as well as women wear earrings, but while women have six or seven holes from which heavy copper rings are suspended, a boy wears only one small ring from his left ear. This small ring and his plaited hair are his distinctive ornamentation, the *suka,* a term which designates both the boy and the young man still in a position to contract marriage. The day his children begin to participate in dances and to establish their own families, he removes this ring. . . . The ornamentation of women has an equivalent significance. It is not only the sign of her social status, it is also a rite destined to assure her fecundity. Thus as she gives birth she takes off her earrings and anklets one by one.

The Fulani themselves are very conscious of applying the same concepts of virility and fecundity to animals and people. Marking their animals' ears is not simply a means to distinguish those belonging to different families; it is also a ritual act with magical implications, designed to encourage their increase.[130]

The same close association between animal and human fecundity is implied in the Zaghawa ceremony referred to in the preceding chapter. Here the skin of a heifer is used to cover the royal copper drums played during the sacrifice of a pregnant camel in rites aimed at insuring rain and a good harvest.[131] A headdress worn by certain Zaghawa groups also combines connotations of rank and wealth with those of fertility. The *mamur* was a coiffure built up with red beads on an arc of copper which was not itself visible. Its opulence varied according to the standing of the wearer, but formerly every woman was given some sort of mamur on her wedding day to wear until she was widowed or divorced, with risk of mortal danger to her husband if she ever took it off.[132]

In the Lemba society and elsewhere, copper bracelets were closely tied to notions of fertility, but among the Bakweri of coastal Cameroon the role is more complex. When many children begin to die, the diviner explains that "a woman of the matrilineage has seen a shiny bangle in her farm and has said nothing about it." The copper bangle is, in fact, believed to be killing the children, so that certain rituals must be followed to "discover the bangle, to render its destructive powers harmless and to transform it, in effect, into a fertility fetish;" once this is done, it becomes a ritual object in the custody of the lineage, insuring both the fertility and the wealth of the family. [133]

Apropos of a maternity figure in copper in the royal house of Tekyi-man, Delange observes that it is the object of sterile women's prayers, very much like the wooden *akua-ba,* and questions which form came first: were the wooden statues substituted for those in copper or is it simply that the images in metal have been reserved for noble families? [134] In her study of brass-studded Chokwe thrones, Kauenhoven-Janzen demonstrates how the motifs and materials reinforce each other to convey a message about leadership and fertility—the multiple domains of power. [135] Similarly, the application of brass or copper rosettes, tacks, and strips of metal to the majestic *nimba* figures used in Baga and Nalu agrarian rites augmented their power (see fig. 22, p. 224), [136] just as the cast figurines worn around their waists by female slaves of the Niele region or the "banana leaf" castings favored by the Kapsiki of North Cameroon were supposed to bring children (see color illust. 4). [137] Another type of cache-sexe, also worn by Kapsiki women, seems more conspicuously phallic (fig. 38). One of the most curious objects in the undoubtedly overstuffed category of "fertility symbols" is a sword with two arching blades found in parts of Zaire and the Central African Republic. Sometimes both blade and handle are of copper, but more commonly the sword has an iron blade with the handle wrapped in copper wire (fig. 39). Vansina asserts that the Tio import these swords simply as prestige items, oblivious of the fact that to their Ngbwaka manufacturers they symbolize the female genitalia. [138]

Time and time again we have noted that much of the evidence of the use of copper in the more distant past comes from burials. If our estimates for the total amounts of cuprous metals absorbed by African societies are at all correct, we must assume that hundreds of thousands of tons still lie buried under the red earth, most of it in graves. As long as copper signified wealth, its very presence testified to the affluence of the deceased. Hutchinson and Talbot describe the quantities of copper rods, manillas, and basins inhumed with rich Kalabari and Ijo traders, and the same was true of important Tio men of affairs. [139] The vast cemeteries of the Upemba Depression are replete with croisettes; throughout the Zimbabwe Plateau and Zambia, copper bangles are standard grave goods.

Nevertheless one suspects that even where wealth was a primary consideration, there was, in some cases at least, a ritualization of its forms. We see from Fagan's careful tables, for example, that at Ingombe Ilede the copper crosses were buried only at the head, or in one case at the feet, of the body; the trade wire in burials 1 and 3 was also found at the head,

38. Cache-sexe, Kapsiki, Cameroon. Brass, leather, fiber, beads

as were the bronze bar and three lumps of copper ore in the latter burial —
that is, all the forms in which copper was traded.[140] In like manner, de
Maret found a consistency in the placement of the various sizes of croisettes in the Upemba burials: the large and very large ones were *only* found
on the thorax, for instance, the very small ones *never* on the thorax.[141]
Just what this means we do not know, but it was probably not accidental.
Another sort of ritualization of currency is evident in the more recent in-
sistence on using older forms for burial, and incidentally for bridewealth
payments, in southern Nigeria. Certain types of manillas were used exclusively for burial, and conversely, proper burial required them.[142] So indis-

39. Ceremonial knives, Monjombo, Ngbwaka, Zaire, and Central African Republic. Iron, copper, brass, wood

pensable were they for both uses that the government was forced to allow each individual to retain 200 manillas for ritual purposes in the wake of Operation Manilla in 1948.[143]

There was nonetheless latitude for innovation. As the ultimate in status symbols, two eastern Delta "palm oil potentates" ordered enormous brass coffins, each weighing 600 pounds, from a Birmingham manufacturer.[144] Mostly, however, grave goods tended to be the same as status indicators above ground: copper, brass, and iron rings of all sorts and sizes; weapons and staffs; crowns, bells. The queen mother of Bamum was buried with the brass pipe she alone among women was allowed to smoke and "a staff for her wanderings whose handle was a cast bird in brass."[145] Some rulers were buried sitting upright on stools robed in finery with all their panoply in hand, like the burial at Igbo Richard, others were decked with appropriate insignia, then wrapped in cloth.[146] Pairault, to be sure, makes a distinction between *bracelets de parure* and *bracelets rituels:* in the funerals he describes, ritual bracelets are always removed from the corpse before inhumation.[147] The copper bracelets emblematic of chieftaincy in the Lower Congo were also not buried with the defunct chief; instead, stone copies were made for the burial, while the copper ones were passed on to his successor.[148]

Sometimes, too, it was relatives of the deceased who donned prescribed ornaments of brass as part of the mourning ritual: among the Efik, each individual wore three brass anklets on each leg and three ivory wristlets on each arm, along with special clothes and hairstyles.[149] In the Degema region of southeastern Nigeria, women of certain families were permitted to wear the large "king" and "queen" manillas as part of funeral ceremonies. At the "second burial" of an important chief, these became part of the family shrine.[150] On the other hand, the Sundi take off all ornaments as a sign of mourning: large copper or brass rings that cannot be removed are covered with dark cloth.[151]

A symbol of authority that is also central to ancestral rituals is the Ibo *ofo* and its cognates among Delta peoples. The ofo is simply a bundle of twigs from the ofo tree, symbolizing "the link between the living holder of family or ruling authority and their ancestors." It is kept by the eldest living male in each Ibo family. Cast bronze ofo are all of the same sort: a cylindrical bar with a spoon-like projection at one end, mirroring the peculiar shape of the ofo twig, and a double-looped handle at the other end.[152] As we have noted, this formed part of the regalia of the eze nri. Analogous bronze *ovo* are also found in Isoko shrines, where tradition often links them to Benin, even though Ibo manufacture seems more likely.[153]

A last word about ancestral shrines. In centralized monarchies like Benin, of course, the cult of the royal ancestors becomes the national cult, and the array of commemorative brass sculptures are the cornerstone of its rituals. While nothing is actually known about the purpose of the Ife heads, it has been suggested that they may have been part of effigies used in "second burials" or similar ceremonies connected with kingship.[154] The Mossi have also made effigies of defunct rulers, but they were hedged with taboos implying an ambivalent relationship between past and present occupants of the throne. When a *mogho-naba* died, a brass caster was called in to make a statue of him and also of one of his wives, a page, and a royal drummer. The new ruler was never supposed to see these castings nor to set eyes on the caster, who was exiled forthwith from Wagadugu in a state of ritual danger.[155]

In the forest regions of equatorial Africa, political units were often small and dispersed, and it was important members of the lineage rather than kings who were the objects of veneration and who were commemorated in copper and brass-decorated figures. The most impressive of these are the *bwété,* the metal-covered reliquaries found among various Kota and Kota-related groups in eastern Gabon and neighboring Congo Republic (see fig. 25, p. 229). The bwété were attached to baskets containing relics and medicines. Copper wire, ribbon, or sheet covers the visible surface of the wooden figure, just as it covers the bones that are preserved, along with brass rings, bracelets, and beads, hidden from view inside the basket. The reliquaries were kept sheltered from the rain and tended carefully. Bwété rituals aimed at placating the ancestors in order to gain prosperity: good health, wealth, numerous offspring, good hunting.[156]

Siroto has insisted on another aspect also which he feels has been underestimated or missed entirely in the discussion of ancestor cults, namely their efficacy against witchcraft. He argues that such effectiveness is related to achievement more than ascription, hence that it is not so much the genealogical link that is important but the attainments of the ancestor, his embodiment of power in his own right. This in oversimplified summary is what he sees as the purpose of the skull cults widespread in this region of Africa.[157] Possibly witchcraft became a more pressing concern in the rapidly changing world ushered in by the imposition of colonial rule, as Ardener has shown so beautifully in his case study of the Bakweri;[158] be that as it may, the antiwitchcraft and proprosperity functions of ancestor veneration do not seem fundamentally contradictory. Thus the *ngongo munene,* a mask of beaten copper symbolizing the ancestors of the chief of the earth in extreme northeastern Angola, was also used for a variety of purposes: for the funeral of a chief of the earth and in ceremonies marking the designation of his successor, in rites of ancestral propitiation during times of epidemic or calamity, in the rites of passage for boys reaching puberty.[159] The copper-clad figures of the Songye and Salampasu, on the other hand, are unequivocal statements of aggressive power. The Songye "fetish" figure stationed at the entrance to a village protected it from evil spirits (see fig. 24, p. 228).[160] The most dangerous of all the Salampasu masks are those whose entire face is covered with copper disks and brass nails.[161]

In all these cases, the addition of copper and brass to a wooden form — just as to a human form — augments the statement of power, with all the ambivalence bound up in that word. In the last chapter, we will explore the qualities ascribed to copper and suggest the cosmological framework in which we must attempt to read them.

## Chapter 11

# Shango and Nommo: Copper and the Language of Materials

Mais si le Nommo est l'eau, il produit aussi du cuivre. Dans le ciel couvert on voit se matérialiser les rayons du soleil sur l'horizon de brume; ces rayons, excréments des génies, sont de cuivre et sont lumière. Ils sont aussi d'eau, car ils supportent l'humidité terrestre dans son cheminement ascendant.

—*Dieu d'eau: Entretiens avec Ogotemmêli*

Shining brass, the hot color of ultra-luminosity, the hue that brings down the thunder, announces the most extraordinary types of command . . .

—ROBERT FARRIS THOMPSON, *Black Gods and Kings*

When Schweinfurth pictured the copper-drenched court of the Mangbetu king, "the gleam of the metal" catching the rays of the noontide sun, and when a few pages later he noted the king's obsession with constantly increasing his hoard of the "red ringing metal,"[1] he put his finger, perhaps unwittingly, on the intrinsic qualities that, I believe, gave copper its peculiar role in African societies. Without minimizing the importance of scarcity, durability, and workability, I suggest a further triad of complementary importance: redness, luminosity, and sound. All of these qualities serve to embed copper in ritual and mythological systems which classify the world, and through classification, aim for a measure of control. And here we must at last explore distinctions between copper and brass and the relation of these metals to others, primarily iron and gold.

## REDNESS, LUMINOSITY, SOUND

It was not only the royal hall of the Mangbetu king that was red with the mass of copper implements, it was also the king himself. In addition to his copper ornaments and insignia, he wore a hat plumed with red par-

277

rots' feathers, and his "entire body was smeared with the native unguent of powdered cam-wood."[2] The Mangbetu court (fig. 32) is one of the most lavish, only equalled perhaps by the panoply surrounding the oba of Benin, but time and again accounts of all sorts juxtapose copper with red body decoration (camwood, ochre, even red clay), red cloth, red beads, red feathers. In a sense, the same statement is being repeated in different words, the same message of power. Ritual objects themselves may be rubbed or painted with red to augment their force. Several of the Ife heads and the smaller figures from Ita Yemoo have traces of red and black paint, as do the terra cottas. Willett reminds us that "originally they must have presented a very vivid appearance."[3] In like manner, red powder was commonly rubbed on the inside of Lemba bracelets, and on bracelets and other copper cult objects in the Cameroon grasslands.[4] The ultimate reinforcer of redness was of course sacrificial blood.

Red, white, and black are the triad of primary colors common to most of sub-Saharan Africa. But though their use is quasi-universal, their meaning is not. Even if there is almost always the immediate association of red with blood, one cannot assume the implications to be the same in every case. Color functions as part of a larger system, and like all symbolic language, its meaning is latent rather than explicit, depending on the entire web of beliefs the user and viewer bring to it and to the nexus in which it is embedded. As Vansina observes, the most powerful symbols are often the most ambiguous, while those that are most obvious may be the least important. Thus one can generalize that for the Tio, as for other African peoples, red symbolizes life, blood, power, fire, conflict, just as white represents sacredness and peace, but the precise meaning is affected by the situation and by the combination with other colors — hence the frequent association of red and white, for example. Nor are meanings static: Vansina notes that whereas in the 1880s black was only partially associated with death (along with red), it has become increasingly so in more recent times. Ordinary red denotes power, but a particular shade indicates misery or grief and is worn as a sign of mourning — one thinks of the burnt sienna color of mourning among the Aşante or the salmon barkcloth of the Ganda. Even among the reds indicative of power, the Tio distinguish the higher reds of the king's insignia from those worn by lords and inferiors.[5]

The pioneering work of Turner on Ndembu color classification has been expanded by that of Fu-Kiau, Janzen, and Jacobson-Widding on the symbolism of color in Kongo cosmology and ritual. Where black is equated with the imperfect world of the living and white, *mpemba,* with the world of the dead, red occupies the transitional, intermediate position between them. "Red indicates the passage from this world to the other, as for example, with the rising and setting of the sun. More abstractly it is identified with all passage in a social sense, all ambivalence associated with states or substances such as power, anger, fire, blood, etc."[6]

But Jacobson-Widding emphasizes that for the Kongo these colors have one set of associations when used alone, another when used in combination. Thus red by itself expresses, in particular, "emotional qualities or physical force attributed to the person who is using it,"as well as the element of magic power. The common denominator, she suggests, is that none of these qualities are designated as evil or good; they are free from moral associations. The combination of red and white, on the other hand, is intimately connected with rituals of healing and protection. Red and white can also be used to play off male and female against each other or to signify a complementarity. In some contexts red represents qualities of the female, in others it may represent her husband (rather than male qualities generically).[7] In Ndembu thinking, too, white and red are opposed in some situations but can also stand for the same object, participate in each other's meaning. Where they are complementary rather than antithetical Turner suggests that it is because they are part of an implicit triadic relationship of which black is the "null" member: red and white are jointly life, opposed to an invisible black which is death and negativity.[8]

There is then no single meaning for red, nor can one assume that the complexes of meanings found among the Kongo and Ndembu are to be found in all cultures. But by and large the ideas of transition and ambiguity as well as of blood, power, and heat seem widespread, and as Jackson asserts apropos of the Kuranko, threshold states, conditions of ambiguity, are usually regarded as dangerous. They must be dealt with by ritual process, by sacrifice, by *rites de passage,* in sum, the full repertoire of counter powers.[9]

This ambiguity extends to copper by virtue of its redness. As we have noted, many African languages have no specific word for copper; it is simply identified as red metal or red iron, so that color is seen as its most salient characteristic. It carries the manifold connotations of blood: sacrifice, execution, war on the one hand; fertility and vitality on the other. It marks the transition from child to adult, from adult to ancestor. Its presence is frequently a statement of agressivity, of the power to take life, as in the copper inlay and wire on the Kuba war-knife or the Mondjumbo *mvango,* the knife formerly used in human sacrifice.[10] Probably the brass sheathing on the Akuapem executioner's drum, illustrated by Cole, has these same connotations,[11] just as the *wango-tabuka,* the royal copper drum of Buganda, is meant to evoke the saying, "The Kabaka is like a leopard. When you pass him you say you have been in danger of being killed."[12] And the "great Gaga Calando," the Jaga leader whom Andrew Battell described as wearing "a peece of Copper crosse his nose, two inches long, and in his eares also," must have produced much the same aggressive effect as a Songye mask.[13]

The shininess of copper and brass adds to this effect. As Ben-Amos says, "the significance of brass [in Benin], at least in the modern Edo view, derives from its red colour and shiny surface, qualities which are considered both beautiful and frightening—a particularly appropriate symbol for the monarchy."[14] Shango, the powerful and wily king of Oyo, lived in a palace "built all of glittering brass" and wore ornaments of the same metal. His undoing came when he used the shining brass of kingship to reflect the light of heaven and bring down the lightning: it struck his palace and killed his wife. In horror he went and hung himself. A brass chain marks the spot where he is supposed to have sunk into the ground. Legends of the historical Shango, the king-who-did-not-die-and-will-return, have become absorbed into the cult of the most violent of natural phenomena, the tropical thunderstorm. Many of the cult objects of the thundergod, both in Africa and in its New World extensions, are of brass and copper, especially in oṣe Shango, the wand carried by adepts.[15] In the nineteenth-century wars against the Fulani, the priests of Shango put on the hideously death-like masks of hammered brass and polished it "so that it would glare hotly in the sun and the enemies would see the glare and think it is the sun and be afraid."[16]

Virtually all descriptions agree that copper and brass were kept highly polished, even that used by ordinary mortals, whether Kota reliquaries, Khoikhoi and Ibo bracelets, Ogboni edan, or Benin bronzes. While the word for copper in many African languages emphasizes its redness, the Kuba words for copper and brass derive from roots concerned with luminosity, with what attracts the eye.[17] The implications of luminosity—both of glare and of reflecting power—help to explain the frequent use of bright metal in the eyes of masks and statues: it attracts, dazzles, repels, looks beyond. The almost life-sized bronze mask, the most sacred object of Igala regalia, is known as "the eye that brings fear to other eyes."[18]

But aggressivity, "the hue that brings down the thunder," is only one possible meaning of shining brass and copper. The copper-covered reliquaries found in eastern Gabon make a complex statement that combines power and wealth with vitality and increase. The color is probably meant to augment the power of the ancestral figure as well as to suggest his mediating position between the living and the dead. Formal elements reinforce this image: the elliptical shape of the Obamba figures in particular, with the suggestion of a cross in the banding of the face, the lozenge-shape below the head—all are variants of the Kongo paradigm of the universe. Even the opposition of concavity and convexity echoes this opposition of life and death.[19] The shining surface suggests not only the watery divide between the two worlds but also the power to deflect witchcraft and other malefic forces and to see into the beyond. This is only the visible part of the reliquary: within the basket are bones covered with copper bands or wires, together with rings, bracelets, and beads of copper and brass. These objects are particularly charged; they are far more than simple grave goods.

In the same way, we must assume a special force inherent in the copper which may provide the *matérial de base* of a *komo* shrine for the Bambara: it is always stipulated that such copper must be taken from a dead woman.[20] This would seem to be a contradiction at a certain level, since the Bambara see copper as a symbol of the placenta, the living substance par excellence, but it reminds us precisely of the inherent ambiguity in all symbolism and particularly in symbols associated with both life and death. In the case of the Tio *ilua,* for example, copper seems in a certain sense to be a male counterpart to the placenta, or at least the umbilical cord. Every Tio, according to Vansina, has two *mpiini* or "life containers," one from the father and one from the mother. That from the father was the ilua, a ring generally made of copper, while the mpiini from the mother was generally the umbilicus. If either was lost, captured, or destroyed, it meant death. To complicate things still further, the ilua had a mysterious link with a particular but unknown animal in the bush.[21] The ilua seems thus to go beyond the amulet or charm to contain the blood of life itself. This is equally true in the close association of copper with menstrual blood and hence with fertility. The association is not usually as explicit as in Burundi, where a smith designated molten copper with the word usually meaning the "coagulated blood of a cow,"[22] but the common practice of signifying puberty and nubility by donning copper jewelry and other forms of red body ornamentation underscores the overriding importance of pro-creativity.

Let us turn for a moment now to sound, which ultimately also has connotations of fertility. We have already discussed the obvious points—the role of copper and brass instruments and especially bells, as well as the importance accorded the sound of manillas, for example, in determining their value or even acceptability. Like brilliant surfaces or bright red, bells, vibrators, and the rings attached to drums and other instruments both attract and repel: they force attention. Their presence is intended to summon the deities or ancestors, to ward off evil spirits, to proclaim status. In Bambara belief, "To ring a bell is to make [the God] Faro hear the sound of copper; it calls him and flatters him at the same time."[23] This is a view with well-nigh universal variations, from the Roman *tintinnabulum* through the medieval West, North Africa, and the Near East, as well as Africa,[24] but it seems characteristically African to emphasize the pleasure implicit in the sound, not only its power to call and bend and protect.

The associations go further, however. The copper drum used in the Turrti (Darfur) ceremonies referred to earlier adds its mysterious power to the rites of fecundity,[25] and the same is true of the "vibrateurs" of copper and brass with their motifs of fertility found in Mauritania,[26] or the ring of copper bells on the Mande marriage calabash.[27] It is part of the message, too, of the small bells and jangling *cache-sexes* often worn by women of childbearing age, and implicit in the sound of the copper bracelets of Lemba. But there is a more subtle association, focusing on the ear as the receptor of sound. The Bambara see the ear as the complement to the mouth and tongue, the means by which the word is received. When they decorate the ear with copper rings, it is "to hear and to compel the spirits to hear, and secondarily to foil the liar or bearer of false and wicked news by putting him in a position to be heard and judged by invisible and supernatural forces." Indeed, they serve essentially the same purpose as the copper rings attached to Bambara musical instruments. The ear is also a sexual metaphor, however, and formerly the number of rings worn had multiple meanings. Thus men wore three rings on the right ear, four on the left, three being the male number and four the female, with seven representing the total being. Women wore four rings on each ear, or if they could manage it, twenty-two, symbolizing the twenty-two stages of creation. Or a single ring might be fixed to the earlobe of both men and women, representing the "mother of the other mouth."[18] Undoubtedly similar layers of meaning lie behind the Bororo earrings discussed earlier. Arkell has shown that the double spiral amulet is widely used in North Africa and the Sudan and that it commonly carries connotations of fertility.[29] He sees it primarily as a charm, however, and seems unaware how commonly it is worn as an earring. In East Africa it is worn not only by Masai upon marriage: among the neighboring Kikuyu, old men who are headmen but also have begotten many children are entitled to hang a coil of brass wire from the slit of the earlobe.[30]

## COPPER IN MYTH AND LEGEND

Rouch has said of Songhay ritual objects that all are connected with myth in a precise fashion: "They are nothing more than an illustration of it, a material proof."[31] This is equally true of ritual objects everywhere, but in the rudimentary state of our knowledge the mythological framework is often missing. Where it does exist we can begin to see the rich systems of correspondences in which something like copper is embedded.

In the Dogon myth of creation, the sun is surrounded by eight spirals of copper which are light and which give it its daily movement. But these spirals which are the excrement of the God Nommo are equated also with water and with the Word. The rays of the sun are called *mênn di,* "water of copper," and just as water is the generative force in the natural world, so the Word is the fertilizing agent in human relationships, the cornerstone of social organization. Mêndi is the name given to a mountain two days north of the Dogon village of Sanga, because it contains both copper and water. It is here that the souls of the dead are believed to go before they begin their journey south, "to provide themselves with copper to drink on their long voyage."

It is because of the correspondence of copper with the Word that the drum banded with copper is more easily heard by Nommo. The helix of copper "is the conduit of sound, the conduit of the word." When the drum is beaten, it activates the copper and the word interlaced by Nommo through the tension thread and the metal band. It reverberates between the drum and the ears of the deity. Sound is compared to weaving: the pattern of words is like the warp and weft making up the whole cloth. This is strikingly reminiscent of the *oriki* to Orisạ Popo, the form of Obatala, the High God, in Ogbomoso:

> Orisa Popo, owner of Ogbomosa, possesses the powerful word.
> He strikes copper and weaves cloth.

The oriki goes on to identify him as the "father who knows copper."[32] This is all the more interesting because white is the main color associated with Obatala and his metals are customarily lead or tin — once again a reminder that the hard and fast, either-or categories typical of western thinking are simply too restrictive.

Dogon mythology is reflected in both architecture and ornament. Just as the granary is the universe in microcosm, so the individual should embody the myth of creation. A woman's mouth, for example, is material to be woven; her teeth are filed to points like the sharp teeth of Nommo through which the threads were drawn. The copper stud through her lower lip is the bobbin of thread. At the same time the zigzag of her teeth symbolizes water and the Word. Copper jewelry is prescriptive, invoking at every point the primordial associations:

> The bracelets of copper on the wrists and bend of the arm have the form and the position of the circular bones that distend the skin of the spirit . . . for his arms are flexible even though they consist of long, unjointed bones. These bracelets number four, the number of woman.
>
> The row of beads or the ring of copper on the right ankle recalls the circular bone at the end of the tail of the spirit. Normally the left ankle should not be ornamented.

Rings of copper are worn on the index finger, the ring finger and the little finger because they are the only fingers in the webbed hand which have circular swellings in place of joints, and the rings imitate the swellings. In contrast, the thumb and middle finger remain bare because in the spirit they are lithe and supple so that a ring would not stay on.

Rings are never worn on the toes because the spirit has no feet. . . . The ear is bi-sexual for both men and women. The auricle is the penis which protects the auditory canal, image of the female sex organ. The triangular lobes, red in color, are the testicles. The eight copper rings in the form of a large crescent attached around the circumference of the helix are the eight ancestors.[33]

And so it goes for clothing, scarification, coiffure, the creation of woman as a work of art: "To be naked is to be without words."

Still another aspect of the myth links the Hogon, the priest, to copper. The Hogon mediates between mankind and Lébé, the serpent, descendant of both the seventh and eighth ancestors, who gives life to both man and the land by coming to the Hogon at night and licking him. When the Hogon dies, a copper ring is put around each ankle and arm. These rings come from the grave of Lébé and are made of metal excreted by Nommo in the form of rays from the clouds which are then changed into copper deep in the earth. The rings are removed after burial and given not to the immediate successor but to the next in line, who holds them while his predecessor is in office. The Hogon "is impregnated with copper. He is thus like copper and cannot cross any water"—because Nommo is the owner of copper he takes back any copper passing over the waters reserved to him. That is, water and copper are of the same essence and both belong to Nommo: Nommo gave copper to man and Nommo takes it away. Dogon thought was explained to Griaule as a series of correspondences, but the foundation of the entire religious system rests on the quadripartite correspondence "voice-spiral-copper-rain."

We have explored the role of copper in Dogon mythology at extraordinary length because of its intrinsic fascination and also because it has parallels in other systems of thought. Skeptics have raised questions about the work of the Griaule school, it is true, hinting that it reveals more about the Gallic mind than the African; but as the results of more and more careful fieldwork become available, they confirm the remarkable richness and complexity of African cosmologies and show the Dogon and Bambara belief systems as no longer the isolated cases they once seemed to be.

Bambara mythology imagines Faro, the bisexual or asexual deity of the Niger, as half-albino, half-copper. Like Nommo, he/she is master of water and of the spoken word. All metals belong to Faro, but most especially copper and gold. Copper descends from the heavens with each clap of thunder and represents the "sounds of Faro." These sounds are enrolled in the spirals of earrings, and penetrate into the tympanum so that words may be heard. Similarly, a piece of star-shaped copper on the harp of Bambara *soma* diviners represents the Word. Because of Faro's twin essence, albinos and copper are the sacrifices and offerings of choice, but conversely, one wears jewelry of copper only at one's peril when crossing the Niger or attending ceremonies of the *komo* society, whose masks have "hooks impregnated with the black mud of the Niger and whose copper, the metal of Faro, has been steeped in the venom of a viper." Appropriately, too, copper is part of the paraphernalia of the *kworé* cult, which is particularly concerned with rain.[34]

The Bozo, Songhay, and Kotoko also identify copper with *génies de l'eau* and by extension with fertility of all sorts.[35] Kotoko mythology compares the shimmering copper with "l'eau poissonneuse," fish-filled water, and with the pupils of the eye. Harakoy Dikko, the Songhay mistress of the Niger, glides over the river in a copper pirogue, reminiscent of the Tsoede legend. Whether the "well of copper" central to various versions of the legend of Wagadu is also part of some *Ur* stock of Sudanese myths associating water with shining metal is impossible to say, but it would not be surprising if it were.[36]

Such associations extend well beyond the Middle Niger–Lake Chad area to the Yoruba, Edo, and Delta peoples of southern Nigeria, but with a difference. Here the glittering sands and fish scales that conjure up visions of shining metal have become conflated with the undreamed of quantities of copper and brass brought across the water in European ships — the early European almost an incarnation of Faro, half-albino, half-copper! The Yoruba river goddess Oşun, the favorite wife of Shango, is worshipped with sacred figures of cast brass, the *edan Oşun,* and with shrine furniture of beaten brass. As the climax of her annual festival, a virgin is possessed by the goddess and leads the procession to the river named after her carrying the edan on her head, then returns and prophesies for the coming year.[37] In Brazil, Oşun has become syncretized with Our Lady of the Immaculate Conception, or in Bahia with the Candlemas Virgin, but retains her attributes of brass and copper; in Cuba, she has metamorphosed into the Virgin of Cobre who owns the fresh waters and brass and gold, possibly suggesting an amalgamation of Mande and Yoruba beliefs. Other riverain *orişa* of the Yoruba are also identified by brass bracelets.[38]

In Benin and particularly throughout the Delta itself, brass is even more intimately associated with the water spirits:

> Among the coastal Ijo, and especially among Kalabari and Nembe, brass is regarded as a rather miraculous substance associated with the spirits. Tales of the water people often describe their realm as amply furnished with brass-

work; and women who claim to have been taken as wives by the water people
sometime produce as evidence a brass manilla or torque which they say was
given them by their spirit husbands. The original cult-objects of certain spirits
are said to have been brasses made by the spirits themselves. Sometimes, it
is said that the pollution of human contact caused these original cult-objects
to disappear. Hence their replacement by the wooden cult-objects that stand
in the shrines today.[39]

As among the Akan, these brasses are sometimes tied to founding heroes
such as Kenin Ala, who is supposed to have descended from heaven by
sliding down a giant python, bringing his brass objects with him: a plaque
with three human figures in low relief and more than a dozen manillas
and torques. Others are insignia of Pere title holders. Among the Oprozo
Ijo, the small bell fragments are known solely by the names of the water
spirits they represent in local dances.[40]

Some local traditions insist that these objects were made by the water
spirits themselves, others ascribe them to Benin, although only a minority
of the objects show stylistic affinities with Benin metalwork. Of the Delta
peoples, only the Isoko appear to have any traditions of working in brass,[41]
so that, as Horton observes, the external origin would have served "to enhance the aura of mystery and value surrounding cast work."[42] But Martha Anderson's work among the Central Delta Ijo is offering another dimension to the understanding of the connection between brass and water
spirits. Here, as elsewhere, brass "found" objects end up in shrines as the
depiction or insignia of the various spirits, but they are part of a fundamental opposition between bush and water spirits in which the latter now
embody an "esthetic of imports": they eat European food, they emphasize
wealth and success. The opposition between bush and water is undoubtedly very old and widespread—in Benin it takes the form of an opposition
of dry land and water—but it was reinforced as maritime contacts with
European traders became synonymous with an influx of luxury materials,
especially brass and copper, and with a commercial ethic, to the point that
among the Ijo, the water spirits have become virtually identified with Europeans. This is all the more ironic because during the early centuries of
trading, the contacts were mostly indirect, thanks to the warlike reputation of the Ijo.[43] Ben-Amos' studies in Benin would seem to corroborate
these findings. The Edo also associate wealth with Olokun, the God of
Waters and specifically of the seas, which are supposed to have their source
in the Olokun (Ethiope) River. This view would have been reinforced by
trade with Europe and especially by the "rain of brass" that coincided with
the revival of kingly power and foreign trade in the first half of the eighteenth century.[44]

Far to the south, an echo of this association of copper and water can be found in Bantu genesis myths. In Kuba myth, Mweel, the primordial sister, finds copper ornaments in the Kasai River, then disappears into it. Her praisename still links water, woman, copper, and tattoos.[45] Similarly, there are suggestive correspondences of copper and water in the Luba genesis myth discussed in the previous chapter.

Thus far we have talked about copper generically and the connotations attaching to its physical properties. How this translates into a single object is suggested by Volavka's provocative study of *ngunda,* the insignia of divine authority in the old Ngoyo kingdom of the Lower Congo. Her detective work in tracking it down to the storerooms of the Musée de l'Homme, where it had been accessioned as a fishing basket, is an interesting story itself, but our concern here is with her elucidation of the iconography of the crown in the context of myth and history. This dome-shaped object was made by coiling "some 100 pieces, totalling about 75 meters, of forged copper strip" and winding them around a horizontal armature of 41 circular copper semicircles, and around its circumference four copper bands of projecting flanges of metal.

The ngunda formerly constituted "the ritual core of the shrine where the climax of royal investiture took place." It is, Volavka argues, an oversize version of the fiber cap of the traditionally invested Kongo chief. But beyond this, she shows that the leopard iconography of the copper semicircles, the red color of the object (though it is now green with oxidation), the metal itself, and the shape are all female within the framework of Kongo language and thought. The crown makes a series of statements signifying the authority of the king to cause suffering and death, but also signifying his symbolic marriage with his own *kanda* or matrilineal group, the crown being interchangeable with a young woman in Kongo myth: "Every chief's investiture is . . . a re-enactment of the myth. . . . Being invested as *mfumu* means committing symbolic incest" — the ultimate crime for humans, the model for deities. The ngunda thus materializes concepts of divine authority and the sacred continuity of the matrilineage, invoking myths of Ne Kongo, the great father, to unify two seemingly antithetical ideas: hierarchical power and a decentralized model of social organization. The Kongo prefer to marry rather than to conquer, to make love not war, so that the marriage symbolism is equal to the statement of power. In Volavka's historical reconstruction, the ngunda embodies ideas of divine chieftancy which precede not only the arrival of the Portuguese but also the development of the centralized Kongo kingdom, and hence may date from the thirteenth or fourteenth century.[46]

Vansina, it is true, is not convinced by Volavka's reconstruction, preferring to stick with the original interpretation of the object as a fishing basket:

not an actual basket but a shrine to the Loango goddess of fish and the sea. Be that as it may, Volavka has raised an extremely important point in showing that metals are ascribed a gender. In this instance copper is female, as it is in the Mweel myth. Lead is also female in the context of ngunda, but elsewhere copper-lead and copper-iron may represent gender opposites, with copper customarily seen as female.

In some cases, an object may be considered female for reasons we simply do not know: the spears in the regalia of the Emir of Biu in northern Nigeria, for example, are classified as male and female, and one female spear in particular is "emphatically the *tsafe* (fetish), regarded with awe and referred to with reluctance." Tradition relates that it miraculously sprang from the ground to block the Biu invaders from the east and was only possessed when its secret was revealed to the Biu leader by the daughter of the local chief.[47] A brass mounting joins the iron blade to the wooden shaft of the spear, which may or may not have some connection with its classification and its power. Stayt sees the ascription of gender to metals in Venda as an extension of color classification: a child receives red blood from its mother and white bones from its father, so that by analogy the mixing of red copper and white lead symbolizes the mixing in marriage of the woman (red) and the man (white). But as he notes, this does not prevent men from wearing red or women white for some rituals.[48] On the other hand, in Bambara and Senufo cosmology red copper is identified as male, yellow copper (brass) as female.[49] Just as in western alchemical tradition metals and metallurgy have been highly sexualized — indeed, the alchemical sign for copper is the female symbol itself, and the metal is associated with Cyprean Aphrodite — so one suspects that in many African societies metals are or would once have been incorporated into a classification of the world by gender. On the analogy of color classification, however, the gender ascription would probably also have been determined in part by the context.

## COPPER, BRASS, AND IRON

Thus far we have noted preferences in the demand for copper and brass or bronze and specified which was used where without trying to draw distinctions between the metals. But even if they tended to be used in the same way, we cannot assume that they were interchangeable. Differences were widely recognized, at least on the basis of color. Sometimes this meant gender differentiation as well, but there has been little exploration of these distinctions. The problem is somewhat simplified in large areas of Central and Southern Africa where brass came in so late that there would scarcely have been time to integrate it into any very complex symbolic system. To the extent that it was ritualized at all in these areas, this would probably have been because of its foreignness and its value. A Natal tradition, for example, relates that when about 1820 an epidemic struck the native population, doctors [sic] ordered all brass ornaments to be destroyed. About 500 pounds of broken European trade bracelets and neck rings were later found on the banks of the Umvolosi River, apparently substantiating the tradition and suggesting, according to Cline, that brass was viewed as something strange or dangerous.[50] On the analogy of the subsequent cattle-killings, however, it may well have been simply because of its value that the brass had to be sacrificed.

The case is different where metallurgy was highly developed and where both copper and copper alloys had been available for a longer period. To be sure, the first consideration might be no more than a practical one: copper would be chosen for cold-hammering and annealing and brass or bronze for casting, as at Igbo-Ukwu. But what are we to make of the Ife castings and the seated figure from Tada (fig. 9)? Was brass at hand only for some and not for others, or was there something about copper that made it preferable in spite of the greater technical difficulty in casting it? Is the use of the two metals evidence of a time difference in their manufacture, despite the stylistic homogeneity?

What are we to make, further, of instances where copper and brass are used in or on the same object? Nupe beaten brasswares, for example, frequently mix copper and brass; so do the very different reliquary figures from eastern Gabon, some of which combine sheet copper and brass, others intricate patterns of wire of the two metals. Weapons and insignia of office may alternate decoration of brass and copper wire, ribbon, or plates. Similarly, there are a number of descriptions of humans, male and female, wearing alternating bracelets of copper and brass on their arms, or in the case of Masai women, necklace-breastplates consisting of coiled circles of heavy brass wire within a circle of finer copper wire coiled at right angles around it.[51] Speke describes Kabaka Mtesa as adorned with alternate brass and copper rings on all ten toes and fingers.[52] Bracelets and rings may also be made of intertwined brass and copper or an inlay of copper on bronze, as in the Kotokoli arm ring in the Berlin Museum (Dahlem).

Two cases of such juxtaposition are particularly intriguing. Certain classes of Akan cast-brass goldweights which Garrard ascribes to the Early Period (c. 1400–1700 A.D.) have copper plugs or insets. The same is true of some gold-dust spoons which seem to belong equally to this period, but there seems to be no explanation for either use of the insets.[53] The second case concerns Benin hip masks being treated for corrosion at the Detroit Institute of Art. In the course of cleaning one of the masks it was found that in "virtually all corroded areas, almost pure copper had been applied over dirt and sand" as a fill and to correct casting flaws. In the same piece, however, thin layers of copper were found over the original cast surface in areas free of damage and flaws: "The mask displays copper around the edges of the headdress, beyond the corroded areas, and large traces also exist around all the features of the face where no repairs were needed." Weston and Johnson, who carried out the treatment, assume that this was done for decorative purposes "to develop areas of contrasting metals into a design, thereby parlaying an expedient into an asset."[54] But one suspects that more than expediency was involved: traces of copper were used around the eye, for example, and bands of copper are sometimes found running vertically down the faces of pectorals as more visible additions to objects cast in brass.[55] This could be explained in terms of color symbolism, which in turn might be gender-linked, except that there is as yet no evidence for this, and in fact, Ben-Amos insists that the Edo see brass as "red" and hence do not make a color distinction between brass and copper.[56]

The plot thickens still further when we consider that iron is also added occasionally to Benin heads: strips of iron are often embedded in the forehead above the bridge of the nose, and pinpoints of iron in the pupils of the eyes (fig. 40). Clearly, we cannot isolate a discussion of copper and brass from iron, for throughout black Africa it is used in many of the same objects and in combination with them. Time and again we have noted that these metals seem to be almost interchangeable in jewelry and implements or that two or even three of them may be used together, adorning the human body, weapons, sculptured objects. They may be interwoven, alternated or inlaid in each other, with alternating bands of copper and iron on the shaft of a spear, for example, paralleling the succession of bracelets on the human arm. Schweinfurth describes an old woman who "had almost an arsenal of metal, links of iron, brass, and copper, strong enough to detain a prisoner in his cell" on her wrists and ankles.[57]

But these metals are not, or were not, interchangeable, nor is their combination ultimately dictated by esthetics. When Miner became curious about the tong amulettes or *kambu* of Timbuktu and why they could be made of different metals, he discovered that "*kambu* made of iron are considered all-powerful. Those made of copper are only effective in witchcraft against children or in their protection. *Kambu* of brass can only protect health and wealth." But he also discovered that the metals alone were not sufficient: "The colors of the *kambu* cords have special significance. When the fetish is to be used to make a victim sicken or die, the particular colored cord selected to tighten around the *kambu* depends upon the skin color of the victim. Thus the black strand is used against Negro Bela and Gabibi, the red against Arabs, and the yellow against the French."[58] A

40. Queen Mother head, early period, Benin, Nigeria. Brass

classic case of basic ideas about color and material being adapted to local conditions! Similarly, the Nyamwezi explained that a particular bracelet was made of intertwined iron and brass because "the former protected against dangers from in front, the latter against dangers behind," though Blohm seems to suspect that the union of the metals was aimed more at influencing different ancestors.[59]

Williams illustrates a Yoruba hunter's doublet laden with charms and medicines, including a horn containing three metal pins — copper, brass, and iron — each of which can be used as a pick to transfer "medicines" to his tongue with curses aimed at delivering the enemy into his hands.[60] Such combinations are not unique among the Yoruba. Although brass is the metal most obviously associated with the Ogboni society, X-rays of free-standing *edan* have shown that a small piece of iron is hidden in their core which, unlike the iron pin of the spiked edan, has no functional purpose. Even thin Ogboni sword blades of brass contain a very small inset of iron. "This might indicate that in Ogboni thought, the well-known female symbolism of the earth" — exemplified by brass — "is doubled by the male symbolism of iron, linked with Ogun, and the blacksmith." Just as Ogboni paraphernalia is closely related to ceremonial objects used in the cult of Ogun, the god of iron, so Ogun insignia include objects of brass and brass and iron.[61] Williams declares that while iron was the first metal to be worked in sub-Saharan Africa and therefore the first to be ritualized as indispensable to the pursuits of agriculture, hunting, and war, "bronze is significant . . . principally in the appurtenances of priest and king, of ritual and ceremony; on the one hand subject to the metaphysical ordering of the universe, on the other to institutions of divine kingship."[62] This "metaphysical ordering of the universe" comes out most clearly in the association of brass with the edan as the embodiment of the spirit of the earth because, in contrast to iron, it does not corrode:

> The *edan* does not die, rocks never crumble.
> The *ogri sakan* does not die from year to year.
> I become the hill, I become the rock beneath the sea,
> I die no more.
> May it please God that I become like the rock beneath the sea.

Like the earth, brass is indestructible, or nearly so.[63]

An Ifa verse offers a mythological explanation for these properties. Brass, lead, and iron were all children of the same mother and all were told to sacrifice against death. Brass and lead did so, but iron said that the diviners were telling lies and that the Sky God had ordained things to last forever. The sacrifice that iron refused to make is what is eating him away;

he begins to rust and spoil if he is buried in the ground for as long as four years. But the sacrifice made by brass and lead is what prevents them from spoiling, even if they are left in the ground for many years.[64] In Edo thought, this quality of permanence symbolizes the continuity of kingship, while iron has "the mystical power of *ase* to insure that whatever proclamations are made will come to pass."[65] Thus iron and brass in Benin art emphasize different aspects or attributes of power.

There may be associations of brass with the earth implicit also in the Igala *okwute* ceremony in which a cast-brass cylinder is used as a stool and a small brass bowl, *ane,* represents the land. The invocation begins: "Land that eats up the chief who wears copper [anklets] that eats up the chief who wears [fine slippers]." However, though these rituals acknowledge the original owners of the land, it is not at all clear how the different parts fit together—one of the objects used in the ceremony, for example, is an iron cannonball.[66] The cannonball is consistent with the view of Ogu, the Igala god of iron, as a god of violence and sudden death, as well as the provider of the tools of civilization. He represents the ambivalent nature of metals, their creative and destructive force. No doubt this is why Igala shrines are painted in both red and white stripes, though in Benin, the deity himself is always in red, indicating violence—and ambiguity.[67]

For the Bambara, on the other hand, Zahan equates "black iron" with raw, unworked metal which when fashioned into rings indicates "malleable and profound thoughts and words," as distinguished from rings of copper, which represent the perfection of the word, its "ressemblance parfaite avec Faro."[68] In a very different vein, Van Warmelo describes Venda puberty ceremonies, where iron and brass have opposing significations. Each girl performs various rites to enhance her attractiveness and emphasize her nubility; then "the older women . . . inspect her as to her virginity and plait brass rings into her hair if they find her intact. A girl that has lost her maidenhead has black (iron) rings plaited into her hair, so that all may know it."[69]

We have very little to go on in interpreting the frequent addition of copper and brass to iron weapons, beyond the obvious connotations of wealth and prestige. But it is highly likely that these additions are often amuletic and apotropaic, as Morel so carefully documents in the case of the Tuareg. The Tuareg apply thin rectangular strips of iron, red copper, and brass in alternate layers (or sometimes just iron and brass) to the pommel of their swords, making a sort of pyramid of metals, at the base of which is an ornament entirely of brass. This is a plaque of brass in the form of a truncated lozenge which looks something like a shield: "it is in fact a shield, a necessary amulet which communicates to the takouba [sword] the supernatural violence needed to penetrate the real shield of the enemy."

Indeed, the word for brass is derived from the words for copper and for shield. When the sword is first made, the smith as "virtual magician" performs a "veritable rite of copper": he verifies the pommel and its plaque and then melts a little "eau de cuivre" which he pours into the designs etched into the iron blade. Or, "*he may only pretend to do this* by touching the engraving with any object of the same metal."[70]

Morel explains the addition of these metals as having not only an offensive but also a defensive purpose. Copper and especially brass are protective, but the primary role of the metal, "hidden from the profane, is not forgotten by the maallem [the smith]: it is to neutralize the 'break-iron amulet' that hangs from the neck of the adversary," an amulet which can cause even the best swordblades to break in the midst of combat or, even worse, to separate from their handles at the moment they are unsheathed. For this reason, too, two bits of copper are applied to the extremities of leather sheath. To the Tuareg, then, "a sword without copper on the hilt is destined for the demons of solitude."[71] Further, both Tuareg and Moors consider iron an impure metal and neutralize it by inlaying copper and brass on anvils, sugar tongs, hammers, locks, and the like, as well as on knives and other weapons. Far from opposing such views, Islam reinforces them, just as it supports the belief among many Berber peoples that gold is to be feared, attracting misfortune to the wearer.[72]

In spite of corrosion, iron and copper are found together so frequently in burials that we must assume that their complementary relationship is a long-established one. Further, the placement of these objects is usually so careful, when the grave has not been disturbed, that it seems clearly part of a complex symbolic language which, though largely undeciphered, seems to link the metals with each other, with notions of right and left, male and female, with different parts of the body. The reconstruction of a Kisalian grave in the museum at Tervuren, for example, shows the skeleton laid out fully covered with iron rings on its arms and legs, a tangle of heavily oxidized copper rings in the area of the groin. De Maret's comments about the positioning of the copper croisettes in the Upemba sites and the arrangement of metal objects at Ingombe Ilede have already been mentioned, but perhaps the most intriguing description of all comes from a burial unearthed at Hampden Farm near Harare (Zimbabwe) and dated to about the thirteenth century A.D. Here one leg had three simple iron anklets, the other two. One arm (we are not told whether right or left) was lavishly adorned with a series of some sixteen bangles and bracelets of four different types in the following sequence from the wrist upwards: two iron bangles, an iron bead bracelet, an iron bangle, a copper and iron bead bracelet, an iron bangle, an iron bead bracelet, an iron bangle, five copper and iron bead bracelets, a single copper-iron-glass bead bracelet (an additional copper and iron bead bracelet either above or below this), and a final copper and iron bead bracelet—plus fragments that could not be assigned a position. In the bead bracelets, the iron and copper beads were in almost equal proportions.[73]

So common are such combinations and associations of copper and iron in both the archaeological and ethnographic literature that they cannot be fortuitous. They remind us that, as with colors, one cannot interpret a single metal any more than a single color without seeing it in its full context with other colors or other materials. And as colors may have what seem to be almost contradictory significations but in fact turn out to be perfectly coherent alternative meanings, the same is undoubtedly true of metals. Investigation into color systems, in fact, may provide the most useful methodology for the study of the language of materials, because it has taught us to be more comfortable with ambiguity and to look at context rather than isolated phenomena. It has taught us, too, to go beyond perception. Thus when the Edo see brass as red we can note that the same is true for the Kongo: we no longer assume that they do not perceive a distinction between red and yellow but realize that in their conceptual and linguistic framework yellow may be equivalent to red.[74]

Or, since copper and iron are sounding metals, we may look to music for clues to their understanding. Like the Songhay violin used in the *culte des génies,* with its bow of copper and blade of steel added to augment its spiritual power,[75] sounds reinforce, modify, and neutralize each other. Sometimes they must be played together to be coherent, or we may find ourselves in the position of the Ewe drummer who was at a loss to get the beat when he tried to play alone without the competing rhythms of his fellow musicians.[76]

# Red Gold

[Les Serer] ne font aucun cas de l'or; ils préfèrent
le cuivre rouge à ce métal si précieux ailleurs.
— Pruneau de Pommegorge (1789)

Gold is no longer considered by the [Gold
Coast] negroes in the careless light it was when
the Europeans first traded with them.
— J. Hippisley (1764)

"It is curious," wrote Walter Cline in 1937, "that the metal most active
in drawing the attention of the Arab and European worlds to Negro Africa
was the one which the Negroes themselves generally valued the least."[1]
He was only echoing a refrain that had been a virtual litany over almost
exactly a millennium of contact between these worlds and Africa. From
al-Husayn about 950 A.D. to the Benin Punitive Expedition in 1897, outsiders never ceased to wonder at the odd preference of Africans for cuprous
metals. To some it seemed to confirm their benighted state, yet another
area requiring improvement. Thus the explorer Speke took Kabaka Mtesa
of Uganda aside and gave him his silk necktie and gold crest-ring "explaining their value, which he could not comprehend, and telling him we gentle-
men prided ourselves on never wearing brass or copper."[2] Others had long
accepted the fact that gold could be gotten in exchange for copper and
similar "baubles" and simply made the best of it.

One could cite a host of sources to buttress the view that copper was
valued more than gold in African societies generally, but it would seem
to be a case of gilding the scholarly lily, since we have shown at such length
how closely the uses of copper in these societies paralleled the uses of gold
in the western and Islamic worlds. We could also point to the geological
record, which amply demonstrates how much more widespread are occurrences of gold in Africa than is commonly realized — alluvial gold as well
as the reef gold that would have required greater technical skill.[3] With the
exception of the justly famous mines of Bambuk-Buré, the Akan forest,
and Zimbabwe, these occurrences were largely ignored before the colonial
period, while those of copper and iron were exploited to the hilt. It may
be argued that working the deposits might not always have been commercially feasible, but Curtin and Garrard have shown how relative a term
that is in societies where time is not equated with money.[4]

296

But what about the exceptions to the rule, those cultures in which gold did play a major role? How do they fit into this model? Can one really argue that their valuation of gold represented a shift over time, a response to outside stimulus?

In the case of Zimbabwe, we have already laid out much of the evidence for such an evolution in chapter 5: the absence of gold in Early Iron Age sites in contrast to the virtual omnipresence of copper; the uneven exploitation of gold deposits in comparison to copper; the apparent dichotomy between production of gold for export and copper for internal consumption; the relatively late thesaurization of gold after a long period of contact with Indian Ocean traders and in the face of heavy-handed Portuguese attempts to control commerce and production. Even then, testimony of travellers such as dos Santos and Lacerda suggests that gold was still not valued very highly in parts of the Zambezi Valley and the northern plateau.[5] Caton-Thompson has proven to be well ahead of her time in generally down-playing the role of gold in the rise of Great Zimbabwe, a salutary corrective to the obsession with gold that long distorted the understanding of these stone-building cultures. Robinson, the excavator of Khami and other plateau sites, concluded that gold was valued in early Zimbabwe only as a result of Asiatic and European contacts, but he sees this as evidence of greater sophistication, a notion very similar to that expressed by the engineer who interpreted the indigenous concentration on copper rather than gold in the Transvaal as a sign of "more primitive mining."[6] Some have even been prompted to theorize that although Africans may have worked copper deposits in these regions, gold must have been worked by foreigners, since it was held in such low esteem by the natives![7]

In the western Sudan and among the Akan, the case is a good deal more tentative because of the difficulties of constructing a chronology. The finds of gold at Rao and other protohistoric sites of the Senegambia would appear to date to the early second millennium A.D. They are accompanied by objects of copper and brass which would indicate trade with Akjoujt, Morocco, or possibly Aïr for the former, North Africa for the latter. Garrard's belief that the trans-Saharan gold trade predates the Arab conquest looks more and more credible in light of Descamps' work in Senegambia and that of the McIntoshes at Jenne-Jeno. The comparative richness of some of the Senegambian sites in comparison with the early phases of Jenne, however, suggests that the extreme western routes across the desert may have been the earliest to be developed and were related to the consolidation and Islamization of states in the Senegal Valley.[8] Later, the Wolof became famous for their gold jewelry. Indeed, Gamble claims that when the Serer fell under Wolof domination, they were forbidden to wear gold and silver—which may not have been too onerous a prohibition, since Pruneau insists that in the eighteenth century they preferred copper anyway.[9]

Elsewhere in the Sudan, the incorporation of gold into indigenous systems of value and ritual may have occurred somewhat later. Except for the lone earring, no gold has turned up at Jenne-Jeno, which according to the McIntoshes was abandoned about 1100 A.D., nor in the tumuli of the Internal Delta (tentatively dated to the very early second millennium A.D.), nor at Daima or other "Sao" sites in the Lake Chad region. Granted, archaeology is barely beginning in much of this area, but myth and ritual would appear to lend support to this hypothesis. Thus gold is strongly associated with the "génie des eaux" in Senegambia and as far south as the Casamance,[10] whereas among the Dogon, largely cut off from early commercial currents of the western Sudan, it hardly figures in creation myths and the rituals deriving from them. Interestingly enough, the Bambara seem to be midway between, just as we would expect: here gold is *one* of the metals of Faro, the deity of the Niger, and is worn in jewelry as the symbol of purity and changelessness. In the cosmology of the Word, it seems to have preempted the primacy of copper, enabling Faro to hear the most secret and powerful utterances.[11] But Zahan notes that the quantity of gold ornaments worn by Bambara women is a recent phenomenon and that formerly they were reserved for the wives of kings.[12] Dogon thought classifies gold as the "younger brother" of copper, and this may symbolize exactly what happened historically.[13] Even the Dogon were not entirely isolated from the far-reaching cultural contacts of the Niger Valley. In Bambara thought, gold would characteristically have been assigned a classification based on its multiple properties, but was also seen as reinforcing the other metals when used in combination.[14] Possibly the linguistic confusion between copper and gold among the Kotoko, supposed to be the descendants of the "Sao," also hints at a comparable evolution and the need to embed metals in a cosmological framework as they become significant.[15]

Precisely because myth and ritual are no more static than any other aspects of culture, they must be used with caution, but along with archaeology they provide one of the few means of counterbalancing the biases of Arabic sources, with their medieval picture of Sudanese kings and courts already heavily influenced by trans-Saharan contacts, Islam, and the "golden trade."

It may be an act of sheer folly to suggest that the same sort of historical evolution could have taken place among the Akan, that there, too, the primacy of gold might have come after the ritualization of iron and copper or more likely, brass. Certainly gold has been prized long enough to saturate Akan kingship and to have become the symbol of the life-giving quality of Nyame, the sky god.[16] When the Portuguese landed at Elmina on the coast in 1471 they were met by Caramansa and his retinue decked out in a dazzling display of gold ornaments.[17] And yet we have seen the central role, also, of brass basins and cast-brass *kuduo* in Akan ritual and in local myths of origin. It is true, too, that no gold has been found in a stratified and securely datable archaeological context anywhere in this region, although relatively few sites have been excavated, and one always has to take into account the possibility of grave robbers in the case of burials.

In fact, Akan culture is extremely eclectic. Both the use of brass and copper and the valuation of gold seem to be intimately linked to Mande influence. According to tradition, gold was not used as currency by the Akan before the arrival of Mande traders in the late fourteenth or fifteenth century. Before that, small bits of iron in the form of discs or rods were used, as in other parts of Africa. Enciso's account of the littoral between Cape Verde and Cape Three Points, written in 1518, describes "pieces of copper shaped at the end like crosses" which were used as money, but it is not clear exactly which part of the coast this refers to and there is no other evidence for such a currency, although the avidity of Gold Coast peoples for copper bracelets has been dealt with at length. Both Hair and Garrard have suggested that the reference may be a somewhat garbled description of early brass goldweights marked with crosses.[18] In any event, Islamic weight standards and many of the Akan words associated with the gold trade are derived from Mande — even the word for gold mine. This is not really surprising if the fields were in fact opened up by *numu* smiths from the Middle Niger. Tekyiman traditions, possibly intended to underscore the backwardness of Aşante, insist that the latter knew nothing about gold and its uses until enlightened by Tekyiman in the early eighteenth century. Even Aşante informants told Garrard that gold-dust currency began to supersede iron only from the 1690s on.[19]

Since Wilks has shown that Mande traders had reached the coast at Elmina before the Portuguese arrived, local peoples would already have been made aware of the insatiable demand for gold to be funneled northward.[20] This awareness would have been augmented by the fanatical preoccupation with gold on the part of Europeans on the coast. Hippisley's comment that the Africans had lost their innocence about the value of gold through long contact with Europeans may be nothing more than the romantic nostalgia of the business man for a golden age that never existed, but it may also contain more than a germ of truth. A century earlier Barbot observed:

> I should not proceed to speak of the proper gold weights, but must first observe as to the gold itself, that the *Blacks* in former times, as appears by the accounts of the most rational persons among them, had nothing near so great

a value for it as they have now. The greediness the *Portuguese* showed for it, whilst they were the sole traders on that coast, for above an hundred years together, . . . and the same eagerness for it in the other *Europeans,* who have since expelled them, by degrees brought the natives to have more esteem for it: and this increasing from one generation to another successively, they have now so great an opinion of its worth, that their whole study in all places on the coast, is either to seek for it in the bowels of the earth, or in rivers, or to purchase it by trading.[21]

Barbot adds that when he reproached some Africans for their eagerness to grow rich in gold and for undervaluing the goods offered by European traders, "they very pertinently answered, That considering the great eagerness the *Europeans* had always shown in fetching gold from those parts of the world, they were apt to believe it was their principal deity, and that our country must be very poor, since we left it, exposing ourselves to so many perils and fatigues to fetch it from among them, at so great a distance."[22] With Mande *dyula* slogging through the rain forest a thousand miles from home and Europeans braving tropical pestilence and the terrors of the deep for it, how could Africans not see gold in a new light? It became increasingly expensive in terms of European goods, and ultimately so highly valued that by the middle of the eighteenth century payment for slaves on the Gold Coast was being demanded in gold.[23] More and more it was being hoarded by the Akan peoples, especially the Aşante and Baulé.

A strong case can therefore be made that Mande traders and craftsmen provided the initial catalyst for the expansion, if not the original exploitation, of Akan gold resources, and that this stimulus was reinforced by the centuries of European presence on the coast. But since the earliest stocks of brasswares as well as the technique of casting also seem now to have been introduced by these same Mande, it is difficult to know whether the role of both metals grew hand in hand or whether in fact brass — perhaps because of its exotic origin — was more highly valued at first and was only gradually eclipsed by gold, not only under the stimulus of trade but also as part of the wholesale borrowing of regalia from the north.[24] Of course valuation is not synonymous with ritualization, and it is still open to question whether brass itself, and not simply brass objects, was ritualized. Until that is better understood, we can only point to two examples that illustrate the close historical connections between brass and gold. Every week, according to tradition, the king of Bono received a brass bowl full of gold dust from the workings near the Tain River.[25] And when the Golden Stool of Aşante was hidden in 1896 to prevent its capture by the British, it was buried "enclosed between two great brass pans."[26]

Arabs and Europeans alike tended to apply a double standard in their trade with Africa: what they brought to the continent — metals, beads and cowries, textiles — were baubles, "merchandise of little value," as al-'Umari put it;[27] what they took from Africa — gold, ivory, slaves — were goods of consummate worth. The slaves do indeed represent a difference of incalculable dimensions, comparable in some degree only to the iron imports which would have directly affected African productivity. But is there any reason to consider copper bracelets and beads any more primitive than gold necklaces and ivory bangles? The purpose of luxury goods the world over is to serve as visible symbols of wealth, status, and power. "Gold and silver are not only negatively superfluous, i.e. dispensable articles," wrote Marx, "but their esthetic properties make them the natural material of luxury, ostentation, splendor, festive occasions, in short, the positive form of abundance and wealth."[28] They are appropriated and controlled by elites precisely to secure or maintain dominance in the social hierarchy. If they become too plentiful, they may still serve ritual and esthetic functions, but something else will replace them as the ultimate signifier of value.

As Marx recognized, these goods must by definition be useless in a conventional sense. Even imported textiles were largely unnecessary in the African climate, and it may even be that the greater part ended up underground in burials just as must have been the case with copper. Gold is even more useless than copper because it is so soft, as Cameron's informants in Katanga noted in explaining why, although they knew of the gold deposits of the region, they preferred "the red copper to the white."[29] But this comment brings us back again to the subject of color symbolism. In many parts of the world gold is valued not only because of its unchangeableness, its resistance to corrosion and oxidation, but also because it represents the ultimate purity of sun and light and whiteness. Curiously enough, however, Marx goes on in the passage quoted above to declare of gold and silver, "They appear, in a way, as spontaneous light brought out from the underground world, since silver reflects all rays of light in their original combination, and gold only the color of highest intensity, viz., red light." Like Marx, the Baulé also see gold as red,[30] and it would be interesting to know if the same is true of other Akan peoples; if so, it would suggest that the appreciation of gold and copper in those parts of Africa is more similar than we might imagine, at least on a symbolic level. This seems to be equally implicit in the myths of "living gold" which the So are said to have introduced into the Central Sudan, a mysterious metal of deep, red richness.[31]

In his study of Mbundu state formation, Joseph Miller emphasizes the role of "symbolic objects to confer authority over men."[32] Janzen makes the same point when he refers to copper in Lemba as "both substance and symbol of authority and power."[33] What we have lost in our industrial age is the dynamism of these symbols. For us, they have become passive signifiers rather than the actual containers of power that they represented in precolonial Africa. We cannot imagine the linguist's staff ornamented with copper or gold literally speaking for the king, or that investiture is infinitely more than handing over a gavel.

The problem for the historian is that while the ideas behind such emblems or other ritual objects may stay relatively constant (although perhaps less than we imagine), the emblems themselves are subject to change, particularly as new materials become available through wider trading contacts. In some cases, it may simply be an interchangeability within the same framework of belief: for example, Bamum royal statuary in wood may be sheathed in copper or in red beads. Since both are durable, red, shiny, and were once scarce, they may simply represent two ways of conveying the same message. Brass and copper entered Kuba regalia presumably because they were originally rare materials, brought from a great distance, and because they could easily be absorbed into the Kuba language of authority. But is this an adequate explanation for the shift among some Kongo chiefs from iron bracelets to a single armlet of copper?[34] The same questions arise with objects not associated directly with kingship: how are they fitted into a prescriptive framework and what, in fact, is involved in the ritualization of materials?

We are far from being able to answer these questions. Often we can do no more than fall back on their usefulness as economic documentation, helping us to understand better the domestic economy and regional patterns of trade. Or they may help us with dating: thus certain imported alloys of copper, such as Muntz metal, were not produced before the nineteenth century, while aluminum did not become cheap enough to find its way into African jewelry until the very end of the century.

Above all, the history of copper in Africa reminds us once again how little Africa was an "island, entire to itself." The huge quantities of copper and brass from Europe and the Near East that flowed into sub-Saharan Africa over the centuries grew to be integral to all aspects of African life, complementing and eventually competing with copper produced indigenously. Cuprous metals became the support of divine authority, the augmenter of fertility, the propitiator of the ancestors, and the repeller of witches. But the impact was not one-way. The African demand for copper and brass provided a major stimulus to industry abroad. We know little about the scale of production for the African market in North Africa and the Near East, but in the Lowlands and in the metallurgical empire of the Fugger, the opening up of sea routes to Africa had an immediate impact. The unheard-of intensification of the slave trade in the eighteenth century was closely linked to the growth of the British brass industry: by the later decades of that century copper and brass goods were second in value only to textiles as a constituent of slaving cargoes.[35]

But as we have tried to suggest, economic history is not simply concerned with material needs; it is inseparable from the values people live by. "Minerva rather than fluctuations of consumer demand governed the fortunes of most industries," wrote Ogilvie of ancient Rome.[36] It is in no sense a denial of *homo oeconomicus africanus* or a return to simplistic nineteenth-century views of fetish-ridden Africa to suggest that we need to know much more about African religious systems, defined in their broadest sense, before we can begin to understand the languages of materials and their full implications for economic behavior.

# ■■ REFERENCE MATERIAL

# ABBREVIATIONS USED IN NOTES AND BIBLIOGRAPHY

| | |
|---|---|
| *Annales* | *Annales: Economies, sociétés, civilisations* |
| ASA | African Studies Association |
| *BIFAN* | *Bulletin de l'Institut français d'Afrique noire* (Dakar) |
| *IJAHS* | *International Journal of African Historical Studies* |
| *JA* | *Journal des africanistes* (formerly *Journal de la Société des africanistes*) |
| *JAH* | *Journal of African History* |
| *JAS* | *Journal of the African Society* |
| *JCMMSSA* | *Journal of the Chemical, Metallurgical and Mining Society of South Africa* |
| *JHSN* | *Journal of the Historical Society of Nigeria* |
| *JRAI* | *Journal of the Royal Anthropological Institute* |
| *JSA* | *Journal de la Société des africanistes* |
| *JSAIMM* | *Journal of the South African Institute of Mining and Metallurgy* |
| MRAC | Musée Royal de l'Afrique Centrale |
| *NA* | *Notes africaines* |
| *NADA* | *Native Affairs Department Annual* (Salisbury) |
| *SAAB* | *South African Archaeological Bulletin* |
| *SAJS* | *South African Journal of Science* |
| *THSG* | *Transactions of the Historical Society of Ghana* |
| *TLS* | *Times Literary Supplement* |
| *UJ* | *Uganda Journal* |
| *WAJA* | *West African Journal of Archaeology* (formerly *West African Archaeological Newsletter*) |

# NOTES

## PROLOGUE

1 Cyril Stanley Smith, "Into the Smelting Pot," review of R. F. Tylecote's *A History of Metallurgy, TLS,* 4 Nov. 1977, 1301.

2 Quoted by I. Bognar-Kutzian, "The Origins of Early Copper-Processing in Europe," in *To Illustrate the Monuments: Essays on Archaeology Presented to Stuart Piggott,* ed. J. V. S. Megaw (London, 1976), 70.

3 Clair Patterson gives earlier dates for the major stages of metallurgy than those customarily found in the literature, basing his estimates on corrections of standard radiocarbon dates: hammering and annealing, from 7300 B.C.; reduction smelting, melting, and casting, from 5000 B.C.; tin-bronze, from 3700 B.C.; and smelting of sulphide ores, from 2500 B.C. Clair Patterson, "Native Copper, Silver, and Gold Accessible to Early Metallurgists," *American Antiquity* 36, no. 3 (July 1971): 286–321. Cf. R. F. Tylecote, *A History of Metallurgy* (London, 1976), ix, 5ff.

4 Heather Lechtman, "Issues in Andean Metallurgy" (Paper presented to the Conference on South American Metallurgy, Dumbarton Oaks, Washington, D.C., 18–19 Oct., 1975), 23.

5 Wladimir W. Krysko, *Lead in History and Art* (Stuttgart, 1979).

6 Tylecote, *History of Metallurgy,* 46. Cf. Leslie Aitchison, *A History of Metals,* 2 vols. (London, 1960), 1:103.

7 Tylecote, 4.

8 Colin Renfrew, *Before Civilization: The Radiocarbon Revolution and Prehistoric Europe* (New York, 1975), 167.

9 J. E. G. Sutton, "Archaeology in West Africa: A Review of Recent Work and a Further List of Radiocarbon Dates," *JAH* 23, no. 3 (1982): 296–97; D. Calvocoressi and N. David, "A New Survey of Radiocarbon and Thermoluminescence Dates for West Africa," *JAH* 20, no. 1 (1979): 1–29.

10 Sutton, 297.

11 See, in addition to Sutton, above, S. K. and R. J. McIntosh, *Prehistoric Investigations in the Region of Jenne, Mali,* 2 vols. (Oxford, 1980), 1:188; G. Connah, *Three Thousand Years in Africa* (New York, 1981), 146–47; F. Treinen-Claustre, "Nouveaux éléments de datation absolue pour l'âge de fer de la région de Koro-Toro (nord du Tchad)," *L'anthropologie* 82 (1978): 103–9.

12 P. Schmidt and D. H. Avery, "Complex Iron Smelting and Prehistoric Culture in Tanzania," *Science* 201, no. 4361 (22 Sept. 1978).

13 D. W. Phillipson, "The Chronology of the Iron Age in Bantu Africa," *JAH* 16, no. 3 (1975): 321–42; T. N. Huffman, "African Origins," *SAJS* 75 (1979): 233–37.

14 R. J. Mason, "Early Iron Age Settlement at Broederstroom 24/73, Transvaal," *SAJS* 77 (Sept. 1981): 401–16.

15 P. de Maret and F. Nsuka, "History of Bantu Metallurgy: Some Linguistic Aspects," *History in Africa* 4 (1977): 43–65.

16 Christopher Ehret, personal communication.

17 R. F. Tylecote, lecture, Massachusetts Institute of Technology, 3 Oct. 1977.

18 Raymond Mauny, "Essai sur l'histoire des métaux en Afrique occidentale," *BIFAN* 14 (1952): 545–95.

19 Nicole Lambert, "Les industries sur cuivre dans l'ouest saharien," *WAJA* 1 (1971): 9–21; cf. idem, "Medinet Sbat et la protohistoire de Mauritanie occidentale," *Antiquités africaines* 4 (1970): 15–62.

20 Paul Huard, "Introduction et diffusion du fer au Tchad," *JAH* 7, no. 3 (1966): 377–405.

21 Christopher Ehret, personal communication.

22 Roland Oliver and Brian Fagan, *Africa in the Iron Age* (Cambridge, 1975), 7.

23 Henri Lhote, "La connaissance du fer en Afrique occidentale," *Encyclopédie d'outre-mer* (Paris, 1952), 269–72; L. M. Diop, "Métallurgie et âge de fer en Afrique," *BIFAN* 30 (1968): 10–38.

24 See, for example, Lechtman, "Andean Metallurgy," *passim*.

25 Cinemathèque, Musée de l'Homme, Paris.

26 For example, Mauny, "Histoire des métaux," 573; idem, "Enquête sur les noms de métaux dans les langues africaines," *NA,* no. 50 (April 1951): 61; Jean Rouch, *La religion et la magie songhay* (Paris, 1960), 124*n*; W. Burchell, *Travels in the Interior of Southern Africa,* 2 vols. (1824; London, 1967), 2:575; Heinrich Vedder, *South West Africa in Early Times,* trans. and ed. C. G. Hall (London, 1966), 28. Cf. [Cardoso], "História do reino do Congo" (c. 1624), in L. Cordeiro, ed., *Memórias do ultramar,* 6 vols. (Lisbon, 1881), 2:81; Lalouel, "Les forgerons mondjombo," *Bulletin de l'Institut d'études centrafricaines* 2 (1974): 108.

27 Brian Fagan, lecture, Yale University, 17 Feb. 1971.

28 N. J. Van der Merwe, "The Advent of Iron in Africa," in *The Coming of the Age of Iron,* ed. T. A. Wertime and J. D. Muhly (New Haven, 1980), 463–506.

29 Leo Frobenius, *The Voice of Africa,* trans. R. Blind, 2 vols. (New York, 1913), 1:14.

30 A. C. P. Gamitto, *King Kazembe and the Marave, Cheva, Bisa, Bemba, Lunda and Other Peoples of Southern Africa . . .,* trans. Ian Cunnison (Lisbon, 1960), 56. Cf. David and Charles Livingstone, *Narratives of an Expedition to the Zambesi and Its Tributaries . . . 1858–1864* (London, 1865), 536; R. F. Burton, *Two Trips to Gorilla-Land and the Cataracts of the Congo,* 2 vols. (London, 1876), 1:227; J. Matthews, *A Voyage to the River Sierra Leone . . . 1788* (London, 1966), 52 inter alia, concerning the high quality of African iron.

31 Basil Davidson, *Old Africa Rediscovered* (London, 1959), 75. Cf. idem, *The Lost Cities of Africa,* rev. ed. (Boston, 1970), 20.

32 Herodotus, *The Histories,* trans. A. de Selincourt (Hammondsworth, 1954), 38.

**CHAPTER 1**

1  J. A. Bancroft, *Mining in Northern Rhodesia,* ed. T. D. Guernsey (n.p., 1961), 36, 63; cf. R. A. Pelletier, *Mineral Resources of South Central Africa* (London, 1964), 268.

2  Ibn Battuta, *Travels in Asia and Africa, 1325–54,* trans. and ed. H. A. R. Gibb (London, 1929), 336.

3  G. Brouin, "Du nouveau au sujet de la question de Takedda," *NA,* no. 47 (1950), 90–91.

4  R. Mauny, *Tableau géographique de l'ouest africain au moyen âge* (Dakar, 1961), 140–41; Henri Lhote, "Recherches sur Takedda, ville décrite par le voyageur arabe Ibn Battuta et située en Air,"*BIFAN* 34 (1972): 435–70.

5  S. Bernus and P. Gouletquer, "Du cuivre au sel: Recherches ethnoarchéologiques sur la région d'Azelick (campagnes 1973–1975)," *JA* 46, nos. 1–2 (1976): 7–68. See also Richard Bucaille, "Takadda, pays du cuivre," *BIFAN* 37, no. 4 (1975): 719–78.

6  Sutton, "Archaeology in West Africa," 296–97.

7  Nicholas De Kun, *The Mineral Resources of Africa* (Amsterdam, 1965), 371; Mauny and Hallemans, "Préhistoire et protohistoire de la région d'Akjoujt," *Proceedings of the Third Pan-African Congress of Prehistory and Protohistory,* Livingstone, 1955 (London, 1957), 257.

8  Nicole Lambert, "Exploitation minière et métallurgie protohistoriques du cuivre au Sahara occidental" (Paper presented to the African Studies Associations of the United States and Canada, Montreal, 1969), *passim;* and idem, "L'apparition du cuivre dans les civilisations préhistoriques," in *200 ans d'histoire africaine: Le sol, la parole et l'écrit,* ed. J. Devisse et al. (Paris, 1981), 1:214–15; and "Les industries sur cuivre," 13; Calvocoressi and David, "Radiocarbon and Thermoluminescence Dates," 1–29.

9  L. Baud, "Notice explicative sur la feuille Kayes-Est," *Carte géologique de reconnaissance* (Dakar, 1950), 23–25; Mauny, *Tableau,* 308 ff.

10  Al-Omari, "Le royaume du Mali," *NA,* no. 82 (1959): 63.

11  Mauny, *Tableau,* 310.

12  C. Christy, "The Bahr el-Ghazal and Its Waterways," *The Geographical Journal* 61, no. 5 (1923): 317, 320–321; ibid 45 (1907): 606; D. C. E. Comyn, *Service and Sport in the Sudan* (London, 1911), 169–70.

13  Quoted in W. G. L. Randles, *L'ancien royaume du Congo des origines à la fin du XIXe siècle* (Paris, 1968), 35; cf. Pierre Kalck, *Histoire de la République centrafricaine* (Paris, 1974), 34.

14  Comyn, *Sudan,* 168.

15  J. G. Bower, "Native Smelting in Equatorial Africa," *The Mining Magazine* (London) 37, no. 3 (Sept. 1927): 137, 146; A. E. Robinson, "The Arab Dynasty of Dar For (Darfur)," *JAS* 28 (1928): 381.

16  W. G. Browne, *Travels in Africa, Egypt and Syria* (London, 1799), 266–67, 472.

17  Christy, "Bahr el-Ghazal," 320. Recently the area has been intensively surveyed, with a view to resuming mining of both copper and iron if problems of trans-

port can be resolved: A. R. A. el-Bashir, personal communication, 1978.

18 Mauny, *Tableau,* 309–10.

19 De Kun, *Mineral Resources,* 371–72; cf. G. Savonnet, "Habitations souter-raines bobo ou anciens puits de mines en pays wilé?" *BIFAN* 36, no. 2 (1974): 228 ff.

20 G. Dieterlen and M. Griaule, *Le renard pâle* (Paris, 1965), 14.

21 W. Allen and T. R. H. Thomson, *Expedition to the River Niger,* 2 vols. (London, 1848), 1:404; K. Strumpell, "Bericht über eine Bereisung des Ostgrenz-gebietes der Residenz Adamaua im Jahre 1909," *Mitteilungen aus den deutschen Schutzgebieten* 24 (1911): 25; S. Passarge, *Adamaua* (Berlin, 1895), 470; Lars Sundström, *The Exchange Economy of Pre-Colonial Tropical Africa* (repr. ed. of *The Trade of Guinea)* (New York, 1974), 217; P. A. Talbot, *The Peoples of Southern Nigeria,* 3 vols. (London, 1926), 1:18; W. B. Cline, *Mining and Metallurgy in Negro Africa* (Menasha, Wis., 1937), 72; E. E. Evans-Pritchard, *The Azande* (Oxford, 1971), 94; J.-P. and A. M. Lebeuf, *Les arts des sao* (Paris, 1977), 77; but cf. De Kun, *Mineral Resources,* 100, and M. A. and B. O. On-weujeogwu, "The Search for the Missing Links in Dating and Interpreting the Igbo-Ukwu Finds," *Paideuma* 23 (1977): 174–75.

22 Pelletier, *Mineral Resources,* 223; G. Bigotte, *Contribution à la géologie du Niari* (Paris, 1959), 124 ff.

23 Victor Babet, *Observations géologiques dans la partie méridionale de l'Afrique equatoriale française* (Paris, 1932), 133 ff.; Naval Intelligence Division, Great Britain, *French Equatorial Africa,* Geographical Handbook Series (London, 1942), 433; V. Thompson and R. Adloff, *The Emerging States of French Equatorial Africa* (Palo Alto, 1960), 243–44.

24 A. Le Chatelier, *Comptes rendus de l'Académie des sciences,* 24 April 1893 (Paris), 116:894; Babet, *Observations,* 133–35; Bigotte, *Géologie du Niari,* 124–27; E. Dupont, *Lettres sur le Congo* (Paris, 1889), 337–38; J. Lombard and P. Nicolini, eds., *Gisements stratiformes de cuivre en Afrique . . .,* Symposium held in Copenhagen, 1960 (Paris, 1962), 110–11; M. Barrat, *Sur la géologie du Congo française* (Paris, 1895), 82–87; G. Bruel, *L'Afrique équatoriale française* (Paris, 1918), 386–87.

25 Dupont, *Lettres,* 340.

26 F. Pigafetta and D. Lopes, *Description du royaume de Congo et des contrées avoisinantes,* ed. Willy Bal (1591; Paris, 1965), 32.

27 Duarte Pacheco Pereira, *Esmeraldo de Situ Orbis,* trans. and ed. G. H. T. Kimble (London, 1937), 144.

28 Pigafetta, *Description,* 46, 79; Andrew Battell, *The Strange Adventures of Andrew Battell of Leigh in Angola and Adjoining Regions,* ed. E. G. Ravenstein (1859: London, 1901), 17.

29 J. Denucé, *L'Afrique au XVIe siècle et le commerce anversois* (Antwerp, 1937), 48; Rebello, in Cordeiro, *Memórias,* 2:20; Francisco Travassos Valdez, *Six Years of a Traveller's Life in Western Africa,* 2 vols. (London, 1861), 2:81–82, 111; David Birmingham, *Trade and Conflict in Angola* (Oxford, 1966), 44, 82.

30 Battell, *Strange Adventures,* 17. A Portuguese document of 1619 denies the existence of copper in the Benguela region (copper had been one of the main

arguments for conquest), but the denial seems to be based on misinformation: Alfredo de Albuquerque Felner, *Angola,* 3 vols. (Coimbra, 1933), 1:478.

31 Rebello, in Cordeiro, *Memórias,* 2:15, 18–19; cf. Castelo Branco, in Cordeiro, 1:12–13, 30.

32 H. Capello and R. Ivens, *From Benguella to the Territory of Yacca . . .,* 2 vols. (London, 1882), 1:22. See also G. Tams, *A Visit to the Portuguese Possessions in Southwestern Africa,* trans. H. Evans, 2 vols. (London, 1845), 2:117–18.

33 J. J. Monteiro, *Angola and the River Congo,* 2 vols. (London, 1875), 1:201, 204–5.

34 Ibid., 255; Capello and Ivens, *From Benquella,* 2:233.

35 Travassos Valdez, *Six Years,* 2:328.

36 Pigafetta, *Description,* 36, 39.

37 Rebello, in Cordeiro, *Memórias,* 2:15.

38 A. Verbeken, *Contribution à la géographie historique du Katanga et des régions voisines,* Institut royal colonial belge, Mémoires, vol. 36, sect. 1 (Brussels, 1954): 52–53.

39 F. Lekime, *Katanga: Pays du cuivre* (Verviers, 1966), 42; cf. G. L. Walker, "Ancient Copper Mining in Central America," *Engineering and Mining Journal-Press,* no. 120 (1925): 813 and rebuttal.

40 Bancroft, *Mining,* 27; Andrew Roberts, "Pre-Colonial Trade in Zambia," *African Social Research* 10 (1970): 729; cf. D. Livingstone, *Livingstone's African Journal 1853-1856,* ed. I. Schapera, 2 vols. (London, 1963), 2:255–56.

41 Verbeken, *Contribution,* 52–53; A. Verbeken and M. Walraet, eds., *La première traversée du Katanga en 1806: Voyage des "Pombeiros" d' Angola aux rios de Sena* (Brussels, 1953), 31.

42 According to Bradley, the name Katanga means "smelted copper," but Verbeken shows that its etymology is less certain and that its use was variable and confusing in the nineteenth century. He theorizes that it was initially a territorial designation which was taken over as a title by the chief of the country; if true, this would be the reverse of customary practice in Africa. Kenneth Bradley, *Copper Venture: The Discovery and Development of Roan Antelope and Mufulira* (London, 1952), 67*n*; Verbeken, *Contribution, passim,* esp. 62–64. Cf. J. E. "Chirupula" Stephenson, ms. 1 Jan. 1950, Yale University Archives and Manuscripts, box 49. I am grateful to Moore Crossey for bringing Stephenson's papers to my attention.

45 Michael Bisson, "Copper Currency in Central Africa: The Archaeological Evidence," *World Archaeology* 6, no. 3 (Feb. 1975): 283–84; Tim Maggs, "Some Recent Radiocarbon Dates from Eastern and Southern Africa," *JAH* 18, no. 1 (1977): 179, 181.

46 M. Bisson, "Prehistoric Copper Mining in Northwestern Zambia," *Archaeology* 27, no. 4 (1974): 245.

47 Raymond Brooks to W. V. Brelsford, 20 Oct. 1950, and Stephenson to Brelsford, 20 Sept. 1956, Yale University Archives and Manuscripts.

48 Bancroft, *Mining,* 37–39; P. L. A. O'Brien, "Copper Deposits and Their Environment in Northern Rhodesia," *Commission on Technical Cooperation* (Leopoldville, 1958), 133.

49 Bancroft, 37-38.

50 Stephenson to Brelsford, 20 Sept. 1956.

51 D. W. Phillipson, *The Later Prehistory of Eastern and Southern Africa* (London and New York, 1977), 150.

52 Roger Summers, *Ancient Mining in Rhodesia and Adjacent Areas* (Salisbury, 1969), 105.

53 Bancroft, *Mining,* 36; but cf. R. Tyndale-Biscoe and J. W. Stagman, "Copper Deposits in Southern Rhodesia," *Committee on Technical Cooperation* (Leopoldville, 1958), 188.

54 Bancroft, 36; cf. Chandler, in Summers, *Ancient Mining,* 28.

55 Summers, 87.

56 P. S. Garlake, "Iron Age Sites in the Urungwe District of Rhodesia," *SAAB* 25, no. 97 (June 1970): 25-44; W. G. L. Randles, "La fondation de l'empire du Monomotapa," *Cahiers d'études africaines* 54 (1974): 232.

57 Summers, *Ancient Mining,* 87.

58 Burchell, *Travels,* 2:567-68.

59 David Livingstone, *Family Letters 1841-1856,* ed. I. Schapera, 2 vols. (London, 1959), 1:117-18, 145, 187.

60 Summers, *Ancient Mining,* 77-78, 101-2.

61 T. G. Trevor, "Some Observations on Ancient Mine Workings in the Transvaal," *JCMMSSA* 12 (1912): 268-70. Cf. N. Van der Merwe: "An old prospector, Isaac (Ike) Lombard, tells me that he has found only one surface mineralization in the Northern and Eastern Transvaal (i.e. the Lowveld and Bushveld) in 65 years which did *not* have an 'ancient' in it. This represents diligence of a high order on the part of Iron Age prospectors and strengthens the view that only the small supply of secondary ore could be used." Personal communication.

62 N. Van der Merwe and R. Scully, "The Phalaborwa Story: Archaeological and Ethnographic Investigation of a South African Iron Age Group," *World Archaeology* 3 (1971): 179-81; cf. T. M. Evers, "Recent Iron Age Research in the Eastern Transvaal, South Africa," *SAAB* 30, nos. 119, 120 (1975): 71-74; and R. J. Mason, "Background to the Transvaal Iron Age: New Discoveries at Oliphantspoort and Broederstroom," *JSAIMM* 74, no. 6 (1974), n.p.

63 E. O. M. Hanisch, "Copper Working in the Messina District," *JSAIMM* 74, no. 6 (1974): 250; H. A. Stayt, *The BaVenda* (Oxford, 1931), 64; N. J. van Warmelo, ed., *The Copper Miners of Musina and the Early History of the Zoutpansberg,* Union of South Africa, Department of Native Affairs, Ethnological Publication no. 8 (Pretoria, 1940), 81-83.

64 Martin Hall and J. C. Vogel, "Some Recent Radiocarbon Dates from Southern Africa," *JAH* 21, no. 4 (1980): 450-51.

65 R. H. Steel, "Iron Age Copper Mine 47/73," *JSAIMM* 74, no. 6 (1974): 244; Mason, "Background." Cf. Mason, *Prehistory of the Transvaal* (Johannesburg, 1962), 388, 406, 412; idem, "Early Iron Age Settlement," 401-16.

66 Georg Bürg, *Die nutzbaren Minerallagerstätten von deutsch-Südwestafrika* (Freiberg and Berlin, 1942), 67-68, 120-21; Vedder, *South West Africa,* 39, 309. In general, units of measurement have been left in their original form

except where it has seemed necessary to give English equivalents to metric values.

67 A. J. H. Goodwin, "Metal Working among the Early Hottentots," *SAAB* 11, no. 42 (1956): 48.

68 Vedder, *South West Africa,* 18, 21; Pelletier, *Mineral Resources,* 85; M. Delesse, "Notice sur les mines de cuivre du cap de Bonne-Espérance," *Annales des mines,* 5th ser., 8 (1855): 20–21; J. M. Smalberger, *Aspects of the History of Copper Mining in Namaqualand, 1846–1931* (Cape Town, 1975), *passim;* F. Le Vaillant, *Voyage de F. Le Vaillant dans l'intérieur de l'Afrique par le cap de Bonne-Espérance,* 5 vols. (Paris, 1798–1803), 2:96–97, 134; but see Vedder, p. 31, concerning Le Vaillant's authenticity.

69 Bancroft, *Mining,* 36.

70 For example, H. B. Thomas and R. Scott, *Uganda* (London, 1935), 216, 221; J. W. Barnes, *Bulletin of the Geological Survey of Uganda: Mineral Resources of Uganda* (Entebbe, 1961), 12–15.

71 L. Cahen, personal communication.

72 David Livingstone, *Last Journals,* 2 vols. (London, 1874), 2:123.

## CHAPTER 2

1 Summers, *Ancient Mining,* 152.

2 Trevor, "Ancient Mine Workings," 267–75; cf. J. Chambers, "Reply to Woodburn," *JCMMSSA* 14 (1913): 194.

3 R. A. Dart, "The Ancient Mining Industry of South Africa," *South African Geographical Journal,* Dec. 1924, 7–13.

4 H. A. Stayt, "Notes on the Balemba," *JRAI* 61 (1931): 236–38.

5 Van Warmelo, *Copper Miners,* 63–64. Cf. G. Bloomhill, "The Ancient Copper Miners of Africa," *African World,* 1963, 6–7, who makes much of the supposedly Semitic features and customs of the Lemba and who notes that they are considered by some to be descended from the Falasha of Ethiopia.

6 T. A. Rickard, "Curious Methods Used by the Katanga Natives in Mining and Smelting Copper," *Engineering and Mining Journal* 123 (1927): 51–58.

7 G. L. Walker, "Ancient Copper Mining in Central Africa," ibid. 120 (1925): 811–16.

8 Bancroft, *Mining,* 27.

9 Summers, *Ancient Mining,* 87. Fagan (lecture, Yale University, 17 Feb. 1971) is also skeptical of Indian influence in Zimbabwe, for similar reasons.

10 Denucé, *L'Afrique,* 48. The "Mafulamengo" of the oral traditions collected in the Lower Congo 1931–41, who were supposed to have been skilled ironworkers, brass casters, and cathedral builders, may represent a telescoped memory of Flemish artisans of the Portuguese period, according to R. L. Wannyn, *L'art ancien du métal au Bas-Congo* (Champles-par-Wavre, 1961): 23–24.

11 J. L. Vellut, "Notes sur le Lunda et la frontière luso-africaine (1700–1900)," *Etudes d'histoire africaine* 3 (1972): 88.

12 T. G. Trevor, "Some Observations on the Relics of Pre-European Culture in Rhodesia and South Africa," *JRAI* 60 (1930): 389–99.

13  Cf. T. Evers and R. Van den Berg, "Ancient Mining in Southern Africa, with Reference to a Copper Mine in the Harmony Block, Northeastern Transvaal," *JSAIMM* 74, no. 6 (1974): 225–26; for Katanga, the conclusion of Roland Oliver, *Cambridge History of Africa* (Cambridge, 1978), 2:398; as well as J.-P. Warnier and Ian Fowler, "A Nineteenth-Century Ruhr in Central Africa," *Africa* 49, no. 4 (1979): 329–47, concerning large-scale iron production in Cameroon.

14  Cline, *Mining and Metallurgy,* 140.

15  *La vie au Sahara,* exhibition catalogue, Musée de l'Homme (Paris, 1972), 45.

16  A. Ndinga-Mbo, "Quelques réflexions sur la civilisation du cuivre au Congo," *Cahiers congolais d'anthropologie et d'histoire* 1 (1976): 37. Cf. Wyatt MacGaffey, *Custom and Government in the Lower Congo* (Berkeley, 1970), 226.

17  Y. Cissé, "Notes sur les sociétés des chasseurs malinke," *JSA* 34 (1964), 196. On the other hand, it is worth noting that in the Cameroon grassland where iron production reached a protoindustrial scale, it was almost deritualized: Warnier and Fowler, "Nineteenth-Century Ruhr," *passim.*

18  Rouch, *Religion et magie songhay,* 277.

19  G. Dieterlen, "Contribution à l'étude des forgerons en Afrique occidentale," *Annuaire,* Ecole pratique des hautes études, Section des sciences religieuses, 73 (1965–66): 10.

20  Ibid.; cf. D. Zahan, *Sociétés d'initiation bambara, le n'domo, le kore* (Paris, 1960), 110–11, 127; Ousmane Silla, "Quelques particularités de la société sénégalaise," *NA,* no. 122 (1969): 40.

21  Jan Vansina, "Anthropologists and the Third Dimension," *Africa* 39 (1969): 65; J. E. G. Sutton in P. L. Shinnie, eds., *The African Iron Age* (Oxford, 1971), 182; G. Célis and E. Nzikobanyanka, *La métallurgie traditionelle au Burundi* (Tervuren, 1976), 5.

22  For a more detailed discussion of the role of the smith, see Mircea Eliade, *Forgerons et alchimistes* (Paris, 1956); Luc de Heusch, "Le symbolisme du forgeron en Afrique," *Reflets du monde,* no. 10 (1956): 57–70; and Cline, *Mining and Metallurgy,* chap. 13.

23  Ladame makes no distinction between the priest and the master smelter: "Le droit des indigènes sur les mines de cuivre du Katanga," *Congo* 2 (1921): 685–91; cf. Cline, 120.

24  Msgr. de Hemptinne, *Les "mangeurs de cuivre" du Katanga* (Brussels, 1926; extract from *Congo* 7[1926]), 10, 14, 15. Cf. Vannoccio Biringuccio, *Pirotechnica* (1540; Cambridge, Mass., 1966), 14, 17–18, concerning Christian rites carried out at mining sites for the protection of workers and a "fortunate outcome."

25  R. Marchal, "Renseignements historiques relatifs à l'exploitation des mines de cuivre par les indigènes de la région de Luishia," *Bulletin des juridictions indigènes et du droit coutumier congolais* 7, no. 1 (1939): 11.

26  Ndinga-Mbo, "Quelques réflexions," 38. It is interesting to compare German mining, technically the most advanced of any in the sixteenth century, where it was also assumed that evil demons must be propitiated and beneficent spirits won over: Harry A. Miskimin, personal communication.

27  Ndinga-Mbo, 38.

28 De Hemptinne, *Mangeurs,* 17 ff.
29 Brian Fagan, lecture, Yale University, 17 Feb. 1971. On copper-smelting rituals, see also Ladame, "Le droit," and Bloomhill, "Ancient Copper Miners," as well as Bancroft, *Mining,* 29.
30 Cline, *Mining and Metallurgy,* 128.
31 Philip Dark, *An Introduction to Benin Art and Technology* (Oxford, 1973), 52.
32 G. Neher, "Brasscasting in Northeast Nigeria," *Nigerian Field* 29, no. 1 (1964): 26.
33 Denis Williams, *Icon and Image* (New York, 1974), 238 ff.
34 Célis and Nzikobanyanka, *Métallurgie,* 175-76.
35 Ibid., 5-7.
36 A. F. C. Ryder, *Benin and the Europeans 1485-1897* (London, 1969), 6-7; J. V. Egharevba, *A Short History of Benin* (Ibadan, 1960), 12.
37 R. Bradbury, personal communication to Marion Johnson; Dark, *Benin Art,* 52-53.
38 Egharevba, *Short History,* 66.
39 R. F. Thompson, personal communication; M. J. Herskovits, *Dahomey: An Ancient African Kingdom,* 2 vols. (New York, 1938), 1:68.
40 S. F. Nadel, *A Black Byzantium* (London, 1965), 74-75.
41 L. W. G. Malcolm, "A Note on Brass-Casting in the Central Cameroons,"*Man* 23, no. 1 (1923): 2.
42 E. Torday, *On the Trail of the Bushongo* (1925; New York, 1969), 156. Cf. Stayt's comment that the Lemba copper workers of Messina were eventually permitted to wear the ornaments which they at first made only for the chief's family: *The BaVenda,* 62.
43 A. Mahieu, "L'exploitation du cuivre par les indigènes au Katanga . . .," *Congo* 6, no. 1 (1925): 123-25.
44 D. Williams, "The Iconology of the Yoruba *Edan Ogboni,*" *Africa* 24 (1964): 139-66.
45 Travassos Valdez, *Six Years,* 1:82, 111.
46 Ibid., 82; Monteiro, *Angola,* I:106.
47 Dupont, *Lettres sur le Congo,* 337-38.
48 M. Capello and R. Ivens, "Les mines de cuivre du Katanga," *Le mouvement géographique* (Brussels) 5, no. 29 (1888): 112; Verbeken and Walraet, *La première traversée,* 53-54 and note.
49 Sundström, *Exchange Economy,* 218. Cf. de Hemptinne, *Mangeurs,* 10. Not surprisingly, Hufrat en-Nahas proves an exception to this principle, at least in the nineteenth century. A. E. Robinson claims that in 1854 these mines were worked under license from the Sultan Huseyn by Shenuda, a Copt of Assiut: "The Arab Dynasty of Dar For (Darfur)," *JAS* 28 (1928): 171.
50 P. A. Möller, *Journey in Africa . . .,* trans. Ione and Jalmar Rudner (Cape Town, 1974), 148; Vedder, *South West Africa,* 140.
51 Verbeken and Walraet, *La première traversée,* 856; J. D. Clark, "Pre-European Copper Working in South Central Africa," *Roan Antelope,* May 1957, 5. Cf. Ladame's rather dubious comment that there may have been no fixed owner-

ship of larger mines, that anyone could work them, and that there was no evidence of warfare to gain control of them: "Le droit," 687-88.

52 Marchal, "Renseignements," *passim.*

53 De Hemptinne, *Mangeurs,* 6-7, 10; Sundström, *Exchange Economy,* 220-21. The situation is somewhat analogous to that in which immigrant agriculturists are dependent on autochthonous earth priests for rituals to insure the fertility of the land; in the same way, autochthonous or at least antecedent priests must be invoked to propitiate the spirits of the mine.

54 Marchal, "Renseignements," 15 ff.

55 De Hemptinne, *Mangeurs,* 14-15; Bancroft, *Mining,* 28; K. Laman, *The Kongo,* 3 vols. (Uppsala, 1953-68), 1:123; "Das deutsche Minengebiet von Tsumeb," *Deutsche Kolonialblatt* 18 (1907): 33-34. Woodcuts in Agricola's *De re metallica* also show women washing and sorting ores.

56 Ladame, "Le droit," 689; Marchal, "Renseignements," 12.

57 Quoted in Bancroft, *Mining,* 28. An English mining engineer claims that at Dikuluwe, metallurgical secrets were kept by the old women of the village, but this is not corroborated by any other sources: cited in Cline, *Mining and Metallurgy,* 119.

58 Narrowness of trenches and shafts:
    *Kansanshi:* trench averages only 45 cm, narrowing at one point to 27 cm (Bisson, "Prehistoric Copper Mining," 244).
    *Rhodesia:* ancient workings often in the form of long, narrow, very deep trenches (Summers, *Ancient Mining,* 19, 35).
    *Messina:* shafts narrow and underground stopes so small as to make it hard to imagine who the miners were (Hanisch, "Copper Working," 251).
    *Phalaborwa:* vertical shafts, some as deep as 70 feet with diameters as small as 20 inches. Child labor, probably girls? (Van der Merwe and Scully, "The Phalaborwa Story," 181; cf. C. M. Schwellnus, "Short Notes on the Phalaborwa Smelting Ovens," *SAJS* 33 [1937]: 906: average width of some stopes only 15 inches.) Compare T. A. Rickard, *Man and Metals,* 2 vols. (New York, 1932), 1:427, concerning the Rio Tinto mines in Spain.

59 J. F. Schofield, "The Ancient Workings of South-east Africa," *NADA* 3 (1925): 6-7. On children in ancient mining, see J. F. Healy, *Mining and Metallurgy in the Greek and Roman World* (London, 1978), 134. On women in European mining, see *La documentation photographique: Métiers, mines et manufactures du XVIe au XVIIIe siècle,* no. 6003 (Paris), which includes a seventeenth-century painting of women working underground.

60 N. J. Van der Merwe, personal communication.

61 J. F. A. Ajayi and M. Crowder, eds., *History of West Africa,* 2 vols. (London, 1971), 1:358-59. But cf. Dumett's refutation of Terray's model of a state-controlled slave labor force in the Akan region: "Precolonial Gold Mining and the State in the Akan Region," *Research in Economic Anthropology* 2 (1979): 37-68.

62 Ibn Battuta, *Travels in Asia and Africa,* trans. and ed. H. A. R. Gibb, 3 vols. (London, 1929), 3:336. Probably the most notorious use of slaves was in the

Athenian-controlled silver mines of Laurion and in the Peruvian mines of the New World.

63 Vedder, *South West Africa,* 260.

64 Gessi Pasha [R. Gessi], *Seven Years in the Soudan* (London, 1892), 259. Robinson claims that earlier in the century the mines at Hufrat were also worked at least partly by slaves: "Arab Dynasty," 168.

65 Marchal, "Renseignements," 14.

66 D. Crawford, *Thinking Black* (London, 1913), 149.

67 De Hemptinne, *Mangeurs,* 9, 16. De Hemptinne, however, seems to overlook the percentage that would have been due the smelters. Ball reports that after smelting, ingots of copper were divided as follows: 20 percent belonged to the smelter, 20 percent to the miners, 20 percent to the tribal chief, and 40 percent to the village chief of the miners, but the region of Katanga referred to is not specified: in Bancroft, *Mining,* 29.

68 De Hemptinne, 10.

69 Van Warmelo, *Copper Miners,* 81, 82. It should be noted that the traditions of the Musina appear to be at odds with those which attribute mining at Messina to the Lemba, tributaries of the local Venda chiefs: see Hanisch, "Copper Working," 250.

70 L. Tauxier, *Le noir du Soudan* (Paris, 1912), 516; Anita Glaze, *Art and Death in a Senufo Village* (Bloomington, Ind., 1981), chap. 1, esp. 34–40. According to Monteil, copper workers formed a group separate from smiths among the Bambara: *Les bambara du Segou et du Kaarta* (Paris, 1924), 220.

71 Dark, *Benin Art,* chap. 4 *passim;* Timothy Garrard, *Akan Weights and the Gold Trade* (London, 1980), chap. 4; A. Mischlich, *Über die Kulturen im Mittel-Sudan* (Berlin, 1942), 70; Nadel, *Black Byzantium,* 269–73.

72 Robert Moffat, *Missionary Labours and Scenes in South Africa,* 3d ed. (New York, 1843), 310.

73 K. G. Lindblom, *Wire Drawing, Especially in Africa* (Stockholm, 1939), 7. Cf. Célis and Nzikobanyaka, *Métallurgie,* 165.

74 E. Mangin, "Les Mossi," *Anthropos* 9 (1914): 718.

75 J. C. Froelich, "Les Konkomba du Nord-Togo," *BIFAN* 11 (1949): 409–19.

76 Nadel, *Black Byzantium,* 272–73.

77 A. E. Afigbo, *Conch* (1970), 213.

78 M. J. Rowlands, "The Archaeological Interpretation of Prehistoric Metalworking," *World Archaeology* 3, no. 2 (Oct. 1971), *passim.* Cf. H. M. Friede, "Socio-Economic Aspects of Metal Production in the Western Transvaal," *Nyame Akuma* 21 (Dec. 1982): 41.

79 Bisson, "Prehistoric Copper Mining," 244–45.

80 Crawford, *Thinking Black,* 117.

81 Henry Junod, "The Balemba of the Zoutpansberg (Transvaal)," *Folk-Lore* 19 (1908): 279–80.

82 V. Lebzelter, *Rassen und Kulturen in Südafrika,* 2 vols. (Leipzig, 1930–34), 2: 203–4.

83 F. I. Ekejiuba, "Preliminary Notes on Brasswork of Eastern Nigeria," *African*

*Notes* (Ibadan) 4, no. 2 (Jan. 1967): 13-14; David Northrup, "The Growth of Trade among the Igbo before 1800," *JAH* 13, no. 2 (1972): 227-28; Nancy Neaher, "Awka Who Travel: Itinerant Metalsmiths of Southern Nigeria," *Africa* 49, no. 4 (1979): 352-66.

84 Glaze, *Art and Death,* 37.


## CHAPTER 3

1 Wagner and Gordon argue that Blaubank (Transvaal) smiths failed to recognize the azurite deposits close at hand and imported malachite ores to mix with locally produced tin to make bronze: "Further Notes on Ancient Bronze Smelters in the Waterberg District, Transvaal," *SAJS* 26 (1929): 563-74.

2 Belluci claims the Azande smelted chrysocolla, but this is highly dubious: see Cline, *Mining and Metallurgy,* 72.

3 Bernus and Gouletquer, "Du cuivre au sel," 20.

4 Ibid., 17.

5 Capello and Ivens, "Les mines de cuivre," 112.

6 Jules Cornet, "Mines de cuivre du Katanga," *Le mouvement géographique* 12, no. 1 (June 1895): 4.

7 C. Coquery-Vidrovitch, *Brazza et la prise de possession du Congo* (Paris, 1969), 155, 406; cf. O. Baumann, "Beiträge zur Ethnographie des Congo," *Mittheilungen der Anthropologischen Gesellschaft in Wien* 17 (1887): 164.

8 De Hemptinne, *Mangeurs de cuivre,* 12-26.

9 Ibid., 31-32.

10 Ladame, "Le droit," 689-90. Cf. Ball in Bancroft, *Mining,* 29.

11 Schmidt and Avery encountered similar conflicts over procedure in reenacting iron smelting in Buhaya, west of Lake Victoria: personal communication.

12 J. H. Chaplin, "Notes on Traditional Smelting in Northern Rhodesia," *SAAB* 16, no. 62 (June 1961): 56-57; J. D. Clark, "Pre-European Copper-Working," 16. Cf. F. L. Coleman, "Some Notes on the Native Development of Copper-Ore Deposits in Central Africa," *South African Journal of Economics* 27, no. 3 (1969): 262-63.

13 De Hemptinne, *Mangeurs,* 12.

14 F. S. Arnot, *Garenganze or, Seven Years' Pioneer Mission Work in Central Africa* (1889; London, 1969), 238-39.

15 Carnahan, quoted in Bancroft, *Mining,* 28.

16 Eugène Rasson, personal communication.

17 Bisson, "Prehistoric Copper-Mining," 243-44; the following description of the Kansanshi Hill site is based on the same article, *passim.*

18 Bancroft, *Mining,* 37-38.

19 Ibid., 39.

20 Summers, *Ancient Mining,* 163-65.

21 Chandler, quoted in Summers, 28-30, but cf. 48.

22 Donald Avery, personal communication.

23 Van der Merwe and Scully, "Phalaborwa," *passim,* quotation 182.

24 C. M. Schwellnus, "Short Notes on the Phalaborwa Smelting Ovens," *SAJS* 33 (1937): 908–9; Van der Merwe and Scully, 192, 197.

25 Evers and Van den Berg, "Ancient Mining," *passim.*

26 Hanisch, "Copper-Working," 251.

27 Stayt, *The BaVenda,* 64–65.

28 Steel, "Iron Age Copper Mine," 244.

29 Mason, *Prehistory,* 388, 406; idem., "Background," n.p.

30 A. J. H. Goodwin, "Metal Working," 48–49. Possibly the cow dung was simply a dressing applied to the furnace to give it a smooth finish, while the small size could indicate a refining rather than a smelting furnace: M. Johnson, personal communication.

31 Bürg, *Die nutzbaren Minerallagerstätten,* 67–68, 102, 120–21.

32 Monteiro, *Angola,* 1: 106.

33 Capt. Pleigneur, "Extrait des notes du Capitaine Pleigneur sur la reconnaissance des mines de Mboko-Songho," *Revue ethnographique* 7 (1888): 276–80.

34 Dupont, *Lettres sur le Congo,* 337, 340.

35 Cholet, in E. Maquet, *Outils de forge du Congo, du Rwanda et du Burundi* (Tervuren, 1965), 33.

36 Laman, *The Kongo,* 1: 122.

37 Tylecote, *History of Metallurgy,* 128.

38 John Harris, *The Copper King: A Biography of Thomas Williams of Llanlidan* (Liverpool, 1964), 170–71. In Japan, 0.1–0.2% lead was traditionally added to copper after it was refined, to give it a brilliant color: Tylecote, 95.

39 Pleigneur, "Extrait des notes," 280.

40 Barrat, *Géologie du Congo français,* 82.

41 M. S. Afia and A. L. Widatalla, *An Investigation of Hofrat en Nahas Copper Deposit, Southern Darfur,* 2 vols., Sudan Geological Survey Bulletin no. 10 (1961), 1: 50.

42 Ibid., 4.

43 Christy, "Bahr el-Ghazal," 321–22.

44 Bower, "Native Smelting," 38–39, 146.

45 W. G. Browne, *Travels in Africa, Egypt and Syria* (London, 1799), 267.

46 Quoted in Afia and Widatalla, *Investigation,* 2.

47 Christy, "Bahr el-Ghazal," 321. Charles Cuny, "Notice sur le Dar-Four et sur les caravanes qui se rendent de ce pays en Egypte, et vice-versa," *Bulletin de la Société géographique de Paris,* 4th ser., 8 (1854): 94, puts the gold content at 10 percent, probably an exaggeration: see Afia and Widatalla, 123.

48 N. Lambert, "Exploitation minière et métallurgique protohistoriques du cuivre au Sahara occidentale" (Paper presented to the African Studies Associations of the United States and Canada, Montreal, 1969), *passim.*

49 Bernus and Gouletquer, "Du cuivre au sel," 17–21.

50 Ibid., 21.

51 Bucaille, "Takadda," 760.

52 Van der Merwe and Scully, "Phalaborwa," 181.

53 Van der Merwe, personal communication.

54 Summers, *Ancient Mining,* 174.
55 Rickard, *Man and Metals,* 1: 120.
56 Cline, *Mining and Metallurgy,* 71; Tylecote, *History of Metallurgy,* 70; and Tylecote, Ghaznavi, and Boydell, "Partitioning of Trace Elements between the Ores, Fluxes, Slags and Metal during the Smelting of Copper," *Journal of Archaeological Science,* 4 (1977): 312.
57 Cline, 72.
58 G. H. Stanley, "Primitive Metallurgy in South Africa," *SAJS* 26 (1929): 738; Trevor, "Relics," 395.
59 F. E. B. Fripp, "An Engineer's Notes on the Mine-Workings of Transvaal and Rhodesia," *Proceedings of the Rhodesian Scientific Association* 11, no. 3 (1912): 178.
60 Bower, "Native Smelting," 146.
61 Donald Avery, personal communication; N. Van der Merwe, in Th. Wertime and J. Muhly, *The Coming of the Age of Iron* (New Haven, 1980), 483.
62 Bernus and Gouletquer, "Du cuivre au sel," 16–17.
63 Barrat, *Géologie du Congo français,* 83.
64 Mauny, *Tableau,* 308.
65 Trevor, "Relics," 395–96; cf. idem, "Ancient Mine Workings," *passim;* Leo Fouché, ed., *Mapungubwe* (London, 1937), 117.
66 J. Chambers, reply to Woodburn, *JCMMSSA* 14 (1913): 192 ff.
67 L. C. Thompson, "Ingots of Native Manufacture," *NADA* 26 (1949):7–19. Cf. Schwellnus, cited in Summers, *Ancient Mining,* 102. Baumann's reference to the working of "Schwefelkupfererzen" north of Manyanga in the Middle Congo is so vague that we cannot deal with it seriously, especially given his own admission that the people in question (identified as Bakongo) maintained the utmost secrecy about their metalworking: "Beiträge," 164.
68 Van der Merwe and Scully, "Phalaborwa," 179–81.
69 Quoted in Stayt, *BaVenda,* 63.
70 P. G. Söhnge, *The Geology of the Messina Copper Mines and Surrounding Country,* Geological Survey of South Africa, memoir no. 40 (1945): 14–51, 176, 182, 184–85. Cf. C. B. Coetzee, ed., *Mineral Resources of the Republic of South Africa,* 5th ed. (Pretoria, 1976): 126, 145.
71 Van der Merwe, personal communication.
72 H. Friede, personal communication.
73 Bradley, *Copper Venture,* 71.
74 De Hemptinne, *Mangeurs,* 24.
75 C. W. Domville Fife, *Savage Life in the Black Sudan* (London, 1927), 182.
76 Evers and Van den Berg, "Ancient Mining," 224.
77 Clark, "Pre-European Copper-Working," 16.
78 Lambert, "Les industries sur cuivre," 9.
79 H. Friede, "Notes on the Composition of Pre-European Copper and Copper-Alloy Artefacts from the Transvaal," *JSAIMM* 75 (1975): 187. Cf. Stanley, "Composition of Prehistoric Bronzes," *SAJS* 26 (1929): 48.
80 Olfert Dapper, *Naukeurige Beschrijvinghe der Afrikaensche Gewesten* (Amsterdam, 1668), 328; J. Barbot," "A Description of the Coasts of North and South

Guinea," in *A Collection of Voyages and Travels,* ed. Awnsham Churchill, 6 vols. (London, 1732), 5: 473.
81 Lambert, "Les industries sur cuivre," 2.
82 In Bancroft, *Mining,* 27.
83 Mauny, *Tableau,* 308.
84 Calderwood, cited in Stayt, *BaVenda,* 64; Trevor, "Ancient Mine Workings," 270; idem, "Ancient Tin Mines of the Transvaal," *JCMMSSA* 19 (1919): 282–88. Cf. Clark in Bradley, *Copper Venture,* 28.
85 Clark, "Pre-European Copper-Working," 16.
86 Marchal, "Renseignements," 15.
87 Pleigneur, "Extrait des Notes," 277.
88 Cline, *Mining and Metallurgy,* 61, 70.
89 R. J. Forbes, *Metallurgy in Antiquity* (London, 1950), 325.
90 J. F. Healy, *Mining and Metallurgy in the Greek and Roman World* (London, 1978), 195.
91 Alan Bateman, *Economic Mineral Deposits,* 2d ed. (New York, 1950), 481.
92 Beno Rothenberg, *Timna: Valley of the Biblical Copper Mines* (London, 1972), esp. chap. 9 *passim.*

## CHAPTER 4

1 Célis and Nzikobanyanka, *Métallurgie traditionnelle,* 175. Cf. H. A. Bernatzik, *Gari-Gari: The Call of the African Wilderness,* trans. V. Ogilvie (New York, 1936), 93–94. It seems curious, as Célis and Nzikobanyanka observe, that the Burundi smith does not cast the bracelet directly in an open mould rather than casting the ingot, then working the ingot into a bracelet.
2 Jan Vansina, *The Tio Kingdom of the Middle Congo 1880–1892* (New York, 1973), 142–43; and idem, *The Children of Woot* (Madison, Wis., 1978), 183.
3 Frobenius, *Voice of Africa,* 1: 642–43, 2: illus., esp. pls. I–III.
4 Göbel, "Gelbschmiedarbeiten der Nupe im Museum für Völkerkunde zu Leipzig," *Jahrbuch des Museums für Völkerkunde Leipzig* 27 (1970): 315 ff.
5 A. R. A. el-Bashir, personal communication.
6 Doran Ross, "Ghanaian Forowa," *African Arts* 8, no. 1 (Autumn 1974): 40–49; Garrard, *Akan Weights,* 186.
7 Garrard, 320.
8 E. Maquet, *Outils de forge du Congo, du Rwanda et du Burundi* (Tervuren, 1965), 94; Laman, *The Kongo,* 1:123. Cf. Dapper, *Naukeurige Beschrijvinghe,* 151.
9 Humphrey Fisher in *Cambridge History of Africa* (Cambridge, 1977), 3: 278. Cf. Frederick Horneman, *The Journal of F. Horneman's Travels from Cairo to Mourzouk . . . in Africa* (London, 1802), 10.
10 G. Bloomhill, "The Ancient Copper Miners of Africa: Lemba Tribe's Secret 'Mutsuku' Rites," *African World,* 1963, 6. Cf. Ladislaus Magyar, "Ladislaus Magyar's Erforschungen von Inner-Afrika," *Petermanns Geographische Mitteilungen* 6 (1860): 231.
11 Livingstone, *Last Journals,* 2: 331.

12 Krantz, quoted in Lindblom, *Wire Drawing,* 20.
13 Capello and Ivens, "Les mines de cuivre," 112.
14 Clark, "Pre-European Copper Working," 5. Froelich noted the same keen appreciation of telegraph wires among the Konkomba of northern Togo until the Administration was able to make them aware of the "inconvenients" of this usage: "Les Konkomba du Nord Togo," *BIFAN* 11 (1949): 419.
15 R. H. Steel, "Ingot Casting and Wire Drawing in Iron Age Southern Africa," *JSAIMM* 75 (1975): 244.
16 Lindblom, *Wire Drawing,* 24-25; Cline, *Mining and Metallurgy,* 111; De Hemptinne, *Mangeurs,* 28; Stayt, *BaVenda,* 65; Moffat, *Missionary Labours;* Livingstone, *Last Journals,* 2: 331.
17 Lindblom, *passim;* Cline, 110 ff.; Célis and Nzikobanyanka, *Métallurgie,* 182.
18 J. Hiernaux, E. de Longrée, and J. DeBuyst, *Fouilles archéologiques dans la vallée du Haut-Lualaba* (Tervuren, 1971), 1, *passim;* P. de Maret, "Sanga: New Excavations, More Data, and Some Related Problems," *JAH* 18, no. 3 (1977): 321-38.
19 Cline, *Mining and Metallurgy,* 112; H. Lichtenstein, *Travels in Southern Africa . . .,* 2 vols. (Cape Town, 1928), 2:412-13.
20 J. O. Vogel, *Kamangoza: An Introduction to the Iron Age Cultures of the Victoria Falls Region* (Nairobi and New York, 1971); idem, *Kumadzulo: An Early Iron Age Site in Southern Zambia* (New York and London, 1971), *passim;* Brian Fagan et al., *Iron Age Cultures in Zambia,* 2 vols. (London, 1967), 1: 91, 123-24, and 2: 43-44; K.R. Robinson, *The Iron Age of the Upper and Lower Shire, Malawi,* Department of Antiquities Publication No. 13 (Zomba, Malawi, 1973), 109-10; T. M. O'C. Maggs, *Iron Age Communities of the Southern Highveld* (Pietermaritzburg, 1976), 121, 123.
21 J. Nenquin, *Excavations at Sanga,* 1957 (Tervuren, 1963), 191-95 and illustrations; Hiernaux et al, *Fouilles,* 38-39, 54; de Maret, "Sanga," *passim.*
22 Fagan et al., *Iron Age Cultures,* 2: 102-5.
23 See, for example, G. Caton-Thompson, *The Zimbabwe Culture* (1931; London, 1971), 208, 231, fig. 26, pl. XLI; P. Garlake, *Great Zimbabwe* (London, 1973), 115; K. R. Robinson, *Khami Ruins* (Cambridge, 1959), 146; Fouché, *Mapungubwe,* 18-19, pl. XXXVIII; R. Summers, *Inyanga* (Cambridge, 1958), 127.
24 Caton-Thompson, 64.
25 De Hemptinne, *Mangeurs,* 29.
26 Burchell, *Travels,* 2: 568.
27 Stayt, *BaVenda,* 58. Cf. K. Hechter-Schulz, "Wire Bangles, a Record of a Bantu Craft," *SAJS* 59:2 (1963): 51-53; B. Fagan, "Wire-Drawing," *SAJS* 59, no. 11 (1963): 525-26.
28 Thurstan Shaw, *Igbo-Ukwu: An Account of Archaeological Discoveries in Eastern Nigeria,* 2 vols. (London, 1970), 1: 98, 158 ff., 204, 232, pl. 311. Some two hundred copper wires were collected at Azelick from the surface of the ground. They appear to be angular in section and therefore were probably not drawn: Bucaille, "Takadda," 750.
29 Dapper, *Naukeurige Beschrijvinghe,* 510; cf. Barbot, "Description," 382.

30 P. A. Talbot, *The Peoples of Southern Nigeria*, 3 vols. (London, 1926), 3: 924, 927.

31 T. J. Hutchinson, *Narrative of the Niger, Tschadda Binue Exploration* (London, 1855), 246, 172.

32 Lindblom, *Wire Drawing*, 6.

33 W. H. Bentley, *Pioneering on the Congo*, 2 vols. (London, 1900), 1: 464.

34 Louis de Mas Latrie, *Relations et commerce de l'Afrique septentrionale ou Maghreb avec les nations chrétiennes du moyen âge* (Paris, 1886), 328. The fragmentary finds of copper wire at Nyarko (Begho) and dated to the twelfth to fifteenth centuries A.D. would likewise imply a northern source: T. Garrard, "Brass in Akan Society to the Nineteenth Century" (Master's thesis, University of Ghana, 1980), 120–23.

35 Tylecote, *History of Metallurgy*, glossary.

36 John Harris, personal communication.

37 De Hemptinne, *Mangeurs,* 25–26.

38 Ibid., 26.

39 H. Deleval, "Les tribus kavati du Mayombe," *La revue congolais* 3 (1912): 261. I am grateful to John Janzen for supplying this reference.

40 Cline, *Mining and Metallurgy*, 84; Torday, *On the Trail*, 212; Mason, *Prehistory*, 421.

41 James Walton, "Some Features of the Monomatapa Culture," in *Third Pan-African Congress on Prehistory*, ed. J. D. Clark and Sonia Cole (London, 1957), 338.

42 Caton-Thompson, *Zimbabwe Culture,* pl. LIII, pp. 1, 2.

43 Cline, *Mining and Metallurgy*, 84.

44 Charles T. Wilson and Robert Felkin, *Uganda and the Egyptian Soudan,* 2 vols. (London, 1882), 1: 180, 216.

45 H. M. Stanley, *Through the Dark Continent,* 2 vols. (New York, 1878), 1: 473–74. Cf. J. H. Speke, *Journal of the Discovery of the Source of the Nile* (London, 1863), 206.

46 Cline, *Mining and Metallurgy*, 85 ff.

47 Dark, *Benin Art,* 50; Merrick Posnansky, "Brass Casting and Its Antecedents in West Africa," *JAH* 18, no. 2 (1977): 289; Cline, 86–87.

48 Malcolm, "Note on Brass-casting, 2. Cf. Max Fröhlich, *Gelbgiesser in Kameruner Grasland* (Zurich, 1979), *passim.*

49 Neher, "Brasscasting," 23.

50 Cline, *Mining and Metallurgy*, 85.

51 Frank Willett, review of Shaw, *Igbo-Ukwu, JAH* 12 (1972): 515; Posnansky, "Brass Casting, *passim;* Cline, 85–86. Willett argues that the combined crucible-mould technique must have been used to cast the Ife heads of pure copper. Much of the air would have been driven out through the porous clay of the investment, producing a partial vacuum to draw the metal quickly into the mould when the whole was inverted. The seated figure from Tada, also in copper, was too large for this method and had to be cast instead from metal heated in separate crucibles, resulting in a number of flaws which were subsequently repaired: "Africa's Bronzes: The Art of a Lost Technology,"

*Newscientist* 98, no. 1353 (April 1983), 65–68. I am grateful to Prof. Willett for sending me a photocopy of this article.

52 Williams, *Icon and Image,* chap. 18 *passim.*

53 Thurstan Shaw, "An Analysis of West African Bronzes," *Ibadan* 28 (1970): 88.

54 Williams, *Icon and Image,* 183–85.

55 Posnansky, "Brass Casting," 297–98.

56 F. Willett, *Ife in the History of West African Sculpture* (London, 1967), 176.

57 Cf. Nancy C. Neaher, "Igbo Metalsmithing Traditions of Southern Nigeria" (Ph.D. diss., Stanford, 1976), 49, 160 ff.

58 Posnansky, "Brass Casting," 297–98.

59 E. Maquet, *Outils de forge, passim;* Cline, *Mining and Metallurgy,* 87.

60 Laman, *The Kongo,* 1: 76, 124.

61 John Janzen, personal communication. This type of mould, from Boma, is illustrated in the catalogue of the Leiden Museum, ed. Marquart, Schmetz, et al., no. 11, pl. 68.

62 Wannyn, *L'art ancien,* 31 ff. Bentley in 1879 was visited by two Kongo chiefs, each with a brass-covered stick, "one being surmounted by a square brass cross, and above each a bird in brass": *Pioneering,* I:120. Cf. 123: King Pedro holding a crucifix and sceptre.

63 Bisson, "Copper Currency," 283.

64 Vogel, *Kamangoza,* 99. Cast rings can be distinguished from smithed rings because there is no join.

65 De Maret, "Sanga," 321–38.

66 Robinson, *Khami Ruins,* 153.

67 Cline, *Mining and Metallurgy,* 85–87; Willett, *Ife,* 176; Denise Paulme, *Les sculptures de l'Afrique noire* (Paris, 1956), 39 ff; L. G. Binger, *Du Niger au golfe de Guinée par le pays de Kong et le Mossi . . . 1887–1889,* 2 vols. (Paris, 1892), 1: 191–92; A. Teixeira da Mota, "Descoberta de bronzes antigos na Guiné portuguêsa," *Boletim cultural da Guiné portuguêsa* 15, no. 59 (1960): 625–34; René Bravmann, *Open Frontiers: The Mobility of Art in Black Africa.* Exhibition Catalogue, University of Washington (Seattle, 1973), 32.

68 T. Shaw, *Nigeria: Its Archaeology and Early History* (London, 1978), chap. 7.

69 J.-P. and A. M. Lebeuf, *Les arts des Sao* (Paris, 1977), *passim.*

70 Neaher, "Igbo Metalsmithing," 126.

71 Posnansky, "Brass Casting," 294, 298; Mauny in Shinnie, *African Iron Age,* 79–80; idem, in *Cambridge History of Africa* (Cambridge, 1978), 2: 321.

72 Lebeuf and Lebeuf, *Les arts,* 88; but see Mauny, *Cambridge History,* 2: 328.

73 Posnansky, "Brass Casting," 297.

74 Shaw, *Igbo-Ukwu,* 1: 272.

75 Cf. ibid.; and J. Bertho and R. Mauny, "Archéologie du pays yoruba et du Bas-Niger," *NA,* no. 51 (1952): 113; as well as A. J. Arkell, "Gold Coast Copies of V–VIIth Century Bronze Lamps," *Antiquity* 3 (1950): 38–40.

76 F. Willett and S. Fleming, "A Catalogue of Important Nigerian Copper-Alloy Castings Dated by Thermoluminescence," *Archaeometry* 18 (1976): 135–46.

77 Quoted in Shaw, *Nigeria,* 119.

78 T. Shaw, "A Note on Trade and the Tsoede Bronzes," *WAJA* 3 (1973): 235; cf. Posnansky, "Brass Casting," 296, 299.

79 Williams, *Icon and Image,* chaps. 17–18 *passim.* Werner also proposes a later dating for the heads, on the basis of zinc content; this will be discussed in the next section.

80 Posnansky, "Brass Casting," 297.

81 Willett and Fleming, "Catalogue," 139–40.

82 Posnansky, "Brass Casting," 298–99.

83 Ibid., 298.

84 Arnold Rubin, review of Willett's *Ife in the History of West African Sculpture, Art Bulletin* 52 (1970): 352–53.

85 Idem, "Bronzes of the Middle Benue," 221–31.

86 Neaher, "Igbo Metalsmithing," 119, 123.

87 Vid. Shaw, *Nigeria,* 163 ff., 179, 184 ff.

88 Neaher, 126–31.

89 Cf. H. Coghlan, *Notes on the Prehistoric Metallurgy of Copper and Bronze in the Old World,* Occasional Papers on Technology no. 4 (Oxford, 1975), 65–67. But see also n. 51 above.

90 O. Werner, "Metallurgische Untersuchungen der Benin-Bronzen des Museums für Völkerkunde Berlin," *Baessler-Archiv,* n.s. 18 (1970): 71–153; S. Wolf, "Neue Analysen von Benin-Legierungen in vergleichender Betrachtung," *Abhandlungen und Berichte des staatlichen Museums für Völkerkunde Dresden* 28 (1968): 91–153; O. Werner and F. Willett, "Spectographic Analysis of Nigerian Bronzes," *Archaeometry* 7 (1964): 81–83.

91 Shaw, *Igbo-Ukwu,* 1: app. 1.

92 Idem, "A Note on Trade," 273.

93 Robert F. Thompson, *Black Gods and Kings* (Los Angeles, 1971), appendix.

94 Shaw, *Igbo-Ukwu,* 1: 277.

95 Lebeuf and Lebeuf, *Les arts,* 76–77, apps. 1, 2.

96 Posnansky, personal communication.

97 Shaw, *Igbo-Ukwu,* 1: 278.

98 Ibid.

99 Lebeuf and Lebeuf, *Les arts,* 76–77.

100 B. Fagg, personal communication.

101 Shaw, *Igbo-Ukwu,* 1: app. 1; M. S. Afia and A. L. Widatalla, *An Investigation of Hofrat en-Nahas Copper Deposit,* 1: 123.

102 Stayt, *BaVenda,* 64; Bloomhill, "Ancient Copper Miners," 6.

103 Hutchinson, *Narrative,* 131, 146; Samuel Ajayi Crowther, *Journal of an Expedition up the Niger and Tshadda Rivers . . .* (London, 1855), 141–42.

104 Albert Maesen, personal communication.

105 Wannyn, *L'art ancien,* 31.

106 Caton-Thompson, *Zimbabwe Culture,* 211; H. M. Friede, "Notes on the Composition of Pre-European Copper and Copper-Alloy Artefacts from the Transvaal," *JSAIMM* 75, no. 5 (1975): 190.

107 Caton-Thompson, 64–65 and inventory, *passim;* Garlake, *Great Zimbabwe,*

115. Cf. Antonio Gomes' account of the kingdom of Monomatapa (1648): "There is a great quantity of copper. . . . they make an alloy of this copper with a metal like tin, but somewhat different which, if it were reckoned in carats would be better than tin, and which in India is called *calam* (motane) by the Kaffirs of Goa." Quoted in Fagan et al., *Iron Age Cultures*, 105. This metal has not yet been identified, but tin was shipped from Cambay to Sofala as early as 1519: Caton-Thompson, 64.

108 A fifteenth-sixteenth century date for tin mining has recently been published in Maggs, "Some Recent Radiocarbon Dates," 182.

109 P. A. Wagner, "Bronze from an Ancient Smelter in the Waterberg District," *SAJS* 22 (1926): 899–900; Wagner and Gordon, "Further Notes," 563–74.

110 "Notes on the Composition," Friede, 818–90; Stanley, "Primitive Metallurgy," 740.

111 Theal, cited in F. R. Paver, "Trade and Mining in the pre-European Transvaal," *SAJS* 30 (1933): 606–7.

112 Moffat, *Missionary Labours*, 310.

113 Friede, "Notes on the Composition," 188.

114 W. C. Aitken, "Brass and Brass Manufactures," in *Birmingham and the Midland Hardware District 1865,* ed. Samuel Timmins (London, 1866), 225 *et seq.* Some lead and zinc accompany copper mineralization in northwest Angola, in Central Africa, and at Cavallo, near Bône in Algeria, but there is no evidence that these ores were ever smelted directly for brasses: De Kun, *Mineral Resources,* 387, 390, 397; Lucien Cahen, *Géologie du Congo belge* (Liège, 1954), 494.

115 Tylecote, *Mining and Metallurgy,* pp. 58–59, 71–72; cf. Werner and Willett, "Spectographic Analysis," 145–47.

116 Theodore Monod, "Le Ma'den Ijâfen: Une épave caravanière ancienne dans la Majâbat al-Koubrâ," *Actes du Premier colloque international d'archéologie africaine* (Fort Lamy, 1969), 304.

117 R. Castro, "Examen métallographique d'un fragment de baquette de laiton coulé provenant d'une épave cravanière, 'Ma'den Ijâfen'," *BIFAN* 36, no. 3 (1974): 497, 510.

118 Graham Connah, *The Archaeology of Benin* (Oxford, 1975), 231–33.

119 Werner, "Metallurgische Untersuchungen," *passim;* and idem, "Benin-Messinge," *Baessler-Archiv,* n.s. 26, no. 2 (1978): 333–439.

120 Great Britain, Parliamentary Papers, *Report from the Select Committee on the State of the Copper Trade. . . .* Commons Committee Reports X (1799).

121 Aitken, "Brass," 225 *et seq.*

122 O. O. Amogu, "The Introduction into and the Withdrawal of Manillas from the 'Oil Rivers' as seen in the Ndoki District," *Nigeria Magazine* 38 (1952): 134–39.

123 Cline, *Mining and Metallurgy,* 80.

124 Sven-Olof Johansson, *Nigerian Currencies,* trans. J. Learmonth (Norrköping, Sweden, 1967), 21; M. E. Elechi, personal communication.

125 W. C. Aitken, *The Early History of Brass and the Brass Manufactures of Birmingham* (Birmingham, 1866), 49.

126 "Bamenda Brass," *Nigeria* (1957): 348.
127 R. Burton, *The Lake Regions of Central Africa,* 2 vols. (1860; New York, 1961), 2: 65–395. In the appendix to his *Through Masai Land,* Joseph Thomson gives the analysis of ear ornaments collected near Kilimanjaro, which proved to be brasses of approximately 81 percent copper, 17 percent zinc. Thomson was told by the natives that the metal was picked up in dry stream beds after the rains and hammered into ornaments, and adds that this was corroborated by coastal traders who bought these ornaments from the Chagga to barter with the people beyond, but this information must rest on misunderstanding or deliberate obfuscation: 577–80.
128 Paver, "Trade and Mining," 610; Friede, "Notes on the Composition," 190. Cf. Tylecote, *Mining and Metallurgy,* 102.
129 Candice Goucher, Jehanne Teilhet, Kent Wilson, and Tsaihwa Chow, "Lead Isotope Studies of Metal Sources for Ancient Nigerian 'Bronzes,'" *Nature* 162, no. 5564 (1976): 130–31.

## CHAPTER 5

1 Garlake, "Iron Age Sites," 42.
2 Vogel, *Kamangoza,* 36.
3 On copper in Iron Age Zambia see Bisson, "Copper Currency," 276–92; Vogel, *Kamangoza,* 52–55, 99, 105; *Kumadzulo,* 36; B. Fagan et al., *Iron Age Cultures in Zambia,* 2 vols. (London, 1967), *passim;* E. A. C. Mills and N. T. Filmer, "Chondwe Iron Age Site, Ndola, Zambia," *Azania* 7 (1972): 135–36; Phillipson, *Later Prehistory,* 148ff.
4 Vogel, *Kumadzulo,* 36.
5 Bisson, "Copper Currency," 281.
6 On Ingombe Ilede, see Fagan et al., *Iron Age Cultures,* 2, esp. chap. 5, p. 8; D. W. Phillipson and B. M. Fagan, "The Date of the Ingombe Ilede Burials," *JAH* 10, no. 2 (1969): 199–204; Garlake, "Urungwe," 25–44; Bisson, 284–86, and David Birmingham in *Cambridge History of Africa* (Cambridge, 1977), 3: 528–30.
7 Bisson, 285.
8 K. Robinson, "An Early Iron Age Site from the Chibi District," *SAAB* 16, no. 63 (1961): 75–102; idem, *Khami Ruins;* and "Further Excavations in the Iron Age Deposits at the Tunnel Site, Gokomere Hill, Southern Rhodesia," *SAAB* 18, no. 72 (1963): 155–71; Caton-Thompson, *Zimbabwe Culture;* Garlake, *Great Zimbabwe;* idem, "Chitope: An Early Iron Age Village in Northern Mashonaland," *Arnoldia* 4, no. 19 (1969): 1–14; "Iron Age Burials at Mount Hampden, Near Salisbury, Rhodesia," *Arnoldia* 3, no. 10 (1967): 1–11; and "An Early Iron Age Site near Tafuna Hill, Mashonaland," *SAAB* 26, nos. 103, 104 (1971): 155–63; Summers, *Ancient Mining,* 215; P. A. Robins and Anthony Whittey, "Excavations at Harleigh Farm, near Rusape, Rhodesia, 1958–1962," *SAAB* 21, no. 82 (1966): 51–60; J. R. Crawford, "Report on Excavations at Harleigh Farm, near Rusape (National Monument No. 72) 1961–1962," *Arnoldia* 3, no. 6 (1967): 5; D. F. Monro and C. W. Spies, "Excavations at

Musimbira, Bikita District, Rhodesia," *Arnoldia* 7, no. 22 (1975): 6–10; Phillipson, *Later Prehistory, passim.*

9   R. Summers, *Inyanga, passim,* esp. 126–29.

10   Phillipson, *Later Prehistory,* 149.

11   Robinson, *Khami,* 6–8, 121.

12   Caton-Thompson, *Zimbabwe Culture,* 21.

13   R. J. Forbes, *Studies in Ancient Technology,* no. 9 (Leiden, 1964), 327; Clément Huart, ed., "Documents persans sur l'Afrique," in *Receuil de mémoires orientaux* (Paris, 1905), 94–95n.

14   Martin Fernandez de Figueroa, in *Documents on the Portuguese in Mozambique and Central Africa,* Centro de estudos históricos ultramarinos (Lisbon, 1964), 3: 599.

15   R. W. Dickinson, "The Archaeology of the Sofala coast," *SAAB* 30 (1975): 84–104.

16   Summers, *Ancient Mining,* 192, 194.

17   Ibid., 194.

18   Garlake, *Great Zimbabwe,* 110.

19   Caton-Thompson, *Zimbabwe Culture,* 198; cf. Robinson, *Khami,* 8; Garlake, 10.

20   Caton-Thompson, 190–91.

21   Summers, *Ancient Mining,* 87.

22   Ibid.

23   Garlake, "Urungwe," 42–43.

24   *Documents on the Portuguese in Mozambique and Central Africa* (Lisbon, 1962), 3: 185.

25   *Documents,* 4: 289, 293.

26   Garlake, "Urungwe," 42.

27   See, for example, F. E. B. Fripp, "An Engineer's Notes on the Mine-workings of Transvaal and Rhodesia," *Proceedings and Transactions of the Rhodesia Scientific Association* 11, no. 3 (1912): 178.

28   T. M. Evers, "Iron Age Trade in the Eastern Transvaal, South Africa," *SAAB* 29, nos. 113, 114 (1974): 35.

29   See, for example, R. Mason, *Prehistory,* 375–77, 415, 421; Maggs, *Southern Highveld, passim;* Elizabeth Voigt, "Preliminary Report on Welgegund: An Iron Age Burial Site," *SAAB* 27, nos. 107, 108 (1973): 163; Jalmar Rudner, "Radiocarbon Dates from the Brandberg in Southwest Africa" *SAAB* 27, nos. 107, 108 (1973): 164; S. F. LeRoux, "Some Iron Age Cultural Remains from the Southern Transvaal," *SAAB* 21, no. 82 (1966): 88–91; Shula Marks and Richard Gray in *Cambridge History of Africa* (Cambridge, 1975), 4: 409; R. Inskeep and T. Maggs, "Unique Art Objects in the Iron Age of the Transvaal, South Africa," *SAAB* 30, nos. 119, 120 (1975): 135; Evers, "Recent Iron Age Research," 71–83; and idem, "Iron Age Trade," 33.

30   Maggs, *Southern Highveld,* 321.

31   *Documents,* 1: 13.

32   David Birmingham and Shula Marks in *Cambridge History of Africa* (Cambridge, 1977), 3: 605.

33 In E. Axelson, ed., *South African Explorers* (London, 1954), 4.

34 On Mapungubwe, see Fouché, *Mapungubwe;* and G. A. Gardner, ed., *Mapungubwe* (Pretoria, 1963); B. Fagan, "The Greefswald Sequence: Bambandyanalo and Mapungubwe," *JAH* 5, no. 3 (1964): 337–61; and Hall and Vogel, "Radiocarbon Dates," 451–52.

35 Fouché, 1–4.

36 Summers, *Ancient Mining*, 111, 152–55.

37 On Sanga, see J. Nenquin, *Excavations at Sanga, 1957* (Tervuren, 1963); J. Hiernaux, E. de Longrée, and J. DeBuyst, *Fouilles archéologiques dans la vallée du Haut-Lualaba* (Tervuren, 1971); P. de Maret, "Sanga," 321–38; Bisson, "Copper Currency," 286–88.

38 Pierre de Maret, "Sanga," 335; idem, "Luba Roots: The First Complete Iron Age Sequence in Zaire," *Current Anthropology* 20, no. 1 (1979): 233–35; and "L'évolution monétaire du Shaba central entre le 7e et le 18e siècle," *African Economic History* 10 (1981): 117–49.

39 See, for example, David Livingstone to Lord Clarendon, Dec. 10, 1867, in *Last Journals,* 1: 265–66; V. L. Cameron, *Across Africa,* 2 vols. (London, 1877), 2: 329; Alfred Sharpe, "Alfred Sharpe's Travels in the Northern Province and Katanga," *Northern Rhodesia Journal* 3 (1957): 216; as well as geological surveys of Katanga.

40 K. R. Robinson, *The Iron Age of the Upper and Lower Shire, Malawi* (Zomba, Malawi, 1973), 109–11; idem, *The Early Iron Age in Malawi* (Zomba, Malawi, 1969), *passim.*

41 Knut Odner, "Usangi Hospital and Other Archaeological Sites in the Northern Pare Mountains, Northeastern Tanzania," *Azania* 6 (1971): 89–130; B. Fagan and J. E. Yellen, "Ivuna: Ancient Salt-Working in Southern Tanzania," *Anzania* 3 (1968): 1–43.

42 See, for example, E. C. Lanning, "Excavations at Mubende Hill," *UJ* 30, no. 2 (1966): 153–63; J. Hiernaux, *L'âge de fer à Kibiro (Uganda)* (Tervuren, 1968), *passim.* A small copper tube was found at Engaruka, but the dating is not clear: H. Sassoon, "Engaruka: Excavations during 1964," *Azania* 1 (1966): 90.

43 J. E. G. Sutton, "The Archaeology and Early Peoples of the Highlands of Kenya and Northern Tanzania," *Azania* 1 (1966): 53.

44 F. Hirth and W. W. Rockhill, eds., *Chau-ju-kua: His Work on the Chinese and Arab Trade in the Twelfth and Thirteenth Centuries Entitled Chu-fan-chi,* repr. ed. (New York, 1966), p. 126.

45 Neville Chittick, *Kilwa: An Islamic Trading City on the East African Coast,* 2 vols. (Nairobi, 1974); idem in Shinnie, *African Iron Age,* 123–24.

46 Eric Axelson, *South-East Africa, 1488–1530* (New York, 1940), 77.

47 Cited in Mauny, "Histoire des métaux," 565.

48 Robert Hess, "The Itinerary of Benjamin of Tudela," *JAH* 6, no. 1 (1965): 17.

49 Al-Bakri, *Description de l'Afrique septentrionale,* trans. M. de Slane (Paris, 1965), 290, 296, 301, 306, 325, 331, 335.

50 Al-Idrisi, *Géographie d'Edrisi,* trans. A. Jaubert, 2 vols. (Paris, 1836), 1:76; cf. 3, 87.

51  Leo Africanus, *Description de l'Afrique,* trans. A. Epaulard, 2 vols. (Paris, 1956), 1: 115–7; 2: 421.

52  Mas Latrie, *Relations et commerce,* 106–7, 328.

53  In G. R. Crone, trans. and ed., *The Voyages of Cadamosto and Other Documents on Western Africa in the Second Half of the Fifteenth Century* (London, 1937), 89.

54  Mas Latrie, *Relations,* 274.

55  V. Magalhães Godinho, *L'économie de l'empire portugais aux XVe et XVIe siècles* (Paris, 1969), 123.

56  Monod, "Le Ma'den Ijâfen," 286–320.

57  Al-'Umari, "Le royaume de Mali," *NA,* no. 82 (1959): 63.

58  Ibn Battuta, *Les voyages d'Ibn Battoutah,* trans. and ed. C. Defrémery and B. R. Sanguinetti, 4 vols. (Paris, 1862), 4: 441.

59  H. A. R. Gibb, trans. and ed., *Ibn Battuta, Travels in Asia and Africa* (London, 1929), 383*n.*

60  Jan Vansina, personal communication.

61  J. Devisse, "Routes de commerce et échange en Afrique occidentale en relation avec la Méditerranée," *Revue d'histoire économique et sociale* 50 (1972): 361–63. Devisse may base this suggesion on Magalhães Godinho's unsupported reading of Ibn Battuta, *L'économie,* 123. But cf. Terence Walz, *Trade between Egypt and Bilad as-Sudan, 1700–1820* (Cairo, 1978), 17, 107*n.*

62  Connah, *Three Thousand Years in Africa,* 165 and *passim.* See also Treinen-Claustre, "Nouveaux éléments," 103–9, but no copper is mentioned for these Haddadian sites.

63  Shaw, *Igbo-Ukwu, passim.*

64  See esp. B. Lawal, "The Igbo-Ukwu 'Bronzes': A Search for the Economic Evidence," *JHSN* 6, no. 3 (1972): 313–21.

65  F. N. Anozie, "Excavations at Onyoma and Ke, Niger Delta," *WAJA* 6 (1976): 89–96: the finds at Ke have been dated to c. 870–1190 A.D., those at Onyoma to c. 1330–1490 A.D. Ceremonial objects of cast bronze as well as a wire-bound sword hilt were found at Ifeka Garden site, dated to c. 1495 A.D.: D. Hartle, "Bronze Objects from the Ifeka Garden Site, Ezira," *West African Archaeological Newsletter* 4 (1966): 25–28.

66  J. D. Fage, in *Cambridge History of Africa* (Cambridge, 1977), 3:475.

67  E. Herbert, "Portuguese Adaptation to Trade Patterns, Guinea to Angola (1443–1640)," *African Studies Review* 17, no. 2 (1974): 411–23.

68  Pacheco Pereira, *Esmeraldo de Situ Orbis,* 132, 134. Cf. B. Paludanus, *Beschrijvinge van de Gantsche Kust van Guinea,* in Linschoten, *Itinerario,* ed. C. P. Burger and F. W. T. Hunger (The Hague, 1934), 7. Markwart suggested the Lower Congo as a possible source of Benin copper in arguing for the African origins of Benin art: *Die Benin Sammlung des Reichsmuseums für Völkerkunde in Leiden* (Leyden, 1913) p. xlviii.

69  K. David Patterson, *The Northern Gabon Coast to 1875* (Oxford, 1975), 22; Paul Du Chaillu, *Exploration and Adventures in Equatorial Africa* (1856; London, 1945), 15.

70 J. Barbot, "Description," 5: 266, 393.

71 Mauny, *Tableau,* 92–114, 524–25; L. Desplagnes, "Etude sur les tumuli du Killi dans la région de Goundam," *L'anthropologie* 14 (1903): 151–72; idem, "Fouilles du tumulus d'El Oualedji," *BIFAN* 13, no. 4 (1951): 1159–73; and *Le plateau central nigérien* (Paris, 1970).

72 S. K. and R. J. McIntosh, *Prehistoric Investigations in the Region of Jenne, Mali,* 2 vols. (Oxford, 1980), 1: 164–66 and pl. XII.

73 Desplagnes, *Plateau,* 151–72; J. Joire, "Découvertes archéologiques dans la région de Rao (Bas Sénégal)," *BIFAN* 17 (1955): 249–333; Cyr Descamps, *L'archeologie et l'histoire en Afrique de l'ouest,* Documents pédagogiques audiovisuels, AUDECAM (Paris, 1977), 26–31; A. Diop, "Datations par la méthode du radiocarbone, série IV," *BIFAN* 39 (1977): 461–70; and Calvocoressi and David, "A New Survey," 14.

74 D. S. Robert, "Les fouilles de Tegdaoust," *JAH* 11, no. 4 (1970): 471–93; M. Posnansky and R. McIntosh, "New Radiocarbon Dates for Northern and Western Africa," *JAH* 17, no. 2 (1976): 182.

75 Roger Bedaux, "Tellem, reconnaissance archéologique d'une culture," *JSA* 42 (1972): 174 ff.; and Bedaux et al., "Recherches archéologiques dans le delta intérieur du Niger," *Palaeohistoria* 20 (1978): 146–47.

76 H. Labouret, "Le mystère des ruines du Lobi," *Revue d'ethnographie et des traditions populaires* 1 (1920): 178 *et seq.* See also the copper anklets and pendant found by Savonnet in the Guéguéré region just to the north: "Habitations souterraines bobo ou anciens puits de mines en pays wilé?" *BIFAN* 36, no. 2 (1974): 227–45.

77 Merrick Posnansky, *The Origins of West African Trade* (Accra, 1971), 11; cf. idem, "Excavation at the D2 Site on the Dwinfuor Quarter of Beeo," *Nyame Akuma* (Calgary) 7 (1975): 17–18.

78 Posnansky, *Origins,* 7–8.

79 "Trouvaille archéologique en Côte d'Ivoire," *NA,* no. 16 (1942): 1–2; R. Mauny, "Datations au Carbon 14 d'amas artificiels de coquillages des lagunes de basse Côte d'Ivoire," *WAJA* 3 (1973): 207–14; D. A. Breternitz, "Rescue Archeology in the Kainji Reservoir Area, 1968," *WAJA* 5 (1975): 91–151.

80 Connah, *Archaeology of Benin,* 142–43, 146–47.

81 Shaw, *Nigeria,* chap. 8 *passim.* See also E. Herbert, "Copper in the Iron Age: The Archaeological Evidence in a Comparative Context" (Paper presented to the Twenty-fifth Annual Meeting of the African Studies Association, Washington, D.C., 1982).

82 Frank Willett, "Baubles, Bangles and Beads: Trade Contacts of Medieval Ife" (Thirteenth Melville J. Herskovits Memorial Lecture, Centre of African Studies, Edinburgh, 1977). I am grateful to Prof. Willett for sending me a copy of this lecture.

83 Robert, "Tegdaoust," 490; Descamps, *L'archéologie,* 27.

84 Mauny, *Tableau,* 163.

85 Descamps, *L'archéologie,* 28, 31.

## CHAPTER 6

1 Marion Johnson, "Paleocolonialism," unpublished paper.
2 Matthews, *Voyage to the River Sierra Leone,* 140–41. Cf. Edward Bold, *The Merchants' and Mariners' African Guide* (London, 1822), 60: ". . . What is quite the rage one year will the following one, most probable [sic], be rejected with the greatest disdain."
3 H. H. Johnston, *The River Congo from Its Mouth to Bolobo* (London, 1884), 131–32.
4 A. G. Hopkins, *An Economic History of West Africa* (London, 1973), 111. See also M. Johnson, "The Ounce in Eighteenth-Century West African Trade," *JAH* 7, no. 2 (1966): 197–214.
5 William Bosman, *A New and Accurate Description of the Coast of Guinea,* new ed. (1704; London, 1967), 91.
6 Victor Dupont [Marquis de Compiègne], *L'Afrique équatoriale: Okanda, Bangouens-Osyéba* (Paris, n.d.), 242.
7 John Atkins, *A Voyage to Guinea* (London, 1735), 159.
8 Barbot, "Description," 382.
9 United Africa Company, "Merchandise Trading in British West Africa," *Statistical and Economic Review,* March 1950, 13. Cf. L. Finigan, "The Life of Peter Stuart," in *Trading in West Africa, 1840–1920,* ed. P. N. Davies (London, 1976), 176.
10 H. Ling Roth, *Great Benin: Its Customs, Arts and Horrors* (Halifax, 1903), 5*n;* John Vogt, *Portuguese Rule on the Gold Coast, 1469–1682* (Athens, Ga., 1979), 69.
11 John Adams, *Sketches Taken during Ten Voyages to Africa between the Years 1786 and 1800* (London, 1823), 263.
12 See, for example, Johnson, "The Ounce"; K. G. Davies, *The Royal African Company* (London, 1957), 232ff; D. Richardson, "West African Consumption Patterns and Their Influence on the Eighteenth-Century English Slave Trade," in *The Uncommon Market: Essays in the Economic History of the Atlantic Slave Trade,* ed. H. Gemery and J. Hogendorn (New York, 1979); P. D. Curtin, *Economic Change in Precolonial Africa* (Madison, Wis., 1975).
13 Herbert, "Portuguese Adaptation," 411–23. Cf. John Vogt, "Notes on the Portuguese Cloth Trade in West Africa, 1480–1540," *IJAHS* 8, no. 4 (1975): 632 *et seq.*
14 J. W. Blake, *Europeans in West Africa, 1450–1560,* 2 vols. (London, 1942), 1: 109–10.
15 Vogt, *Portuguese Rule,* 69.
16 Eustache de La Fosse, *Voyage à la côte occidentale d'Afrique en Portugal et en Espagne (1479–*1480), ed. R. Foulché-Delbosc (Paris, 1897), p. 12.
17 In Blake, *Europeans in West Africa,* 2: 367, 374, 379–82.
18 Ibid., 1: 107. Small wonder that the officers of the Casa da Guiné complained that the "counting and weighing of the manillas and the brass . . . require much handling": 1: 101.

19 A Braamcamp Freire, ed., *Archivo histórico portuguêz,* 11 vols. (Lisbon, 1903–16), 1: 200–201.
20 Blake, *Europeans in West Africa,* 1: 97.
21 Ryder, *Benin,* 40.
22 Ibid., 53.
23 Blake, *Europeans in West Africa,* 1: 111.
24 Ibid., 1: 107.
25 Braamcamp, *Archivo,* 1: 200–201.
26 Garrard, *Akan Weights,* chap. 2 *passim.*
27 Vogt, *Portuguese Rule,* 76.
28 "The Portuguese Gold Trade: An Account Ledger from Elmina, 1529–1531," *THSG* 14, no. 1 (June 1973): 93–98. Cf. Roger Barlow, *A Brief Summe of Geographie,* ed. E. G. R. Taylor (London, 1932), 106. Vogt notes that the variety of metalwares had simplified by 1529 to six basic items: brass manillas, three kinds of brass bowls (*bacias*), and lidded and unlidded large cooking pots (*caldeiras* and *caldeirões*).
29 Magalhães Godinho, *L'économie de l'empire portugais,* 275.
30 At Cochin on the Malabar Coast, pepper could only be obtained against at least one-third payment in copper: L. Schick, *Un grand homme d'affaires au début du XVIe siècle, Jacob Fugger* (Paris, 1957), p. 277.
31 Vogt, *Portuguese Rule,* p. 76.
32 Magalhães Godinho, 373. *L'économie de l'empire portugais,* 373.
33 J. A. Goris, *Étude sur les colonies marchandes méridionales (portugais, espagnols, italiens) à Anvers de 1488 à 1567* (Louvain, 1925), 239–43. Cf. J. van Houtte, "Anvers aux XVe et XVIe siècles," *Annales* 16, no. 2 (1961): 253–54.
34 In Jakob Strieder, *Aus Antwerpener Notariatsarchiven: Quellen zur deutschen Wirtschaftsgeschichte des 16. Jahrhunderts* (Stuttgart and Leipzig, 1930), 451–53.
35 In J. Strieder, "Negerkunst von Benin und deutsches Metallexportgewerke im 15. und 16. Jahrhundert," *Zeitschrift für Ethnologie* 64 (1932): 252.
36 Vogt, *Portuguese Rule,* 77; Magalhães Godinho, *L'économie,* 375.
37 Vogt, app. A, p. 221.
38 Ibid., 74. Cf. Godinho, *L'économie,* 373.
39 Garrard, "Brass in Akan Society," 70–71.
40 Godinho, *L'économie,* 375.
41 Blake, *Europeans in West Africa,* 1: 235–36.
42 *Documentos sobre os portugueses em Moçambique e na Africa central* 1: *passim.*
43 Alexandre Lobato, *A expansão portuguêsa em Moçambique de 1498 a 1530,* 3 vols. (Lisbon, 1954–60), 3: 48–50, 69–70.
44 Ibid., 313.
45 Garrard, "Brass," 166.
46 Pacheco, *Esmeraldo,* 80–81.
47 Ibid., 120–21.
48 Vogt, *Portuguese Rule,* 72.

49 Ludovico Guicciardini, *Descrittione delli tutti i Paesi Bassi* (Antwerp, 1567), 121.
50 J. Strieder, *Die Inventur der Firma Fugger aus dem Jahre 1527* (Tübingen, 1965), 46–47.
51 Denucé, *L'Afrique;* Strieder, *Aus Antwerpener Notariatsarchiven,* xviii, xxxvi–xxxvii; H. van der Wee, *The Growth of the Antwerp Market and the European Economy,* 2 vols. (Louvain, 1963), 2: 126.
52 On the Fugger, see in addition to the works by Strieder above, his *Die deutsche Montan-und Metallindustrie im Zeitalter der Fugger* (Berlin, 1931); and Schick, *Jacob Fugger.*
53 Vogt, *Portuguese Rule,* 89–90.
54 On the European copper trade see, in addition to the works cited above, E. Herbert, "The West African Copper Trade in the Fifteenth and Sixteenth Centuries," in *Precious Metals in the Age of Expansion,* ed. H. Kellenbenz, Papers of the Fourteenth International Congress of Historical Sciences (Stuttgart, 1981).
55 Pierre Jeannin, "Le cuivre, les Fugger et la Hanse," *Annales* 10 (1955): 233–34.
56 E. Westermann, "Tendencies in the European Copper Market in the Fifteenth and Sixteenth Centuries," in *Precious Metals in the Age of Expansion,* 74.
57 Pacheco, *Esmeraldo,* 110.
58 Ryder, *Benin,* 40, 53, 55–56.
59 Vogt, *Portuguese Rule,* 74–75.
60 In R. Hakluyt, *Principal Voyages of the English Nation,* 12 vols. (London, 1903–5), 6: 218; Vogt, 76, 112.
61 Cf. Vogt, 211.
62 Ibid., 153, 196–97.
63 K. Ratelband, ed., *Vijf dagregisters van het kasteel São Jorge da Mina (Elmina) aan de Goudkust (1645–1647)* (The Hague, 1953), xcix. This same figure was cited by a representative of the Swedish Crown—which may tend to support this remarkably high figure or may simply be based on Blommaert's estimate. I am grateful to Prof. Harvey Feinberg for help in translating Ratelband.
64 K. Y. Daaku, *Trade and Politics on the Gold Coast 1600–1720* (Oxford, 1970), 11.
65 Davies, *Royal African Company,* 351.
66 Ibid., 232–33.
67 See, for example, Daaku, *Trade and Politics,* 47.
68 See Barbot, "Description," 273.
69 Kristof Glamann, *Dutch-Asiatic Trade, 1620–1740* (Copenhagen, 1958), 171–74. See also N. W. Posthumus, *Inquiry into the History of Prices in Holland,* 2 vols. (Leiden, 1946–64), tables 173 *et seq.*
70 On the effects of the Thirty Years' War on the Central European copper industry, see Günther Probst, "Absatzmärkte und Verkehrswege der niederungarischen Bergstädte," *Zeitschrift für Ostforschung* 3 (1954): 551.
71 Ratelband, *Vijf dagregisters,* xcix.
72 Candice Goucher, "Iron is Iron 'til it rusts: Trade and Ecology in West African Iron-Working," *JAH* 22, no. 2 (1981): 179–90.

73 Aitchison, *History of Metals,* 2: 320.
74 Blake, *Europeans in West Africa,* 2: 380; Hakluyt, *Principal Voyages,* 6: 252.
75 Ratelband, *Vijf dagregisters,* 386.
76 Elizabeth Donnan, *Documents Illustrative of the History of the Slave Trade to America,* 4 vols. (Washington, D.C., 1930–35), 2: 450. Marion Johnson suggests that pewter may sometimes have been a substitute for silver: personal communication.
77 W. J. Mueller, *Die Africanische auf der Guineischen Guldkust gelegene Landschaft Fetu* (1673; Graz, 1968), 149.
78 Barbot, "Description," 35, 45; Dapper, *Naukeurige Beschrijvinghe,* 352.
79 Dapper, 360; Barbot, 75.
80 Dapper, 432.
81 Ratelband, *Vijf dagregisters,* 390–91.
82 Daaku, *Trade and Politics,* 38.
83 Dapper, *Naukeurige Beschrijvinghe,* 481.
84 Donnan, *Documents,* I: 396.
85 Garrard, "Brass," 7.
86 Donnan, 1: 237.
87 Ibid., 1: 404–5.
88 Ryder, *Benin,* 86, 95–97; Barbot, "Description," 382; Dapper, *Naukeurige Beschrijvinge,* 500.
89 Dapper, 510.
90 Barbot, 465.
91 Dapper, 510 (cf. Ratelband, *Vijf dagregisters* 386); Barbot, 465.
92 Dapper, 513; K. David Patterson, *The Northern Gabon Coast to 1875* (Oxford, 1975), 10, 14–15.
93 Dapper, p. 575; Pieter van den Broecke, *Reizen naar West-Afrika, 1605–1614,* ed. K. Ratelband (The Hague, 1950), xcv; Randles, *Ancien royaume du Congo,* 173, 180.
94 R. Elphick, *Kraal and Castle* (New Haven, 1977), 65–66, 77, 160–66; R. Elphick and H. Giliomée, *The Shaping of South African Society 1652–1820* (Cape Town, 1979), 9; Jan van Riebeeck, *Journal of Jan van Riebeeck,* ed. H. B. Thom, 3 vols. (Cape Town, 1958), 1: 79; Richard Gray, ed., *The Cambridge History of Africa* (Cambridge, 1975), 4: 439, 442–43; G. Harinck, "Interaction between Xhosa and Khoi: Emphasis on the period 1620–1750," in L. Thompson, ed., *African Societies in Southern Africa,* repr. ed. (London, 1978), 164–66.
95 Monica Wilson and Leonard Thompson, eds., *Oxford History of South Africa,* 2 vols. (New York, 1969), 1: 81, 114; cf. Elphick and Giliomée, 301; and C. R. Boxer, *The Tragic History of the Sea* (Cambridge, 1959), 213–15.
96 Nicholas Buckeridge, *Journal and Letter Book of Nicholas Buckeridge 1651–1654,* ed. J. R. Jensen (Minneapolis, 1973), 32.
97 Ibid., 76.
98 Barbot, "Description," 465.
99 Cf. David Birmingham, "Early Trade in Angola and its Hinterland," in *Pre-Colonial African Trade,* ed. Richard Gray and David Birmingham (London,

1970), 163–64. The Congolese had manufactured manillas of copper before the arrival of the Portuguese: J. Cuvelier and L. Jadin, *L'ancien Congo d'après les archives romains (1578–1640)* (Brussels, 1954), 119n.

100 J. Cuvelier, *L'ancien royaume du Congo* (Bruges, 1946), 44, 108–9, 111–12, 126–27, 145, 227–28; A. Brásio, *Monumenta missionaria africana,* 8 vols. (Lisbon, 1952–68), 1: 303–5, 476.

101 Ryder, quoted in Shaw, *Igbo-Ukwu,* 1:78.

102 Battell, *Strange Adventures,* 16.

103 Birmingham, "Early Trade," 166; Baltasar Rebello in Cordeiro, *Memorias,* 2: 15, 18–19; Castello Branco, ibid., 1: 12–13, 30, 31; Brásio, *Monumenta,* 6: 524, 528–29, 566. Albuquerque Felner, on the other hand, reprints a Portuguese document of 1619 which denies that there is copper in Benguela: *Angola,* 3 vols. (Coimbra, 1933), 1: 478.

104 Van den Boogart and Emmer, in Gemery and Hogendorn, *Uncommon Market,* 358–59.

105 J. Barbot, "Description," 383–84; Phyllis Martin, *The External Trade of the Loango Coast, 1576–1870* (Oxford, 1972), 63.

106 M. J. Paiva Manso, *História do Congo* (Lisbon, 1872), 68.

107 Cuvelier, *Ancien royaume,* 240–42.

108 Randles, *Ancien royaume du Congo,* 107, 112, 118–20.

109 S. van Brakel, "Eene memorie over den Handel der West-Indische Compagnie Omstreeks 1670," *Historisch Genootschap te Utrecht, Bijdragen en mededeelingen* 35: 97–98; Donnan, *Documents,* 1: 193.

110 Eric Axelson *The Portuguese in Southeast Africa, 1600–1700* (Johannesburg, 1960), 32, 55, 65, 119, 130, 178.

111 Battell, *Strange Adventures,* 43.

112 Van den Broecke, *Reizen,* 64, 70, 335. Cf. Samuel Brun, *Schiffarten* (1624; Graz, 1969), 16–17; Denucé, *L'Afrique,* 55; Jules de Saint-Genois, *Voyageurs belges,* 2 vols. in 1 (Brussels, 1846), 2: 61.

113 Martin, *External Trade,* 51, 56–57, 59. Donnan reprints an agreement for a shipment of Loango copper and ivory to Curaçao in 1663: 4:422–26.

114 E.g. Barrat, *Géologie du Congo français,* 72 ff.; Babet, *Observations géologiques,* 12.

115 Dapper, *Naukeurige Beschrijvinghe,* 532. Barbot virtually repeats Dapper's account: "Description," 5, 472.

116 Dapper, 571; Ratelband, *Vijf dagregisters,* Bijlage K, 386.

117 Lt. Pleigneur, "Mines de cuivre et de plomb de Mbokô-Songhô," *Revue d'Ethnologie* 7 (1888), p. 280.

118 Martin, *External Trade,* 36, 41–42; idem, "Loango in the Seventeenth and Eighteenth Centuries," in Gray and Birmingham, *African Trade,* 141, 143.

119 Along the same lines, Latham argues that the copper rod currency of the Cross River antedated the arrival of the Europeans, but he does not speculate about the source of the copper: "Currency, Credit and Capitalism on the Cross River in the Pre-Colonial Era," *JAH* 12, no. 4 (1971): 599. See also chap. 8 below.

120 A. Raponda Walker, *Notes d'histoire du Gabon* (Brazzaville, 1960), *passim,* esp. 55, 78, 94–95.

121 Martin, *External Trade,* 50–51, 64–65.

122 Martin, "Loango," 147–48.

123 L. Degrandpré, *Voyage à la côte occidentale d'Afrique* . . . *1786 et 1787,* 2 vols. (Paris, 1801), 1:38–39.

124 Burton, *Gorilla-Land,* 2:6.

125 Alan Smith, "Delagoa Bay and the Trade of Southeastern Africa," in Gray and Birmingham, *African Trade,* 265, 271; E. C. Godee Molsbergen, ed., *Reizen in Zuid-Afrika in de Hollandse Tijd,* 4 vols. (The Hague, 1922), 3:130.

126 G. Liesegang, "New Light on Venda Traditions: Mahumane's Account of 1730," *History in Africa* 4 (1977): 170, 177n21; Evers, "Iron Age Trade," 33.

127 In G. M. Theal, ed., *Records of South-Eastern Africa,* 9 vols. (Cape Town, 1898–1903), 1:413.

128 Smith, "Delagoa Bay"; and idem, "The Trade of Delagoa Bay as a Factor in Nguni Politics 1750–1835," in *African Societies in Southern Africa,* ed. L. Thompson (London, 1978), 173–74.

129 Smith, "Delagoa Bay," 274–75.

130 Ibid., 271.

131 Hopkins, *Economic History,* 93–94.

132 PRO CUST/3 and 17. I am deeply indebted to Marion Johnson for providing computer print-outs of these records. Note that they also include *imports* of copper and brass from Africa, largely shruff from North Africa.

133 Henry Hamilton, *The English Brass and Copper Industries to 1800* (London, 1926), 112.

134 Ibid., 112; John Morton, personal communication.

135 Hamilton, *English Brass and Copper,* 112.

136 Davies, *Royal African Company,* 172.

137 On the rise of the British brass and copper industry, see, in addition to Hamilton, M. B. Donald, *Elizabethan Copper* (London, 1955); John Harris, *The Copper King: A Biography of Thomas Williams of Llanidan* (Liverpool, 1964), 1–12, 115; John Latimer, *The Annals of Bristol: Eighteenth Century* (Bristol, 1893), 89, 270; Joan Day, *Bristol Brass: The History of the Industry* (Newton Abbot, 1973); G. Grant-Francis, *The Smelting of Copper in the Swansea District of South Wales* (London, 1881).

138 *Report from the Select Committee on the State of the Copper Trade* . . . (1799), Commons Committee Reports, X.

139 See Eric Williams, *Capitalism and Slavery* (Chapel Hill, 1944), esp. 83–84 concerning the role of British brass and copper manufactures in the slave trade. On the relative positions of Bristol and London in the eighteenth-century African trade, see James A. Rawley, "The Port of London and the Eighteenth-Century Slave Trade," *African Economic History* 9 (1980): 85–100.

140 John Morton, personal communication.

141 Deeds of the Cheadle and Warrington Companies, 12 July 1755. I am grateful to Prof. John Harris for access to this ms. Cf. Hamilton, *Brass and Copper,* 150, 259.

142 Day, *Bristol Brass,* 90.

143 Grant-Francis, *Smelting of Copper,* 113; Harris, *Copper King,* 177–79; Cheadle

Brass Wire Minute Books, 29 March 1788–1 July 1831: 8 Oct. 1790. I am grateful to Prof. Harris for access to these books.

144 Cheadle Minute Books, 23 Aug. 1790 and 9 Aug. 1791.

145 Day, *Bristol Brass,* 199.

146 Harris, *Copper King,* 9–10.

147 Donnan, *Documents,* 2:536.

148 Richardson, "Consumption Patterns," 312–14.

149 Ibid., *passim.*

150 Atkins, *Voyage to Guinea,* 159.

151 Ryder, *Benin,* 144.

152 Egharevba, *Short History,* 42. The brass stool may, however, have been a European import, according to Irwin Tunis: "A Study of Two Cire-Perdue Cast Copper Alloy Stools," *Baesssler-Archiv,* n.s. 29, no. 1 (1982): 1–66.

153 J-F. Landolphe, *Mémoires du capitaine Landolphe,* ed. J. S. Quesné, 2 vols. (Paris, 1823), 1:126–27.

154 Donnan, *Documents,* 2:540.

155 Daaku, *Trade and Politics,* 163.

156 Atkins, *Voyage to Guinea,* 163; M. Johnson, personal communication.

157 Richardson, "Consumption Patterns," 317–19.

158 J. E. Inikori, "The Import of Firearms into West Africa, 1750–1807: A Quantitative Analysis," *JAH* 18, no. 3 (1977): 340.

159 *Report of the Select Committee . . . 1799,* pp. 668, 673; Harris, *Copper King,* 11–12. See also Georg Nørregard, *Danish Settlements in West Africa, 1658–1850,* trans. S. Mannem (Boston, 1966), 161; cf. L. F. Roemer, *Tilforladelig Eftervetning om Kysten Guinea* (Copenhagen, 1760), 27, 318.

160 Sundström, *Exchange Economy,* 235.

161 P. Labarthe, *Voyage à la côte de Guinée* (Paris, 1803), 34, 45; A. Pruneau de Pommegorge, *Description de la nigritie* (Paris, 1789), 128–30.

162 Pruneau de Pommegorge, 12–13, 36, 123.

163 Dieudonné Rinchon, *Pierre-Ignace-Liévin van Alstein, capitaine négrier* (Dakar, 1964), *passim.*

## CHAPTER 7

1 Pierre de Maret, "New Survey of Archaeological Research and Dates for West-Central and North-Central Africa," *JAH* 23, no. 1 (1982): 9.

2 Thomas Q. Reefe, *The Rainbow and the Kings* (Berkeley, 1981), 95–102, quotations 95, 100, 101.

3 Vansina, *Children of Woot,* 192–93.

4 Joseph Miller, *Kings and Kinsmen* (Oxford, 1976), 37.

5 Vellut, "Notes sur le Lunda," 88.

6 Ibid., 89.

7 *Cambridge History of Africa,* 4 (Cambridge, 1975): 374, 377–78; and 5 (1976): 228.

8 Vellut, "Notes sur le Lunda," 88–89.

9  David Livingstone, *Livingstone's African Journal 1853–1856,* 2:255–56; idem, *Missionary Travels and Researches in South Africa* (London, 1857), 459.

10  *Cambridge History,* 5:378–80; Verbeken and Walraet, *Première traversée, passim.*

11  See, in addition to Verbeken and Walraet, 75, 96–97, Andrew Roberts, *A History of the Bemba* (Madison, Wis., 1973), 107, 192; Lacerda's "Journey," in Richard Burton, trans. and annot., *The Lands of Cazembe* (London, 1873), 130; E. A. Alpers, *Ivory and Slaves in East Central Africa* (Berkeley and Los Angeles, 1975), 200, 224; Ian Cunnison, "Kazembe and the Portuguese, 1798–1832," *JAH* 2, no. 1 (1961): 75; David and Charles Livingstone, *Narrative of an Expedition to the Zambezi,* 389.

12  Clark, "Pre-European Copper-Working," 5.

13  See, for example, Livingstone, *Last Journals,* 2:62, 67; Monteiro, *Angola,* 305; J. M. Moubray, *In South Central Africa* (London, 1912), 117; Laman, *The Kongo,* 1: 122. "Chirupula" Stephenson notes that the Swahili mixed powdered copper carbonate, that is, malachite, with fat to treat venereal disease, which was rampant on the Copperbelt: Letter to J. D. Clark, Jan. 2, 1956. In the same letter he claims that Chiwala, an African trader who established the settlement in what became Ndola township, tried to keep the Bwana M'Kubwa mine a secret from European prospectors by pretending that he was working it only for medicine.

14  D. and C. Livingstone, *Narrative,* 128. In 1616 Bocarro had travelled overland from Maravi country south of Lake Nyasa to Kilwa, using copper bracelets as gifts for the chiefs of the villages through which he passed. The copper came from the Zambezi, but its ultimate source is not known: see *The East African Coast,* ed. G. S. P. Freeman-Grenville (Oxford, 1962), 165–68.

15  Livingstone, *Last Journals,* 2: 67, 73, 106, 119, 120. See also Andrew Roberts, "Nyamwezi Trade," in *Pre-Colonial African Trade,* ed. R. Gray and D. Birmingham (London, 1970), pp. 54–57.

16  Livingstone, *Last Journals,* 1: 344; 2: 44; cf. 2: 31, 37; and idem, *African Journal,* 1: 98.

17  Idem, *Last Journals,* 1875 ed., 266.

18  Israel K. Katoke, *The Making of the Karagwe Kingdom,* Historical Association of Tanzania Paper no. 8 (Nairobi, 1970), 22.

19  Célis and Nzikobanyanka, *Métallurgie,* 101, 164, 180.

20  F. L. Van Noten, *Les tombes du roi Cyirima Rujugira et de la reine-mère Nyirayuhi Kanjogera* (Tervuren, 1972), *passim,* esp. 24–27. Van Noten is inclined to place Cyirima's death at around 1635 A.D. ± 30 on the strength of radiocarbon dates. He also seems to accept the tradition collected by Kagame that bars of copper and brass from the east coast reached Rwanda about 1650 (p. 55).

21  Dugald Campbell, *In the Heart of Bantuland* (London, 1922), 262.

22  John Tosh, "The Northern Interlacustrine Region," in Gray and Birmingham *African Trade,* 111.

23  A. C. Pedroso Gamitto, *King Kazembe and the Marave, Cheva, Bisa, Bemba,*

*Lunda and Other Peoples of Southern Africa . . .,* trans. Ian Cunnison, 2 vols. (Lisbon, 1960), 2: 98-99.

24 *Cambridge History,* 5: 244-45; Reefe, *Rainbow,* chap. 13 *passim.*

25 Burton, *Lake Regions,* 1: 150-51; 2: 65; (1872), 2: 413, 415. Speke noted simply that the "dark rich red" copper of Katanga was more appreciated than imported copper: *What Led to the Discovery of the Source of the Nile* (London, 1864), 199.

26 Letter of Mwenda II to Son Altesse Royale, Prince de Belgique, reprinted in translated abridgement in G. E. Tilsley, *Dan Crawford: Missionary and Pioneer in Central Africa* (London, 1929), 136-40. On Msiri generally, see Auguste Verbeken, *M'siri, roi du Garenganze* (Brussels, 1956).

27 De Hemptinne, *Mangeurs,* 32.

28 Marchal, "Renseignements," 14-15; *Cambridge History,* 5: 247; but cf. de Hemptinne, 9.

29 De Hemptinne, 4.

30 [Reichard] "The Copper Mines of Katanga," *Proceedings of the Royal Geographical Society* 7, no. 8 (1885): 540.

31 Cornet, "Mines de cuivre du Katanga," 4.

32 The best account of the political history of this region in the later nineteenth century is Reefe, *Rainbow,* chap. 13.

33 Robert W. Harms, *River of Wealth, River of Sorrow* (New Haven, 1981), 23.

34 Stanley, *Through the Dark Continent,* 2:359. Cf. Livingstone, *Last Journals,* 151.

35 Vansina, *Tio Kingdom,* 272.

36 Dupont, *Lettres sur le Congo,* 334-35.

37 H. M. Stanley, *The Congo and the Founding of Its Free State,* 2 vols. (New York, 1885), 2:356-57; Giles Sautter, *De l'Atlantique au fleuve Congo: Une géographie du sous-peuplement,* 2 vols. (Paris, 1966), 1:374.

38 H. M. Stanley, *Five Years in the Congo, 1879-1884* (New York, 1885); cf. Bentley, *Pioneering,* 1:401.

39 Sautter, *De l'Atlantique,* 1:377.

40 Dupont, *Lettres,* 340.

41 I am grateful to Jeffrey E. Hayer for first alerting me to the importance of Hufrat en-Nahas.

42 Afia and Widatalla, *Investigation,* 1: 2.

43 Wilson and Felkin, *Uganda and the Egyptian Sudan,* 2:164.

44 Afia and Widatalla, *Investigation,* 1: 2.

45 Robert C. Collins, "Sudanese Factors in the History of the Congo and Central West Africa in the Nineteenth Century," in *Sudan in Africa,* ed. Y. F. Hasan (Khartoum, 1971), 162-63.

46 Heinrich Barth, *Travels and Discoveries in North and Central Africa 1849-1855,* 2d ed., 5 vols. (London, 1857-58), 2:141. See also Sundström, *Exchange Economy,* 233. According to Newbury, 5,000 cowries were equal to about 10 francs in Kano at this period: "North African and Western Sudan Trade in the Nineteenth Century: A Re-evaluation," *JAH* 7, no. 2 (1966): 237.

47 Barth, 3:557.

48 Ibid., 2:141.
49 Frederick Horneman, *The Journal of Frederick Horneman's Travels from Cairo to Mourzouk . . . 1797–1798* (London, 1802), 64, 113.
50 MacGregor Laird and R. A. K. Oldfield, *An Expedition into the Interior of Africa by the River Niger, 1832, 1833, and 1834,* 2 vols. (London, 1837), 231.
51 Samuel Ajayi Crowther, *Journal of an Expedition up the Niger and Tshadda Rivers* (London, 1855), 118.
52 Hutchinson, *Narrative,* 130–31.
53 E. M. Chilver, "Nineteenth-Century Trade in the Bamenda Grassfields, Southern Cameroon," *Afrika und Übersee* 45 (1961): 238.
54 Heinrich Barth, "An Account of Two Expeditions," *Journal of the Royal Geographical Society* 23 (1853): 120; A. R. A. el-Bashir, personal communication.
55 Barth, *Travels,* 2:141.
56 Newbury, "Sudan Trade," 242.
57 John E. Lavers, "Trans-Saharan Trade circa 1500–1800: A Survey of Sources" (Paper presented at the Seminar on Economic History of the Central Savanna of West Africa, Kano, Nigeria, 5–10 Jan. 1976), 9.
58 Walz, *Trade between Egypt and Bilad as-Sudan,* 4 ff., 17–19.
59 Browne, *Travels in Africa,* 302, 349. Walz is dubious about Browne's claim that copper was exported to Egypt: Walz, 39.
60 Walz, 43.
61 Muhammad ibn 'Umar al-Tunisi, *Voyage au Ouaday* (Paris, 1851), 338–39, 351–52.
62 G. Schweinfurth, *The Heart of Africa,* 2 vols. (London, 1873), 1:176, 502; cf. O. Antonori, in *Inner-Afrika nach dem Stande der geographischen Kenntniss in den Jahren 1861 bis 1863,* ed. A. Petermann and B. Hassenstein, *Petermanns Mitteilungen, Ergänzungsheft* 2 (1863):83; Charles de la Kethulle De Ryhove, "Deux années de résidence chez le sultan Rafai: Voyage et exploration au nord du Mbomou," *Bulletin de la Société royale belge de géographie* 19 (1895): 538; Wilson and Felkin, *Uganda and the Egyptian Sudan,* 2:216.
63 Schweinfurth, 2:372.
64 Ibid., 1:502.
65 Ibid., 1:487; 2:38, 87, 148.
66 Ibid., 1:502; 2:43 ff. Cf. idem, "Das Volk der Monbuttu," *Zeitschrift für Ethnologie* 5 (1873): 19–20.
67 Browne, *Travels in Africa,* 267.
68 In Afia and Widatalla, *Investigation,* 1:2.
69 Christy, "Bahr el-Ghazal," 321; cf. Afia and Widatalla, 1:123; and Charles Cuny, "Notice sur le Dar-Four et sur les caravanes qui se rendent de ce pays en Egypte, et vice-versa," *Bulletin de la Société géographique de Paris,* 4th series, 8 (1854): 94.
70 Schweinfurth, *Heart of Africa,* 2:43, 87.
71 Bradley, *Copper Venture,* 71.
72 Bisson, "Prehistoric Copper Mining," 245.
73 Roberts, "Pre-Colonial Trade," 721.
74 Ibid., 742.

75  Livingstone, *African Journal,* 2:287; cf. Chapman's account of Dongwe copper (1953) in Roberts, "Pre-Colonial Trade," 723–24.

76  Alpers, *Ivory and Slaves,* 252.

77  M. D. D. Newitt, *Portuguese Settlement on the Zambesi* (London, 1973), 75; C. S. Lancaster and A. Pohorilenko, "Ingombe Ilede and the Zimbabwe Culture," *IJAHS* 10 (1977): 1–30 *passim.*

78  Roberts, "Pre-Colonial Trade," 728.

79  Nicola Sutherland-Harris, "Zambian Trade with Zumbo in the Eighteenth Century," in Gray and Birmingham, *African Trade,* 233–35.

80  Alpers, *Ivory and Slaves,* 124.

81  Sutherland-Harris, "Zambian Trade," 238–39.

82  Ibid., 241.

83  Alpers, 124; Sutherland-Harris, 233.

84  Garlake, *Great Zimbabwe,* 114; Dos Santos, in Theal, *Records of South-Eastern Africa,* 7:285. Cf. D. N. Beach, *The Shona and Zimbabwe 900–1850* (New York, 1980), 98.

85  Nicola Sutherland-Harris, "Trade and the Rozwi Mambo," in Gray and Birmingham, *African Trade,* 249.

86  S. I. Mudenge, "The Role of Foreign Trade in the Rosvi Empire: A Re-appraisal," *JAH* 15, no. 3 (1974): 386.

87  Lancaster and Pohorilenko, "Ingombe Ilede," *passim.*

88  Sutherland-Harris, "Rozwi Mambo," 260.

89  Theal, *Records,* 7:378, 379, 380.

90  Elphick, *Kraal and Castle,* 67.

91  Van Warmelo, *Copper Miners,* 4, 80–82.

92  M. Delesse, "Notice sur les mines de cuivre du cape de Bonne-Espérance," *Annales des mines,* 5th series, 8 (1855): 201; cf. Elphick, *Kraal and Castle,* 77.

93  H. J. Wikar, Jansz J. Coetsé, and W. van Reenew, *The Journal of Hendrik Jacob Wikar (1779),* trans. A. W. van der Horst and E. E. Mossop, ed. E. E. Mossop (Cape Town, 1935), 149, 155; Wilson and Thompson, *Oxford History of South Africa,* 1:143.

94  Wilson and Thompson, *Oxford History,* 1:143; Burchell, *Travels,* 2:567–68.

95  Lichtenstein, *Travels in Southern Africa,* 2:409.

96  Livingstone, *Family Letters,* 1:117–18, 145, 187.

97  Van der Merwe and Scully, "The Phalaborwa Story," 95; Van Warmelo, *Copper Miners,* 83.

98  P. G. Söhnge, *The Geology of the Messina Copper Mines and Surrounding Country,* Geological Survey of South Africa, memoir no. 40 (1945), 14.

99  Van Warmelo, *Copper Miners,* 83.

100  John M. Smalberger, *Aspects of the History of Copper Mining in Namaqualand, 1846–1931* (Cape Town, 1975), *passim.*

101  Vedder, *South West Africa,* 35–38.

102  Sir Francis Galton, *Narrative of an Explorer in Tropical South Africa* (London, 1889), 136; Karl Johan Andersson, *Lake Ngami* (London, 1856), 182, 202–3; B. Heintze, "Buschmänner und Ambo," *Journal. Südwest-Afrikanische Wissenschaftliche Gesellschaft* (Windhoek) 26 (1971–72): 47–49.

103 Vedder, *South West Africa,* 264-65, 281-85.

104 John Leighton Wilson, *Western Africa* (New York, 1856), 245, 350-51; Monteiro, *Angola,* 106. Copper ore may have been more desired than smelted metal because of the demands of the Swansea process, which mixed oxides and other ores.

105 George Brooks, *Yankee Traders, Old Coasters and African Middlemen* (Brookline, Mass., 1970), 286-87.

106 Monteiro, *Angola,* 88-89.

107 Douglas L. Wheeler, *The Portuguese in Angola, 1836—1891: A Study in Expansion and Administration* (Ann Arbor, Mich.: University Microfilms, 1966), app. 6, p. 407.

108 Roger Anstey, *Britain and the Congo in the Nineteenth Century* (Oxford, 1962), 23.

109 Wheeler, *Portuguese in Angola,* 205.

110 Great Britain, House of Commons, *Report from the Select Committee on West Africa,* 1842, app. no. 36, p. 502.

111 Louis Edouard Bouët-Willaumez, *Commerce et traite des noirs aux côtes occidentales d'Afrique* (Paris, 1848), 49.

112 Ibid., 89, 98; Bold, *African Guide,* 43, 46-47, 58.

113 Adams, *Sketches,* 111, 113; Bold, 67, 72, 78; Bouët-Willaumez, *Commerce,* 140-1, 147.

114 Du Chaillu, *Exploration,* 52, 90, 145, quotation 93; Bouët-Willaumez, 154; Wilson, *Western Africa,* 246; T. Boteler, *A Narrative of a Voyage of Discovery to Africa and Arabia,* 2 vols. (London, 1835), 2:394-95; Dupont, *L'Afrique équatoriale: Okanda,* 123, 132, 144, 234 ff., 240; Coquery-Vidrovitch, *Brazza,* 208, 394-95; A. Walker and R. Reynard, "Anglais, espagnols et nord-américains au Gabon au XIXe siècle," *Bulletin de l'Institut d'études centrafricaines* 12 (1956): 266.

115 Coquery-Vidrovitch, *Brazza,* 208.

116 Ibid., 204-5.

117 Ibid., 471.

118 Ibid., 208-9, 242-47.

119 Henri Brunschwig, "Les factures de Brazza, 1875-1878," *Cahiers d'études africaines* 13 (1963): 17.

120 Coquery-Vidrovitch, *Brazza,* 42-43; cf. C. Coquilhat, *Sur le haut Congo* (Brussels, 1888), 532-33.

121 A. Courboin, "Les populations de l'Alima: Congo français," *Bulletin de la Société royale de géographie d'Anvers* 28 (1904): 282.

122 Sir Harry Johnston, *George Grenfell and the Congo,* 2 vols. (London, 1908), 2:801-2, 806.

123 Vansina, *Tio Kingdom,* 282-83, 285-86.

124 Elphick, *Kraal and Castle, passim;* Wilson and Thompson, *Oxford History,* 1:81, 114, 151-52.

125 Elphick, 77.

126 Cited in *Oxford History,* 1:238; Ludwig Alberti, *Account of the Tribal Life and Customs of the Xhosa in 1807,* trans. William Fehr (Cape Town, 1968), 71, 72.

127  Burchell, *Travels,* 1:164.
128  Smith, "Delagoa Bay," 188; Henry Francis Fynn, *The Diary of Henry Francis Fynn* (Pietermaritzburg, 1950), *passim;* Cline, *Mining and Metallurgy,* 80.
129  Smith, "Delagoa Bay," 188.
130  Leonard Thompson, *Survival in Two Worlds: Moshoeshoe of Lesotho, 1786–1870* (Oxford, 1975), 34, 192.
131  T. Baines, *Gold Regions of South-East Africa,* facs. ed. (London, 1968), 9.
132  Gerald W. Hartwig, *The Art of Survival in East Africa: The Kerebe and Long Distance Trade, 1800–1895* (New York, 1976), 80; *Cambridge History,* 5:273.
133  Burton, *Lake Regions,* 2:409; cf. Aitken, "Brass and Brass Manufactures," 309; Stanley, *Through the Dark Continent,* 249, 273; Emin Bey, *Société normande de géographie* (1879), 174, 263; J. L. Krapf, *Travels, Researches and Missionary Labours . . . in Eastern Africa* (London, 1860), *passim,* esp. 124.
134  Speke, *Sources of the Nile,* 19, 94, 200; Wilson and Felkin, *Uganda and the Egyptian Sudan,* 1:48.
135  Burton, *Lake Regions,* 2:410; Speke, *Sources of the Nile,* 94. Even beads had to be restrung to a precise length and cloth cut to precise measurements to be acceptable to the Masai: J. Thomson, *Through Masai Land* (London, 1885), 101.
136  Burton, *Lake Regions,* 1:145.
137  Speke, *Sources of the Nile,* app. B.
138  Thomson, *Masai Land,* 227.
139  Burton, *Lake Regions,* 1:150–51.
140  Marion Johnson, personal communication.
141  In *Les grandes voies maritimes dans le monde, XVe–XIXe siècles* (Paris, 1965), 195–201.
142  Newbury, "Sudan Trade," 233–46. Cf. Marion Johnson, "Calico Caravans: The Tripoli-Kano Trade after 1880," *JAH* 17, no. 1 (1976): 95–118.
143  Leo Africanus, *Description de l'Afrique,* trans. A. Epaulard, 2 vols. (Paris, 1956), 2:424.
144  Merrick Posnansky, "Archaeology, Technology and Akan Civilization," *JAS* 2 (1975): 32–33.
145  Mueller, *Die Africanische,* 149; Garrard, "Brass in Akan Society," 66. York speculates that the cuprous metals found at New Buipe in northern Ghana and dated to about the sixteenth century came from the north, since there is no evidence of European goods, with the possible exception of beads, which could also have come from the north: "Excavations at New Buipe," *WAJA* 3 (1973): 181. At this period, however, much the same goods were traded by both land and sea.
146  Sundström, *Exchange Economy,* 247. See, for example, R. Jobson, *The Golden Trade* (1623; Teignmouth, 1904), 117, 130. Dapper and Barbot's accounts of the desert trade are largely based on Marmol and therefore not very reliable in their own right.
147  J. L. Miège, *Le Maroc et l'Europe (1830–94),* 4 vols. (Paris, 1961–62), esp. 2:150–52, 3:86–87, 366.

148 James Grey Jackson, *An Account of the Empire of Marocco . . . and an Interesting Account of Timbuctoo, the Great Emporium of Central Africa* (London, 1814), 289–90; Auguste Beaumier, "Lettre de M. Auguste Beaumier," *Bulletin de la Société de géographie,* Sept. 1870, p. 366; Jacopo Gråberg de Hemso, *Spècchio geográfico e statístico dell'imperio di Marocco* (Genoa, 1832), 144–45; Oskar Lenz, "Voyage du Maroc au Sénégal," *Bulletin de la Société de géographie,* 7th series, 1 (1881): 217; Philip Curtin, *Africa Remembered* (Madison, Wis. 1967), 183; A. Adu Boahen, *Britain, the Sahara and the Western Sudan, 1788–1861* (London, 1964), 122.

149 L. G. Binger, *Du Niger au golfe de Guinée par le pays de Kong et le Mossi . . . 1887–1889,* 2 vols. (Paris, 1892), 1:79; 316, 320; 2:50, 92, 168; L. Tauxier, *Le noir du Soudan* (Paris, 1912), 516–17; idem, *Le noir du Bondouku* (Paris, 1921), 60; Muhammad Akbar, "The Samorian Occupation of Bondoukou: An Indigenous View," *IJAHS* 10 (1977): 243.

150 P. Staudinger, *Im Herzen der Hausaländer* (Berlin, 1889), 595–96.

151 Landolphe, *Mémoires,* 2:86; Ryder, *Benin,* 225.

152 Anene, 195; J. F. A. Ajayi, in Ajayi and Crowder, eds., *History of West Africa,* 2 vols. (London, 1974), 2:135; cf. Thurstan Shaw, "A Note on Trade and the Tsoede Bronzes," *WAJA* 3 (1973): 237.

153 Allen and Thomson, *Expedition to the River Niger,* 1:321.

154 Aitken, "Brass," 319.

155 Thomson, *Masai Land,* 579–80; Célis and Nzikobanyanka, *Métallurgie,* 165–66.

156 By mid-century some zinc was being imported into Africa for the local manufacture of brass, but until then virtually all brass was foreign-made.

157 Vogt, *Portuguese Rule,* 69.

158 Elphick, *Kraal and Castle,* 77–78.

159 Torday, *On the Trail,* 211–12.

160 Stanley, *Through the Dark Continent,* 2:286.

161 Schweinfurth, *Heart of Africa,* 1:202.

162 Vogt, *Portuguese Rule,* 69.

163 Speke, *Sources of the Nile,* app. B.

164 Dupont, *Lettres,* p. 340; G. Brouin, "Du nouveau au sujet de la question de Takedda," *NA,* no. 47 (July 1950): 91.

165 Vansina, *Tio Kingdom,* p. 272.

166 Candice Goucher, "Iron is Iron 'til It Is Rust: Trade and Ecology in the Decline of West African Iron-Smelting," *JAH* 22, no. 2 (1981): 179–90.

## CODA

1 Cited in Bancroft, *Mining in Northern Rhodesia,* 27.

2 Roan Antelope Mining Company, *Africans at RoanAntelope,* 3d ed. ([Luanshya], 1961), 16; Bradley, *Copper Venture* 28.

3 N. Lambert, "Exploitation minière et métallurgique protohistoriques du cuivre au Sahara occidentale" (Paper presented to the African Studies Associations of the United States and Canada, Montreal, 1969), 2.

4 Fripp, "An Engineer's Notes," 169.

5 De Hemptinne, *Mangeurs,* 24.

6 Warnier and Fowler, "Nineteenth-Century Ruhr," 329–51.

7 Pleigneur, "Extrait des notes," 276–80.

8 Marchal, "Renseignements," 16 ff.

9 De Hemptinne, *Mangeurs,* 34.

10 Livingstone, *Last Journals,* 373.

11 Timothy Garrard, "Akan Metal Arts," *African Arts* 13, no. 1 (Nov. 1979): 38.

12 Barth, *Travels,* 2:141.

13 See above, chap. 6.

14 Aitken, "Brass," 319.

15 [Hallet], "The Manilla Problem: Post Scriptum," *Statistical and Economic Review* 4 (1949): 59.

16 Frank Willett, "Baubles, Bangles and Beads: Trade Contacts of Medieval Ife" (Thirteenth Melville J. Herskovits Memorial Lecture, Edinburgh University, 1977), 14.

17 Fynn, *Diary,* 157–58.

18 F. I. Ekejiuba, "The Aro System of Trade in the Nineteenth Century," *Ikenga* 1, no. 2 (1972): 15.


**CHAPTER 8**

1 Philip Grierson, "The Origins of Money," *Research in Economic Anthropology* (1978), 8.

2 Marion Johnson, lecture, Yale University, 24 Oct. 1977.

3 D. F. Allen, "Wealth, Money and Coinage in a Celtic Society," in *To Illustrate the Monuments: Essays on Archaeology Presented to Stuart Piggott,* ed. J. V. S. Megaw (London, 1976), 208. For an excellent discussion of the issues raised in the study of African currencies, see Curtin, *Senegambia,* 233–37. Curtin emphasizes not only the importance of local and regional differences but also the necessity of taking historical change into account. Failure to do this has been a major weakness of economic anthropologists.

4 The two fragments of copper bar found at Kumadzulo (6th–7th century A.D.) may have been an early form of currency, but any generalization is obviously premature: Vogel, *Kumadzulo,* 36.

5 Bisson, "Copper Currency," 286–88; de Maret, "Sanga," 334–35; and idem, "L'évolution monétaire du Shaba central," 132–33.

6 Garlake, "Iron Age Sites," 31–32, 37–38, 42; Fagan, in Fagan et al., *Iron Age Cultures,* 2:102–3.

7 Garlake, "Iron Age Sites," 43; idem, *Great Zimbabwe,* 134.

8 Bisson, "Copper Currency," 285.

9 Dos Santos, in Theal, *Records of South-Eastern Africa,* 7:270.

10 De Maret, "Luba Roots," 233–34; and idem, "L'évolution monétaire," 117–49.

11 Arnot, *Garenganze,* 238.

12 Bisson, "Copper Currency," 284; Maggs, "Some Recent Radiocarbon Dates," 179; Malawi Department of Antiquities, *Kukumba Mbiri MuMalawi* (1973),

48, 71–72; pl. VII. I am grateful to David Killick for bringing this reference to my attention. See also E. Anciaux de Faveaux and P. de Maret, "Vestiges de l'âge de fer dans les environs de Lubumbashi," *Africa-Tervuren* 26 (1980): 13–19, concerning two types of ingot moulds found in undated contexts in this area.

13 De Hemptinne, *Mangeurs,* 8; A. Mahieu, "L'exploitation du cuivre par les indigènes au Katanga . . .," *Congo* 6 (1925): 112. Ladame claims that bars were also cast in the shape of a double *T,* reaching a length of 1.5 m and a width of 10 cm: "Le Droit," 690–91.

14 Livingstone, *Last Journals,* 1:265; cf. 2:179, where he puts the weight at 60–70 lbs.

15 David and Charles Livingstone, *Narratives of an Expedition to the Zambesi,* 508.

16 Verney Lovett Cameron, *Across Africa,* 2 vols. (London, 1877), 1:319–20; Thompson, "Ingots of Native Manufacture," 11; Monteiro, *Angola,* 1:270–71.

17 See, for example, Cameron and Thompson, n. 16 above; Cornet, "Mines de cuivre," 4; E. Verdick, *Les premiers jours au Katanga (1890–1903)* (Brussels, 1952), 132–33; Ladislaus Magyar, "Ladislaus Magyars Erforschungen von Inner-Afrika," *Petermanns Geographische Mitteilungen* 6 (1860), 227; Campbell, *Bantuland,* 119.

18 Vogel, cited in Bisson, "Copper Currency," 280.

19 De Hemptinne, *Mangeurs,* 26–29, 34–35. Cf. Campbell, *Bantuland,* 119.

20 Friede, "Notes on the Composition," 185.

21 Although Thompson's informants claimed that the musuku were made by peoples working copper on both sides of the Limpopo: Louis Thompson, "The Mu-tsuku," *SAJS* 35 (1938), 396.

22 Fripp, "An Engineer's Notes," 171.

23 Thompson, "Mu-Tsuku," 396–98.

24 B. H. Dicke, "A Bavenda Sacred Object," *SAJS* 23 (1926): 935–36. In fact, as Thompson observed, they most resemble the trunk of a baobab tree with its branches lopped off.

25 George W. Stow, *The Native Races of South Africa* (New York, 1905), ill. following 518.

26 Cited in Fripp, "An Engineer's Notes," 171.

27 R. H. Steel, "Ingot-Casting and Wire-Drawing in Iron Age Southern Africa," *JSAIMM* 75 (Nov. 1975), no pagination. Cf. Stanley, "Primitive Metallurgy," 738.

28 A. C. Haddon, "Copper Rod Currency from the Transvaal," *Man,* no. 65 (1908): 121–22; H. D. Hemsworth, "Note on Marali Currency," *Man,* no. 66 (1908): 122; Thompson, "Ingots," 13; H. Junod, "The Balemba of the Zoutpansberg (Transvaal)," *Folklore* 19 (1908): 280.

29 G. Lindblom, "Copper Rod 'Currency' from Palabora, N. Transvaal," *Man,* no. 90 (1926): 146; Hemsworth, "Note," 122.

30 Van der Merwe and Scully, "The Phalaborwa Story," 183.

31 Stayt, *BaVenda,* 67.

32 Ibid., 67–68. Cf. Thompson, "Mu-Tsuku," 396.

33 Hemsworth, "Note," 122.
34 Van der Merwe and Scully, "The Phalaborwa Story," 192.
35 See, for example, Haddon, "Copper Rod Currency," 121; Hemsworth, "Note," 122; Van der Merwe and Scully, 190; Stayt, *BaVenda,* 67.
36 *Ibn Battuta in Black Africa,* ed. and trans. Said Hamdun and Noël King (London, 1975), 58.
37 *Oxford English Dictionary; Larousse Classique.*
38 Mauny, *Tableau géographique,* 311; Bucaille, "Takadda," 772–73.
39 Bucaille, 750.
40 S. Bernus and P. Gouletquer, "Du cuivre au sel," 47–49 and fig. 16.
41 Mauny, *Tableau,* 312 and fig. 61. Mauny also summarizes the information about ingots found elsewhere in the southern Sahara. See, in addition, G. Brouin, "De nouveau au sujet de la question de Takedda," *NA,* no. 47 (1950): 90–91, for a description of the small bar of copper found at Annissamane.
42 Mauny, *Tableau,* 312–13.
43 Latham, "Currency, Credit and Capitalism," 599.
44 Dapper, *Naukeurige Beschrijvinghe,* 510.
45 John Morton, personal communication. Cf. Fynn's comment that the Zulu liked the mark of the hammer to appear on brass bracelets and necklaces to show that they were newly made: *Diary,* 273.
46 The Rev. Hope M. Waddell, *Twenty-Nine Years in the West Indies and Central Africa* (London, 1863), 247; A. J. H. Latham, *Old Calabar 1600–1891* (Oxford, 1973), 76–79; David Northrup, *Trade without Rulers: Pre-Colonial Economic Development in South-Eastern Nigeria* (Oxford, 1978), 163.
47 Bold, *African Guide,* 78; cf. Capt. Hugh Crow, *Memoirs of the Late Hugh Crow of Liverpool* (London, 1830), 283.
48 Latham, *Old Calabar,* 76–79. According to Aitken, the standard "Guinea rod" manufactured in Birmingham for export to the "Gold Coast" and Old Calabar was 3 feet long, of nos. 4 and 5 gauge wire, and packed in cases of 100: "Brass and Brass Manufactures," 319.
49 Jean Gabus, *L'art nègre* (Neuchâtel, 1967), 67.
50 P. A. Talbot, *Life in Southern Nigeria* (London, 1923), 319–20; Latham, *Old Calabar,* 29; Neaher, "Awka Who Travel," 362–63; Simon Ottenberg, "The Development of Credit Associations in the Changing Economy of the Afikbo Igbo," *Africa* 38 (1968): 239.
51 D. C. Dorward, "Pre-Colonial Tiv Trade and Cloth Currency," *IJAHS* 9 (1976): 583–85.
52 A. E. Afikpo, "Trade and Trade Routes in Nineteenth-Century Nsukka," *JHSN* 7, no. 1 (1973): 88.
53 Vansina, *Tio Kingdom,* 283.
54 Bentley, *Pioneering,* 2:44.
55 Pleigneur, "Extrait des notes," 280; Vansina, *Tio Kingdom,* 282–83; E. Maquet, *Outils de forge du Congo, du Rwanda et du Burundi* (Tervuren, 1965), 33; J.-F. Vincent, "Dot et monnaie de fer," *Objets et mondes* 3 (1963): 290; Coquery-Vidrovitch, *Brazza,* 68n; Cline, *Mining and Metallurgy,* 82.
56 Laman, *The Kongo,* 1:122–23.

57 Vansina, *Tio Kingdom,* 282.

58 T. Obenga, *La cuvette congolaise, les hommes et les structures* (Paris, 1976), 104–9 and pls. XXI, XXI *bis,* XXII, XXIX. Vansina points out that many currencies in this area took exotic shapes and were of iron: personal communication.

59 Coquery-Vidrovitch, *Brazza,* 336.

60 J. H. Weeks, *Among the Primitive Bakongo* (1914; New York, 1969), 202. See Vansina, *Tio Kingdom,* 285, chart 14: "Decline of the mitako in length: 1881–93." Curtin describes a similar decline in the weight of the iron-bar'currency in the Senegambia during the eighteenth century: *Senegambia,* 243–44.

61 Bentley describes these rods as 21 inches long and 0.18 inches in diameter, equivalent to no. 7 gauge wire: *Pioneering,* 2:230, 334. Other writers give the diameter as 2–5 mm: Vansina, 285. Like the Calabar "black coppers," they were generally bent double and tied together in bundles of ten.

62 Weeks, *Bakongo,* 202, and Vansina, *Tio,* 285.

63 Obenga, *Cuvette,* 109; Vansina, *Tio,* 285; Sautter, *De l'Atlantique,* 1:375n2; Weeks, *Bakongo,* 213.

64 Vansina, *Tio,* 286–87.

65 Ibid., 288–89; Coquery-Vidrovitch, *Brazza,* 315, 462, 470–71; Johnston, *The River Congo,* 153; Bentley, *Pioneering,* 2:333.

66 Al-Bakri, *Description de l'Afrique septentrionale,* trans. M. de Slane (Paris, 1965), 325.

67 Shaw, *Igbo-Ukwu,* 1:160–68; 2: pls. 309–23; Connah, *Archaeology of Benin,* 142.

68 [Bill Hallet], "The Manilla Problem," United Africa Company Ltd. *Statistical and Economic Review* 3 (Mar. 1949): 44.

69 Vogt, "Portuguese Gold Trade," 94.

70 Strieder, *Aus Antwerpener Notariatsarchiven,* 452–53.

71 K. Ratelband, *Vijf dagregisters van het kasteel São Jorge da Mina (Elmina) aan de Goudkust (1645–1647)* (The Hague, 1953), xcviii. Cf. Dapper, *Naukeurige Beschrijvinghe,* 501.

72 Grant-Francis, *Smelting of Copper,* 27n.

73 Aitken, *Early History of Brass,* 5.

74 Ibid., 49; idem, "Brass and Brass Manufactures," 313.

75 R. F. A. Grey, "Manillas," *The Nigerian Field* 14 (1951): 54. The 1948 analysis of the *okpoko* manilla gave the following results, in percentages: copper, 62.68; lead, 30.05; bismuth, 0.05; arsenic, 0.65; antimony, 2.81; tin, 2.05; zinc, 0.98; nickel, 0.48. Other chemical analyses in this century have all shown a composition of roughly 65 percent copper and 25 percent lead, but some have turned up as much as 8 percent tin and traces of silver and gold, as well as 6 percent antimony.

76 John Morton, personal communication.

77 Aitken, "Brass and Brass Manufacture," 49–50. Iron manillas also circulated on the Ivory Coast: "Afrique: Les monnaies indigènes de la côte d'Ivoire," *La géographie* 21 (1910): 209; and in the eighteenth century on the Gambia: Francis Moore, *Travels into the Inland Parts of Africa* (London, 1738), 128.

78  I am grateful to M. E. Elechi, Senior Ethnographer, Federal Department of Antiquities, Port Harcourt, Nigeria, and to D. H. Griffin, UAC International, for information on the metal content of manillas.
79  Elechi, personal communication.
80  Griffin, personal communication.
81  In Talbot, *Peoples of Southern Nigeria,* 3:875–76. See also Johansson, *Nigerian Currencies,* for a useful summary of sources about the manilla.
82  Grey, "Manillas," 56.
83  Mary Kingsley, *West African Studies* (London, 1899), 82.
84  *La géographie* 21 (1910): 209.
85  O. O. Amogu, "The Introduction into and the Withdrawal of Manillas from the 'Oil Rivers' as seen in the Ndoki District," *Nigeria Magazine* 38 (1952), *passim.*
86  Talbot, *Life in Southern Nigeria,* 132; K. C. Murray, "Pottery of the Ibo of Ohuhu-Ngwa," *Nigerian Field* 37 (1972): 150; Grey, "Manillas," 63–65.
87  Grey, 57.
88  [Hallet], "The Manilla Problem," 46 ff.
89  Lichtenstein, *Travels,* 417; Alberti, *Xhosa,* 71; Fynn, *Diary,* 270; Sundström, *Exchange Economy,* 209; A. J. H. Goodwin, "Some Copper Weapons from Katanga," *SAJS* 32 (1935): 476–78. Kakanda copper dagger and axe, used as currencies: Pitt-Rivers Museum, Oxford; cf. copper spear and dagger, Cambridge Archaeology and Ethnography Museum, 1908 E.91 and 92.
90  Al-'Umari, in *Corpus of Early Arabic Sources for West African History,* trans. J. F. P. Hopkins, ed. and annot. N. Levtzion (Cambridge, 1981), 260; *Cambridge History of Africa,* 3:278; Barth, *Travels,* 2:310; "Capt. Percival's Surveys in the Bahr el-Ghazal Province," *Geographical Journal* 30 (1907): 606; Schweinfurth, *Heart of Africa,* 2:372; M. Posnansky, "Kilwa: An Islamic Trading City on the East African Coast," *IJAHS* 11 (1978): 501.
91  Martin, *External Trade,* 645; Monteiro, *Angola,* 1:9; George Brooks, *Yankee Traders, Old Coasters and African Middlemen* (Brookline, Mass., 1970), 283–84.
92  Coquery-Vidrovitch, *Brazza,* 77, 208, 253.
93  See, for example, Marquis de Compiègne, *L'Afrique equatoriale: Gabonais, Pahouins-Gallois* (Paris, 1876), 237; G. Kaptein, "Familieleven en zeden bij de inboorlingen van den Evenaar," *Congo* 3 (1922): 542–43; H. Deschamps, *Traditions orales et archives au Gabon* (Paris, 1962), 55, 107; Walker, *Notes d'histoire du Gabon,* 122; Burton, *Gorilla-Land,* 1:75–76; E. Anderson, *Contribution à l'ethnographie des kuta,* 2 vols. (Upsala, 1953, 1974), 1:101, 141.
94  Bisson, "Copper Currency," 285.
95  Latham, "Currency," 601, 604–5.
96  Dos Santos, in Theal, *Records,* 7:270.
97  Talbot, *Peoples of Southern Nigeria,* 3:877–79.
98  Weeks, *Bakongo,* ill. opp. 202.
99  In P. N. Davies, *Trading in West Africa, 1840–1920* (London, 1976), 51.
100 Vansina, *Tio,* 288 and chart 15. See also Harms, *River of Wealth,* 86 ff. Cf. Curtin, *Senegambia,* 237–40.

101 F. I. Ekejiuba, "The Aro Trade System in the Nineteenth Century," *Ikenga* 1, no. 1 (1972): 16.

102 Ibid., 23. In this case the fact that the payment consists of "one of each" plus multiples of four undoubtedly has ritual significance: see Curtin's interesting discussion of gift-giving in *Senegambia,* 287 ff.


## CHAPTER 9

This chapter is based on extensive study of museum collections and special exhibitions, in particular those of the Musée de l'Homme (Paris), the Museum of Mankind (London), the Smithsonian Institution (Washington), the Brooklyn Museum, the Field Museum (Chicago), the Museum of Cultural History (University of California at Los Angeles), the Detroit Institute of Arts, the Musée Ethnographique de Neuchâtel (Switzerland), and the Pitt-Rivers Museum (Oxford).

1 See, for example, the journal of the *James,* Royal Africam Company, June 5, 1675 (PRO t/70 1211; I am grateful to Marion Johnson for this reference); Adams, *"Sketches,"* 35; Crow, *Memoirs,* 250–51; Martin, *External Trade,* 14; Deschamps, *Traditions,* 30; Sundström, *Exchange Economy,* 233. Alagoa, however, disputes the nineteenth-century European accounts that derived the name "Brass," applied to the Nembe kingdom, from the huge basins imported for salt-making; in fact, he claims there is no local memory of such basins: "Long-distance Trade and States in the Niger Delta," *JAH* 11, no. 3 (1970): 325.

2 Dapper, *Naukeurige Beschrijvinghe,* 481; Crow, *Memoirs,* 253–54; Sundström, *Exchange Economy,* 233.

3 Dapper, 481; Mueller, *Die Africanische,* 149; Sundström, 233. Cf. Landolphe, *Mémoires,* 1:98.

4 Burton, *Lands of Cazembe,* 63.

5 Abbé Proyart, *Histoire de Loango, Kakongo, et autres royaumes d'Afrique* (Paris, 1776), 14. Cf. Monteiro's description of drying manioc on sheets of copper or iron above a woodfire in the region of Luanda: *Angola,* 1:159–60.

6 See, for example, Phillips, in Donnan, *Documents,* 1:404; K. Ratelband, ed., *Vijf dagregisters van het kasteel São Jorge da Mina (Elmina) aan de Goudkust (1645–1647)* (The Hague, 1953), VI; Sundström, *Exchange Economy,* 233; Deschamps, *Traditions,* 80.

7 Garrard, *Akan Weights,* 130, 143.

8 See, for example, A. A. de Andrade, *Relações de Moçambique setecentista* (Lisbon, 1955), 334–35; P. de Marees, "Description of Guinea," in *Purchas His Pilgrimes,* 20 vols. (Glasgow, 1905), 6:302; Barbot, "Description," 5:154–55 and *passim;* Dapper, *Naukeurige Beschrijvinghe,* 483; Bosman, *Coast of Guinea,* 74, 82–83; George E. Brooks, *Yankee Traders, Old Coasters and African Middlemen* (Brookline, Mass., 1970), 239. Adams wrote (*Sketches,* 105): "I have heard of those, who, depending on their own judgement, have brought to England, what they conceived to be boxes of [gold] and which, on inspection, proved to be almost wholly the filings taken from brass pans."

9 De Hemptinne, *Mangeurs,* 30.

10  Herodotus, *The Histories,* trans. A. de Selincourt (Hammondsworth, 1954), 299.

11  R. J. Forbes, *Metallurgy in Antiquity* (Leiden, 1950), 327.

12  *Géographie d'Edrisi,* trans. A. Jaubert, 2 vols. (Paris, 1836), 1:5–6.

13  M. F. de Figueroa, in Centro de estudos ultramarinos, *Documents,* 3:591.

14  Pacheco Pereira, *Esmeraldo,* 132.

15  Quoted in C. S. Lancaster and A. Pohorilenko, "Ingombe Ilede and the Zimbabwe Culture," *IJAHS* 10 (1970): 11.

16  Quoted in Goodwin, "Metal Working," 48.

17  Blake, *Europeans in West Africa,* 2:343.

18  Paludanus, in *Het Itinerario,* 7.

19  Du Chaillu, *Exploration,* 9.

20  Bentley, *Pioneering,* 2:69; Johnston, *Grenfell and the Congo,* 2:585, 588. Cf. Courboin, "Populations de l'Alima," 277 ff.; and Wannyn, *L'art ancien,* 49.

21  Coquilhat, *Haut Congo,* 154.

22  Harms, *River of Wealth,* 192.

23  A. T. Gutersohn, "Het Economisch Leven van den Mongo-Neger," *Congo* 1 (1920): 97. Concerning the heavy jewelry worn in Cabinda and Angola, see Monteiro, *Angola,* 1:52; and A. O. Saldanha da Gama, *Memória sobre as colônias de Portugal situadas na costa ocidental de Africa* (Paris, 1839), 84.

24  C. H. Stigand, *The Land of Zinj* (London, 1913), 222; Burton, *Gorilla-Land,* 1:70–71; and idem, *Lake Regions,* 1:150–51. Cf. Campbell, *Bantuland,* 141; J. C. Okello-Oloya, "Acholi Costume," *UJ* 36 (1972): 53; Wilson and Felkin, *Uganda and the Egyptian Sudan,* 1:41.

25  George Célis, The Decorative Arts in Rwanda and Burundi," *African Arts* 4, no. 1 (Autumn 1970): 42.

26  Campbell, *Bantuland,* 142. Cf. The Rev. John Campbell, *Travels in South Africa . . . Second Journey,* 2 vols. (1822; London, 1967), 1:124, for a description of a woman at Old Lattakoo wearing fifty copper rings on her arm.

27  De Marees, in *Purchas,* 6:364–65.

28  Talbot, *Peoples of Southern Nigeria,* 2:395–96, 405; G. T. Basden, *Among the Ibos of Nigeria* (1921; London, 1966), 91–92.

29  See, for example, the pieces in the Jos Museum, Nigeria. I am very grateful to Nancy Neaher for sharing her extensive files on brasswork of the Benue-Cameroon area with me, as well as those collected by Tim Chappel.

30  Lt. Lalouel, "Les forgerons mondjombo," *Bulletin de l'Institut d'études centrafricaines* 2 (1947): 113. Cf. Degrandpré, *Voyage,* 1:74; Monteiro, *Angola,* 1: 52; Burton, *Gorilla-Land,* 1:70–71; Coquilhat, *Haut Congo,* 151.

31  Livingstone, *Missionary Travels,* 187.

32  Dapper, *Naukeurige Beschrijvinghe,* 510; Shaw, *Igbo-Ukwu, passim.*

33  See, for example, the Tiv bracelets in the Pitt-Rivers Museum (Oxford), and Arnold Rubin, "Notes on Regalia in Biu Division, North-Eastern State, Nigeria," *WAJA* 4 (1974): 161–75. Cf. Hutchinson, *Narrative of the Niger,* 146, 172, concerning the diffusion of brass wire jewelry into the interior from Old Calabar.

34  Margaret Trowell, *African and Oceanic Art* (New York, 1968), 214, ill. 222.

35  A. J. Arkell, "The Double Spiral Amulet," *Sudan Notes and Records* 20 (1937): 151-55.

36  Maggs, *Southern Highveld,* 122; Burchell, *Travels,* 2:566-67; S. Daniell, *African Scenery and Animals* (London, 1804-5), 37-38.

37  F. R. Rodd, *People of the Veil* (London, 1926), 57; M. Dupire, "Contribution à l'étude des marques de propriété du bétail chez les pasteurs peuls," *JSA* 24 (1954), 129.

38  See, for example, Joseph Thomson, *Through Masai Land* (London, 1885), 422; Herbert M. Cole, "Vital Arts in Northern Kenya," *African Arts* 7, no. 2 (Winter 1974): 19. Cf. Du Chaillu's description of the Fan earrings, which were so heavy that a finger could pass through the hole they made: *Exploration,* 75.

39  Vienna, Museum für Völkerkunde, no. 3, 69. Cf. J. C. Froehlich, "Les Konkomba du Nord-Togo," *BIFAN* 11 (1949): 420, for Konkomba head ornaments.

40  See, for example, the collection of head ornaments in the Museum of Cultural History, University of California at Los Angeles.

41  Dupont, *L'Afrique équatoriale: Okanda,* 146; idem, *L'Afrique équatoriale: Gabonais, Pahouins-Gallois* (Paris, 1872), 158; Du Chaillu, *Exploration,* 67.

42  Stanley, *Through the Dark Continent,* 1:90-91, 141. Cf. V. L. Cameron, *Across Africa,* 2 vols. (London, 1877), 1:95-98, for Gogo use of copper and brass on their heads and hair.

43  See esp. Goodwin, "Metal Working," 47-49; Ruth E. Gordon and Clive J. Talbot, eds., *From Dias to Vorster: Source Material on South African History 1488-1975* (Goodwood, Republic of South Africa, n.d.), 63, 69; Le Vaillant, *Voyage,* 1:194, 2:96, 161-62; Campbell, *Travels,* 2:302; Burchell, *Travels,* I:291.

44  Barth, *Travels,* 4:292.

45  See, for example, Willett, *Ife,* 105; Jan Vansina, "*Ndop*: Royal Statues among the Kuba," in *African Art and Leadership,* ed. Douglas Fraser and Herbert M. Cole (Madison, Wis., 1972); Chokwe standing and seated figures, UCLA; Pascal Imperato, "The Dance of the Tyi Wara," *African Arts* 4, no. 1 (Autumn 1970), cover and 78-79. Cf. Marilyn H. Houlberg, "Ibeji Images of the Yoruba," *African Arts* 7, no. 1 (Autumn 1973), fig. 2; Sakata (Congo) figure with brass rings, Smithsonian.

46  Glaze, *Art and Death,* pl. 38.

47  Robin Horton, "Notes on Recent Finds of Brasswork in the Niger Delta," *Odu* 2, no. 1 (July 1965): 77-91, esp. pl. 1.

48  Wannyn, *L'art ancien,* 27.

49  See esp. the collections of the Musée de l'Homme.

50  See esp. Warren Robbins, *African Art in American Collections* (New York, 1966), figs. 72, 72a; René Bravmann, *West African Sculpture* (Seattle, 1970), 32; and the statues in the Musée du Centre des Sciences Humaines, Abidjan, Ivory Coast, many of which are illustrated in B. Holas, *Arts traditionnels* (Ceda, 1967), and idem, *Craft and Culture in the Ivory Coast* (Paris, 1968).

51  M. Posnansky, "Brass Casting," 298. Cf. A. Kyerematen, *Panoply of Ghana* (London, 1964), 89.

52  M. and F. Herskovits, "The Art of Dahomey, I: Brasscasting and Appliqué

Cloths," *American Magazine of Art,* Feb. 1934, 67–68; cf. Bravmann, *West African Sculpture,* 46.

53 Garrard, *Akan Weights,* chaps. 9–10.
54 On Senufo brass casting, see esp. Glaze, *Art and Death,* 34–40, chap. 2 *passim,* 130; and also G. Bochet, "Les masques senoufo, de la forme à la signification," *BIFAN* 27 (1965): 662; and G. Clamens, "Le serpent en pays senoufo," *NA,* no. 56 (1956): 14.
55 Sultan Njoya, *Histoire et coutumes des bamum,* trans. H. Martin (Dakar, 1952), dates the introduction of brass casting into Bamum to the reign of Mbuembue, i.e., earlier in the nineteenth century.
56 R. F. Thompson, "African Influence on the Art of the United States," in *Black Studies in the University,* ed. A. L. Robinson, C. S. Foster, and D. H. Ogilvie (New Haven, 1969), 148.
57 A Boom (Kuba) "masque cloche" in the Musée des Arts Océaniens et Africains (Paris) has thin copper sheets over the forehead and mouth and strips rounded over the cheeks. The copper is overpainted brown so that it looks like wood.
58 Some writers differentiate Marka from Bambara masks, in fact, by the layer of metal hammered onto the surface of the wood: Robert Goldwater, *Bambara Sculpture from the Western Sudan* (New York, 1960), 17; Franco Monti, *African Masks* (London, 1969), 20.
59 F. M. Olbrechts, *Les arts plastiques du Congo belge* (Brussels, 1959), 77. An exceptional statue is entirely of forged copper: pl. 211.
60 Joseph Cornet, *A Survey of Zairian Art* (Raleigh, N.C., 1978), pl. 159.
61 Ibid., pl. 101.
62 Alain and Françoise Chaffin, *L'art kota* (Meudon, 1979).
63 L. Perrois and G. Pestmal, "Note sur la découverte et la restauration de deux figures funéraires kota-mahongwe (Gabon)," *Cahiers* de l'Orstom, série, sciences humaines, 8 no. 4 (1971): 367–86. See also E. Herbert, "Images of the Ancestors: the Bwété of the Mahongwe" (Paper presented to the ASA, Philadelphia, 1980).
64 M.-L. Bastin, "Un masque en cuivre martelé des Kongo du nord-est de l'Angola," *Africa-Tervuren* 7, no. 2 (1961–62): 31–34; H. Baumann, *Afrikanische Plastik und Sakrales Königtum* (Munich, 1969), 29.
65 Thompson, *Black Gods and Kings,* chap. 3, p. 5, figs. 12–15.
66 Stanley, *Through the Dark Continent,* 2:145.
67 Tamara Northern, *The Ornate Implement* (Hanover, N.H., 1981), 3–4.
68 Barbot, "Description," 5:38.
69 Richard Andrée, "Seltene Ethnographica des stadtischen Gewerbe-Museums zu Ulm," *Baessler-Archiv* 4 (1913): 34–35.
70 See, for example, the comparative exhibits of the Pitt-Rivers Museum, Oxford, and the Musée Océanien, Paris; C. Singer, E. J. Homyard, and A. R. Hall, *A History of Technology,* 3 vols. (Oxford, 1954), 1:618; Jean Herbert, *La mythologie hindoue* (Paris, 1953), pl. XXIX.
71 Curt Morgen, *Durch Kamerun von Süd nach Nord* (Leipzig, 1893), 200.
72 G. Lienhardt, *Divinity and Experience* (Oxford, 1961), 252–53.

73 Schweinfurth, *Heart of Africa*, 2:110.
74 See S. Passarge, *Adamaua* (Berlin, 1895), 440-41.
75 See, for example, Travassos Valdez, *Six Years*, 1:212; Mary Kingsley, *Travels in West Africa* (London, 1898), 204; Monteiro, *Angola*, 1:143; L. Van de Velde, "La région du Bas-Congo et du Kwilou-Niadi," *Bulletin de la Société royale belge de géographie* 10 (1886): 376; Coquery-Vidrovitch, *Brazza*, 103n; Victor Turner, *Lunda Rites and Ceremonies*, Rhodes-Livingstone Museum Occasional Papers (1953), 41.
76 Ryder, *Benin*, 321; Sundström, *Exchange Economy*, 199.
77 L. Siroto, "The Face of the Bwiiti," *African Arts* 1, no. 3 (Spring 1968): 86.
78 Francis Galton, *Narrative of an Explorer in Tropical South Africa . . .* (London, 1889): 136.
79 Carl Mauch, "Reisen im Inneren von Süd-afrika, 1865-72," *Petermanns Geographische Mitteilungen* 8, Ergänzungsheft 37 (1874): 47.
80 Stanley, *Through the Dark Continent*, 2:308.
81 Quoted in C. van Overberghe, *Les basonge* (Brussels, 1908), 223. Cf. Frobenius, *Voice of Africa*, 1:14, about the technical and esthetic perfection of Songye weapons.
82 Vansina, *Tio Kingdom*, 156.
83 Leo Africanus, *Description de l'Afrique*, trans. A. Epaulard, 2 vols. (Paris, 1956), 1:237-38.
84 Muhammad ibn 'Umar al-Tunisi, *Voyage au Ouaday* (Paris, 1851), 396-97.
85 A. E. Robinson, "The Arab Dynasty of Dar For (Darfur)," *JAS* 30 (1929): 67.
86 M.-J. Tubiana, *Survivances pré-islamiques en pays zaghawa* (Paris, 1964), 35-36, 182-83; idem, "Danses zaghawa," *Objets et mondes* 6, no. 4 (1966): 290-91.
87 A. J. Lush, "Kiganda Drums," *UJ* 3, no. 1 (1935): 14; Wilson and Felkin, *Uganda and the Egyptian Sudan*, 1:216.
88 *Cambridge History of Africa*, 1:388.
89 De Marees, *Description of Guinea*, 6:338, 343.
90 In H. Ling Roth, *Great Benin: Its Customs, Art and Horrors* (Halifax, 1903), 80. Cf. Du Chaillu, *Exploration*, 201.
91 Schweinfurth, *Heart of Africa*, 2:38.
92 Robert G. Armstrong, "A Possible Function for the Bronze Roped Pot of Igbo-Ukwu," *WAJA* 4 (1974): 177-78.
93 Viviana Pâques, "Origine et caractères du pouvoir royal au Baguirmi," *JSA* 37 (1967): 190-91.
94 J. Lombard, "L'intronisation d'un roi bariba," *NA*, no. 62 (April 1954): 45-47; D. F. Heath, "Bussa Regalia," *Man* 37 (1937), 77-80.
95 In Thomas Hodgkin, *Nigerian Perspectives* (Oxford, 1960), 77-80.
96 M. Palau-Marti, *Le roi-dieu au Benin* (Paris, 1964), 38.
97 *Annual Report*, Musée Ethnographique de Neuchâtel, 1966, 66.4.66.
98 Wilson and Felkin, *Uganda*, 1:216.
99 Bravmann, *West African Sculpture*, 56.
100 Van Warmelo, *Copper Miners*, 27.
101 Gilberto Freyre, *The Masters and the Slaves*, trans. S. Putnam (New York, 1956), 317.

102 Matthews, *Voyage to the River Sierra Leone,* 105.
103 See, for example, *La vie du Sahara,* exhibition catalogue, Musée de l'Homme (Paris, 1960), 76, and the Cambridge University Museum of Archaeology and Ethnology: Bagam (Malcolm).
104 Dapper, *Naukeurige Beschrijvinghe,* 540.
105 In Churchill, *Voyages,* 6:217, 239.
106 Jean Rouch, "Le culte des génies," *JSA* 15 (1945): 29.
107 Cole, "Vital Arts," 19. Italics mine.
108 B. Lembezat, *Kirdi: Les populations paiennes du Nord-Cameroun* (n.p., 1950), 97.
109 John Janzen, personal communication.
110 Chinua Achebe, *Things Fall Apart* (London, 1958), 107.
111 De Marees, *Description of Guinea,* 6:338.
112 Wilson and Felkin, *Uganda,* 1:290–91.
113 *Vie du Sahara,* 63; Holas, *Craft and Culture,* 127.
114 R. G. Clough, *Oil River Trader* (London, 1972), 80–161.
115 See esp. Neaher, "Igbo Metalsmithing," 146–47.
116 Degrandpré, *Voyage,* 1:71.
117 Barbot, "Description," 5:383.
118 Kenneth Murray, "Idah Masks," *Nigerian Field,* 14, no. 3 (1949): 86; Holas, *Craft and Culture,* 127, fig. 32; Robbins, *African Art,* figs. 62, 63.
119 C. K. Meek, *A Sudanese Kingdom* (London, 1931) opp. 134; R. Burton, *Gorilla-Land,* 1:67–68.
120 G. Rouget, "Notes et documents pour servir à l'étude de la musique yoruba," *JSA* 35 (1965): 67–107; G. Dieterlen and Z. Ligers, "Notes sur les tambours-de-calebasse en Afrique occidentale," *JSA* 33 (1963): 258.
121 A. Kyerematen, *Panoply of Ghana,* 24.
122 R. S. Rattray, *Ashanti* (Oxford, 1923), 289.
123 A. Kyerematen, "The Royal Stools of Ashanti," *Africa* 39 (1967): 2–3.
124 See esp. Nancy Neaher, "Nigerian Bronze Bells," *African Arts* 12, no. 3 (May 1979): 42–47, 95. Peek comments that clapperless bells sounded by striking other metal, not by being struck internally by a clapper: "Isoko Bronzes and the Lower Niger Bronze Industries," *African Arts* 13, no. 4 (August 1980): 64.

## CHAPTER 10

1 Daniel Biebuyck, "Textual and Contextual Analysis in African Art Studies," *African Arts* 8, no. 3 (Spring 1975): 50.
2 Denise Paulme, in E. de Rouvre, *Parures africaines* (Paris, 1956), 23–24.
3 Anita J. Glaze, "Senufo Ornament and Decorative Arts," *African Arts* 12, no. 1 (Nov. 1978): 63.
4 Betty Gubert, "Three Songye and Kongo Figures," *African Arts* 15, no. 1 (Nov. 1981): 46.
5 Gutersohn, "Het Economisch Leven," 92–105.
6 G. Célis and E. Nzikobanyanka, *La métallurgie traditionnelle au Burundi: Techniques et croyances* (Tervuren, 1976), 182. Cf. Wilhelm Blohm, *Die Nyam-*

*wezi,* 3 vols. (Hamburg, 1931), 2:87; Vedder, *South West Africa,* 68; Burton, *Gorilla-Land,* 1:70–71.

7 Wannyn, *L'art ancien,* 48.

8 G. Loyer, *Relation du voyage au royaume d'Issiny* (Paris, 1714), 156.

9 Célis and Nzikobanyanka, *Métallurgie,* 170; cf. Burton, *Gorilla-Land,* 1:71; Campbell, *Bantuland* (London, 1922), 142; Gerald Hartwig, *The Art of Survival: The Kerebe and Long-Distance Trade, 1800–1895* (New York, 1976), 114. Jacques Maquet comments that "in Rwanda, the wives of great chiefs wear ornaments in copper which recall the horns [of cattle] and their walk has a bovine rhythm": *Afrique* (Paris, 1962), 158.

10 Heinrich Vedder, "The Herrero," in his *The Native Tribes of South West Africa* (Cape Town, 1928), 182. Cf. Eberhard Fischer and Hans Himmelheber, *Die Kunst der Dan,* Museum Rietberg (Zurich: 1976), 177.

11 Livingstone, *Last Journals,* 304. On the other hand he noted with admiration that in the case of the female slaves in Tippu Tip's caravan, "the many pounds' weight of fine copper leglets seemed only to help the sway of their walk": ibid., 241.

12 Elphick, *Kraal and Castle,* 166–68.

13 Vedder, *South West Africa,* 219.

14 Moffat, *Missionary Labours,* 248.

15 Coquilhat, *Haut Congo,* 154; Stanley, *Through the Dark Continent,* 2:319–20.

16 Nadel, *Black Byzantium,* 363.

17 C. de Chavannes, *Le Congo français* (Paris, 1937), 390; cf. Lichtenstein, *Travels in Southern Africa,* 1:336–37; G. Tams, *A Visit to the Portuguese Possessions in Southwestern Africa,* trans. H. Evans, 2 vols. (London, 1845), 1:124.

18 M. J. and F. S. Herskovits, "The Art of Dahomey, I: Brasscasting and Appliqué Cloths," *American Magazine of Art,* Feb. 1934, 70. In the Cameroon grasslands, brass pipes were a comparable gift exchanged among royalty: Chilver, "Nineteenth-Century Trade in the Bamenda Grassfields," 241.

19 Barbot, "Description," 5:349.

20 B. Holas, *Arts Traditionals, Musée de la Côte d'Ivoire* (Ceda, 1967), pl. 7; Neaher, "Igbo Metalsmithing Traditions," 121. Brass was a standard gift to northern Nguni chiefs in the late eighteenth and early nineteenth centuries: Fynn, *Diary,* 2, 77, 195.

21 Bravmann, *West African Sculpture,* 48.

22 E. C. Chubb, "The Zulu Brass Armlet 'Ingxota'," *Man,* Nov. 1936, 185.

23 Möller, *Journey to Africa,* 126 and ill. facing 83. Compare the Mangbetu sabres illustrated by Schweinfurth (*Artes Africanae,* pl. XVIII, fig. 8): the holes in the blade hold copper knobs, the number of these indicating the rank the owner holds in the army.

24 See, for example, Allen and Thomson, *Expedition to the River Niger,* 1:232, on the daughters of the *atta* of Idah. See also the Verre chiefs pictured in the Jos Museum.

25 Sultan Njoya, *Histoire et coutumes des bamum,* trans. H. Martin (Dakar, 1952), 130.

26 See esp. H. Baumann and L. Vajda, "Bernhard Ankermanns völkerkundliche

Aufzeichnungen im Grasland von Kamerun, 1907–1909," *Baessler-Archiv,* n.s.
7 (1959): 236, 262, 303; H. Baumann, *Afrikanische Plastik und sakrales Königtum* (Munich, 1969), 23, 25; Bravmann, *West African Sculpture,* 64; P. Har-
ter, "Four Bamileke Masks: An Attempt to Identify the Style of Individual
Carvers or Their Workshops," *Man,* Sept. 1969, 416; "Bamenda Brass," *Nigeria* 55 (1957): 348; F. Thorbecke, *Im Hochland von Mittel-Kamerun,* pt. 3
(Hamburg, 1919), 51 ff.; Roy Sieber, *Sculpture of Black Africa* (Los Angeles,
1968); and Tamara Northern and Leonard Kahan, personal communication.

27 C. Tardits, "Panneaux sculptés bamoun," *Objets et mondes* 2, no. 4 (1962):
253. On Benin, see esp. Paula Ben-Amos, *The Art of Benin* (New York, 1980),
and Willett, *Ife,* 162–63; for Nupe, see Nadel, *Black Byzantium,* 270; for
Dahomey, Paul Mercier, "Evolution de l'art dahoméen," *Présence africaine*
10, no. 1 (1950): 185–87, and M. and F. Herskovits, "Brasscasting," 68.

28 See esp. A. F. C. Ryder, "A Reconsideration of the Ife-Benin Relationship,"
*JAH,* 6, no. 1 (1965): 34–35, but also Arnold Rubin, "Bronzes of the Middle
Benue," *WAJA* 3 (1973).

29 Shaw, *Igbo-Ukwu,* 1:268–70 and *passim.*

30 E. A. Alpers, "Trade, State and Society among the Yao in the Nineteenth Century," *JAH* 10, no. 3 (1969): 410.

31 Roberts, "Nyamwezi Trade," 25, 62; Van Warmelo, *Copper Miners,* 65.

32 Stayt, *BaVenda,* 25, 62; Van Warmelo, 65.

33 Robinson, *Khami Ruins,* 110, 114, 152–54.

34 G. Gutzeit, "La fonte de la monnaie (croisettes) chez les baluba du territoire
de Musonoï (Haut-Katanga Ouest)," *Archives suisses d'anthropologie générale*
7, no. 1 (1934): 74 ff.

35 Vansina, *Children of Woot,* 65, 191.

36 Torday, *On the Trail,* 156, 179–80, 192. Certain notables were entitled to wear
hatpins of red copper: Vansina, *Children of Woot,* 133.

37 Torday, *On the Trail,* 156.

38 Célis and Nzikobanyanka, *Métallurgie,* 5–13, 168. Njoya also refers to a lance
with a blade of copper and a knife of copper which were apparently part of
the Bamum regalia: *Bamum,* 128. See the associations of copper with kingship and blacksmithing paraphernalia in Vansina, *Children of Woot,* 50–51,
121.

39 Schweinfurth, *Heart of Africa,* 2:43.

40 Reefe, *Rainbow,* 86, 92. Note Reefe's description of the royal ceremony, known
as "striking the anvil," which recalls that the royal ancestor introduced iron-
smelting to the area: p. 82.

41 Nadel, *Black Byzantium,* 72–74.

42 Willett, *Ife,* 172.

43 For a summary of the controversy surrounding the provenance of the Tsoede
bronzes, see esp. Douglas Fraser, "The Tsoede Bronzes and Owo Yoruba Art,"
*African Arts* 8, no. 3 (Spring 1975): 30–35.

44 Egharevba, *Benin,* 12.

45 Personal communication.

46 In Ryder, "Reconsideration," quotation p. 26. Concerning the wide use of

brass crowns analogous to the Benin "headpiece of shining brass," see R. F. Thompson, "The Sign of the Divine King," *African Arts* 3, no. 3 (Spring 1970).

47 Ben-Amos, *Art of Benin.*

48 See, for example, Speke, *Sources of the Nile,* 405–6; Stanley, *Through the Dark Continent,* 1:205; Sir John Gray, "The Diaries of Emin Pasha–Extracts I," *UJ* 25, no. 1 (1961): 6; and 16, no. 1 (1962): 78–79; Lush, "Kikanda Drums," 14; Hamo Sassoon, *Guide to Kasubi Tombs* (Kampala, 1970). Cf. Wilson and Felkin, *Uganda and the Egyptian Sudan,* 1:202, and the ceremonial knife attributed to Kabaka Mwanga in the Wilson Museum, Dartmouth College.

49 I. K. Katoke, *The Making of the Karagwe Kingdom* (Nairobi, 1970), 24; Speke, *Sources of the Nile,* 202, 206.

50 Stanley, *Dark Continent,* 1: 460, 473–74.

51 Katoke, *Karangwe Kingdom,* 24.

52 H. Sassoon, "Iron Cows and Copper Spears: The Royal Insignia of Karagwe," *UJ* 34, no. 2 (1970): 200. Cf. Trowell, *African and Oceanic Art,* 241.

53 Vansina, *Children of Woot,* 49–51, 121. The anvil has remained one of the symbols essential to Kuba government, and miniature anvils were sewn into the tops of caps. According to Vansina, anvils also figured with Tio *nkobi,* the secret boxes of the lords which enhanced their power: *Tio Kingdom,* 326.

54 Reefe, *Rainbow,* 77.

55 Cited in Randles, *Ancien royaume du Congo,* 143.

56 G. P. Murdock, *Africa* (New York, 1959), 35: 14.

57 Joseph Mertens, *Les chefs couronnés chez les bakongo orientaux* (Brussels, 1942), 68 ff.

58 See esp. Van de Velde, "Région du Bas-Congo," 374–75; Wannyn, *L'art ancien,* 51–52, pl. XXIX: Obenga, *Cuvette congolaise,* 41–42. Randles notes the confusion in the European sources on this score. De Barros says the Kongo *nlunga* or royal bracelet was made of copper at the time of the first Portuguese embassies, while Ruy de Pina claims it was of ivory, and a text of 1624 describes it as iron: p. 48.

59 Basden, *Among the Ibos,* 256–61; V. C. Uchendu, *The Igbo of Southeast Nigeria* (New York, 1965), 83.

60 Neaher, "Igbo Metalsmithing," 139–40; idem, "Nigerian Bronze Bells," 45.

61 Horton, "Finds of Brasswork," 83.

62 T. J. Hutchinson, *Impressions of Western Africa* (London, 1858), 141–42; Talbot, *Peoples of Southern Nigeria,* 3:786; D. Forde, *Efik Traders of Old Calabar* (New York, 1956), 138–39.

63 Janzen, personal communication. See also idem, *The Quest for Therapy in Lower Zaire* (Berkeley, 1978), 24, 45–46.

64 J. Janzen and W. MacGaffey, *Anthology of Kongo Religions* (Lawrence, Kansas, 1975), 96–97

65 Deleval, "Tribus kavati," 174.

66 Janzen and MacGaffey, *Anthology,* 97–106, quotation 102; Deleval, 261. The Royal Ethnographic Museum in Leiden has a casting mould of clay for a bracelet from Boma which could have been used for Lemba bracelets, except that

Deleval is quite specific about the preparation of sand moulds. See J. Marquart et al., *Ethnographisch Album van het Stroomgebied van den Congo* (The Hague, 1904–16), series 2, no. 11, p. 68.

67  Thompson, *Black Gods and Kings,* chap. 6, pp. 1–2.

68  On Ogboni, see in addition to Thompson, chap. 6, Denis Williams, "The Iconology of the Yoruba *Edan Ogboni,*" *Africa* 24 (1964): 139–66, and idem, *Icon and Image,* 237–42; P. Morton-Williams, "The Yoruba Ogboni Cult," *Africa* 30, no. 4 (1960): 34–40; Robert Smith, "Yoruba Armament," *JAH* 8, no. 1 (1967): 93; L. E. Roache, "Psychophysical Attributes of the Ogboni Edan," *African Arts* 4, no. 2 (Winter 1971): 48–53. There may be a parallel to the three-ness of Ogboni in the Kulango representation of the earth as a three-headed snake: Labouret, "Le mystère des ruines du Lobi," 196. See also Talbot, *Peoples of Southern Nigeria,* 2:45, who claims that among the Aro Ibo, the earth is typified by three stones enclosing a small square, the fourth side of which is occupied by an old currency rod.

69  Dennis M. Warren, "Bono Royal Regalia," *African Arts* 8, no. 2 (Winter 1975): 16.

70  M. D. McLeod, *The Asante* (London, 1981), chap. 9 and *passim;* P. Ozanne, in Shinnie, *African Iron Age,* 61; and R. Silverman, "A Vestige of the Trans-Saharan Gold Trade" (Paper presented to the ASA, Bloomington, Ind., 1981).

71  M. Posnansky, *Origins of West African Trade* (Accra, 1971), 7–8. Cf. Binger, *Du Niger,* 2: 223, concerning a similar legend about a copper kettle in Anno country.

72  C.-H. Perrot, "Ano Asema: Mythe et histoire," *JAH* 15, no. 2 (1974): 202.

73  J. R. Anquandah, "An Archaeological Survey of the Techiman-Wenchi Area," in Goody and Arhin, eds., *Ashanti and the Northwest* (Legon, 1965).

74  M. Johnson, personal communication.

75  Posnansky, *West African Trade,* 7–8; Eva Meyerowitz, *The Sacred State of the Akan* (London, 1951), 49; *British Museum Quarterly* 8 (1933): 52.

76  Eva Meyerowitz, *Akan Traditions of Origin* (London, 1952), 47 and 95 *nl.*

77  Warren, "Bono Royal Regalia," 18.

78  Meyerowitz, *Sacred State,* 133.

79  Warren, "Bono Royal Regalia."

80  Silverman, "Vestige"; Meyerowitz, *Sacred State,* 48.

81  Rattray, *Ashanti,* 142, 147.

82  Ibid., 99–100, 128, 145–49, 177, 199–200, 210; and idem, *Religion and Art in Ashanti* (Oxford, 1927), 127, 179–80. Cf. H. M. Cole, "The Art of Festival in Ghana," *African Arts* 8, no. 3 (Spring 1975), 17 and fig. 7; and McLeod concerning the large basin serving as a "market fetish" in Kumasi: *Asante,* 52.

83  Rattray, *Religion and Art,* 113–14, 150. Cf. T. E. Bowdich, *Mission from Cape Coast Castle to Ashantee,* 3rd ed. (London, 1966), 278–79, 280, 284, 289, 297.

84  Ozanne, in Shinnie, *African Iron Age,* 52, 57.

85  De Marees, *Description of Guinea,* 6:261. Cf. Anquandah, "Survey," 128.

86  Landolphe, *Mémoires,* 2:55. There are a number of descriptions from various parts of West Africa of the use of copper basins and plates to adorn or to hold the head of a corpse: see, for example, Talbot, *Life in Southern Nigeria,*

157; Vansina, *Tio,* 209; C. K. Meek, *Tribal Studies in Northern Nigeria,* 2 vols. (London, 1931), 1:187–88; M. Jackson, "Sacrifice and Social Structure among the Kuranko," *Africa* 47, no. 2 (1977): 136*n16.*

87 J. Delange, *Arts et peuples de l'Afrique noire* (Paris, 1967), 56.

88 Rattray, *Ashanti,* 313–15.

89 J. Delange, "Un *kuduo* exceptionnel," *Objets et mondes* 5, no. 3 (1965): 202; Rattray, *Ashanti,* 128.

90 H. Gundert, cited in Sundström, *Exchange Economy,* 233.

91 See, for example, John Duncan, *Travels in Western Africa in 1845 and 1846,* 2 vols. (London, 1847), 1:253; Matthews, *Voyage to the River Sierra Leone,* 66–67, 134; J. Sorie Conteh, "Mining and Secret Societies," *Kroniek van Afrika* 2 (1972): 205; Landolphe, *Mémoires,* 1:98, 118, 125–26; Ryder, *Benin,* 67, 202; J. S. Boston, *The Igala Kingdom* (Ibadan, 1968), 199–200, 204, 221; "Efik Dances," *Nigeria* 53 (1957): 151; Ekejiuba, "Preliminary Notes," 14–15; Philippa Payne, "Calabar Coronation," *Nigerian Field* 19, no. 2 (April 1954): 95–96; Burton, *Gorilla-Land,* 1:82.

92 Shaw, *Igbo-Ukwu,* 1:131, pls. 249, 250.

93 Ibid., 1:268–70.

94 William Bascom, *Ifa Divination* (Bloomington, Ind., 1969), 29–30, 31, 34.

95 Rouch, *Religion et magie songhay,* 291–92. The handle of the sabre forms the motif on the cover of his book.

96 Célis and Nzikobanyanka, *Métallurgie,* 177.

97 Charles Jeannest, *Quatre années au Congo* (Paris, 1886), 113; J. L. Krapf, *Travels, Researches and Missionary Labours in Eastern Africa* (London, 1860), 76–77.

98 A. Dim Delobsom, *Les secrets des sorciers noirs* (Paris, 1934), 41–42.

99 Yves Person, "Un cas de diffusion: Les forgerons de Samori et la fonte à la cire perdue," *Revue française d'histoire d'outremer* 54, no. 194 (1967): 219–26.

100 G. Clamens, "Les nyi-kar-yi de Watyene (senufo du cercle de Korhogo)," *NA,* no. 60 (Oct. 1953): 108–10; Glaze, *Art and Death,* 22.

101 Glaze, 54–79, pls. 24–27.

102 Paulme, *Sculptures,* 12.

103 R. F. Thompson, personal communication.

104 Bravmann, *West African Sculpture,* 62.

105 See, for example, Musée de l'Homme D.67.163.493 (Collection Hartmann); R. Wente-Lukas, *Die materielle Kultur der nicht-islamischen Ethnien von Nord Kamerun und Nordostnigeria* (Wiesbaden, 1977), 129; Lembezat, *Kirdi,* 80.

106 W. S. Simmons, "The Supernatural World of the Badyaranke of Tonghia (Senegal)," *JAS* 37, no. 1 (1967): 58.

107 Wannyn, *L'art ancien,* 58.

108 Jean Gabus, *Au Sahara,* 2 vols. (Neuchâtel, 1955–58), 2:45.

109 Ibid., 2:95.

110 "Some Yoruba Customs," *Nigerian Field* 14, no. 3 (1949): 115.

111 Y. Cissé, "Notes sur les sociétés des chasseurs malinke," *JSA* 34 (1964), 175–226.

112 Cambridge University Museum of Archaeology and Ethnology: Sara (Nar) *nunga do,* 75-5 A/B.

113 Neaher, "Nigerian Bronze Bells," 45.

114 On the *pinces amulettes,* see esp. B. Holas, "Pince amulette des guerzé (Haute-Guinée française)," *NA,* no. 48 (Oct. 1950): 123-34; G. Szumoski, "Notes sur la grotte préhistorique de Bamako," *NA,* no. 58 (April 1953): 39; J. Daget and M. Konipo, "La pince-amulette chez les bozo," *NA,* no. 51 (July 1951): 80-81; H. Miner, *The Primitive City of Timbuctoo,* rev. ed. (New York, 1965), 109-12, 309; Patrick McNaughton, "The Bamana Blacksmiths," (Ph.D. diss., Yale University, 1977), 146-47.

115 "Some Yoruba Customs," *Nigerian Field* 14, no. 2 (1949): 78, and 14, no. 3 (1949): 114-15; Labouret, "Ruines des lobi," 195-96; G. Clamens and A. Adandé, "Poignard et haches de parade de cuivre senufo ancien," *NA,* no. 58 (April 1953): 49; A. Lériche, *NA,* no. 60 (Oct. 1953): 116, citing Appia.

116 Schweinfurth, *Artes Africanae,* 2:figs. 1, 3, 7, 10. Cf. E. Torday and T. A. Joyce, *Notes ethnographiques sur des populations habitant les bassins du Kasai et du Kwango oriental* (Brussels, 1922), 35, 103, 194, 213, 331, 332; Lucienne Chapoix, "Les anneaux en cuivre jaune au Bas-Congo," *Africa-Tervuren* 5, no. 1 (1959): 75; Edwin W. Smith and A. M. Dale, *The Ila-speaking Peoples of Northern Rhodesia,* 2 vols. (London, 1920), 1:101-2.

117 Wannyn, *L'art ancien,* 51 and pl. XXIX.

118 Hornimann Museum (London), 25.117.

119 James Thomson, *Through Masai Land* (London, 1885), 442, ill. Cf. C. H. Stigand, *The Land of Zinj* (London, 1913), 222, 248, 251.

120 P. Imperato, "Songoni Koun," *African Arts* 14, no. 2 (Feb. 1981): 43.

121 Delange, *Arts et peuples,* 43.

122 Geoffrey Parrinder, *African Mythology* (London, 1967), 78.

123 See, for example, C. Béart, "Sur les bassari de Haute-Gambie," *NA,* no. 49 (Jan. 1951): 4; and B. Holas, "Aspects modernes de la circoncision rituelle et l'initiation ouest-africaines," *NA,* no. 49 (Jan. 1951): 5.

124 Basden, *Among the Ibos,* 73-74, 92, ill. 89; Talbot, *Peoples of Southern Nigeria,* 2:395-96, 405.

125 Talbot, 2: 408; Neaher, "Igbo Metalsmithing," 138; Forde, *Efik Traders,* 62.

126 Anders Sparrman, *A Voyage to the Cape of Good Hope . . . 1772-1776,* new ed. (Cape Town, 1975), 90 and footnote.

127 Célis and Nzikobanyanka, *Métallurgie,* 169.

128 Van de Velde, *Région du Bas-Congo,* 375.

129 De Marees, in *Purchas,* 6:269-70.

130 M. Dupire, "Contribution à l'étude des marques de propriété du bétail chez les pasteurs peuls," *JSA* 24 (1954): 129.

131 Tubiana, *Survivances pre-islamiques,* 35-36.

132 Idem, "Une coiffure d'apparat," *Objets et mondes* 8, no. 2 (1968): 129-43. This coiffure may be extremely old: two rock paintings at Ennedi seem to depict something similar to the mamur.

133 Edwin Ardener, *Coastal Bantu of the Cameroons* (London, 1956), 100-101, and personal communication.

134 Delange, *Arts et peuples,* 58-59.

135  R. Kauenhoven-Janzen, "Chokwe Thrones," *African Arts* 14, no. 3 (May 1981): 72–73.
136  See esp. the examples in the Musée de l'Homme and the Brooklyn Museum. Sometimes, as in the case of the nimba in the Art Institute of Chicago, the metal has been removed, leaving a pattern of verdigris. On the nimba, see B. Thiam, "'Nimba' déesse de la fécondité," *NA*, no. 108 (Oct. 1956): 128–30.
137  Binger, *Du Niger*, I: 250; Leonard Kahan, personal communication.
138  Vansina, *Tio*, 272. Cf. examples in the Brooklyn Museum and in *Detroit Collects African Art*, exhibition catalogue, Detroit Institute of Arts (1977), no. 166.
139  Hutchinson, *Impressions*, 147–48; Talbot, *Peoples of Southern Nigeria*, 3:488, 506, 509, 513; idem, *Life in Southern Nigeria*, 149, 199; Vansina, *Tio*, 209–212. Cf. Coquilhat, *Haut Congo*, 64, 172; Burton, *Gorilla-Land*, 2:124; Boteler, *Voyage of Discovery*, 2:386–87.
140  Fagan, in Fagan et al., *Iron Age Cultures*, 2: chap. 5.
141  Pierre de Maret, "L'évolution monétaire du Shaba central entre le 7e et le 18e siècle," *African Economic History* 10 (1981): 138–39.
142  Grey, "Manillas," 63–66; Talbot, *Life in Southern Nigeria*, 139–40; D. Forde, in *Essays on the Ritual of Social Relations*, ed. Forde et al. (Manchester, 1962), 116.
143  Grey, 66.
144  Aitken, *Early History of Brass*, 59–60. Neaher cites Partridge's description of a royal coffin made of brass plates by local smiths for the *atta* of Igala: "Igbo Metalsmithing," 120.
145  Anna Rein-Wuhrmann, *Mein Bamumvolk im Grasland von Kamerun* (Stuttgart, 1925), 55–56.
146  See, for example, M. Littlewood, in M. McCulloch, M. Littlewood, and I. Dugast, *Peoples of the Central Cameroons* (London, 1954), 125, and "Basoga Death and Burial Rites," *UJ* 2, no. 2 (1934): 122; Coquilhat, *Haut Congo*, 64; Vansina, *Tio*, 209–212; Talbot, *Peoples of Southern Nigeria*, 3:506.
147  C. Pairault, "Boum Kabir (Chad) en présence de la mort," *JSA* 34, no. 1 (1964): 149.
148  R. F. Thompson, personal communication.
149  Forde, *Efik Traders*, 23–24.
150  Grey, "Manillas," 66; cf. the Kalabari Abbonema torque in the Pitt-Rivers Museum, Oxford. Cf. also de Marees in *Purchas*, 6: 343; and Coquilhat, *Haut Congo*, 168.
151  Laman, *The Kongo*, 1:71.
152  N. Neaher, "Igbo Metalsmiths," *African Arts* 19, no. 4 (July 1976): 48.
153  Peek, "Isoko Bronzes," 63–64.
154  Willett, *Ife*, 26–27.
155  A. Dim Delobsom, *L'empire du Mogho-Naba* (Paris, 1932), 134–35.
156  On the bwété, see esp. Siroto, "Face of the Bwiiti"; L. Perrois, "Note sur les figures du bwété des kota-mahongwe (Gabon): Réponse à L. Siroto," *African Arts* 2, no. 4 (Winter 1969): 65–67; idem, "Redécouverte d'un style africain: Le 'bwété' des mahongwe du Gabon," ORSTOM, Libreville, 1966; and "Le bwété des kota-mahongwe," ORSTOM, Libreville, 1969; also Alain and Fran-

çoise Chaffin, *L'art kota* (Meudon, 1979); and E. Herbert, "Images of the Ancestors: The Bwété of the Mahongwe" (Paper presented to the ASA, Philadelphia, 1980).

157 L. Siroto, "Witchcraft Belief in the Explanation of Traditional African Iconography," in *The Visual Arts: Plastic and Graphic,* ed. J. Cordwell (New York, 1979), *passim,* esp. 250–54.

158 Edwin Ardener, "Witchcraft, Economics and the Continuity of Belief," in *Witchcraft, Confessions and Accusations,* ed. Mary Douglas (London, 1971).

159 Bastin, "Masque en cuivre martelé," 31–34.

160 T. K. Seligman, "African Art at the de Young Museum," *African Arts* 7, no. 4 (Summer 1974): 20–22, fig. 1; Sieber, *Sculpture of Black Africa.*

161 Joseph Cornet, *Art of Africa* (New York, 1971), 171.


**CHAPTER 11**

1 Schweinfurth, *Heart of Africa,* 2: 43–45, 87, 99. Cf Johnston, *Grenfell and the Congo,* 2 vols. (New York, 1910), 2:536.

2 Schweinfurth, 2: 45.

3 Willett, *Ife,* 22, 50, 70, 105.

4 L. Chapoix, "Les anneaux," 75; T. Northern, *The Sign of the Leopard: Beaded Art of the Cameroon* (Storrs, Conn., 1975), *passim;* Deschamps, *Traditions,* 80, 88, 97, 100, 104.

5 Vansina, *Tio Kingdom,* 219, 235–36, 318, 386–87; G. P. Hagan, "A Note on Colour Symbolism," *Research Review* 7, no. 1 (1970): 8–14.

6 John Janzen, introduction to A. Fu-Kiau kia Bunseki-Lumanisa, *N-Kongo ye Nza Yakun'zungidila: Le mukongo et le monde qui l'entourait* (Kinshasa, 1969), 6–7, 120, 123.

7 Anita Jacobson-Widding, *Red-White-Black as a Mode of Thought* (Uppsala, 1979), *passim,* quotation 179.

8 Victor Turner, "Color Classification in Ndembu Ritual," in *The Forest of Symbols* (Ithaca, N.Y., 1967).

9 Jackson, "Sacrifice and Social Structure," *Africa* 49, no. 2 (1977): 123–39. Cf. D. Zahan, "Les couleurs chez les bambara du Soudan français," *NA,* no. 50 (April 1950): 52–56; A. I. Richards, *Chisungu* (London, 1956); and Brenda E. F. Beck, "Colour and Heat in South Indian Ritual," *Man, JRAI* 4 (1969): 553–72.

10 Torday, *On the Trail,* 212; Lt. Lalouel, "Les Forgerons mondjoumbo," *Bulletin de l'Institut d'études centrafricaines* 2 (1947): 112.

11 Cole, "Art of Festival," 17 and fig. 1.

12 Lush, "Kiganda Drums," 14.

13 Battell, in *Purchas His Pilgrimes,* 6:385.

14 Ben-Amos, *Art of Benin,* 15.

15 L. Frobenius, *Die atlantische Götterlehre* (Jena, 1926), 124, 131; P. Verger, *Notes sur le culte des orisa et vodun à Bahia . . .* (Dakar, 1957), 305, 311–12; M. Palau-Marti, *Le roi-dieu au Bénin* (Paris, 1964), 160, 187; A. Adandé, *Les récades des rois du Dahomey* (Dakar, 1962), 18–19, 85–87; J. Delange, "Sur un oshe

shango," *Objets et mondes* 3, no. 3 (1963): 205–6; D. Crowley and D. Ross, "The Bahian Market in African-Influenced Art," *African Arts* 15, no. 1 (Nov. 1981): 60; Rouch, *Religion et magie songhay*, 161. The Detroit Institute of Arts has a heavy cast-brass wand of Shango. Similar ones are found in Dahomey.

16 Thompson, *Black Gods and Kings,* chap. 3, pp. 5–6, chap. 20, p. 2.

17 Vansina, *Children of Woot,* 275. Cf. Dapper's comments that the shiniest copper rods were considered the best: *Naukeurige Beschrijvinge,* 510.

18 Murray, "Idah Masks," 86.

19 R. F. Thompson, lecture, Yale University, 17 Feb. 1972.

20 Germaine Dieterlen, "Les sociétés initiatiques bambara" (Course given at the École des Hautes Études, section VI, Sorbonne, Paris, 1968–69).

21 Vansina, *Tio Kingdom,* 199–200.

22 G. Célis and E. Nzikobanyanka, *La métallurgie traditionnelle au Burundi* (Tervuren, 1976), 172.

23 G. Dieterlen, *Essai sur la religion bambara* (Paris, 1951), 153.

24 See, for example, Clémence Sugier, *Symboles et bijoux traditionnelles de Tunisie* (Tunis, 1969), 8; and E.A.T. W. Budge, *Amulets and Talismans* (New Hyde Park, N.Y., 1961), 30, 215.

25 Tubiana, *Survivances pré-islamiques,* 182–83.

26 Gabus, *Au Sahara,* 2:94–95.

27 G. Dieterlen and Z. Ligers, "Notes sur les tambours-de-calebasse en Afrique occidentale," *JSA* 33, no. 2 (1963): 258.

28 Dieterlen, *Religion bambara,* 67–68; D. Zahan, *La dialectique du verbe chez les bambara* (Paris, 1963), 24. Cf. H. Zemps, "Poupées des filles dan excisées," *Objets et mondes* 6, no. 3 (1966): 245, concerning Mande influence on the Dan.

29 A. J. Arkell, "The Double Spiral Amulet," *Sudan Notes and Records* 20 (1937): 151–55.

30 C. H. Stigand, *The Land of Zinj* (London, 1913), 248.

31 Rouch, *Religion et magie songhay,* 168.

32 Verger, *Notes sur le culte,* 477.

33 Marcel Griaule, *Dieu d'eau: Entretiens avec Ogotemmêli* (Paris, 1966), 75–76. The following section is from the same source, quotations on 77, 115. In addition to the work by Griaule's students, two superb dissertations have added immeasurably to our understanding of the cultural and cosmological context of two Bamana (Bambara) art forms, ironworking and mud cloth: Patrick McNaughton, "The Bamana Blacksmiths" (Ph.D. diss., Yale, 1977), and Sarah Brett-Smith, "Iron Skin: The Symbolism of Bamana Mud Cloth" (Ph.D. diss., Yale, 1982). Fisher Nesmith has drawn parallels between Dogon sculptures and the creation myth, but they remain speculative, since the antiquity and origins of these bronzes are very uncertain: "Dogon Bronzes," *African Arts* 12, no. 2 (Feb. 1979).

34 Dieterlen, *Religion bambara, passim,* but esp. 41–44, 49, 51, 53, 151, 166, 204, 223. Other societies share this interdiction against crossing water while wearing copper, or more generally, anything red: see Meek, *Sudanese Kingdom,* 291; Burton, *Gorilla-Land,* 1:140; Du Chaillu, *Exploration,* 135. In con-

trast, Doutté cites the North African belief that when the Arabic letter *t* is written 400 times on a leaf of brass, it provides protection against drowning: E. Doutté, *Magie et religion en Afrique du nord* (Alger, 1909), 236.

35 G. Dieterlen, "Le génie des eaux chez les bozo," *JSA* 12 (1942): 150 ff.; Rouch, *Religion,* 67, 80, 157–63, 266; and idem, "L'étude des pêcheurs sorkawa," *Africa* 20 (1950): 21; J.-P. and A. M. Lebeuf, *Les arts des sao,* 78–79. Cf. Delange, *Arts et peuples,* 38.

36 C. Monteil, *La légende du ouagadou et l'origine des soninke,* Mélanges ethnologiques, Mémoires de l'IFAN, no. 23 (Dakar, 1953), 371–72.

37 Ulli Beier, "Oshun Festival," *Nigeria,* no. 53 (1957): 170–87; Verger, *Notes sur le culte,* pl. 110. See also the Oṣun cult furniture of hammered brass in the American Museum of Natural History.

38 Verger, 403, 409–12; William R. Bascom, "The Yoruba in Cuba," *Nigeria* 37 (1951): 15; R. F. Thompson, "Abatan," in *Tradition and Creativity in Tribal Art,* ed. D. Biebuyck (Los Angeles, 1969), 146, 149.

39 Robin Horton, "Notes on Recend Finds of Brasswork in the Niger Delta," *Odu,* 2 (1965): 72.

40 Ibid., *passim;* E. J. Alagoa, "Oprozo and Early Trade on the Escravos: A Note on the Interpretation of Oral Tradition of a Small Group," *JHSN,* 7 (1969): 155.

41 Peek, "Isoko Bronzes," 60–66.

42 Horton, "Recent Finds," 89.

43 Martha Anderson, personal communication and paper presented to the ASA Meetings, Bloomington, Ind., Oct. 1982. Cf. Herskovits' comment that in Dahomey brass is identified with the white man: *American Magazine,* 1934, 70.

44 Ben-Amos, *Art of Benin,* 45–46, and personal communication. Cf. Frobenius, *Voice of Africa,* 1: 306, and G. Parrinder, *African Mythology* (London, 1967), 83.

45 Jan Vansina, personal communication. There are other suggestive associations of copper and water elsewhere in Bantu Africa: among the Bomitaba of equatorial Africa, for example, the "femmes de l'eau," believed to have been possessed by the spirits of the family dead, encircle their arms with spiral copper bracelets: Darre and Le Bourhis, "Notes sur la tribu bomitaba," *Bulletin de la Société des recherches congolaises,* no. 6 (1926): 34. Some of the spears of Dinka masters of the fishing spear have shafts almost entirely overwound with coils of copper (or more recently of aluminum) wire: G. Lienhardt, *Divinity and Experience* (Oxford, 1961), 252–53.

46 Zdenka Volavka, "Insignia of the Divine Authority," *African Arts* 14, no. 3 (May 1981): 43–51.

47 A. Kirk-Greene, "A Note on Some Spears from Bornu, Northern Nigeria," *Man* 63 (Nov. 1963): 174–75.

48 Stayt, *BaVenda,* 260–61; J. Eberhart, "Quelques aspects du mariage chez les venda," *JSA* 25 (1955): 87. Cf. Randles, *L'ancien royaume du Congo,* 44, 47, 49.

49 Dieterlen, *Religion bambara,* 49; G. Calame-Griaule, *Ethnologie et langage* (Paris, 1965), 267–68; A. Maesen, personal communication.

50 Cline, *Mining and Metallurgy,* 80, citing Trevor.

51 Wilson Museum, Dartmouth College.

52 Speke, *Sources of the Nile,* 292.

53 Garrard, *Akan Weights,* 277 ff.; and idem, "A propos," *African Arts* 15, no. 4 (Aug. 1982): 27, 78.

54 Judith Weston and Meryl Johnson, "Benin Bronze Preservation," *African Arts* 8, no. 4 (Summer 1975): 50–51 and fig. 2. An armlet in the Museum of Mankind (1944.Af.4.26) is of cast brass or bronze with inset animals of red copper, but it may be a relatively modern piece.

55 See, for example, the animal-head pectorals in the Pitt-Rivers Museum, Oxford.

56 Ben-Amos, personal communication.

57 Schweinfurth, *Heart of Africa,* 1: 132 and ill.

58 Miner, *Primitive City of Timbuctoo,* 112.

59 Blohm, *Die Nyamwezi,* 2: Tafel 12.

60 Williams, *Icon and Image,* 84 and fig. 41.

61 Hans Witte, review of exhibition, in *African Arts* 10, no. 1 (Oct. 1976): 75; Williams, 84; Thompson, *Black Gods,* chap. 7, pp. 1–2.

62 Williams, *Icon and Image,* 104.

63 Ogboni incantation quoted ibid., 18–19.

64 Bascom, *Ifa Divination,* verse 35–36.

65 Ben-Amos, *Art of Benin,* 15, 64.

66 Boston, *Igala Kingdom,* 199–200, 204.

67 Ibid., 215; Ben-Amos, *Art of Benin,* 49, 51.

68 Zahan, *Dialectique,* 26.

69 N. J. van Warmelo, ed., *Contributions towards Venda History, Religion and Tribal Ritual* (Pretoria, 1950), 43.

70 M.-H. Morel, "Essai sur l'épee touareg de l'Ahaggar (takouba)," *Travaux de l'Institut de recherches sahariennes* 2 (1941): 130–36, 138, 158. Italics his.

71 Ibid.

72 Gabus, *Au Sahara,* 2:45, 48, 92–96, 240–54. See the fine collection of Tuareg tools and utensils in the Musée d'Ethnographie, Neuchâtel, Switzerland, as well as the objects illustrated in the *Vie du Sahara* exhibition catalogue (Paris, 1963). Cf. Ernest Kühnel, *Islamische Kleinkunst* (Braunschweig, 1963), 134.

73 P. S. Garlake, "Iron Age Burials at Mount Hampden, Near Salisbury, Rhodesia," *Arnoldia* 3, no. 10 (1967): 5–6.

74 Jacobson-Widding, *Red-White-Black,* 144, 154.

75 Jean Rouch, "Le culte des génies," *JSA* 15 (1945): 29. Cf. V. Pâques, *Les bambara* (Paris, 1954), 79–80.

76 John Miller Chernoff, *African Rhythm and African Sensibility* (Chicago, 1979), 159.

## CONCLUSION

1 Cline, *Mining and Metallurgy,* 11. Cf. Paulme, *Sculptures,* 17.

2 Speke, *Sources of the Nile,* 341.

3 See, for example, Pelletier, *Mineral Resources, passim;* De Kun, *Mineral Re-*

*sources of Africa, passim;* M. T. W. Morgan, *East Africa* (New York, 1969), 259; V. Thompson and R. Adloff, *Emerging States of French Equatorial Africa* (Palo Alto, 1960), 242–44.

4 Philip Curtin, "The Lure of Bambuk Gold," *JAH* 14, no. 4 (1973); Garrard, *Akan Weights,* 146–48.

5 Dos Santos, in Theal, *Records,* 7:274, 275, 277; cf. ibid., 379: account by Senhor Ferão; Burton, *Lands of Cazembe,* 23.

6 Robinson, *Khami Ruins,* 8; Fripp, "An Engineer's Notes," 178.

7 Pelletier, *Mineral Resources,* 21, 268. Cf. J. F. Schofield, "The Ancient Workings of Southeast Africa," *NADA,* no. 3 (1952): 5–12.

8 Cyr Descamps. "L'archéologie et l'histoire en Afrique de l'ouest," AUDECAM Documents pédagogiques audio-visuels, (Paris, 1977): 26–31; idem, "Sites protohistoriques de la Sénégambie," *Annales de la Faculté de lettres et sciences humaines de Dakar* 9 (1980): 303–13 (I am grateful to Merrick Posnansky for supplying me with copies of these articles); S. K. and R. J. McIntosh, *Prehistoric Investigations;* Timothy F. Garrard, "Myth and Metrology: The Early Trans-Saharan Gold Trade," *JAH* 23, no. 4 (1982): 443–62.

9 Cadamosto, *The Voyages of Cadamosto and Other Documents on Western Africa in the Second Half of the Fifteenth Century,* trans. and ed. G. R. Crone (London, 1937), 68; D. P. Gamble, *The Wolof of Senegambia* (London, 1957), 39, 73, 103; A. Pruneau de Pommegorge, *Description de la Nigritie* (Paris, 1789), 122, 123.

10 B. Appia, "Notes sur le génie des eaux en Guinée," *JSA* 14 (1944).

11 Dieterlen, *Religion bambara,* 41–42.

12 Zahan, *Dialectique,* 24–25.

13 M. Griaule, *Dieu d'eau: Entretiens avec Ogotemmêli* (Paris, 1966), 102–3.

14 Pâques, *Les bambara,* 79–80.

15 J.-P. and A. Lebeuf, *Les arts des sao,* 78–79.

16 E. Meyerowitz, *The Sacred State of the Akan* (London, 1951), chap. 12, "Gold."

17 J. de Barros, "De Asia," in Cadamosto, *Voyages,* 114ff.

18 Garrard, *Akan Weights,* 3–4, 279; P. E. H. Hair, "Some Minor Sources for Guinea, 1519–1559: Enciso and Alfonce/Fonteneau," *History in Africa* 3 (1976): 32.

19 See Garrard, chaps. 2–3.

20 Ivor Wilks, "A Medieval Trade Route from the Niger to the Gulf of Guinea," *JAH,* 3, no. 2 (1962), 337 *et seq.*

21 J. Hippisley, *Essays on the African Trade* (London, 1764), 40; Barbot, "Description," 5:234.

22 Ibid.

23 Johnson, "The Ounce," 204–5; E. Reynolds, *Trade and Economic Change on the Gold Coast, 1807–1874* (London, 1974), 9. Gold was also demanded for slaves on the Whydah coast at this time, and came to be used at the court of Dahomey, but never on the same scale as in Aşante: D. Henige and M. Johnson, "Agaja and the Slave Trade: Another Look at the Evidence," *History in Africa* 3 (1976): 62–64.

24 Garrard, *Akan Weights,* 6, 24, 38.

25 Ibid., 46.

26 Rattray, *Ashanti,* 9. It is hard to know how to interpret the 1740 report that natives in the Egwira region considered it "fetish" to use copper in seeking for gold, "though iron is good": Garrard, 143. It is instructive to compare the Kongo experience with the Aşante. After their conversion to Christianity, the king and court adopted Portuguese fashions and with them a taste for gold jewelry. Subsequently, in an attempt to evade the ritual requirement of investiture with the copper *ngunda* of Ngoyo, a Kongo claimant to the throne requested crowns from the king of Portugal and the Pope. The latter obliged with a gold crown in 1648, but Volavka emphasizes that this was never called *ngunda,* being known rather by words that are a distortion of the Portuguese *coroa.* Neither the crown nor gold in any form was sacralized in Kongo belief. Volavka, "Insignia of the Divine Authority," 51.

27 al-ʿUmari, *Masalik el Absar fi Mamalik el Amsar,* trans. and ed. Gaudefroy-Demombynes (Paris, 1927), 202.

28 Karl Marx, *Contribution to the Critique of Political Economy,* extract in *Marxism and Art,* ed. M. Solomon (Detroit, 1979): 65.

29 V. L. Cameron, *Across Africa,* 2 vols. (London, 1877), 2:329.

30 Susan Vogel, personal communication.

31 *Cambridge History of Africa,* 3:278.

32 Joseph Miller, *Kings and Kinsmen: Early Mbundu States in Angola* (Oxford, 1976), 63.

33 John Janzen, personal communication.

34 Mertens, *Les chefs couronnés,* 82 n1.

35 Harris, *Copper King,* 9–10.

36 R. M. Ogilvie, *The Romans and Their Gods* (London, 1970), 14–15.

# BIBLIOGRAPHY

## UNPUBLISHED SOURCES

### Dissertations

Brett-Smith, Sarah Catharine. "Iron Skin: The Symbolism of Bamana Mud Cloth." Ph.D. diss., Yale University, 1982.

Foss, Perkins. "The Arts of the Urhobo People of Southern Nigeria." Ph.D. diss., Yale University, 1976.

Garrard, Timothy F. "Brass in Akan Society to the Nineteenth Century: a Survey of the Archaeological, Ethnographic and Historical Evidence." Master's thesis, University of Ghana, 1980.

McNaughton, Patrick. "The Bamana Blacksmiths: A Study of Sculptors and Their Art." Ph.D. diss., Yale University, 1977.

Neaher, Nancy C. "Igbo Metalsmithing Traditions of Southern Nigeria." Ph.D. diss., Stanford University, 1976.

### Archives

Birmingham Chamber of Commerce and Industry. Archives.

Bristol City Archives. Shipping: Africa.

Cheadle and Warrington Companies. Deeds.

Cheadle Brass Wire Minute Books, 29 March 1788–July 1831.

Stephenson, J. E. "Chirupula." Manuscript Papers. Yale University Archives and Manuscripts, box 49.

Tervuren (Belgium), MRAC Archives. Luwel. "Notes du Dr. Amerlinck relatives aux mines de cuivre, de fer, etc., au Katanga." N.d. [1891/92]. R.G. 1110-105.

## PUBLISHED SOURCES

### Metals and Metallurgy

Afia, M. S., and A. L. Widatalla. *An Investigation of Hofrat en-Nahas Copper Deposit, Southern Dafur.* 2 vols. Sudan Geological Survey Bulletin no. 10. [Khartoum], 1961.

Aitchison, Leslie. *A History of Metals.* 2 vols. London, 1960.

Andrade, Antonio Alberto de. *Relações de Moçambique setecentista.* Lisbon, 1955.

Babet, Victor. *Observations géologiques dans la partie méridionale de l'Afrique équatoriale française (Bassins du Niari, de la Nyanga, . . .).* Paris, 1932.

"Bamenda Brass." *Nigeria,* no. 55 (1957): 344-55.

Bancroft, J. A. *Mining in Northern Rhodesia.* Edited by T. D. Guernsey, British South Africa Co. N.p., 1961.

Barrat, Maurice. *Sur la géologie du Congo français.* Paris, 1895.

Bernus, S., and P. Gouletquer. "Du cuivre au sel: Recherches ethnoarchéologiques sur la région d'Azélick (campagnes 1973-1975)." *JA* 46, nos. 1-2 (1976): 7-68.

Bigotte, G. *Contribution à la géologie du Niari: Étude sédimentologique et métallogénique de la région minière.* Bulletin de la Direction des mines et de la géologie. Gouvernement général de l'AEF. Paris, 1959.

Bognar-Kutzian, Ida. "The Origins of Early Copper-Processing in Europe." In *To Illustrate the Monuments: Essays on Archaeology Presented to Stuart Piggott.* Edited by J. V. S. Megaw. London, 1976.

Bower, J. G. "Native Smelting in Equatorial Africa." *The Mining Magazine* (London) 37, no. 3 (Sept. 1927), 137-47.

Bradley, Kenneth. *Copper Venture: The Discovery and Development of Roan Antelope and Mufulira.* London, 1952.

Bucaille, Richard. "Takadda, pays du cuivre." *BIFAN* 37, no. 4 (1975): 719-78.

Bürg, Georg. *Die nutzbaren Minerallagerstätten von deutsch-Südwestafrika.* Freiberg and Berlin, 1942.

Camps, G. "Les traces d'un âge du bronze en Afrique du nord." *Revue africaine* 104 (1960): 31-45.

Célis, G., and E. Nzikobanyanka. *La métallurgie traditionelle au Burundi.* Tervuren, 1976.

Chaplin, J. H. "Notes on Traditional Smelting in Northern Rhodesia." *SAAB* 16, no. 62 (June 1961): 53-57.

Cholet, J. "Mission de M. Cholet au Gabon-Congo depuis 1886." *Comptes rendus des séances de la Société géographique.* Paris, 7 Nov. 1890, 455-63.

Christy, Cuthbert. "The Bahr el-Ghazal and its Waterways." *The Geographical Journal* 61, no. 5 (1923): 313-35.

Clark, J. D. "Pre-European Copper Working in South Central Africa." *Roan Antelope,* May 1957.

Cline, Walter B. *Mining and Metallurgy in Negro Africa.* Menasha, Wis., 1937.

Coetzee, C. B., ed. *Mineral Resources of the Republic of South Africa.* 5th ed. Pretoria, 1976.

Coghlan, H. *Notes on the Prehistoric Metallurgy of Copper and Bronze in the Old World.* Occasional Papers on Technology no. 4. Oxford, 1975.

Cohen, Gaston. *Le cuivre et le nickel.* Que sais-je? Paris, 1962.

Cordeiro, Luciano, ed. *Memórias do ultramar: Viagens explorações e conquistas dos portugueses.* 6 vols. Lisbon, 1881.

Cornet, Jules. "Mines de cuivre du Katanga." *Le mouvement géographique* 12, no. 1 (June 1895): 21-25.

Dark, Philip J. C. *An Introduction to Benin Art and Technology.* Oxford, 1973.

_____. "*Cire-perdue* Casting: Some Technological and Aesthetic Considerations." *Ethnologica,* n.s., 3 (1966): 222-30, tables 27-37.

De Kun, Nicolas. *The Mineral Resources of Africa.* Amsterdam, 1965.

Dupont, E. *Lettres sur le Congo: Récit d'un voyage scientifique entre l'embouchure du fleuve et le confluent du Kassai.* Paris, 1889.

Eliade, Mircea. *Forgerons et alchimistes.* Paris, 1956.

Evers, T. M., and R. P. Van den Berg. "Ancient Mining in Southern Africa, with Reference to a Copper Mine in the Harmony Block, Northeastern Transvaal." *JSAIMM* 74, no. 6 (1974): 217–26.

Fagan, Brian M. "Wire-Drawing." *SAJS* 59, no. 11 (1963): 525–26.

Fischer, Eberhard. "Zur Technik des Gelbgusses bei den westlichen Dan." In *Festschrift Alfred Bühler*, 93–115. Basel, 1965.

Forbes, R. J. *Studies in Ancient Technology*, no. 9. Leiden, 1964.

Friede, H. M. "Iron Age Metal Working in the Magaliesberg Area." *JSAIMM* 77 (1977): 224–32.

Friede, H. M., and R. H. Steel. "Notes on Iron Age Copper-Smelting Technology in the Transvaal." *JSAIMM* 75 (1975): 221–31.

———. "Tin Mining and Smelting in the Transvaal during the Iron Age." *JSAIMM* 76 (1976): 461–70.

Fripp, F. E. B. "An Engineer's Notes on the Mine-workings of Transvaal and Rhodesia." *Proceedings and Transactions of the Rhodesia Scientific Association* 11, no. 3 (1912): 168–81.

Fröhlich, Max. *Gelbgiesser im Kameruner Grasland.* Zürich, 1979.

Goodwin, A. J. H. "Metal Working among the Early Hottentots." *SAAB* 11, no. 42 (1956): 46–51.

Gutzeit, Grégoire. "La fonte de la monnaie (croisettes) chez les baluba du territoire de musonoï (Haut-Katanga ouest)." *Archives suisses d'anthropologie générale* 7, no. 1 (1934): 73–81.

Hanisch, E. O. M. "Copper Working in the Messina District." *JSAIMM* 74, no. 6 (1974): 250–53.

Hechter-Schulz, K. "Wire Bangles, a Record of a Bantu Craft: A Note on the Making of Brasswire Bangles by a Shangaan on the Gold Mines Near Springs." *SAJS* 59, no. 2 (1963): 51–53.

Hemptinne, Msgr. de. *Les "mangeurs de cuivre" du Katanga.* Brussels, 1926. Extract from *Congo* 7 (March 1926): 371–403.

Job, A. L. "Mining in Uganda." *Uganda Journal* 31, no. 1 (1967): 43–61.

Justice, J. N. "The Ancient Metal Workings in East Nigeria." *Man* 22, no. 3 (1922): 3–4.

Kandt, R. "Gewerbe in Ruanda." *Zeitschrift für Ethnologie* 36 (1904): 329–72.

Lindblom, K.G. *Wire Drawing, Especially in Africa.* Statens Etnografiska Museum, Smarre-Meddelanden, 15. Stockholm, 1939.

McNaughton, Patrick R. "Bamana Blacksmiths." *African Arts* 12, no. 2 (Feb. 1979): 65–71.

Malcolm, L. W. G. "A Note on Brass-Casting in the Central Cameroons." *Man* 23, no. 1 (1923): 1–4.

Maret, Pierre de, and F. Nsuka. "History of Bantu Metallurgy: Some Linguistic Aspects." *History in Africa* 4 (1977): 43–65.

Mauny, Raymond. "Essai sur l'histoire des métaux en Afrique occidentale." *BIFAN* 14 (1952): 545–95.

———. *Tableau géographique de l'ouest africain au moyen âge*. Dakar, 1961.

Mouta, Fernando. "As minas de cobre do Congo." *Actividade econômica 1*, no. 3 (1936): 9–15.

Ndinga-Mbo, A. "Quelques réflexions sur la civilisation du cuivre au Congo." *Cahiers congolais d'anthropologie et d'histoire* 1 (1976): 31–44.

Neaher, Nancy C. "Awka Who Travel: Itinerant Metalsmiths of Southern Nigeria." *Africa* 49, no. 4 (1979): 351–66.

———. "Igbo Metalsmiths among the Southern Edo." *African Arts* 9, no. 4 (July 1976): 46–49, 91.

Neher, G. "Brasscasting in Northeast Nigeria." *Nigerian Field* 29, no. 1 (1964): 16–27.

Nicolini, P. *Le synclinal de la Nyanga (zone de la boucle du Niari)*. Bulletin de la Direction des mines et de la géologie de l'AEF, no. 10, 1959.

Norddeutscher Affinerie. *Kupfer in Natur, Technik, Kunst und Wirtschaft*. Hamburg, 1966.

Pelletier, René Arthur. *Mineral Resources of South Central Africa*. London, 1964.

Phillipson, D. W. "The Chronology of the Iron Age in Bantu Africa." *JAH* 16, no. 3 (1975): 321–42.

Pleigneur, (Capt.). "Extrait des notes du capitaine Pleigneur sur la reconnaissance des mines de Mboko-Songho." *Revue ethnographique* 7 (1888): 277–80.

Posnansky, Merrick. "Brass Casting and Its Antecedents in West Africa." Review article, *JAH* 18, no. 2 (1977): 287–300.

Renfrew, Colin. *Before Civilization: The Radiocarbon Revolution and Prehistoric Europe*. New York, 1975.

Rickard, T. A. *Man and Metals*. 2 vols. New York, 1932.

Rothenberg, Beno. *Timna: Valley of the Biblical Copper Mines*. London, 1972.

Rowlands, M. J. "The Archaeological Interpretation of Prehistoric Metalworking." *World Archaeology* 3, no. 2 (Oct. 1971): 210–24.

Shinnie, P. L., ed. *The African Iron Age*. Oxford, 1971.

Stanley, G. H. "Composition of Prehistoric Bronzes." *SAJS* 26 (1929): 44–49.

———. "Primitive Metallurgy in South Africa." *SAJS* 26 (1929): 732–48.

———. "Some Observations on Ancient Mine Working in the Transvaal." *JCMMSSA* 12 (1912): 370–72.

Summers, Roger. *Ancient Mining in Rhodesia and Adjacent Areas*. Salisbury, 1969.

Trevor, T. G. "Some Observations on Ancient Mine Workings in the Transvaal." *JCMMSSA* 12 (1912): 267–75.

———. "Some Observations on the Relics of Pre-European Culture in Rhodesia and South Africa." *JRAI* 60, n.s. 33 (1930): 389–99.

Tylecote, R. F. *A History of Metallurgy*. London, 1976.

Van der Merwe, Nikolaas J. "The Advent of Iron in Africa." In *The Coming of the Age of Iron*, edited by T. A. Wertime and James D. Muhly, 463–506. New Haven, 1980.

Wagner, P. A. "Bronze from an Ancient Smelter in the Waterberg District." *SAJS* 22 (1926): 899–900.

Wagner, P. A. and H. S. Gordon. "Further Notes on Ancient Bronze Smelters in the Waterberg District, Transvaal." *SAJS* 26 (1929): 563–74.

Wannyn, R. L. *L'art ancien du métal au Bas-Congo*. Champles-par-Wavre, 1961.

Warnier, Jean-Pierre, and Ian Fowler. "A Nineteenth-Century Ruhr in Central Africa." *Africa* 49, no. 4 (1979): 329–51.

Woodburn, J. Allen. "Mining Copper Ores at Messina." *JCMMSSA* 14 (1913): 53–64.

## Copper in African Trade and Culture

### Archaeological Evidence

Bisson, Michael. "Copper Currency in Central Africa: The Archaeological Evidence." *World Archaeology* 6, no. 3 (Feb. 1975): 276–92.

_____. "Prehistoric Copper Mining in Northwestern Zambia." *Archaeology* 27, no. 4 (1974): 242–47.

Calvocoressi, D., and Nicholas David. "A New Survey of Radiocarbon and Thermoluminescence Dates for West Africa." *JAH* 20, no. 1 (1979): 1–29.

Caton-Thompson, Gertrude. *The Zimbabwe Culture.* 1931; London, 1971.

Connah, Graham. *The Archaeology of Benin.* Oxford, 1975.

_____. *Three Thousand Years in Africa.* New York, 1981.

Descamps, Cyr. "Sites protohistoriques de la Sénégambie." *Annales de la Faculté des lettres et sciences humaines de Dakar,* no. 9 (1980): 303–13.

Desplagnes, L. "Étude sur les tumuli du Killi dans la région de Goundam." *L'anthropologie* 14 (1903): 151–72.

_____. "Fouilles du tumulus d'El Oualedji." *BIFAN* 13, no. 4 (1951): 1159–73.

Evers, T. M. "Iron Age Trade in the Eastern Transvaal, South Africa." *SAAB* 29, nos. 113, 114 (1974): 33–37.

_____. "Recent Iron Age Research in the Eastern Transvaal, South Africa." *SAAB* 30, nos. 119, 120 (1975): 71–83.

Fagan, Brian M., et al. *Iron Age Cultures in Zambia.* 2 vols. London, 1967.

Fouché, Leo, ed. *Mapungubwe: Ancient Bantu Civilization on the Limpopo. Excavation Reports.* London, 1937.

Gardner, G. A. *Mapungubwe.* Pretoria, 1963.

Garlake, Peter S. *Great Zimbabwe.* London, 1973.

_____. "Iron Age Sites in the Urungwe District of Rhodesia." *SAAB* 25, no. 97 (June 1970): 25–44.

Hall, Martin, and J. C. Vogel. "Some Recent Radiocarbon Dates from Southern Africa." *JAH* 21, no. 4 (1980): 431–55.

Hartle, Donald. "Bronze Objects from the Ifeka Garden Site, Ezira." *West African Archaeological Newsletter* 4 (1966): 25–28.

Huffman, T. N. "Ancient Mining and Zimbabwe." *JSAIMM* 74, no. 6 (1974): 238–42.

Joire, J. "Découvertes archéologiques dans la région de Rao (bas Sénégal)." *BIFAN* 17 (1955): 249–333.

Labouret, H. "Le mystère des ruines du Lobi." *Revue d'ethnographie et des traditions populaires* 1 (1920): 178–96.

Lambert, Nicole. "Les industries sur cuivre dans l'ouest saharien." *WAJA* 1 (1971): 9–21.

_____. "Medinet Sbat et la protohistoire de Mauritanie occidentale." *Antiquités africaines* 4 (1970): 15–62.

Lebeuf, J.-P. and A. M. Lebeuf. *Les arts des sao.* Paris, 1977.

McIntosh, S. K., and R. J. McIntosh. *Prehistoric Investigations in the Region of Jenne, Mali.* 2 vols. B.A.R. International Series no. 89. Oxford, 1980.

_____. "Finding West Africa's Oldest City." *National Geographic* 162 no. 3 (Sept. 1982): 396-418.

Maggs, T. M. O'C. *Iron Age Communities of the Southern Highveld.* Publications of the Natal Museum no. 2. Pietermaritzburg, 1976.

_____. "Some Recent Radiocarbon Dates from Eastern and Southern Africa." *JAH* 18, no. 1 (1977): 161-91.

Maret, Pierre de. "L'évolution monétaire du Shaba central entre le 7e et le 18e siè-cle." *African Economic History* 10 (1981): 117-49.

_____. "Luba Roots: The First Complete Iron Age Sequence in Zaire." *Current Anthropology* 20, no. 1 (1979): 233-35.

_____. "New Survey of Archaeological Research and Dates for West-Central and North-Central Africa." *JAH* 23, no. 1 (1982): 1-15.

_____. "Sanga: New Excavations, More Data, and Some Related Problems." *JAH* 18, no. 3 (1977): 321-38.

Mason, R. J. "Early Iron Age Settlement at Broederstroom 24/73, Transvaal, South Africa." *SAJS* 77 (Sept. 1981): 401-16.

_____. *Prehistory of the Transvaal.* Johannesburg, 1962.

Mauny, Raymond. "Un âge de cuivre au Sahara occidentale?" *BIFAN,* 13 (1951): 168-80.

Monod, Theodore. "Le Ma'den Ijâfen: Une épave caravanière ancienne dans la Majâbat al-Koubrâ." *Actes du première colloque international d'archéologie africaine,* 286-320. Fort Lamy, 1969.

Nenquin, Jacques. *Excavations at Sanga.* Tervuren, 1963.

Phillipson, D. W. *The Later Prehistory of Eastern and Southern Africa.* London and New York, 1977.

Phillipson, D. W., and B. M. Fagan, "The Date of the Ingombe Ilede Burials." *JAH* 10, no. 2 (1969): 199-204.

Posnansky, Merrick. "Archaeology in West Africa." In *Into the 80's,* edited by D. Roy, P. Shinnie, and D. Williams, 73-85. Vancouver, 1981.

Posnansky, Merrick, and Roderick McIntosh. "New Radiocarbon Dates for Northern and Western Africa." *JAH* 17, no. 2 (1976): 161-95.

Robert, Denise S. "Les fouilles de Tegdaoust." *JAH* 11, no. 4 (1970): 471-93.

Robinson, K. R. *Khami Ruins.* Cambridge, England, 1959.

Rubin, Arnold. "Bronzes of the Middle Benue." *WAJA* 3 (1973): 221-31.

Shaw, Thurstan. *Igbo-Ukwu: An Account of Archaeological Discoveries in Eastern Nigeria.* 2 vols. London, 1970.

_____. *Nigeria: Its Archaeology and Early History.* London, 1978.

Steel, R. H. "Iron Age Copper Mine 47/73." *JSAIMM* 74, no. 6 (1974): 244.

Summers, Roger, *Inyanga: Prehistoric Settlements in Southern Rhodesia.* Cambridge, England, 1958.

Sutton, J. E. G. "Archaeology in West Africa: A Review of Recent Work and a Further List of Radiocarbon Dates." *JAH* 23, no. 3 (1982): 291-314.

Treinen-Claustre, F. "Nouveaux éléments de datation absolue pour l'âge de fer de la région de Koro-Toro (nord du Tchad)." *L'anthropologie* 82 (1978): 103–9.

Tylecote, R. F. "Early Copper Slags etc. from the Agadez Region of Niger." *Journal of the Historical Metallurgy Society* 16, no. 2 (1982): 59–64.

Van der Merwe, Nickolaas J., and R. T. K. Scully. "The Phalaborwa Story: Archaeological and Ethnographic Investigation of a South African Iron Age Group." *World Archaeology* 3 (1971): 178–96.

Van Noten, Francis L. *Les tombes du roi Cyirima Rujugira et de la reine-mère Nyirayuhi Kanjogera.* Tervuren: MRAC, 1972.

Vogel, Joseph O. *Kamangoza: An Introduction to the Iron Age Cultures of the Victoria Falls Region.* Nairobi and New York, 1971.

———. *Kumadzulo: An Early Iron Age Site in Southern Zambia.* New York and London, 1971.

Willett, Frank. *Ife In the History of West African Sculpture.* London, 1967.

Willett, Frank, and S. J. Fleming. "A Catalogue of Important Nigerian Copper-Alloy Castings Dated by Thermoluminescence." *Archaeometry* 18 (1976): 135–46.

*Historical Evidence: Sources before c. 1900*

Adams, (Capt.) John. *Sketches taken during Ten Voyages to Africa between the Years 1786 and 1800.* London, 1823.

Aitken, W. C. "Brass and Brass Manufactures." In *Birmingham and the Midland Hardware District 1865,* edited by Samuel Timmins. London, 1866.

———. *The Early History of Brass and the Brass Manufactures of Birmingham.* Birmingham, 1866.

Alberti, Ludwig. *Account of the Tribal Life and Customs of the Xhosa in 1897.* Translated by William Fehr. Cape Town, 1968.

Allen, W., and T. R. H. Thomson. *Expedition to the River Niger.* 2 vols. London, 1848.

Arnot, Frederick Stanley. *Garenganze or, Seven Years' Pioneer Mission Work in Central Africa.* 1889; London, 1969.

Atkins, John. *A Voyage to Guinea.* London, 1735.

Barbot, Jean. "A Description of the Coasts of North and South Guinea." In vol. 5 of *A Collection of Voyages and Travels,* edited by Awnsham Churchill. 6 vols. London, 1732.

Barlow, Roger, *A Brief Summe of Geographie.* Edited by E. G. R. Taylor. London, 1932.

Barth, Heinrich. *Travels and Discoveries in North and Central Africa 1849–1855.* 2d ed. 5 vols. London, 1857–58.

Battell, Andrew. *The Strange Adventures of Andrew Batell of Leigh in Angola and Adjoining Regions.* Edited by E. G. Ravenstein. 1589; London: Hakluyt Society, 1901.

Bentley, W. H. *Pioneering on the Congo.* 2 vols. London, 1900.

Binger, L. G. *Du Niger au golfe de Guinée par le pays de Kong et le Mossi . . . 1887–1889.* 2 vols. Paris, 1892.

Blake, J. W. *Europeans in West Africa, 1450–1560.* 2 vols. London: Hakluyt Society, 1942.

Bold, Edward. *The Merchants' and Mariners' African Guide . . .* London, 1822.

Bosman, Willem. *A New and Accurate Description of the Coast of Guinea.* New ed. 1704; London, 1967.

Boteler, T. *A Narrative of a Voyage of Discovery to Africa and Arabia.* 2 vols. London, 1835.

Bouët-Williamez, Louis Edouard. *Commerce et traite des noirs aux côtes occidentales d'Afrique.* Paris, 1848.

Braamcamp Freire, Anselmo, ed. *Archivo histórico português.* 11 vols. Lisbon, 1903–16.

Brásio, Antonio Duarte, ed. *Monumenta missionaria africana, Africa occidental.* 8 vols. Lisbon, 1952–68.

Broecke, Pieter van den. *Reizen naar West-Afrika, 1605–1614.* Edited by K. Ratelband. The Hague, 1950.

Brun (Braun), Samuel. *Schiffarten.* 1624; Graz, 1969.

Buckeridge, Nicholas. *Journal and Letter Book of Nicholas Buckeridge 1651–1654.* Edited by John R. Jensen. Minneapolis, 1973.

Burchell, William J. *Travels in the Interior of Southern Africa.* 2 vols. 1824; London, 1967.

Burton, Richard F. *The Lake Regions of Central Africa.* 2 vols. 1860; New York, 1961.

———. *A Mission to Gelele, King of Dahomey.* 2 vols. London, 1864.

———. *Two Trips to Gorilla-Land and the Cataracts of the Congo.* 2 vols. London, 1876.

———, trans. and annot. *The Lands of Cazembe.* London, 1873.

Cadamosto. *The Voyages of Cadamosto and Other Documents on Western Africa in the Second Half of the Fifteenth Century.* Translated and edited by G. R. Crone. London, 1937.

Campbell, (the Rev.) John. *Travels in South Africa . . . Second Journey.* 2 vols. 1822; London, 1967.

Capello, M., and R. Ivens. "Les mines de cuivre du Katanga." *Le mouvement géographique* (Brussels) 29 (1888); 112–13.

Centro de estudos históricos ultramarinos, Lisbon. *Documentos sobre os Portugueses en Moçambique e na Africa central, 1497–1840; Documents on the Portuguese in Mozambique and Central Africa, 1497–1840.* Documents from the National Archives of Rhodesia and Nyasaland. Lisbon, 1962–

Crow, (Capt.) Hugh. *Memoirs of the Late Hugh Crow of Liverpool.* London, 1830.

Dapper, Olfert. *Naukeurige Beschrijvinge der Afrikaensche Gewesten.* Amsterdam, 1668.

Degrandpré, L. *Voyage à la côte occidentale d'Afrique . . . 1786 et 1787.* 2 vols. Paris, 1801.

Donnan, Elizabeth. *Documents Illustrative of the History of the Slave Trade to America.* 4 vols. Washington, D.C., 1930–35.

dos Santos, João. "Ethiopia Oriental." In *Records of South East Africa,* edited by G. M. Theal. 9 vols. Cape Town, 1898–1903.

Du Chaillu, Paul B. *Exploration and Adventures in Equatorial Africa.* 1856; London, 1945.

Duncan, John. *Travels in Western Africa in 1845 and 1846.* 2 vols. London, 1847.

Enfield, William. *An Essay towards the History of Liverpool.* 2d ed. London, 1774.

Fynn, Henry Francis. *The Diary of Henry Francis Fynn.* Pietermaritzburg, 1950.

Grant-Francis, George. *The Smelting of Copper in the Swansea District of South Wales, from the time of Elizabeth to the Present Day . . .* London, 1881.

Great Britain. *Parliamentary Papers.* 1799. "Report from the Select Committee on the State of Copper Trade. . . ." Commons Committee Reports X.

Great Britain. *Parliamentary Papers.* 1842. "Report from the Select Committee on the West Coast of Africa together with the Minutes of Evidence. Irish University Press Series of British Parliament. Shannon, 1968.

Great Britain. *Parliamentary Papers.* 1865. "Report from the House of Commons Select Committee on the West Coast of Africa."

Hair, P. E. H. "Some Minor Sources for Guinea, 1519–1559: Enciso and Alfonce/Fonteneau." In *History in Africa* 3 (1976): pp. 19–46.

Hopkins, J. F. P., trans., and N. Levtzion, ed. and annot. *Corpus of Early Arabic Sources for West African History.* New York, 1981.

Hutchinson, Thos. J. *Narrative of the Niger, Tschadda Binue Exploration.* London, 1855.

Ibn Battuta. *Travels in Asia and Africa, 1325–54.* Translated by H. A. R. Gibb. 1929.

Labarthe, P. *Voyage à la côte de Guinée.* Paris, 1803.

Landolphe, J.-F. *Mémoires du capitaine Landolphe.* Edited by J. S. Quesné. 2 vols. Paris, 1823.

Latimer, John. *The Annals of Bristol: Eighteenth Century.* Bristol, 1893.

Leo Africanus. *Description de l'Afrique.* Translated by A. Epaulard. 2 vols. Paris, 1956.

Le Vaillant, François. *Voyage de François Le Vaillant dans l'intérieur de l'Afrique par le Cap de Bonne-Espérance.* 5 vols. Paris, 1798–1803.

Lichtenstein, Henry. *Travels in Southern Africa . . .* 2 vols. Cape Town, 1928.

Livingstone, David. *Family Letters 1841–1856.* Edited by I. Schapera. 2 vols. London, 1959.

———. *Last Journals.* 2 vols. London, 1874. 1 vol. ed. New York, 1875.

———. *Livingstone's African Journal 1853–1856.* Edited by I. Schapera. 2 vols. London, 1963.

———. *Missionary Travels and Researches in South Africa.* London, 1857.

Livingstone, David, and Charles Livingstone. *Narrative of an Expedition to the Zambesi and Its Tributaries . . . 1858–1864.* London, 1865.

Loyer, G. *Relation du voyage au royaume d'Issiny.* Paris, 1714.

Marees, Pieter de. "Description of Guinea." In *Purchas His Pilgrimes.* 20 vols. Glasgow, 1905.

Matthews, John. *A Voyage to the River Sierra Leone . . . 1788.* London, 1966.

Meredith, Henry. *An Account of the Gold Coast.* London, 1812.

Moffat, Robert. *Missionary Labours and Scenes in South Africa.* 3d ed. New York, 1843.

Möller, Peter August. *Journey in Africa through Angola, Ovampoland and Damaraland.* Translated by Ione and Jalmar Rudner. Cape Town, 1974.

Monteiro, Joachim John. *Angola and the River Congo.* 2 vols. London, 1875.

Mueller, Wilhelm Johann. *Die Africanische auf der Guineischen Goldkust gelegene Landschaft Fetu.* 1673; Graz, 1968.

Pacheco Pereira, Duarte. *Esmeraldo de Situ Orbis.* Translated and edited by G. H. T. Kimble. London, 1937.

Paiva Manso, Maria Jordão, Visconde de. *História do Congo. Documentos.* Obra posthuma do (Dr. Levy) Visconde de Paiva Manso. Lisbon, 1872.

Paludanus, Bernardus. "Beschrijvinge van de Gantsche kust van Guinea, Manicongo, etc." in *Het Itinerario van Jan Huygen van Linschoten 1579-1592,* edited by C. P. Burger and F. W. T. Hunger. The Hague, 1934.

Pigafetta, F., and D. Lopes. *Description du royaume de Congo et des contrées avoisinantes.* Edited by Willy Bal. 1591; Paris, 1965.

Proyart, Abbé. *Histoire de Loango, Kakongo, et autres royaumes d'Afrique.* Paris, 1776.

Pruneau de Pommegorge, A. *Description de la nigritie.* Paris, 1789.

[Reichard]. "The Copper Mines of Katanga." *Proceedings of the Royal Geographical Society* 7, no. 8 (1885): 540. London.

Roemer, Ludewig Ferdinand. *Tilforladelig Eftervetning om Kysten Guinea.* Copenhagen, 1760.

Schweinfurth, Georg August. *Artes Africanae. Illustrations and Descriptions of the Industrial Arts of Central African Tribes.* Leipzig and London, 1875.

_____. *The Heart of Africa.* 2 vols. London, 1873.

Sparrman, Anders. *A Voyage to the Cape of Good Hope towards the Antarctic Polar Circle round the World and to the Country of the Hottentots and the Caffres from the Year 1772 to 1776.* 1785-86; new ed. Cape Town, 1975.

Speke, John Hanning. *Journal of the Discovery of the Sources of the Nile.* London, 1863.

Stanley, Henry M. *The Congo and the Founding of Its Free State.* 2 vols. New York, 1885.

_____. *Five Years in the Congo, 1879-1884.* 1885.

_____. *Through the Dark Continent.* 2 vols. New York, 1878.

Theal, G. M., ed. *Records of South-Easternern Africa . . .* 9 vols. Cape Town, 1898-1903.

Travassos Valdez, Francisco. *Six Years of a Traveller's Life in Western Africa.* 2 vols. London, 1861.

al-Tunisi, Muhammad ibn 'Umar. *Voyage au Ouaday.* Paris, 1851.

(al-'Umari) Ibn Fadl Allah. *Masalik el Absar fi Mamalik el Amsar.* Translated and edited by Gaudefroy-Demombynes. Paris, 1927.

Van Brakel, S. "Eene Memorie over den Handel der West-Indische Compagnie Omstreeks 1670." *Historisch Genootschap te Utrecht, Bijdragen en mededeelingen* 35: 97-104.

Van de Velde, (Lt.) Liévin. "La région du Bas-Congo et du Kwilou-Niadi." *Bulletin de la Sociéte royale belge de géographie* 10 (1886): 347-412.

Van Riebeeck, Jan. *Journal of Jan van Riebeek.* Edited by H. B. Thom. 3 vols. Cape Town, 1958.

Waddell, (the Rev.) Hope M. *Twenty-Nine Years in the West Indies and Central Africa.* London, 1863.

Wikar, H. J., Jansz J. Coetsé, and W. van Reenen. *The Journal of Hendrik Jacob Wikar (1779)* . . . Translated by A. W. van der Horst and E. E. Mossop, edited by E. E. Mossop. Cape Town, 1935.

Wilson, Charles T., and Robert William Felkin. *Uganda and the Egyptian Soudan.* 2 vols. London, 1882.

Wilson, John Leighton. *Western Africa.* New York, 1856.


*Historical Evidence: Sources after c. 1900*

Abdallah, Yohanna B. *The Yaos.* Edited and translated by M. Sanderson. Zomba, 1919; 2d. ed., London, 1973.

Adandé, Alexandre. "Les récades des rois du Dahomey." *Catalogues et documents de l'Institut français de l'Afrique noire,* no. 15. Dakar, 1962.

Afikpo, A. E. "Trade and Trade Routes in Nineteenth-Century Nsukka." *JHSN* 7, no. 1 (1973): 77–90.

Alagoa, E. J. "Long-Distance Trade and States on the Niger Delta." *JAH* 11, no. 4 (1970): 319–30.

—————. "Oproza and Early Trade on the Escravos: A Note on the Interpretation of Oral Tradition of a Small Group." *JHSN* 7 (1969): 151–56.

Albuquerque Felner, Alfredo de. *Angola.* 3 vols. Coimbra, 1933.

Alpers, Edward A. *Ivory and Slaves in East Central Africa: Changing Patterns of International Trade to the Late Nineteenth Century.* Berkeley and Los Angeles, 1975.

—————. "Trade, State and Society among the Yao in the Nineteenth Century." *JAH* 10, no. 3 (1969): 405–20.

Ankermann, B. "Ethnographische Forschungsreise ins Grasland von Kamerun." *Zeitschrift für Ethnologie* 42 (1910): 288–310.

Appia, Béatrice. "Notes sur le génie des eaux en Guinée." *JSA* 14 (1944): 33–41.

Ardener, Edwin. *Coastal Bantu of the Cameroons.* London, 1956.

Armstrong, Robert G. "A Possible Function for the Bronze Roped Pot of Igbo-Ukwu." *WAJA* 4 (1974): 177–78.

Bascom, William R. *Ifa Divination.* Bloomington, Ind., 1969.

Basden, G. T. *Among the Ibos of Nigeria.* 1921; London, 1966.

—————. *Niger Ibos.* London, 1966.

Bassani, Ezio. "Sono from Guinea Bissau." *African Arts* 12, no. 4 (Aug. 1979): 44–47.

Bastin, M.-L. "Un masque en cuivre martelé des kongo du nord-est de l'Angola." *Africa-Tervuren* 7, no. 2 (1961): 29.

Baumann, H., and L. Vajda. "Bernhard Ankermanns völkerkundliche Aufzeichnungen im Grasland von Kamerun, 1907–1909." *Baessler-Archiv,* n.s. 7 (1959): 217–317.

Beier, H. U. "Oshun Festival." *Nigeria,* no. 53 (1957): 170–187.

Ben-Amos, Paula. *The Art of Benin.* New York, 1980.

Biebuyck, Daniel P. "Textual and Contextual Analysis in African Art Studies." *African Arts* 8, no. 3 (Spring 1975): 48–57.

Blake, J. W. *European Beginnings in West Africa 1454–1578.* London, 1937.

Blohm, Wilhelm. *Die Nyamwezi.* 3 vols. Hamburg, 1931.

Bochet, G. "Les masques senoufo, de la forme à la signification." *BIFAN* 27, nos. 3–4 (1965): 636.

Boston, J. S. *The Igala Kingdom.* Ibadan, 1968.

Bravmann, René A. *Open Frontiers: The Mobility of Art in Black Africa.* Exhibition Catalogue, University of Washington. Seattle, 1973.

———. *West African Sculpture.* Seattle, 1970.

Brincard, M.-T., ed. *The Art of Metal in Africa.* Exhibition Catalogue. New York, 1982.

Browne, W. G. *Travels in Africa, Egypt and Syria.* London, 1799.

Bruel, Georges. *L'Afrique équatoriale française.* Paris, 1918.

Campbell, Dugald. *In the Heart of Bantuland.* London, 1922.

Célis, Georges. "The Decorative Arts in Rwanda and Burundi." *African Arts* 4, no. 1 (Autumn 1970): 40–42.

Chaffin, Alain, and Françoise Chaffin. *L'art kota.* Meudon, 1979.

Chapoix, Lucienne. "Les anneaux en cuivre jaune au Bas-Congo." *Africa-Tervuren* 5, no. 1 (1959): 74–75.

Chavannes, Charles de. *Le Congo français.* Paris, 1937.

Chilver, E. M. "Nineteenth-Century Trade in the Bamenda Grassfields, Southern Cameroon." *Afrika und Übersee* 45 (1961).

Cissé, Youssouf. "Notes sur les sociétés de chasseurs malinke." *JSA* 34, no. 2 (1964): 75–226.

Cole, Herbert M. *African Arts of Transformation.* Santa Barbara, Calif., 1970.

———. "The Art of Festival in Ghana." *African Arts* 8, no. 3 (Spring 1975): 12–23, 60–62, 90.

———. "Vital Arts in Northern Kenya." *African Arts* 7, no. 2 (Winter 1974): 12–23, 82.

Cole, Herbert M., and Doran Ross. *The Arts of Ghana.* Los Angeles, 1977.

Coquery-Vidrovitch, Catherine. *Brazza et la prise de possession du Congo.* Paris, 1969.

Coquilhat, C. *Sur le haut Congo.* Brussels, 1888.

Cornet, Joseph. *Art of Africa.* New York, 1971.

———. *A Survey of Zairian Art.* The Bronson Collection. Raleigh: North Carolina Museum of Art, 1978.

Courboin, A. "Les populations de l'Alima, Congo français." *Bulletin de la Société royale de géographie d'Anvers* 28 (1904): 273–308; and 32 (1908): 648–70.

Crawford, D. *Thinking Black.* London, 1913.

Cunnison, Ian. *The Luapula Peoples of Northern Rhodesia.* Manchester, 1959.

Curtin, Philip D. *Economic Change in Precolonial Africa: Senegambia in the Era of the Slave Trade.* Madison, Wis., 1975.

Cuvelier, Jean. *L'ancien royaume du Congo*. Bruges, 1946.

Daaku, Kwame Yeboa. *Trade and Politics on the Gold Coast 1600–1720: A Study of the African Reaction to European Trade*. Oxford, 1970.

Daget, J., and M. Konipo. "La pince-amulette chez les bozo." *Notes africaines*, no. 51 (1951): 80–81.

Davies, K. G. *The Royal African Company*. London, 1957.

Day, Joan. *Bristol Brass: The History of the Industry*. Newton Abbot, England, 1973.

Delange, Jacqueline. *Arts et peuples de l'Afrique noire*. Paris, 1967.

———. "Un *kuduo* exceptionnel." *Objets et mondes* 5, no. 3 (1965): 197–204.

———. "Sur un oshe shango." *Objets et mondes* 3, no. 3 (1963): 205–10.

Deleval, Henri. "Les tribus kavati du mayombe." *La revue congolaise* 3 (1912): 32–115, 103–115, 170–86, 253–61.

Denucé, J. *L'Afrique au XVIe siècle et le commerce anversois*. Antwerp, 1937.

Deschamps, H. *Traditions orales and archives au Gabon*. Paris, 1962.

Devisse, Jean, et al., eds. *200 ans d'histoire africaine: Le sol, la parole et l'écrit*. Mélanges en hommage à Raymond Mauny. 2 vols. Paris, 1981.

Dieterlen, Germaine. *Essai sur la religion bambara*. Paris, 1951.

———. "Notes sur le génie des eaux chez les Bozo." *JSA* 12 (1942): 149–55.

Dieterlen, Germaine, and M. Griaule. *Le renard pâle*. Paris, 1965.

Dieterlen, Germaine, and Z. Ligers. "Notes sur les tambours-de-Calebasse en Afrique occidentale." *JSA* 33, no. 2 (1963): 255–74.

———. "Un objet rituel bozo: Le maniyalo." *JSA* 28, no. 1 (1958): 33–42.

Dim Delobsom, Antoine Augustine. *L'empire du mogho-naba*. Paris, 1932.

———. *Les secrets des sorciers noirs*. Paris, 1934.

Donald, M. B. *Elizabethan Copper*. London, 1955.

Dupire, M. "Contribution à l'étude des marques de propriété du bétail chez les pasteurs peuls." *JSA* 24 (1954): 123–43.

Dupont, Victor (Marquis de Compiègne). *L'Afrique équatoriale: Okanda, Bangouens-Osyéba*. Paris, n.d.

———. *L'Afrique équatoriale: Gabonais, Pahouins-Gallois*. Paris, 1876.

Egharevba, J. V. *A Short History of Benin*. Ibadan, 1960.

Ehrenberg, Richard. *Das Zeitalter der Fugger*. 2 vols. Jena, 1922.

Ekejiuba, F. I. "Preliminary Notes on Brasswork of Eastern Nigeria." *African Notes*, (Ibadan) 4, no. 2 (Jan. 1967): 11–15.

Elphick, Richard. *Kraal and Castle*. New Haven, 1977.

Eyo, Ekpo, and Frank Willett. *Treasures of Ancient Nigeria*. New York, 1980.

Fage, J. D., and Roland Oliver, eds. *Cambridge History of Africa*. 5 vols. Cambridge, 1975–.

Fagg, William. *Nigerian Images*. London, 1963.

Fischer, Eberhard, and Hans Himmelheber. *Die Kunst der Dan*. Museum Rietberg. Zurich, 1976.

Fischer, Werner, and Manfred A. Zirngibl. *African Weapons*. Passau, 1978.

Forde, Daryll. *Efik Traders of Old Calabar*. New York, 1956.

Fraser, Douglas. "The Tsoede Bronzes and Owo Yoruba Art." *African Arts* 8, no. 3 (Spring 1975): 30–35, 91.

Fraser, Douglas, and Herbert M. Cole, eds. *African Art and Leadership.* Madison, 1972.

Frobenius, Leo. *Die atlantische Götterlehre.* Jena, 1926.

———. *The Voice of Africa.* Translated by Rudolf Blind. 2 vols. New York, 1913.

Fu-Kiau kia Bunseki-Lumanisa, A. *N'Kongo ye Nza Yakun'zungidila: Le Mukongo et le monde qui l'entourait.* Kinshasa, 1969.

Gabus, Jean. *L'art nègre.* Neuchâtel, 1967.

———. *Au Sahara.* 2 vols. Neuchâtel, 1955–58.

———. *Sahara: Bijoux et Techniques.* Neuchâtel, 1982.

Garrard, Timothy F. "Akan Metal Arts." *African Arts* 13, no. 1 (Nov. 1979): 36–43.

———. *Akan Weights and the Gold Trade.* London, 1980.

Gemery, Henry A., and Jan S. Hogendorn, eds. *The Uncommon Market: Essays in the Economic History of the Atlantic Slave Trade.* New York, 1979.

Glaze, Anita J. *Art and Death in a Senufo Village,* Bloomington, Ind., 1981.

———. "Senufo Ornament and Decorative Arts." *African Arts* 12, no. 1 (Nov. 1978): 63–71.

———. "Woman Power and Art in a Senufo Village." *African Arts* 8, no. 3 (Spring 1975): 64–68, 90.

Göbel, Peter. "Gelbschmiedarbeiten der Nupe im Museum für Völkerkunde zu Leipzig." *Jahrbuch des Museums für Völkerkunde Leipzig* 27 (1970): 266–319.

Goris, J. A. *Étude sur les colonies marchandes méridionales (portugais, espagnols, italiens) à Anvers de 1488 à 1567.* Louvain, 1925.

Grey, R. F. A. "Manillas." *The Nigerian Field* 16, no. 2 (April 1981): 52–66.

Griaule, Marcel, *Dieu d'eau: Entretiens avec Ogotemmêli.* Paris, 1966.

Gutersohn, A. T. "Het Economisch Leven van den Mongo-Neger." *Congo* 1 (1920): 92–105.

Hamilton, Henry. *The English Brass and Copper Industries to 1800.* London, 1926.

Harms, Robert W. *River of Wealth, River of Sorrow.* New Haven, 1981.

Harris, John Raymond. *The Copper King: A Biography of Thomas Williams of Llanidan.* Liverpool, 1964.

Heath, D. F. "Bussa Regalia." *Man* 37 (1937): 77–80.

Herbert, Eugenia. "Aspects of the Use of Copper in Pre-Colonia West Africa." *JAH* 14, no. 2 (1973): 179–94.

———. "Images of the Ancestors: The Bwété of the Mahongwe," Paper presented to the twenty-third annual meeting of the ASA, Philadelphia, 1980.

———. "Portuguese Adaptation to Trade Patterns, Guinea to Angola (1443–1640)." *African Studies Review* 17, no. 2 (1974): 411–23.

———. "The West African Copper Trade in the Fifteenth and Sixteenth Centuries." In *Precious Metals in the Age of Expansion,* edited by H. Kellenbenz, pp. 119–30. Papers of the Fourteenth International Congress of Historical Sciences. Stuttgart, 1981.

Hiley, Edgar. *Brass Saga.* London, 1957.

Hilton-Simpson, M. W. *Land and Peoples of the Kasai.* London, 1911.

Holas, B. "Pince-amulette des guerzé (Haute-Guinée française)." *NA,* no. 48 (Oct. 1950): 123–50.

Horton, Robin. "Notes on Recent Finds of Brasswork in the Niger Delta." *Odu* 2, no. 1 (July 1965): 76–91.

Jackson, M. "Sacrifice and Social Structure among the Kuranko." *Africa* 49, no. 2 (1977): 123–39.

Jacobson-Widding, Anita. *Red-White-Black as a Mode of Thought.* Uppsala, 1979.

Janzen, John, and Wyatt MacGaffey. *Anthology of Kongo Religions.* Lawrence, Kansas, 1975.

Jeannest, Charles. *Quatre années au Congo.* Paris, 1886.

Johansson, Sven-Olof. *Nigerian Currencies.* Translated by J. Learmont. Norrköping, Sweden, 1967.

Johnson, Marion. "The Ounce in Eighteenth-Century West African Trade." *JAH* 7, no. 2 (1966): 197–214.

Johnston, (Sir) Harry H. *George Grenfell and the Congo.* 2 vols. London, 1908.

———. *The River Congo from Its Mouth to Bólóbó.* London, 1884.

Kauenhoven-Janzen, Reinhild. "Chokwe Thrones." *African Arts* 16, no. 3 (May 1981): 69–74.

Krieger, Kurt. *Westafrikanische Plastik.* 3 vols. Berlin, 1965–69.

Ladame, F. "Le droit des indigènes sur les mines de cuivre du Katanga." *Congo* 2 (Dec. 1921): 685–91.

Laman, K. *The Kongo.* 3 vols. Uppsala, 1953–68.

Latham, A. J. H. "Currency, Credit and Capitalism on the Cross River in the Pre-Colonial Era." *JAH* 12, no. 4 (1971): 599–606.

Lembezat, B. *Kirdi, les populations païennes du Nord-Cameroun.* Mémoires de l'Institut français de l'Afrique noire (Centre du Cameroun). N.p., 1950.

Lindblom, G. "Copper Rod 'Currency' from Palabora N. Transvaal." *Man* 26 (1926).

Lobato, Alexandre. *A expansão portuguêsa em Moçambique de 1498 a 1530.* 3 vols. Lisbon, 1954–60.

Lombard, J. "L'intronisation d'un roi bariba." *NA,* no. 62 (April 1954): 45–47.

Lush, A. J. "Kiganda Drums." *UJ* 3, no. 1 (1935): 7–25.

McLeod, M. D. *The Asante.* London, 1981.

McNaughton, Patrick R. "The Throwing Knife in African History." *African Arts* 3, no. 2 (Winter 1970): 54–60.

Magalhães Godinho, Vittorino. *L'économie de l'empire portugais aux XVe et XVIe siècles.* Paris, 1969.

Mahieu,A. "La monnaie de cuivre au Katanga." *Congo* 2 (1926): 419–22.

Marchal, R. "Renseignements historiques relatifs à l'exploitation des mines de cuivre par les indigènes de la région de Luishia." *Bulletin des juridictions indigènes et du droit coutumier congolais* (Elizabethville) 7, no. 1 (1939): 10–17.

Martin, Phyllis. *The External Trade of the Loango Coast, 1576–1870.* Oxford, 1972.

Mas Latrie, Louis de. *Relations et commerce de l'Afrique septentrionale ou Maghreb avec les nations chrétiennes du moyen âge.* Paris, 1886.

Meek, C. K. *The Northern Tribes of Nigeria.* 2 vols. London, 1925.

———. *A Sudanese Kingdom.* London, 1931.

———. *Tribal Studies in Northern Nigeria.* 2 vols. London, 1931.

Mertens, Joseph. *Les chefs couronnés chez les bakongo orientaux.* Mémoire, Institut Royal Colonial Belge. Brussels, 1942.

Miner, Horace. *The Primitive City of Timbuctoo.* Rev. ed. New York, 1965.

Morton-Williams, Peter. "The Yoruba Ogboni Cult." *Africa* 30, no. 4 (1960): 34–40.

Murray, Kenneth C. "Idah Masks." *Nigerian Field* 14, no. 3 (1949): 85–92.

Musée de l'Homme. *La Vie du Sahara.* Paris, 1956.

Nadel, S. F. *A Black Byzantium: The Kingdom of Nupe in Nigeria.* London, 1965.

Neaher, Nancy. "Igbo Metalsmiths among the Southern Edo." *African Arts* 9, no. 4 (July 1976): 46–49.

———. "Nigerian Bronze Bells." *African Arts* 12, no. 3 (May 1979): 42–47, 95.

Northern, Tamara. *The Ornate Implement.* Dartmouth College Museum and Galleries. Hanover, N. H. 1981.

———. *Royal Art of Cameroon: The Art of the Bamenda Tikar.* Hopkins Center Art Galleries, Dartmouth College. Hanover, N. H. 1973.

Northrup, David. *Trade without Rulers: Pre-Colonial Economic Development in South-Eastern Nigeria.* Oxford, 1978.

Obenga, T. *La cuvette congolaise, Les hommes et les structures.* Paris, 1976.

Olbrechts, F. M. *Les arts plastiques du Congo belge.* Brussels, 1959.

Pairault, C. "Boum Kabir (Chad) en présence de la mort." *JSA* 34, no. 1 (1964): 141–67.

Pâques, Viviana. "Origine et caractères du pouvoir royal au Baguirmi." *JSA* 37 (1967): 183–214.

Paulme, Denise. *Les sculptures de l'Afrique noire.* Paris, 1956.

Paver, F. R. "Trade and Mining in Pre-European Transvaal." *SAJS* 30 (1933): 603–11.

Peek, Philip M. "Isoko Bronzes and the Lower Niger Bronze Industries." *African Arts* 13, no. 4 (August 1980): 60–66.

Perrois, L. "L'art kota-mahonqwe: Les figures funéraires du bassin de l'Ivindo (Gabon-Congo)." *Arts de l'Afrique noire,* no. 20 (1976).

———. "Le bwété des kota-mahongwe du Gabon: Note sur les figures funéraires des populations du bassin de l'Ivindo." Orstom, 1969.

———. "Note sur les figures du bwéte des kota-mahongwe (Gabon)" (Réponse à Siroto). *African Arts* 2, no. 4 (1969): 65–67.

Perrois, L, and G. Pestmal. "Note sur la découverte et la restauration de deux figures funéraires kota-mahongwe (Gabon)." *Cahiers de l'Orstom,* série, sciences humaines, 8, no. 4 (1971): 367–86.

Perrot, Claude-H. "Ano Asema: Mythe et histoire." *JAH* 15, no. 2 (1974): 199–222.

Pitt-Rivers, Augustus. *Antique Works of Art from Benin.* New York, 1976.

Plass, M. *Seven Metals of Africa.* Philadelphia, 1959.

Posnansky, Merrick. "Ghana and the Origins of West African Trade." *African Quarterly* 11 (1971): 111–14.

Randles, W. G. L. *L'ancien royaume du Congo des origines à la fin du XIXe siècle.* Paris, 1968.

Rattray, R. S. *Ashanti.* Oxford, 1923.

———. *Religion and Art in Ashanti.* Oxford, 1927.

Reefe, Thomas Q. *The Rainbow and the Kings: A History of the Luba Empire to 1891.* Berkeley, 1981.

Richardson, David. "West African Consumption Patterns and Their Influence on the Eighteenth-Century English Slave Trade." In *The Uncommon Market: Essays in the Economic History of the Atlantic Slave Trade,* edited by H. Gemery and J. Hogendorn. New York, 1979.

Roache, L. E. "Psychophysical Attributes of the Ogboni Edan." *African Arts* 4, no. 2 (Winter 1971): 48–53.

Robbins, Warren M. *African Art in American Collections.* New York, 1966.

Roberts, Andrew. "Pre-Colonial Trade in Zambia." *African Social Research* 10 (1970).

―――. "Nyamwezi Trade." In *Pre-Colonial African Trade,* edited by R. Gray and D. Birmingham, 39–74. Oxford, 1970.

Ross, Doran. "Ghanaian Forowa." *African Arts* 8, no. 1 (Autumn 1974): 40–49.

Rouch, Jean. *La religion et la magie songhay.* Paris, 1960.

Rouvre, E. de, with D. Paulme and J. Brosse. *Parures africaines.* Paris, 1956.

Rubin, Arnold. *African Accumulative Sculpture: Power and Display.* New York, 1974.

―――. "Notes on Regalia in Biu Division, North-Eastern State, Nigeria." *WAJA* 4 (1974): 161–75.

Ryder, A. F. C. *Benin and the Europeans 1485-1897.* London, 1969.

―――. "A Reconsideration of the Ife-Benin Relationship." *JAH* 6, no. 1 (1965): 25–38.

Sassoon, Hamo. "Iron Cows and Copper Spears: The Royal Insignia of Karagwe." *UJ* 34, no. 2 (1970): 200.

Sautter, Giles. *De l'Atlantique au fleuve Congo: Une géographie du sous-peuplement.* 2 vols. Paris, 1966.

Shaw, Thurstan. "A Note on Trade and the Tsoede Bronzes." *WAJA* 3 (1973): 233–38.

Schick, Leon. *Un grand homme d'affaires au début du XVI siècle, Jacob Fugger.* Paris, 1957.

Sieber, Roy. "The Insignia of the Igala Chief of Eteh." *Man* 65 (1965).

Siroto, Leon, *African Spirit Images and Identities.* Pace Gallery. New York, 1976.

―――. "The Face of the Bwiiti." *African Arts* 1, no. 3 (Spring 1968): 22–27, 86–89.

―――. "Witchcraft Belief in the Explanation of Traditional African Iconography." In *World Anthropology: The Visual Arts,* edited by Justine Cordwell. The Hague, 1979.

Smith, Alan. "Delagoa Bay and the Trade of South-Eastern Africa." In *Pre-Colonial African Trade,* edited by Richard Gray and David Birmingham, 265–90. London, 1970.

―――. "The Trade of Delagoa Bay as a Factor in Nguni Politics 1750-1835." In *African Societies in Southern Africa,* edited by Leonard Thompson, 171–89. London, 1978.

"Some Yoruba Customs." *Nigerian Field* 13, no. 1, (1948): 24–27; 13, no. 2 (1948): 59–61; 14, no. 1 (1949): 33–35; 14, no. 2 (1949): 74–79; 14, no. 3 (1949): 113–19.

Stayt, H. A. *The BaVenda.* Oxford, 1931.

Stow, George W. *The Native Races of South Africa.* New York, 1905.

Strieder, Jakob. *Aus Antwerpener Notariatsarchiven: Quellen zur deutschen Wirtschaftsgeschichte des 16. Jahrhunderts.* Stuttgart and Leipzig, 1930.

―――. *Das reiche Augsburg: Ausgewählte Aufsätze Jakob Strieders.* Munich, 1938.

Sundström, Lars. *The Exchange Economy of Pre-Colonial Tropical Africa.* New York, 1974. Originally published as *The Trade of Guinea.* Uppsala, 1965.

Sutherland-Harris, Nicola. "Trade and the Rozwi Mambo." In *Pre-Colonial African Trade,* edited by Richard Gray and David Birmingham, 243–64. London, 1970.

————. "Zambian Trade with Zumbo in the 18th Century." in *Pre-Colonial African Trade,* edited by Richard Gray and David Birmingham, 231–42. London, 1970.

Talbot, P. A. *Life in Southern Nigeria.* London, 1923.

————. *The Peoples of Southern Nigeria.* 3 vols. London, 1926.

————. *Tribes of the Niger Delta.* London, 1932.

Teixeira da Mota, A. "Bronzes antigos da Guiné." *Actas do Congresso Internacional de Etnografia* 4 (1963): 149–54.

————. "Descoberta de bronzes antigos na Guiné portuguêsa." *Boletim cultural da Guiné portuguêsa* 15, no. 59 (1960): 625–37.

Thiam, B. "'Nimba' déesse de la fécondité." *NA,* no. 108 (Oct. 1965): 128–30.

Thompson, Louis C. "Ingots of Native Manufacture." *NADA* 26 (1949): 7–19.

————. "The Mu-tsuku." *SAJS* 35 (1938): 396–98.

Thompson, Leonard, *Survival in Two Worlds: Moshoeshoe of Lesotho, 1786–1870.* Oxford, 1975.

Thompson, Robert Farris. *Black Gods and Kings.* Los Angeles, 1971.

————. "The Sign of the Divine King." *African Arts* 3, no. 3 (Spring 1970): 8–17, 74–78.

Torday, E. *On the Trail of the Bushongo.* 1925; New York, 1969.

Torday, E., and T. A. Joyce. "Notes ethnographiques sur des populations habitant les bassins du Kasai et du Kwango oriental: 1. Peuplades de la forêt; 2. Peuplades des prairies." *Annales du Musée du Congo belge,* bk. 2, pt. 2. Brussels, 1922.

Trowell, Margaret. *African and Oceanic Art.* New York, 1968.

Trowell, Margaret, and K. P. Wachsmann. *Tribal Crafts of Uganda.* London, 1953.

Tubiana, M.-J. "Danses zaghawa." *Objets et mondes* 6, no. 4 (1966): 279–300.

————. *Survivances pré-islamiques en pays zaghawa.* Paris: Institut d'Ethnologie, Musée de l'Homme, 1964.

————. "Une coiffure d'apparat." *Objets et mondes* 8, no. 2 (1968): 129–43.

Turner, Victor. "Color Classification in Ndembu Ritual." In *The Forest of Symbols.* Ithaca, N.Y., 1967.

United Africa Company. "The Manilla Problem." *Statistical and Economic Review,* no. 3 (Mar. 1949): 44–56; and no. 4 (Sept. 1949): 59–60.

Van der Wee, H. *The Growth of the Antwerp Market and the European Economy.* 3 vols. The Hague, 1963.

Vansina, Jan. *The Children of Woot.* Madison, Wis., 1978.

————. "Long-Distance Trade-Routes in Central Africa." *JAH* 3, no. 3 (1962): 375–90.

————. "Probing the Past of the Lower Kwilu Peoples (Zaire)." *Paideuma* 19–20 (1973–74): 332–64.

————. *The Tio Kingdom of the Middle Congo, 1880–1892.* New York, 1973.

Vedder, Heinrich. *South West Africa in Early Times.* Translated and edited by C. G. Hall. London, 1966.

Vellut, J. L. "Notes sur le Lunda et la frontière luso-africaine (1700–1900)." *Etudes d'histoire africaine* 3 (1972): 61–166.

Verbeken, Auguste. *M'siri, roi du Garenganze.* Brussels, 1956.

Verbeken, Auguste, and M. Walraet, trans. and annot. *La première traversée du Katanga en 1806: Voyage des "Pombeiros" d'Angola aux rios de Sena.* Mémoires de l'Institut royal colonial belge, no. 30, pt. 2. Brussels, 1953.

Vogt, John. "Notes on the Portuguese Cloth Trade in West Africa, 1480–1540." *IJAHS* 8, no. 4 (1975): 623–51.

————. "The Portuguese Gold Trade: An Account Ledger from Elmina, 1529–1531." *THSG* 14, no. 1 (June 1973): 93–103.

————. *Portuguese Rule on the Gold Coast, 1469–1682.* Athens, Georgia, 1979.

Volavka, Zdenka. "Insignia of the Divine Authority." *African Arts* 14, no. 3 (May 1981): 43–51.

Von Luschan, F. *Die Altertümer von Benin.* 3 vols. Leipzig, 1919.

Walker, A. Raponda. *Notes d'histoire du Gabon.* Mémoires de l'Institut des études centrafricaines, no. 9. Brazzaville, 1960.

Walz, Terence. *Trade between Egypt and Bilad as-Sudan, 1700–1820.* Cairo, 1978.

Warmelo, N. J. van, ed. *The Copper Miners of Musina and the Early History of the Zoutpansberg.* Union of South Africa, Department of Native Affairs, Ethnology Publication no. 8. Pretoria, 1940.

Warren, Dennis M. "Bono Royal Regalia." *African Arts* 8, no. 2 (Winter 1975): 16–21.

————. "Bono Shrine Art." *African Arts* 9, no. 2 (Jan. 1976): 28–34.

Weeks, J. H. *Among the Primitive Bakongo.* London, 1914.

Wente-Lukas, Renate. *Die materielle Kultur der nicht-islamischen Ethnien von Nord Kamerun und Nordostnigeria.* Wiesbaden, 1977.

Westerdijk, H. *Ijzerwerk van Central-Afrika.* Exhibition, Museum voor Land en Volkenkunde Rotterdam. Rotterdam, 1975.

Willett, Frank. *African Art.* New York, 1971.

Williams, Denis. *Icon and Image.* New York, 1974.

————. "The Iconology of the Yoruba *Edan Ogboni.*" *Africa* 24 (1964): 139–66.

Wilson, Monica, and Leonard M. Thompson, eds. *The Oxford History of South Africa.* 2 vols. New York, 1969.

Zahan, Dominique. "Les couleurs chez les bambara du Soudan français." *NA,* no. 50 (April 1951): 52–56.

————. *La dialectique du verbe chez les bambara.* Paris, 1963.

Zeltner, F. de. "La bijouterie indigène en Afrique occidentale." *JSA* 1 (1931): 43–48.

# INDEX

References to illustrations are printed in boldface type. Numbers in italics refer to charts, tables, and maps.

—brass casting, 41–42; rituals, 40; techniques, 84, 85; as derived from European technology, 90–91; as derived from Ife, 90–91, 251; origins of, traditions concerning, 251–52; **color illus.** 1
Benjamin of Tudela, 113
Bent, Theodore, 187, 207
Bentley, W. H., 82, 197–98, 214
Benue region: casting traditions, 77, 91–92; lead in, 95; copper trade, 162–63; massive collars and bracelets, 217
Bergdamas: mining, 27; copper smelting, 168
Bernus, S., 16, 67, 195
Bida: beaten brasswork, 77
Bié: copper deposits, 21
Biebuyck, Daniel, 240
Bini: hammered brasswork, 77; casting large objects, 91; traditions concerning origins of brass-casting, 251–52. *See also* Benin; Edo
Binji: wire, 227
Birmingham, England, as brass center, 149, 176, 181, 201, 202
Bisa: and Kazembe, 157; identified with "Urenje," 166; ingots still kept by, 191
Bisson, Michael, xxii; dating of mine at Kansanshi, 24, 165; on migratory miners at Kansanshi, 47; on techniques used at Kansanshi, 57–58; on openmould casting, 87; on copper trade, extent of, 104; on ingots and currency, 186, 187, 206
Blaauwbank: bronze possibly made at, 96, 97; use of imported malachite, 320n1
"Black coppers," 197
Blacksmiths, and brass casters, 41–42, 46. *See also* Smiths (i.e. coppersmiths)
Blohm, Wilhelm, 292
Blommaert, Samuel, 133, 135, 181, 336n63
Bobangi: collars, 214–15; decorated oars, 232, 234
Bobo: *Do* mask, 225
Bocarro, Gaspar, 187, 341n14
Body decoration. *See* Decorative uses of copper; Jewelry
Bold, Edward, 197
Bomitaba, 368n45
Bono, 257; shrines, 258

Bornu, 162; colonists from, at Hufrat, 163; currency, 205
Bororo: earrings, 218, 270, 282
Bosman, Willem, 124
Botswana: ancient workings, 26
Bouët-Willaumez, Louis Edouard, 170
Boullé Kadié, 17
Bower, J. G., 66, 70
Bowls, ceremonial, 257, 261. *See also* Basins
Bracelets, 76, **212–15**; of telegraph wire, 47, 79, 324n14; of copper wire, 81; of cast copper, 83; for export, Loango coast, 141; at Darfur, from old copper melted down, 164; from Niari Basin, with admixture of lead, 171; worn from wrist to elbow, 173, 216–17; as royal insignia, 248, 253, 274; Lemba, 255, 270, 278, 361–62n66; as amulets, 265; of Masai warrior, 266; of brass and copper, intertwined, 289
Brand, Pieter, 168
Brass: early production of, 5; casting rituals, 40; beaten, 77–78; as alloy, 92; metallic composition of, 97–98; European, metallic composition of, 98–99; shininess of, 176, 280–81; and copper, relative preferences for, 176–78, 288–90; of Ogboni, 255; in Senufo divinations, 262–63; associated with water spirits, 285–86; used with copper and iron, 288–95 *passim*; associated with the earth, 293; and gold, 300; derivation of name, 353n1. *See also* Akan
Brass, English, 146–48; and African trade, *145–47, 148–50,* 149–53; and slave trade, 302–303
Brass casters: in Benin, 41–42; guilds of, 47
Brass imports to Africa. *See* Imports of copper and brass to Africa
Brazza, Pierre Savorgnan de, 161, 170, 171
Brazza Mission (1882), 19
Brew, Richard, 136
Bridewealth payments, 104, 194, 206, 243, 272
Bristol, England, as brass center, 149–51
Broecke, Pieter van den, 141, 142
Broederstroom: 24/73 mine, 27; copper chain found at, purity of, 72

Taruga, 7
Tati region: ancient workings, 26
Tegdaoust, 117, 121
Tekyiman, 271, 299
"Tellem" sites, 117
Termite hills, in furnace construction, 37, 53, 58, 69
Terra cotta sculpture: and cast metal pieces, 89, 90; as amulet, 264; red and black paint on, 278
Tessalit: ancient workings, 18
Theophilus, 69
Thompson, A. P., 66
Thompson, Louis C., 71, 193
Thompson, Robert Farris, 223, 255, 277
Thomson, Joseph, 173, 176, 329n127
Thomson, T. R. H., 175
Tikar: palm wine containers, 230; bells, 239; amulet (wood and brass), 264
Timna, Israel, 75
Tin: in bronze, 92; in Southern Africa, 96; in Zimbabwe, 96
Tio: ornamental collars and bracelets, 76; currency, 197–98; and Ngbwaka swords, 271; symbolism of red for, 278; *ilua* (life containers), 281
Tippu Tip, 159, 359n11
Title societies: copper and prestige of, 253–54; copper and ritual authority of, 254–57
Tiv: body ornamentation, 217; mouth whistles, 235–36
*Tjiwara* headpiece, 266–67, **268**
Tlhaping: smelting by (doubted), 167; earrings, 218
Tongs (pince-amulettes), 265–66, 290
Tools: early manufacture of, 3–4; for mining, 52, 60, 61, 63, 66, 68–69; for wiredrawing, 78
Torday, E., 248
Towerson, William, 126, 132, 136
Trade, intra-African: in Zambia, 104–5, 165–66; in Zimbabwe, 105–8, 166–67; in Transvaal, 109–11, 168; in Katanga, 111–12, 154–60; in East Africa, 112–13; in West Africa, 113–21; in Nigeria, 115–16; quantity of goods traded, 120–21; of European goods imported to coast, 130; and wars, impact of, 134; Vili system, 142–43; nineteenth century, 154–69, *155*; from Niari

Basin, 160–61; from Hufrat, 161–63; from Egypt to the Sudan, 163–65; from Namaqualand, 167–68
Trade, maritime, 123–53; goods involved, 123–25, 135–38, *139*, 151, 170–71; Portuguese (1460–1600), 125–32; competition from interlopers, 129, 132, 145; Dutch (seventeenth century), 132–40; ships' invoices, 133, 151–52; and wars, impact of, 133–34; exports of copper and brass from Africa, 140–44; eclipses trans-Saharan trade, 174–75. *See also* English trade with Africa
Trans-Saharan trade: caravan discovered by Monod, 98, 114, 120, 180; copper in, 113–15, 117; eclipsed by maritime trade, 174–75; quantity of goods traded, 180; gold in, 297. *See also* Arab traders
Transvaal: earliest ironworking in, 8; ancient workings, 26–27, 29–30, 314n61; *mfecane*, 31; Bantu settlement in, dating of, 32; ore deposits in, 71–72; bronze made in, analysis of, 96–97; copper trade, 109–11; currency, **192**, 192–94. *See also* Buisport; Harmony mines; Lolwe Hill; Mapungubwe; Messina; Olifantspoort; Phalaborwa; Uitkomst Cave
Travassos Valdez, Francisco, 42
Trenches. *See* Shafts and trenches in mines
Trevor, T. G.: on ancient workings at Messina, 26, 70, 71, 73, 168; on "foreign" metalworkers, 29–30, 31–32; on Blaauwbank ingot, 97; on musuku, 193
Trumpets and bugles, 235, 250
Tsoede (Nupe culture hero), 42, 250–51
Tsoede bronzes, 91, 94, 220; metallic composition of, 98; bells on, 238; term considered unacceptable, 251. *See also* Jebba, sacred bronze figures; Tada sacred bronze figures
Tsumeb: ancient workings, 15, 27; smelting, 63
Tswana: wiredrawing, 80, 81; cuprous metal worked by, 97, 167; and Dutch traders, 138; earrings, 217–18
Tuareg: weapons, ornate, 232, 293–94; rings as amulets, 265

DESIGNED BY IRVING PERKINS ASSOCIATES
COMPOSED BY METRICOMP, GRUNDY CENTER, IOWA
MANUFACTURED BY KINGSPORT PRESS, KINGSPORT, TENNESSEE
TEXT IS SET IN TIMES ROMAN
DISPLAY LINES ARE SET IN OPTIMA AND TIMES ROMAN

Library of Congress Cataloging in Publication Data

Herbert, Eugenia W.
Red gold of Africa.

Bibliography: pp. 373–391.
Includes index.
1. Industries, Primitive — Africa, Sub-Saharan.
2. Copper industry and trade — Africa, Sub-Saharan.
3. Copper mines and mining — Africa, Sub-Saharan.
4. Copper — Folklore. 5. Africa, Sub-Saharan — Industries.
I. Title.
GN645.H44 1984     669′.3′0967     83-40264
ISBN 0-299-09600-9